COMMON MINDS

Common Minds

Themes from the Philosophy of Philip Pettit

Edited by
GEOFFREY BRENNAN
ROBERT GOODIN
FRANK JACKSON
and
MICHAEL SMITH

CLARENDON PRESS · OXFORD

OXFORD

UNIVERSITY PRESS

Great Clarendon Street, Oxford OX2 6DP

Oxford University Press is a department of the University of Oxford.
It furthers the University's objective of excellence in research, scholarship,
and education by publishing worldwide in

Oxford New York

Auckland Cape Town Dar es Salaam Hong Kong Karachi
Kuala Lumpur Madrid Melbourne Mexico City Nairobi
New Delhi Shanghai Taipei Toronto

With offices in

Argentina Austria Brazil Chile Czech Republic France Greece
Guatemala Hungary Italy Japan Poland Portugal Singapore
South Korea Switzerland Thailand Turkey Ukraine Vietnam

Oxford is a registered trade mark of Oxford University Press
in the UK and in certain other countries

Published in the United States
by Oxford University Press Inc., New York

British Library Cataloguing in Publication Data

Data available

Library of Congress Cataloging in Publication Data

Data available

Typeset by Laserwords Private Limited, Chennai, India
Printed in Great Britain
on acid-free paper by
Biddles Ltd, King's Lynn, Norfolk

ISBN 978–0–19–921816–5

1 3 5 7 9 10 8 6 4 2

Contents

Preface

During a career spanning over thirty years Philip Pettit has made seminal contributions in moral philosophy, political philosophy, philosophy of the social sciences, philosophy of mind and action, and metaphysics. His many contributions would be remarkable enough in themselves, but they are made all the more so by the ways in which Pettit connects them with each other. Pettit holds that the lessons learned when thinking about problems in one area of philosophy often constitute ready-made solutions to problems we face in completely different areas. His body of work taken as a whole provides a vivid example of what philosophy looks like when done with that conviction.

The evaluation of such a whole is difficult, but this volume begins that task by collecting together ten papers by eleven outstanding contemporary theorists—drawn from philosophy, political science, law, and criminology—all of whom grapple with core issues from some part of Pettit's corpus. Although most of the essays do not deal explicitly with his synoptic scheme, the quality of the parts, as perceived by these specialists in the relevant areas, provides a test of the synoptic approach. If Pettit is able to say significant and interesting things across such a broad range of philosophy, this fact surely suggests that the synoptic method is worth pursuing more broadly. In any event, and at our request, Pettit himself has provided an account of how the various parts of his view taken as a whole hang together, forgoing the opportunity to rebut criticisms in a point-by-point fashion in favour of giving broad-brush responses in the context of a more comprehensive overview.

Draft versions of many of the chapters were first delivered at a conference held in Philip's honour at the Australian National University in 2003. Thanks go to the Research School of Social Sciences for making that conference possible, and to Jeannie Haxell and Di Crosse for making it run so smoothly. Peter Momtchiloff's support for this project since its inception is also very gratefully acknowledged, as are the comments on the draft chapters provided by two readers for Oxford University Press. Finally, thanks to Tristram McPherson for compiling the index, and to Catherine Berry, Jean van Altena, and Donald Strachan for their hard work in the production phase.

Geoffrey Brennan
Robert Goodin
Frank Jackson
Michael Smith

List of Contributors

John Braithwaite is Federation Fellow and a member of the Regulatory Institutions Network at the Research School of Social Sciences, Australian National University.

John Ferejohn is Carolyn S. G. Munro Professor of Political Science and Senior Fellow, The Hoover Institution, Stanford University, and Visiting Professor of Law at New York University.

Richard Holton is Professor of Philosophy at MIT. He taught previously at Monash University, the Research School of Social Sciences at the Australian National University, the University of Sheffield, and the University of Edinburgh.

Susan Hurley is Professor of Philosophy at the University of Bristol and Fellow of All Souls College, Oxford. She was formerly Fellow at St Edmund Hall, Oxford, and Professor of Political and Ethical Theory at the University of Warwick.

Nicola Lacey is Professor of Criminal Law and Legal Theory at the London School of Economics. She is also Adjunct Professor at the Research School of Social Sciences, Australian National University, and a member of the Global Law School Faculty, New York University. Prior to joining the LSE, Lacey taught at University College, London; New College, Oxford; and Birkbeck College, London.

Rae Langton is Professor of Philosophy at MIT, having taught previously at Monash University, the Research School of Social Sciences at the Australian National University, the University of Sheffield, and the University of Edinburgh.

Cynthia Macdonald is Professor of Philosophy at Queen's University Belfast and Adjunct Professor of Philosophy at the University of Canterbury, New Zealand, having previously taught at the University of Manchester.

Graham Macdonald is Professor of Philosophy at the University of Canterbury, New Zealand, and Distinguished International Fellow, Institute for Cognition and Culture, Queen's University Belfast. Before moving to Canterbury, he taught at the University of Bradford.

Peter Menzies is Professor of Philosophy at Macquarie University, having previously held a research fellowship in the Research School of Social Sciences, Australian National University.

Alva Noë is Professor of Philosophy at the University of California, Berkeley.

Philip Pettit is Laurance S. Rockefeller University Professor for Politics and the University Center for Human Values at Princeton University. Before moving to Princeton, he was for many years Professor of Social and Political Theory at the Research School of Social Sciences, Australian National University, and prior to that, Professor of Philosophy at the University of Bradford.

Thomas M. Scanlon is Alford Professor of Natural Religion, Moral Philosophy, and Civil Polity at Harvard University.

Jeremy Waldron is University Professor in the School of Law at New York University. Until recently he was University Professor at Columbia University, and before that, he taught at Princeton, Berkeley, Edinburgh, Oxford, and Otago.

1

Beyond Program Explanation

Cynthia Macdonald and Graham Macdonald

In a number of articles over the years, and especially in *The Common Mind* (1993), Philip Pettit has defended a distinctive and influential solution to the so-called problem of mental causation—the problem of how minds can make a causal difference to the world. This view has become known as 'program explanation', hereafter PE. As its name indicates, PE is more than just a proposal purporting to solve the problem of how our minds can influence events in the physical world. It is also an account of how the 'special' sciences can be explanatorily autonomous. The 'problem' addressed by PE is multifaceted, and we cannot deal with all of its aspects here. In what follows, we want to concentrate on that part of the proposal that deals with issues concerning mental causation, since *inter alia* PE is meant to demonstrate how mental properties can be causally relevant to the behaviour they explain. We begin by outlining the problem of mental causation that concerns us. We then give a brief account of Pettit's solution, indicating what we take to be its principal shortcomings, before providing what we take to be the correct solution. We develop our criticism of PE by elaborating on the metaphysics of the preferred alternative. Finally, we reinforce our view by showing how it can be deployed to defeat a powerful argument, mounted by Jaegwon Kim, against the possibility of causally relevant emergent properties.

1. INTRODUCING THE PROBLEM

What is the problem that appeal to PE is meant to solve? Classically, the mental causation problem arises as a consequence of a commitment to non-reductive physicalism, together with some supplementary assumptions

Versions of parts of this paper have been read at a number of venues, including the Research School of Social Sciences at the Australian National University, the Australasian Philosophical Association (NZ Division) Conference at the University of Otago (1999), the South African Philosophical Association Conference (2000), and the University of Massachusetts (Amherst). We are grateful to audiences for their comments. We are also indebted to Tim Elder and Michael Smith for their comments on the penultimate draft. This work has been supported by a grant from the Royal Society of New Zealand Marsden Fund.

concerning causation.[1] The thesis of physicalism entails a monist ontology, which we take minimally to involve the claim that all events are physical events.[2] The non-reducibility claim requires acknowledging that some of these events are also mental events, which we take to be the claim that although every event that has a mental property has a physical property, the mental and physical properties are irreducibly distinct. There are two relevant assumptions concerning causality in play. The first is that mental events—specifically, believings, desirings, hopings, intendings—can cause physical effects. The second is that physical effects have sufficient physical causes. The question that immediately arises is: does the 'mentality' of the mental events contribute to the production of effects thus caused? Prima facie it would appear not; the 'physicality' of those physical causes does all the work.

This problem is sharpened if one accepts, as Pettit seems to do (and we certainly do), a certain metaphysical view of the nature of events involved in the causal transaction. This metaphysics requires that events be exemplifyings or instancings of properties in objects at, or during intervals of, times. This is the Property-Exemplification Account of events (hereafter PEA), one that we describe in more detail later. According to it, a mental event just is the exemplifying of a mental property in an object at a time, and also has various properties, such as the property of being an exemplifying of a mental property in an object at a time. For example, the event which is my thinking of Vienna now just is the exemplifying in me now of the property, *thinks of Vienna* (a property of me), and that event has the property of being a thinking of Vienna. Similarly, a physical event just is the exemplifying of a physical property in an object at a time, and it too will have various properties. Given the physicalist commitment, each mental event, i.e. exemplifying of a mental property, will be (i.e. be identical with) an exemplifying of a physical property.[3]

---

[1] 'Non-reductive physicalism' is anomalous monism without the commitment to there being no psychological or psychophysical laws. We avoid this commitment just because the notion of 'law' at stake is controversial. Nothing hangs on this issue in this chapter.

[2] We speak here of events, but the thesis is intended to cover all mental phenomena, however they are to be analysed in terms of events.

[3] In the terminology preferred by Kim, whose version of the account we describe here and develop further in Section 4, events are *exemplifications* of properties by objects at times. But Kim himself, and many others who take a universalist rather than a tropist view of properties, often use the term 'instance' as an alternative to the term 'exemplification' (and thus claim, e.g., that a mental event is an instance of a property at a time in an object). We ourselves prefer 'exemplifyings' to 'exemplifications' (along the lines of Lombard 1986), since it makes clear that events are fundamentally changes, whose 'constitutive' properties are dynamic rather than static, or its cognate term, 'instancings', since we think that failure to do so blurs the crucial distinction between a substance and an event. Given the universalist (as contrasted with a tropist) view of properties, according to which an exemplification/instance of a property just is the thing that has it, we would have to say that *Jones* is the instance of the property *runs*, since, according to the PEA, as developed by Kim, this is a property of Jones, and so is a constitutive property of the event which is Jones's running. But although Kim wants to say that the subject of that event is Jones, the exemplification of the property, *runs* by Jones is an *event*, a running, not the event's subject. We

Further, events themselves have properties, and have them by instantiating them. Now the problem looks like this: can the mental property of a mental/physical event exercise any causal influence? The assumption that physical effects have physical causes now has the consequence that, in any case where there is putative mental causation of a physical effect, the physical *property* of the mental/physical event must be the one in virtue of which that event causes the physical effect. The mental property looks inert; the only way of rescuing any causal influence on its behalf, so it seems, is to make the physical effect over-determined—brought about both in virtue of the mental/physical event's being an instance of the physical property and in virtue of that event's being an instance of the mental property. Of course, there may well be some cases of causal over-determination, but such *systematic* over-determination is exceedingly implausible, so this way out looks desperate. Another way is to secure the causal effectiveness of the mental property of the event by identifying it with a physical property. But this is a reductive move that looks increasingly implausible; and, in any case, requires the rejection of the position we wish to defend, non-reductive physicalism. Epiphenomenalism looms.

This is the problem that appeal to PE is meant to solve. Or so one might suppose, given Pettit's concentration on the task of making what he calls 'higher-order' intentional states causally relevant to the production of behaviour. In fact, though, Pettit sees the problem as twofold, and we think that part of his reluctance to accept an alternative, metaphysically less baroque, solution lies in his conflation of the two features of the problem, hinted at above. The problem, which he introduces in the form of the question, 'What is the relation between a higher-order [believing that p] and lower-order cause in virtue of which the higher-order counts as causally relevant?' (Pettit 1993: 33), is divided into two parts. First, there is 'the state played a certain causal part' and, second, there is 'it did so in virtue of the property of being a belief that p' (Pettit 1993:

can avoid this problem altogether if we distinguish instances from instancings (i.e. exemplifyings), since we can then maintain (1) that an instance of a property is the thing that has it (whether this is an object or an event), (2) that events just are (i.e. are identical with) exemplifyings of dynamic properties of objects in those objects, *and* (3) that an instance of a property of an event just is the event that has that property. Events, like any other entities, have properties by instantiating them, but their constitutive properties are not, according to PEA, properties that they possess. These distinctions are important to our solution of the problem of causal relevance, since only certain ways of developing the PEA will make that solution possible. We return to this in Section 4. For more on the distinction between static and dynamic properties, and the differences between Kim's and Lombard's versions of the PEA, see C. Macdonald (1989).

We would prefer to avoid the term 'instances' entirely, since it suggests a trope view of properties, which we reject. But, since many parties to the dispute concerning the problem of mental causation, including Pettit and Kim (esp. Kim 2003), regularly talk of events as instances of properties—intending the *universalist* view of properties as multiply exemplifiable entities that can be (wholly) present in many places at the same time—we will, for present purposes, speak in these terms too.

34).[4] We take the first feature (how the state can play a 'causal part') to be the problem of causal *efficacy*, and the second to be the problem of causal *relevance*.[5] Efficacy has to do with causes and effects extensionally conceived. Given that *c* caused *e*, any descriptions referring to *c* and *e* will (suitably arranged) yield a true causal statement. This means that a description of *c* can pick out *c* by specifying *any* property *c* possesses, and likewise for *e*. The extensionality of the causal relation ensures that *whatever these properties are*, the resulting causal statement will be true. Given the profusion of properties possessed by all events (think of 'mere' Cambridge properties), it is clear that not all true causal claims will yield causally illuminating *explanations* of why *e* occurred. This is why there is an issue of causal relevance, as distinct from causal efficacy: only some properties of the event that is the cause are causally relevant to the production of the effect, so only *those* properties, suitably specified, will yield causal explanations of the effect. Keeping this distinction in mind, we can ask: which aspect of the mental causation problem does the PE strategy solve? The problem of causal efficacy, the problem of causal relevance, or both? We think that Pettit is more concerned with causal relevance, but this leads him to adopt an unusual, and ultimately very implausible, approach to the problem of causal efficacy. Or so we shall argue.

---

[4] Again, Pettit and others speak of mental properties as higher-order properties, where we would use the term 'higher-level'. Higher-level properties should not be confused with higher-order ones. Higher-order properties are properties of properties, not properties of the things that have them in virtue of their possession of other properties. It is common, especially in functionalist treatments in the philosophy of mind, to use 'higher-order' rather than 'higher-level' when talking about mental properties such as being in pain, or dispositional properties like solubility. It's important that it's quite different from the contemporary logician's usage (though similar to Russell's and Ramsey's). In contemporary terms, 'solubility', like 'being a number', is a first-order predicate, and so stands for a first-order property, because its instances are particulars. However, both predicates might be classed as impredicative, i.e. specifiable by phrases that include second-order quantification over all properties, including those properties themselves. Thus, '$\lambda x(x$ is soluble)' might be specified by something like '$\exists F(Fx \,\&\, \forall y(Fy \,\&\, y$ is placed in water $\rightarrow y$ dissolves))', where we have a second-order quantifier, '$\exists F$', which ranges over all properties, including solubility (just as the bound variable in '$\iota x(\forall y(x \iota y \rightarrow x$ is taller than $y)$' impredicatively specifies the tallest person). Pettit and others who are functionalists with regard to mental properties use the term 'higher-order' precisely because, in order to give the definitions of such properties, we need to use higher-order quantification. They take a property such as being in pain, e.g., as higher-order because it is the state of being in a state that is causally related to others in the way that is characteristic of pain. However, for reasons just given, we take mental properties of events to be higher-level properties—properties of events that have them in virtue of their possession of other properties, rather than properties of properties of events. Be that as it may, since many of the examples used by Pettit and others in the mental causation debate concern both higher-level and higher-order properties, and since the issue of realization of one property by another that is central to the debate seems to arise with regard to both sorts of properties, we will, for present purposes, use the term 'higher-order' to cover both sorts of case.

[5] Things get a bit confusing, however, since, although Pettit speaks of properties and their instances as we do, sometimes his talk of states is elliptical for talk of property-instances, and sometimes his talk of states is elliptical for talk of properties. Here it looks like he means, by 'state', 'event' (i.e. 'property-instance'), but, as we shall see, at other times he seems to mean 'property'. See especially our discussion of his examples in Section 3.

2. THE PROGRAM EXPLANATION SOLUTION

Fundamentally, the PE strategy construes the notion of a mental property's 'determining an effect' as non-causal. PE thus bites the bullet: mental (and presumably all other special science) properties are *not* causally efficacious, in the sense that events that are instances of them do *not* bring about the effects they do in virtue of being instances of such properties. Mental properties are taken to be higher-order properties that supervene on physical properties of events. In any case where a mental property is thought to be causally efficacious in the production of an action (in the sense just specified), what really happens is that the instantiation of the higher-order (mental) property 'ensures that' a lower-order (physical) property is instantiated, this lower-order property doing the causal work (again, in the sense that the event that is an instance of that lower-order property brings about the action in virtue of being an instance of that property). As Pettit puts the point,

The general idea in the program model . . . is that a higher-order property is causally relevant to something when its instantiation ensures or at least probabilifies, in a non-causal way, that there are lower-order properties present which produce it. (Pettit 1993: 37)

So an instantiation of a mental property will 'program for' the instantiation of those physical properties required for the production of the physical effect. The 'ensuring that' and 'programming for' are non-causal relations, so there is no causal competition between mental and physical properties, and so no over-determination.

In addition to solving the over-determination problem, the PE model is said to have the virtue of presenting intentional causation as like many other cases of higher-order causation. To this end the PE model is supported by various examples in which it is alleged that one finds just such a higher-order programming for lower-order properties whose instantiations then cause the effects that one may have thought were caused by (instantiations of) the higher-order property. Thus, consider an eraser's elasticity, which enables it to bend. Its elasticity is a higher-order property, realized by a lower-order property, its having a certain molecular structure. The elasticity is said to non-causally program for its realization by a relevant molecular-structural property, instances of this lower-order property then producing the bending effect. Thus, it is claimed, 'The dispositional state programs for the bending' (Pettit 1993: 39)[6] We return to this example later.

---

[6] Pettit mentions two other examples, that of boiling water causing a crack in its container, and the failure of a square peg to fit into a round hole. Neither of these is a case of higher-order properties programming for the instantiation of their realizing properties, so we set them aside.

The PE strategy and model works with a number of assumptions, four of which are salient to our discussion. First, the model assumes that the lower-order property that *is* causally effective need not be the most immediate lower-order property; it may be one further down the ladder, so to speak. That is, the model is agnostic concerning the level at which causal efficacy resides. Second, the strategy does not take on board the problem of showing how causation works; it is intended to be compatible with most theories of causation. Third, the model is to be interpreted as an ontological one. 'It is an account of how, in the objective arrangement of things, higher-order causes relate to their lower-order counterparts. It is not an account of how we must subjectively come to know that certain higher-order causes are causally relevant' (Pettit 1993: 35). Fourth, the strategy takes as its metaphysical basis the distinction between properties and their instances: properties are abstract and universal, their instances are worldly, and so only instances of properties are involved in causal transactions.

Brief comments about these background assumptions are in order. We accept the first—that the causal 'grounding' of a higher-order property need not take place at an order immediately 'below' it. However, the second is problematic. On some accounts of causation, the strategy does not work. This becomes apparent when we cite our main complaint against the PE model, in Section 3. We accept the ontological constraint of the third assumption, and also the specific metaphysical commitments made by the fourth assumption. Any account of mental causation should be as ontologically robust as are accounts of any other kind of causation. Otherwise, it risks not being about what it sets out to be an account of, the obvious fact that our minds are causally active (by which we mean here, so as not to beg questions, that mental properties are causally relevant to the events that instances of them 'produce'). The metaphysics of properties as universals has been challenged, but it is common to both PE and our preferred solution, so it will not be questioned here.

3. THE PROBLEM WITH PROGRAM EXPLANATION

With causal explanation we assume that the cause cited in the explanation is crucial to any account of how it works as an explanation. Similarly, the PE strategy will work only if the 'program' part of the account illuminates how the 'explains' part works. This debt is paid by appeal to an analogy with the operation of a computer program, where the implementation of the program requires that lower-order electrical properties are brought into play. So the explanation is secured in similar fashion to the way that appeal to causes secures explanation: the effect is *brought about* by the explaining feature(s). This example makes it look like programming properties secure the causal effectiveness of the lower-order properties they program for in a causal way. But it is clear that this is not how programming properties are envisaged as carrying out their programming work; they are meant to carry out this work in a non-causal way. That is the point of the PE strategy as applied to the problem of mental causation—that it avoids over-determination problems by taking physical properties to carry out the causal work and taking mental properties to *non*-causally ensure that there will be physical properties available to carry out that work.

As we see it, there are two, related problems that make this solution implausible. The first surfaces when one asks how in general such programming is effected. How, exactly, do the higher-order properties non-causally *ensure* that the causally effective lower-order properties are instantiated? The second appears when one considers the most attractive answer to this question.

Consider the first. The problem is that, on a plausible reading of Pettit's account, the higher-order and lower-order properties are instantiated separately, and the most natural way to interpret the *ensuring* relation between *different* property-instances is causally. Clearly this interpretation of *ensuring* depends upon the property-instances being separate (non-identical), so we need to support this understanding of what Pettit says.

There are two reasons for thinking that the program model requires that the property-instances be non-identical. The first derives from how Pettit describes its essential features. Take the three conditions he places on a property's being a 'programming property':

1. Any instantiation of the higher-order property non-causally involves the instantiation of certain properties—maybe these, maybe those—at a lower order.

2. The lower-order properties associated with instantiations of the higher-order, or at least most of them, are such as generally to produce an E-type event in the given circumstances.

3. The lower-order properties associated with the actual instantiation of the higher-order property do in fact produce E. (Pettit 1993: 37)

What these quoted passages make clear is that Pettit's model works with an ontology not only of higher-order and lower-order properties, but also of higher-order and lower-order 'states', or instantiations of properties.[7] It is also clear that if the proper construal of the relation between the instances were that they are identical, it would have been easy to say so, rather than to leave it at the vague and non-defined 'association' between the instances. So we think that a natural reading of these passages forces the non-identity interpretation, and with it the thought that the *ensuring* relation between the separate instances is a causal relation, it being plausible to think that one event (property-instantiation)

---

[7] There is a question of how this can be reconciled with a further view, articulated a few pages earlier in his account of causal relevance, that there is token identity between the role (higher-order) state and the realizer (lower-order) state (Pettit 1993: 33) (though we note that Pettit, rightly in our view, does not think this solves the problem of the causal relevance of properties).

ensures that another occurs only if it causes, or causally contributes to, the occurrence of the latter.

The temptation to interpret 'ensure' causally is strengthened by another locution employed by Pettit: 'The factor that programs for an effect . . . non-causally *arranges things* (it means that things are arranged) so that there will be such a producer state—maybe this, maybe that—available to do the work' (Pettit 1993: 37, italics added).[8] How one property can be such that its instantiation non-causally arranges things so that an instance of another property produces the effect, though, is mysterious. What seems to be required here is a *de re* relation between separate instances of two properties such that the one instance (non-causally) produces (ensures, arranges for) the second instance, this latter instance producing (causing) the effect.[9] The natural reading of *both* 'producing' relations here is causal, and we have been given no reason to think otherwise, apart from the convenient fact that making the first production non-causal avoids causal over-determination. So, on our favoured reading the ensuring relation holds between (separate) property-instances, and this makes it difficult to see this relation in anything other than causal terms.

Our second reason for the 'separate-instance' interpretation arises from considering a different understanding of what is going on, one that says: the 'arrangement' of the higher-order and lower-order *properties* is such that whenever the one is instanced, so is the other. Here the ensuring work is done at the property level, so the accusation that causality is implicated is neatly avoided. And this reading is supported by a functionalist account of the relation between mental and physical properties, a relation of role property to realizing property, where a mental state (such as pain, or the belief that *p*) is the occupant of a certain causal role, the causal role definitive of the mental type in question (in the Ramsey/Lewis style). Now, there is no difficulty understanding the claim that the role properties non-causally ensure the existence of realizing properties, but the most natural way of making metaphysical sense of this connection in these cases is by *identifying* the instantiations, and, for reasons to which we return later, that is a result that Pettit wishes to avoid. For one thing, this result would also ensure that the higher-order property is causally efficacious, contradicting the claims made by

---

[8] Again, by 'producer state' here Pettit seems to mean, not 'property' but 'property-instance'.

[9] Actually, this makes it look as though Pettit might be flirting with a trope conception of properties, rather than a universalist one. Given that, on the latter view, an instance of a property just is the thing that has it, it is difficult to make sense of what is going on here without supposing either that the mental event and the physical event are distinct (in being distinct instances of distinct properties), which Pettit clearly is not supposing, or that the property-instances, in being distinct instances, are tropes. This latter would allow him to say that mental events are physical events, but only by committing him to the view that such events are constituted by both mental tropes and physical tropes. Trope theories of mental causation also suffer from the problem of causal relevance, and we think they are in a worse position than the PEA to resolve it, though we haven't the space to go into the reasons why here. We discuss them in detail in Macdonald and Macdonald (forthcoming, 2007).

advocates of Program Explanation.[10] For another, this co-instantiation account is one we have defended elsewhere (and below), and it has been criticized by Pettit for having the defect that 'it would make a state like the belief that p causally relevant but relevant in virtue of a property other than that of being the belief that p: relevant in virtue of being such and such a neural or electronic state' (Pettit 1993: 38). Although this criticism is couched in terms of causal relevance rather than causal efficacy, it is clear that the identity claim is being rejected, and with it any chance of rescuing the identity of the higher-order and lower-order property instances.[11] We are left with the puzzle as to how the higher-order instance can non-causally ensure the instantiation of the lower-order property.

Friends of the PE strategy might say that we are ignoring Pettit's explanation of how programming works in the case of mental causation. Consider an agent's intentional state, say, S's belief that p, which explains an agent's action of A-ing. The intentional state will program for the A-ing if, no matter how it is realized (variable realization being possible), the realizer (lower-order, physical) state—say, a particular neural state—tends to produce a type-A action. (By 'state' Pettit here must mean 'property' rather than 'property-instance', given that he takes the realization relation to hold between properties. But see n. 5.) That is, all of the possible realizers of the belief that p must be such that they tend to produce A (given certain background conditions). The intentional state, the belief that p, is causally relevant to the agent's A-ing just because it is realized by states, all of which tend to cause A-type actions (given the background conditions). But this fact, that the intentional state is realized only by producers of A-type actions, cannot be just a happy accident, merely fortuitous. If it were, then all cases of mental causation would depend on the huge coincidence that relevant higher-order intentional states are all realized, it so happens, by states with an appropriate causal profile. To reduce such coincidence, Pettit relies on the assumption that agents are *designed* so that their higher-order intentional states will be realized by the appropriate lower-order, causally efficacious neural states. This design assumption underwrites the 'program' part of the PE model: given adequate design, the instance of the higher-order property will ensure that there will be an instance of the lower-order property.

Does this help with the problem of how the higher-order instance non-causally arranges for there to be an instance of the lower-order property? We don't think so. On the contrary, we think that it makes the non-causal aspect of the story more implausible. The natural way to think of design in this context is biological design, and this is the way in which Pettit thinks of it: 'we may readily assume

---

[10] The claim that the identity of instances guarantees the causal efficacy of the higher-order property is defended below, but was first proposed by us in Macdonald and Macdonald 1986. Note that this does not guarantee the causal *relevance* of the higher-order property, but it is not *relevance* that is at issue here. See Section 5 below.

[11] We return to consider this objection, particularly as an objection to an account of causal relevance, at the beginning of Section 5.

that any natural intelligence is going to have been designed, under evolutionary and perhaps cultural pressures, to meet suitable design specifications' (Pettit 1993: 41). One must presume that the designer here is natural selection, where such selection includes cultural selection, whatever that turns out to be. But any selection-style story about design will be resolutely causal, relying on the selection process operating on the effects of the properties it selects. Brutally briefly, the story will be that some properties have instances whose effects in a particular environment make their possessors more likely to replicate themselves (more likely than competitors lacking the relevant properties), thus producing more instances of those properties. This clearly requires that the property-instances be causally efficacious in the selection process, so this part of the PE model strengthens the suspicion that the causal power of the intentional property is being discarded in an unprincipled way, just to avoid the over-determination problem.

A critic may point to cases in which a property is 'non-causally' selected because it is regularly correlated with a property for which one can tell the appropriate causal story. But reliance on such regular correlations is not available to the PE model, as it is trying to *explain* such regular correlations between instances of higher-order properties and instances of appropriate lower-order realizing properties.

This brings us to the second, related problem with the PE model mentioned earlier, which is that many accounts of causality would have trouble denying the status of cause to the instance of the higher-order property. Consider, for example, a counterfactual account. Since the PE model requires that, had the higher-order property not been instanced, the effect would not have occurred, such an account renders the higher-order property a cause of the effect. Or, consider Woodward's recent 'manipulation theory' of cause and causal explanation, which states that 'as a rough approximation, a necessary and sufficient condition for X to cause Y or to figure in a causal explanation of Y is that the value of Y would change under some intervention on X in some background circumstances' (Woodward 2003: 15). This also makes an instance of a higher-order property a cause. In order for the PE strategy to work in the requisite way on this theory, it is necessary for the supposedly non-causally productive instance to be susceptible to interventions that would change instantiations of the lower-order property, and hence change the effect produced. But if so, then Woodward's condition on something's being a cause is met. Again, apart from the convenience of avoiding a problem (over-determination), it is difficult to see why one would want to deny that the instance of the higher-order property is causally efficacious.

4. OUR ALTERNATIVE

Our diagnosis of what goes wrong with the PE model is that it assumes that the higher-order and lower-order properties must have *distinct* (non-identical) instances. This is what generates the puzzle about how it is that the first instance non-causally produces the second instance. Our view is that one can employ the same metaphysics of properties and instances (presuming a universalist, rather than a tropist, view of properties) and rescue the causal efficacy of the mental by rejecting this assumption—i.e. by identifying the instances of the mental and physical properties of events (as well as by identifying the events that exemplify them).

A more comprehensive metaphysical basis for this resolution is supplied by the Property-Exemplification Account of events, PEA.[12] As noted earlier in our discussion, according to it, events are exemplyings of (*n*-adic) act or event properties at (or during intervals of) times in objects. The objects in which such exemplifyings occur are the subjects of those events. And the properties, whose exemplifyings in subjects just are events, are properties, not of events, but of their subjects. For example, the event of Jones's running at noon yesterday just is the exemplifying in Jones of a property of Jones, the property, *runs*, at noon yesterday. Such properties are termed constitutive properties of events, and are so termed because they are the properties of subjects whose exemplifyings by those subjects just are events. Constitutive properties of events are properties whose exemplifying it is of the essence of those events to be.

In addition to constitutive properties, events also have characterizing properties. These are properties that events possess, at least some of which they possess in virtue of 'having' (i.e. being exemplifyings of) constitutive properties. Thus, for example, the event that is the exemplifying of the property, *runs*, by Jones at noon yesterday has as its constitutive property a property of Jones. That event has the property of being a running.

Events construed along these lines are sometimes referred to as 'structured particulars'. They are deemed so because they 'have' not only constitutive properties, but also constitutive objects (or subjects) and constitutive times.[13]

---

[12] We supply the necessary metaphysical details to allay the doubts of those who may think it cannot be supplied. One such person is Stephen Yablo (1992: esp. 259).

[13] The exposition of the PEA here is based on work of Kim's (esp. his 1976). According to Kim, although the first condition on events specified here is indispensable to the theory, the second, as formulated, is not. The theory could proceed, e.g., by defining the predicate 'is an event' over ordered *n*-tuples of objects, properties, and times. In this case, the ordered triple, $< x, P, t >$, would be an event if and only if x has P at t; and the principles of set theory would guarantee the existence of the triple (assuming, of course, that x, P, and t exist). But Kim himself appears to favour the first method over the second, and it is certainly the preferable one from the point of view of the phenomenon of causal interaction between events, where this is assumed to entail their positionality. The claim that events have constitutive objects, properties, and times should not be understood as the claim that they are in some way constituted by or composed of objects, properties, and times, these being related to each other in something like the way that a chair, say, is often viewed as composed of or constituted by its parts arranged in a certain way. This much is clear from the fact that the relationships that the 'components' of events bear to one another are very different from the relations that the components of physical things bear to one another. In the case of an event, one component is *exemplified by* another, *at* yet another; and it is clear that whatever the constituents of a biological organism or an artefact may be, they do not bear this relationship to one another. Given

That is to say, it is in the nature of any event to be an exemplifying of a property (of its subject) in a subject at a time. Two conditions on events are essential to the account, one an existence condition and one an identity condition. These are formulated for monadic events as follows:

Existence Condition: Event $[x,P,t]$ exists if and only if the object x has the property P at time t.

Identity Condition: Event $[x,P,t]$ is identical with event $[y,Q,t']$ if and only if the object x is identical with the object y, the property P is identical with the property Q, and the time t is identical with the time t'.

where x and y, P and Q, and t and t' are variables ranging over objects, properties, and times, respectively.

The PEA construes properties as both abstract and multiply exemplifiable, entities that can have, but are not identical with, their exemplifyings. According to it, to say that a mental event is identical with a physical event is to say that each event which is (= is identical with) an exemplifying of a mental property of a subject in that subject at a time is identical with an exemplifying of a physical property of that subject in that subject at that time. So, to say that a mental event is a physical event is to say that there is just one exemplifying of two properties, one mental and one physical, by an object at a time. Thus, appealing to the PEA in order to rescue causal efficacy for mental events requires simply recognizing that a single event can be (identical with) an exemplifying of both a mental and a physical property.

What is the relation between mental and physical properties of persons—those properties whose exemplifyings just are mental/physical events? On our view, mental properties whose exemplifyings just are mental events are not constitutive properties of those events, but, rather, supervene on physical properties constitutive of such events, and consequently, mental properties of events supervene on physical properties of events.[14] Given the identity condition on events imposed by the PEA, non-reductive physicalism requires rejection of the view that mental properties are constitutive properties of the events that have them, on the assumption that each event has only one constitutive property (but see n. 13). But, independently of this, the position is committed to some kind of supervenience thesis, since without such commitment it is difficult to fend off the charge that the position is irredeemably dualist, because it acknowledges the

all of this, the claim that the components of events are constitutive of them amounts to the claim that they are essential to them. Kim explicitly commits himself to some version of the latter. For more on this, see C. Macdonald 1989. Lombard (1986) agrees with Kim that the identity condition on events, as formulated, is not essential to the account, but for different reasons. According to him, events can have more than one constitutive property, whereas the identity condition as formulated here assumes that each event has just one.

[14] Does the fact that mental properties are not constitutive properties of events show that physical events that are mental events are not in some sense 'genuinely' mental? No, only that physicalism is contingently true.

presence in the natural world, if not of non-physical events, of non-physical properties. Many will think that such a position does not deserve the name 'physicalist'.

What kind of supervenience thesis best captures the relation between mental and physical properties is a thorny issue, as is well known.[15] Still, for present purposes we can say this much. Take supervenience between the mental and the physical to be that relation which holds between a mental property or set of properties, M, and another, physical one, P, such that any two objects/events indiscernible with respect to P cannot diverge with respect to M. Further, following Kim (1978, 1984), let us distinguish weak from strong supervenience. Then we can define a relation of strong supervenience thus:

SS: M-properties strongly supervene on P-properties $=_{df}$. For any possible worlds w and w^*, and any individuals x and y, if x in w is a P-twin of y in w^*, and the actual world's laws of physics hold in both, then x in w is an M-twin of y in w^*.[16]

where any x and y are $M(/P)$-twins if and only if x and y are exactly alike with respect to their $M(/P)$-properties.

What does the issue of causal relevance of mental properties amount to in this context—the issue of whether the mental property *of* an event is causally effective in that event's bringing about the effects it does?[17] Well, according to the PEA, events have (characterizing) properties as well as being the exemplifyings

---

[15] For some sceptical discussion of the value of appeal to psychophysical supervenience, see, e.g., Miller 1990; Melnyk 1995; and Heil 1998. For some examples of work on psychophysical supervenience that seeks to meet objections based on the claim that no satisfactory thesis can be found, see Horgan 1993 and Grimes 1991.

[16] This is an adaptation of the definition of strong supervenience given by Brian McLaughlin (in his 1995). By M-properties ($/P$-properties) we mean the non-empty set, $M(/P)$, of properties. We choose this version over Kim's principally because it is weaker than Kim's, though Kim's entails it. Kim's implies that it is necessarily the case that if something has an M-property, then it has some P-property. But SS could be true if twins had no P-property at all. It thus allows for the possibility that there might be purely mental worlds. We think this consequence desirable, given that we take physicalism to be true and contingent, and given the possibility of variable realization of mental properties. Kim blocks it only by assuming that P-properties are properties of the P-type and by allowing complementation to be a property-forming operator, so that $-P$, a negative property, is a way of being of the P-type. But one might deny that there are any negative properties on the grounds that they have no causal powers, and we think that this is a plausible thing to do. We adapt McLaughlin's definition primarily by introducing the caveat 'and the actual world's laws of physics hold in both' precisely because we take physicalism to be true and contingent. Although we do not take the identity conditions of properties to be given in terms of their causal powers, we do take it that if the identity conditions are identical, they have the same causal powers, and we take it that physical laws relate properties in virtue of their causal powers. So worlds in which there are the same physical properties that there are in the actual world will be worlds in which the same physical laws hold.

[17] Again, as we point out in the text, we take the causal relevance of a property to be more than a matter of its instances being causally effective, i.e. causally efficacious. But we do take this to be a necessary condition on causal relevance, so for present purposes we will not allude to other conditions that we take to be necessary as well. For more on the other conditions, see n. 18 below and Macdonald and Macdonald 1995a.

of properties. They have properties by exemplifying them. Given this, and given the universalist understanding of properties to which PEA subscribes (see n. 3), whereby an instance of a property just is (i.e. is identical with) the thing that has (exemplifies) it, instances of mental properties of mental events are identical with instances of physical properties of physical events (since each mental event is identical with a physical event). We take it that a necessary (but not sufficient) condition on causal relevance of properties is that instances of those properties are causally efficacious.[18] So, to say that a mental property *of* a physical event is causally relevant is at least to say that an instance of that property, i.e. that event, is causally efficacious in bringing about an effect of that event. According to our strategy, this will require that (mental) instance to be a physical instance, i.e. that one and the same event is an instance of both a mental and a physical property.

That requirement would need to be met anyway, since, on the universalist conception presumed by the PEA, things exemplify properties, and a thing just is (i.e. is identical with) an instance of each property that it has. Thus, an event exemplifies its properties, and it is (= is identical with) an instance of each property it has. This alone makes it difficult to see what exactly is going on in the metaphysics of Pettit's PE strategy, since he takes mental events to be identical with physical events, but wants to distinguish instances of higher-order properties (of events) from instances of lower-order ones, apparently using the PEA. We think this isn't possible. So, given the metaphysics of the PEA and Pettit's commitment to psychophysical event identity, there is independent reason to reject the 'distinct property-instances' view.

But we also hold a further thesis, which applies specifically to higher-order and lower-order properties. Things—objects, events, and other individual particulars—exemplify properties, but some properties they exemplify just by exemplifying others. This is not the case with all properties that a thing exemplifies, even given the universalist conception of properties. But it does apply to some. Consider a red, square box. It has the properties of being red and being square. It also has the property of being coloured. It is (identical with) an instance of each property that it has. The box exemplifies the properties of being red, being square, and being coloured. It does not exemplify the property of being

---

[18] It is clearly not sufficient, since, given the view that an exemplification of a property is the thing that has it, every property exemplified by an event would be causally relevant whenever that event caused any effect. So, in addition to (1) causal efficacy of their instances (i.e. events), we place two further conditions on the causal relevance of properties: (2) that the properties participate in a general 'pattern', or network of relations, in nature (one example of which is the nomological pattern), and (3) the generality which the properties display must be of the right type for a given type of effect (e.g. if the pattern is the nomological pattern, the nomological property must be nomological for a certain type of effect). For more on these conditions and our defence of them, see Macdonald and Macdonald 1995*a*.

square just by exemplifying the property of being red. But it does exemplify the property of being coloured just by exemplifying the property of being red.[19]

Similarly, events exemplify properties. But some properties they exemplify just by exemplifying others. In the case of higher-order (mental) and lower-order (physical) properties of events, we claim that this is just what happens. Thus, a mental event can exemplify the property *being a thinking of Vienna* just by exemplifying the property, say, *being neuro-chemical event* α. We claim that this view has an independent plausibility; it is not invoked just to solve a problem of over-determination. Where one property (or properties) of an event is said to *realize* another property (or properties) of that event, this is by far the most plausible way to construe the relation between the properties exemplified.

Call this thesis the Property-Dependence Thesis, to distinguish it from another, weaker thesis that we also hold and which follows from the universalist conception of properties, the Co-instantiation Thesis.[20] According to the latter, a mental property and a physical property of an event can be co-instantiated in a single instance; i.e. there is just one instance of two properties. This thesis is weaker than the Property-Dependence one, because on the universalist conception, *all* properties of an event are co-instantiated in a single instance—an event is just one instance of all of its properties, not just the higher-order and the lower-order ones. Still, since, on our view, the stronger thesis entails the weaker one, it follows that, where P is the physical property realizing mental property M, there will be just one instance of both P and M, P_i: i.e. M_i.[21] Given this, the mental instance, M_i, will be causally efficacious whenever the physical instance, P_i, is—given the assumption we share with Pettit, that causes are worldly events.

In short, our claim is twofold: (1) mental properties of persons supervene on their physical properties, and (2) mental properties of events supervene on their physical properties. This is consistent with the view that an individual event can be an exemplifying of both a mental and a physical property (of a person), can be an instance of both a mental property and a physical property (of an event), and can be an instance of a mental property just by being an instance of a physical property (of an event). Consequently, the epiphenomenalism problem that attaches to mental properties disappears, along with causal over-determination.

---

[19] But note that we do not think that the relation between mental and physical properties is a determinable/determinate relation, as some others (e.g. Yablo 1992) do. So, in the case of the properties of being coloured and being red, the dependence thesis holds because that the object is an instance of the property of being coloured is entailed by the fact that it is an instance of the property of being red. In other cases, of which the mental/physical property case is one, the dependence will hold for a different reason.

[20] See Macdonald and Macdonald 1986.

[21] So, in what follows, when we claim that $P_i = M_i$—i.e. that there is one instance of both a mental property and a physical property where mental properties are not identical with, or reducible to, physical ones—we mean more than that there is just one instance of both a mental property and a physical property (since on the universalist conception of properties, an event is just one instance of *all* of its properties). We mean that a mental event exemplifies M just by exemplifying P.

5. RESISTANCE TO THE PREFERRED ALTERNATIVE

The temptation to resist the suggestion that there is just one instance of two properties, one mental and one physical, is, we think, a result of two separate but related thoughts, both of which we think are mistaken. The first is the thought that distinct (non-identical) properties cannot share their instances, cannot be co-instantiated. But this thought is clearly wrong. Using an analogy we have used before, whenever the property *being red* is instanced, so is the property *being coloured*; it is very implausible to view the situation as anything other than one of a single instance of *both* properties, despite the non-identity of the properties being instanced. In general, in any case of properties related as determinate to determinable, an instance of a determinate property will just be an instance of a determinable property.[22] The property of weighing less than 100 lbs can be instanced by instancing the property of weighing 2 lbs. The latter will also be an instance of the properties of weighing less than 99 lbs, of weighing less than 98 lbs, and so on. (Note that these are also all examples of cases in which the stronger, property-dependence thesis is true.) It seems to us to be ontologically promiscuous to populate the world with extra instances whenever this happens. There is just one instance, which happens to be of many properties.

We stress that this is an analogy only: others have viewed it as no mere analogy, and have modelled the relation of mental to physical properties as a relation between determinable and determinate properties.[23] We do not think that this is a correct analysis of the mental–physical relation. One cannot infer from the fact that a person has a brain-property α that they have a mental property β (at least not without considerable empirical theoretical input), so one cannot infer from the fact that an event (an exemplifying of the brain-property α, i.e. an exemplifying of the mental property β) has the property of being an instance of the brain-property α that it has the property of being an instance of the mental property β. However, one *can* infer from the fact that something has the property of being red that it has the property of being coloured. Still, the determinate–determinable relation is just one example of a supervenience relation, and there are other examples of this latter relation that can underwrite our confidence that mental properties are co-instantiated with the physical properties upon which they supervene. In particular, that higher-order properties are *realized by* lower-order properties makes the identification of their instances compelling. At the very least, the onus is on those who deny this identification to explain how the realizing instances come to be 'separate existences'.

---

[22] We first suggested this analogy in Macdonald and Macdonald 1986. For further elaboration see Macdonald and Macdonald 1995*a*.

[23] See esp. Yablo 1992.

The second thought responsible for resistance to our solution is that, although co-instantiation is possible, it does not provide for the causal relevance of the higher-order property. As we have seen, Pettit expresses the objection that on our view intentional states are given relevance 'through construing them as identical with electronic or neural states', this having the defect that 'it would make a state like the belief that *p* causally relevant but relevant in virtue of a property other than that of being the belief that *p*: relevant in virtue of being such and such a neural or electronic state' (Pettit 1993: 38).[24] We take it that this objection has the following form: being the belief that *p* will be causally relevant when it is capable of explaining an effect that would have been produced by instances of *any* of its realizing properties. Because its relevance is thus 'general' with respect to all of its realizers, the causal relevance of the higher-order mental property cannot be identified with the causal relevance of any particular (lower-order, physical) realizing property. But, so the objection goes, our account, in identifying the *events* as it does, identifies the causal relevance of the mental property of the event with the relevance of a particular physical realizer property of that event.

It is worth clarifying what would be wrong with such an identification from our point of view. One could only identify the causal relevance of an intentional property (say, the property of being the belief that *p*) with that of a particular realizer of that property (say, the property of being neuro-chemical state *a*) if *that* realizer's relevance was shared by all the other (possible) realizers of the intentional state. This identification, if correct, would lead immediately to the reduction of the intentional property to its realizer, there being no other realizers whose causal relevance differed, thus defeating our aim of establishing the possibility of non-reductive monism.

What the criticism does, though, is conflate the requirements on causal efficacy, which concerns events, with those on causal explanation, which concerns what we have been calling causal relevance. As noted above, our view is that the causal efficacy of events is just one condition on the causal relevance of the properties of those events. The notion of 'being relevant *in virtue of* property *P* rather than property *Q*', whether this concerns properties that are co-instanced or whether it concerns properties connected by the 'ensuring' relation, can only be made sense of in terms of the causal power of the property instanced, this power making that property relevant for the causal explanation of (an aspect of) the effect. The property *being the desire that q* will be relevant to the causing of a number of appropriate actions, appropriate given the content of the desire. Those actions will be caused, in part at least, *in virtue of* the agent's having that desire (i.e. exemplifying the property *desires that q*). On different occasions a desire with the same content will be variously realized (given non-reduction) by different

---

[24] We cite Pettit here because of the context, but this objection is common to several critics of our view; see Ehring 1996, 1999, and Yablo 1992, e.g. Note that Pettit's use of 'state' here must mean 'property-instance'.

first-order physical properties, and while those realizers may be relevant to (and so explanatory of) the actions physically described, the claim is that it will be *in virtue of* the desire's being a desire that *q* that the action, intentionally described, is performed.

If this is what is meant by *in virtue of,* and the related notion of causal relevance, then we agree with Pettit that it is only *some* properties of events that are causally relevant to the effects they produce. Which properties they are will depend on which aspects (properties) of the effect one wants explained. But none of this touches on the point about causal efficacy. It is clear that on our account not all properties whose instances are causally efficacious will be causally and so explanatorily relevant (though we do insist that any causally relevant property must be one whose instances are causally efficacious). Thus, suppose that a window has a shattering point of 5 lbs, and shatters because it is struck by a 7 lb rock thrown at it. It is causally relevant that the rock weighs more than 5 lbs, even though this instance of weighing more than 5 lbs is also an instance of weighing more than 2 lbs. The throwing of a rock weighing more than 2 lbs won't explain the window's shattering, though *in this case* the instance of the property *weighing more than 2 lbs* just is an instance of weighing more than 5 lbs (= an instance of weighing 7 lbs), and so the throwing caused the shattering. The property *weighing more than 2 lbs* does not help to explain the shattering because other instances of it in rock throwings won't be ones in which the window will shatter. But this truth about other instances is irrelevant to the causal efficacy of this instance, it being pertinent only to the matter of causal relevance.

It is difficult to see why this outcome should be problematic. *Any* view of the causal relation that takes it to be an extensional relation, relating items 'in the world', will have the consequence that some causally efficacious properties, properties whose instances are causally efficacious, will not illuminatingly explain the effects they bring about. They will not, in these cases, be causally relevant properties. The only way to avoid this result is to change drastically the metaphysics presupposed here, that of properties and instances and the PEA account of events, a metaphysics to which Pettit seems committed.[25] Short of this, one can only avoid this consequence (on the assumption of extensionality) by insisting that no causally efficacious instance can be an instance of more than one property, thus ensuring that causal efficacy and relevance cannot come apart. This is an extraordinarily strong claim to make given the obvious counter-examples presented by instances of different determinates of a determinable. Take the example just given. The rock's weighing more than 5 lbs is relevant to (and so explanatory of) the window's shattering; its weighing more than 2 lbs may be relevant to my toe hurting when it falls on to that toe. Its weighing 7 lbs is both its

---

[25] We explore, and reject, a challenge to this metaphysics stemming from a specific version of trope theory (Robb 1997, 2001), which takes the properties whose causal relevance is in question to be tropes themselves, in Macdonald and Macdonald (forthcoming, 2007).

weighing more than 5 lbs and its weighing more than 2 lbs; one surely multiplies instances beyond necessity by insisting that these are all distinct instances.

Pettit himself needs something like the distinction between efficacy and relevance, even on his account where programming properties are said to be causally relevant but not causally efficacious. On this account, some properties that program for their effects do not figure in illuminating accounts of why those effects occurred. That an eraser is elastic programs for its bending, but its elasticity can be inferred from knowledge of its molecular structure, making the dispositional property (elasticity) 'insignificant'. So, Pettit adds the requirement that the programming property be 'significant', thus ensuring its explanatory relevance. If causal relevance requires 'significance', we can avail ourselves of this resource without going the circuitous and difficult route of 'programming'. We say that only some properties whose instances are causally efficacious are 'significant', or causally relevant, to their effects.[26] That some are not is irrelevant as an objection to our account.

It is worth noting that in the example just cited, that of elasticity, it would be strongly counter-intuitive to insist that when the dispositional property of being elastic is realized, its instances are not instances of the realizing property. In general, we claim, whenever a higher-order property is a functional property, it is co-instanced with its realizing properties—and so is as causally efficacious as they are. That being elastic is not a *significant* programming property is not germane here, since that does not change its status as a programming property. On the PE model, what lack of significance does is render the property causally irrelevant, and so non-explanatory. This might make it look as though no higher-order property *can be* causally relevant, in the sense that it can have a causal profile that cannot be identified with that of its lower-order realizers. But we deny this too, for the reasons given in Section 4 above.

We take it that the above establishes our strategy as intuitively more acceptable than one that makes mental properties causally inert. It secures the causal efficacy of such properties, and avoids over-determination, all in an ontologically parsimonious way. Moreover, its main device, co-instantiation, receives independent support from considerations stemming from the realization relation. However, its claim to be the best available strategy has been challenged (Kim 1999), and this challenge could be seen to provide indirect support for Pettit's view that the higher-order properties are not causally effective in producing the events that they explain. Kim's challenge takes the form of an argument that purports to

---

[26] The conditions for causal relevance are spelled out in more detail in Macdonald and Macdonald (1995*a*). We think that the problem of 'significance' will be inevitable on any account of causal relevance, since relevance has to do with explanatory potential, and this will vary from context to context, depending on the type of effect to be explained. Moreover, even within a single context, there will be properties whose instances are causally efficacious, but the properties themselves will not be causally relevant, as the above examples illustrate. This just goes to show that it is a mistake to think that there is such a thing as causal relevance *tout court*.

show that if supervenient properties have causal powers, then they are reducible to the properties on which they supervene. If correct, this would defeat our aim to show how irreducible mental properties can be both causally efficacious *and* causally relevant, since, in order for our solution to work, it must be possible for there to be emergent properties. We defend this possibility below, again on the basis of the crucial distinction between properties and their instances.

6. THE POSSIBILITY OF CAUSAL RELEVANCE

For some time now Jaegwon Kim has been arguing that the non-reductive monist's picture of the mind is seriously unstable, the instability making the 'non-reductive' aspect untenable. Consider Fodor's non-reductive monism, where the reduction of mental properties is rejected on the grounds that they are variously realized, where this means that their base realizing properties are heterogeneous. Given this heterogeneity, it is claimed that the subvening property formed by disjoining the particular realizing properties will not form a natural kind, thus blocking reduction to that disjunctive property. The lower-order properties cannot form disjunctive antecedents and consequents of a single law, so a bridge law is ruled out.[27] The problem, as Kim sees it here, is that we need an answer to the question of why the supervening property, say pain, is not 'equally heterogeneous and nonnomic as a kind' (Kim 1993: 323). Failing one, we must take seriously the thought that the variably realized supervening properties cannot figure in laws, not even *ceteris paribus* laws, leading to the conclusion that there are no 'special sciences' (on the assumption that all scientific explanation is law-based).

A related argument concentrates on the causal powers of the supervening and subvening properties. This begins by noting that the non-reductive monist is committed to there being a difference between the causal powers of properties at the subvening and supervening levels, those at the subvening level forming a heterogeneous set, those at the supervening level supposedly being homogeneous. The threat that arises is that the supervening properties will have no unified causal powers, thus making them causally irrelevant.[28] Recently Kim has advanced an argument along these lines, coming to a conclusion that has the form of a dilemma: either the supervening mental properties are causally inert, or they are reducible (Kim 1999, 2003). Either way, it is bad news for non-reductive monism, which needs irreducible higher-order properties that possess (independent) causal powers.

---

[27] Thus, he says, 'the lower level disjunctive antecedent is not a natural kind, and so is not law-apt— . . . a badly heterogeneous disjunction is unsuited for laws' (Kim 1993: 318). Note that Kim's most recent view (Kim 1998, 2005) is that bridge laws are neither necessary nor sufficient for reduction, since there is functional reduction (which he endorses).

[28] For an early formulation of such an argument see G. Macdonald 1986.

Such properties would be, in our terminology, emergent ones, having a distinctive causal profile. According to Kim's argument, if there were such emergent properties, then 'downward causation' would be possible, and downward causation is incoherent. The argument for downward causation goes like this. Emergent properties must have distinctive causal powers. They must be capable of being causally effective in bringing about their own distinctive effects. Suppose that they only bring about effects of the same (higher-order) level. These effects will be higher-order effects (given that emergent properties themselves are higher-order). But this means that the higher-order effects will have lower-order realizations. So, it is by causing instances of the lower-order (base) realizing properties that an emergent property will cause a higher-order effect. So higher-order causation presupposes downward causation.

Why, according to Kim, is downward causation incoherent? Consider emergent properties $M1$ and $M2$, where $M1$ causes $M2$'s instantiation, $M1$ being realized by $P1$ and $M2$ realized by $P2$. Given that $M2$ 'arises out of' (is realized by) $P2$, $M2$ would be instantiated by $P2$'s instantiation, regardless of whether $M1$ had caused $M2$. Simplicity dictates that $M1$ causes $M2$'s instantiation by causing $P2$ to be instantiated (the 'Downward Causation' conclusion). But g*iven* that $M1$ is realized by $P1$, and *given* irreducibility (i.e. that $M1 \neq P1$), we now have two sufficient causes of $P2$. This embarrassment of causal power can be resolved only by (a) eliminating $M1$ or $P1$ as a cause of $P2$, or (b) sacrificing irreducibility. Pettit takes the first option, giving up on the causal power of the mental, Kim the second.

Kim concludes that the emergent property $M1$ does not independently cause $P2$'s instantiation: what is doing the causal work is what realizes $M1$: namely, $P1$. So the so-called emergent property has no (distinctive) causal power, and $M1$ has no independent causal relevance. From this, given the previously stated assumptions, we can conclude that the special sciences cannot be defended by relying on the model that takes special science properties to be higher-order properties that are variably realized by, but irreducible to, physical ones. 'If emergent properties exist, they are causally, and hence explanatorily, inert and therefore largely useless for the purpose of causal/explanatory theories' (Kim 1999: 33).[29]

7. A DIFFERENT ARGUMENT AGAINST DOWNWARD CAUSATION

Given the hierarchical picture of the sciences presented here, it might look as though Kim has a sound argument for the causal irrelevance of emergent

---

[29] This argument is updated in Kim 2003. In the earlier paper Kim took the argument to show that the mental was causally inert; in the later paper he stresses the reducibility of the mental. If we can show that the mental can be causally relevant, we will have defused the argument for reducibility.

properties. But we claim that the argument is not sound. In this final section we want to show that there is a *sense* in which it is true that downward causation is incoherent. But the route to that conclusion is significantly different from Kim's, and leads to different consequences. In particular, it rescues the possibility of the causal relevance of (some) higher-order properties, mental ones included.

The argument, as presented, shuttles between talking of the downward causal power of properties and that of their instances. It is not that Kim is unaware of the importance of the property/instance distinction. He recognizes that 'Properties as such don't enter into causal relations; when we say M causes M^*, that is short for "An instance of M causes an instance of M^*" or "An instantiation of M causes M^* to instantiate on that occasion" ' (Kim 2003: 155).[30] But if we keep this distinction in mind, his conclusion that 'higher-order causation is downward causation' does not follow as immediately as he thinks it does. The crucial move in the argument is taken when downward causation is said to be required even for causation at the same (higher-order) level. The higher-order 'effect' ($M2$) is realized in a lower-order property ($P2$), and it is *an instance of* the lower-order property that is caused by (*an instance of*) the higher-order $M1$. As noted above, $M1$ does this by being realized by $P1$, the consequence being, so Kim argues, that either $P1$ does all the causal work, or $M1 = P1$. Kim opts for the latter solution, rescuing the $M1$–$M2$ 'causal' relation by ensuring, via reducibility, that it is the same relation as the $P1$–$P2$ 'causal' relation.[31]

Diagrammatically, his picture of the situation is as shown in Figure 1.1 (Kim 2003: 166): i.e. causation between mental properties just is causation between physical properties, since mental properties are physical properties. But this picture plainly flouts the distinction that Kim explicitly recognizes. The story should go: the putatively higher-order $M1$ has an instance, $M1_i$, that causes an instance of $M2$, $M2_i$, and does this (according to Kim) by means of an instance ($P1_i$) of its realizing base's causing an instance of $M2$'s realizing base, $P2_i$. Read this way, there is a sense in which we agree with Kim's conclusion: the causal relation between $M1_i$ and $M2_i$ is the same as the causal relation between $P1_i$ and $P2_i$. The picture is as shown in Figure 1.2. That is, causation between mental events just is causation between physical events, since mental events are physical events. But the obvious question now is: why is the supervening property said to be either reducible or causally inert, when the natural assumption, one argued for in preceding sections of this chapter, is that the supervening and base properties

---

[30] He also says: 'The fact that properties M and P must be implicated in the identity, or non-identity, of M and P instances can be seen from the fact that "An M-instance causes a P-instance" must be understood with the proviso "in virtue of the former being an instance of M and the latter being an instance of P" ' (Kim 2003: 157). On our view, this conflates causal efficacy with causal relevance.

[31] Our use of scare-quotes around key terms in this paragraph is intended to mark the equivocation we detect in the argument between talk of property-instances and causal efficacy, and talk of properties and causal relevance.

$$M1 \text{----- causes ---} \rightarrow M2$$
$$= \quad \text{is reductively} \quad =$$
$$\text{identical with}$$
$$P1 \text{----- causes ---} \rightarrow P2$$

Fig. 1.1.

$$M1_i \text{----- causes ---} \rightarrow M2_i$$
$$= \quad \text{is identical with} \quad =$$
$$P1_i \text{----- causes ---} \rightarrow P2_i$$

Fig. 1.2.

share instances? If there is just one instance of both the supervening and the base property, then it is true that there is no 'downward causation', where this now means that there are no higher-order *instances* of properties that cause lower-order *instances* of properties. There is no distinction between levels of instances, only between levels of properties. But this is unremarkable, and does not have the consequences drawn by Kim. *This* 'fact' of no downward causation does not lead to the conclusion that the higher-order properties are causally inert; nor does it lead, *without further argument*, to the conclusion that they are reducible. The causal efficacy of the instance is as secure as the causal efficacy of the base instance, given that there is here only one instance. All that is needed to secure the causal power of the supervening property is the plausible additional premiss that if a property has instances that are causally efficacious, then the property has causal powers. And *if* the higher-order property is irreducible, then it will have independent causal relevance; it will have a causal 'profile' different from that of its particular realizing properties. So what drives Kim to his sceptical conclusion?

Kim's sceptical attitude concerns the very idea that properties that are wholly distinct might nevertheless be co-instantiated in a single instance, and it is anchored in his views on the metaphysics of events.[32] These views go beyond commitment to the Property-Exemplification Account (PEA), since, as we have seen in Section 4, that account can be consistently combined with non-reductive monism. Kim's sceptical attitude is due to his further commitment to (1) the view that mental properties of persons are constitutive properties of the events that are (i.e. are identical with) instances of them, and (2) the view that events have only one constitutive property. Given that physical properties are constitutive properties of the events that are instances of them, the identity condition on

---

[32] Thus, when discussing the relation between the mental property M and its subvening P, he says: 'To continue, from *Irreducibility* we have (6) $M \neq P$' and notes that 'this only means that this instance of $M \neq$ this instance of P. Does this mean that a Davidsonian "token identity" suffices here? The answer is no: the relevant sense in which an instance of $M =$ an instance of P requires either property identity $M = P$ or some form of reductive relationship between them' (Kim 2005: 42).

events entails that it can only be that $M1_i = P1_i$ if $M1 = P1$ (and similarly for $M2_i$ and $P2_i$ and $M2$ and $P2$). Given distinctness of the M-properties and the P-ones, distinctness of the instances is assured, and epiphenomenalism, *both* at the level of causal efficacy (of events) *and* at the level of causal relevance, looms.

However, non-reductive monists—even those who commit themselves to the PEA—are free to reject (1) and/or (2), and thereby to block the epiphenomenalist conclusion. If, for example, (2) is rejected, then non-reductive monists can argue that mental/physical events have two constitutive properties, one mental and one physical, both of which need to figure in their identity conditions, and this is possible compatibly with the distinctness of the properties instanced.[33] Taking this line would leave the relation between mental and physical properties unresolved, however, so we prefer to reject (1): mental properties are not constitutive properties of the events that are instances of them, but, rather, supervene on such properties (in the sense specified in Section 4). But this is something that any physicalist who thinks that physicalism is true and contingent should do.

There is an argument in Kim 1999 that looks as though it will still deliver the unwelcome conclusion. The critical move is made by the claim that where the realizing relation holds between properties, the instance of the realized property has causal powers identical to those of the instance of the realizer property (so the causal powers of $M1_i$ and $P1_i$ are the same). Kim construes this as flowing from the causal inheritance principle, which says that, in cases of higher-order/lower-order causation, the instance of the higher-order property 'inherits' all its causal power from the instance of the lower-order property. But this causal inheritance principle is not obviously derivable from the less controversial claim that identical instances have identical causal powers, and even this is controversial enough. Let's consider the identity claim first, before returning to the inheritance claim.

The identity claim *looks* uncontroversial; indeed, it looks like it provides the ground for the conclusion that the supervening property is causally efficacious,

---

[33] One might think that this is inconsistent with the existence and identity conditions of events as stated by the PEA, but it is not (though it is inconsistent with Kim's claims on behalf of that account). As Lombard points out:

Suppose that an event, e_1, is x's exemplifying of F at t, and that an event, e_2, is x's exemplifying of G at t, where F and G are distinct properties. Despite the fact that Kim's criterion of identity for events says that events are identical only if they are exemplifyings of the same property, that condition does *not* imply that e_1 and e_2 are distinct events. Nothing in that condition or in Kim's existence condition for events says that e_1 could not, in addition to being an exemplifying of F, be an exemplifying of G, and that e_2 could not, in addition to being an exemplifying of G, be an exemplifying of F. And if those were the facts, then e_1 and e_2 would be exemplifyings of the same properties by the same objects at the same times, and hence would be, according to Kim's criterion, identical. . . . that latter idea [that an event can be an exemplifying of only one property] is a consequence, not of the view that events are exemplifyings of properties by objects at times, but of the view that events are explicanda, a view from which Kim's property-exemplifying account is ultimately derived. (Lombard 1986: 55)

and hence has causal power. It provides support for the efficacy claim because, as we have remarked before, '. . . is causally efficacious' is an extensional context. If *this* is all that is entailed by the causal inheritance principle, then there can be no objection to it. But there is a way of reading the attribution of causal power to an instance that suggests that it is the *property* instanced, and not the instance itself, whose causal power is in question. What this ambiguity can do is camouflage an inference from the identity of what we will call *instance causal power* to a conclusion about the identity of causal powers of the property instanced. This inference would enable one to move from accepting the picture as presented in Fig. fig1.2 to accepting the picture as presented in Fig. fig1.1. And it is in fact this further inference that Kim needs in order to arrive at his sceptical conclusion concerning the impossibility of emergent properties. But this inference is infirm, so the scepticism is unwarranted. Additional argument is required in order to be entitled to conclude, from a claim about the identity of the causal power of the instance of co-instanced properties, that the two properties thus co-instanced have the same causal power. So, in our example, $M1_i = P1_i$, it is clear that *as instances* they have the same causal power. But this does not by itself license the inference to the conclusion that $M1$ and $P1$ have the same causal power, since this has to do with instances of $M1$ and $P1$ in addition to $M1_i$ and $P1_i$. Further, given the possibility of variable realizability, it is clear that we are not entitled to conclude, from the fact that $M1_i = P1_i$, that every instance of $M1$ is an instance of $P1$.

In the case being considered by Kim, it is unlikely that an argument to this conclusion can be mounted that will not beg the question about the coherence of the notion that emergent properties have distinctive causal powers. Ironically, some of the points made by Pettit in favour of program explanation support this view. As we noted earlier, Pettit has made a convincing case for there being supervening properties that are explanatorily *significant*. Such properties are, on the PE model, those that ensure their realization in properties from which one cannot just 'read off' the causal relevance of the higher-order property. The model being examined is one of higher-order property causation, and we are assuming, consistent with Kim's starting-point, that the higher-order property is co-instanced in different situations with different base (lower-order) properties. These base properties have, *ex hypothesi*, different causal powers, and on the plausible assumption that the causal powers of each such property differ from those of any other, it is impossible for the higher-order property to possess the same causal power of each lower-order realizing property. Connected to this is the point alluded to by Pettit, that the difference in causal power can be detected by counterfactualizing: a mental property—say, intending to pay that bill—can cause the action of paying the bill, and without that intention the action would not have occurred. But it may be false that without the particular realizer property being instanced, the bill would not have been paid. The intention could have been realized by a different base property. So the causal powers of supervening properties can have different profiles from that of the properties supervened upon. There can be emergent properties, properties that are causally relevant to the effects they produce, even though there is no 'pernicious' downward causation.

8. CONCLUSION

We have examined Program Explanation and found its metaphysics suspect: resistance to the co-instantiation of realized and realizing properties is unmotivated, and it causes needless problems with the interpretation of the essential 'ensuring' relation. In addition, it renders instances of intentional properties causally inefficacious, a strongly counter-intuitive result. Giving up this non-identity should be palatable to Pettit once the distinction between causal efficacy and causal relevance is recognized and respected, given that his objection to our view appears to depend only on a conflation of the two. We have argued that the preferred alternative reinstates the causal efficacy of the mental while avoiding the problem of causal over-determination. This, however, still leaves open the possibility that, though not causally inert, mental properties may be causally irrelevant, so explanatorily inert. We therefore concluded by addressing an argument of Kim's to the effect that higher-order properties *could not be* causally relevant, as they could not have distinctive causal powers. Kim's conclusion, it was argued, derived from an equivocal premiss. Disambiguating that premiss destroyed the pessimistic conclusion that such properties are 'largely useless for the purpose of causal/explanatory theories' (Kim 1999: 33). There can be higher-order properties with distinctive causal powers, and so non-reductive monism lives on.

REFERENCES

Brand, M., and Walton, D. 1976 (eds.). *Action Theory*. Dordrecht: D. Reidel.

Ehring, D. 1996. 'Mental Causation, Determinables and Property Instances'. *Nous* 30(4): 461–80.

——— 1999. 'Tropeless in Seattle: The Cure For Insomnia'. *Analysis* 59(1): 19–24.

Grimes, T. 1991. 'Supervenience, Determination, and Dependency'. *Philosophical Studies* 62: 81–92.

Heil, J. 1998. 'Supervenience Deconstructed'. *European Journal of Philosophy* 6: 146–55.

Horgan, T. 1993. 'From Supervenience to Superdupervenience: Meeting the Demands of a Material World'. *Mind* 102: 554–86.

Kim, J. 1976: 'Events as Property Exemplifications'. In Brand and Walton 1976: 159–77.

——— 1978. 'Supervenience and Nomological Incommensurables'. *American Philosophical Quarterly* 15: 149–56.

——— 1984. 'Concepts of Supervenience'. *Philosophy and Phenomenological Research* 45: 153–76.

——— 1993. *Supervenience and Mind*. Cambridge: Cambridge University Press.

―― 1998. *Mind in a Physical World*. Cambridge, Mass.: MIT Press.

―― 1999. 'Making Sense of Emergence'. *Philosophical Studies* 95: 3–36.

―― 2003. 'Blocking Causal Drainage and Other Maintenance Chores with Mental Causation'. *Philosophy and Phenomenological Research* 67: 151–76.

―― 2005. *Physicalism, or Something Near Enough*. Princeton: Princeton University Press.

Lombard, L. 1986: *Events: A Metaphysical Study*. London: Routledge & Kegan Paul.

Macdonald, C. 1989: *Mind–Body Identity Theories*. London: Routledge.

―― and Macdonald, G. 1986. 'Mental Causation and Explanation of Action'. *Philosophical Quarterly* 36: 145–58.

―― ―― 1995*a*. 'How to Be Psychologically Relevant'. In Macdonald and Macdonald 1995*b*: 60–77.

―― ―― 1995*b* (eds.). *Philosophy of Psychology: Debates on Psychological Explanation*. Oxford: Blackwell.

―― ―― forthcoming, 2007. 'The Metaphysics of Mental Causation'. *Journal, of Philosophy*.

Macdonald, G. 1986. 'The Possibility of the Dis-unity of Science'. In Macdonald and Wright 1986: 219–46.

―― and Wright, C. 1986 (eds.). *Fact, Science, and Morality*. Oxford: Basil Blackwell.

McLaughlin, B. 1995. 'Varieties of Supervenience'. In Savellos and Yalcin 1995: 16–59.

Melnyk, A. 1995. 'Two Cheers for Reductionism: Or, The Dim Prospects for Non-reductive Materialism'. *Philosophy of Science* 62: 370–88.

Miller, R. 1990. 'Supervenience is a Two-Way-Street'. *Journal of Philosophy* 87: 695–701.

Pettit, P. 1993. *The Common Mind: An Essay on Psychology, Politics, and Society*. Oxford: Oxford University Press.

Robb, D. 1997. 'The Properties of Mental Causation'. *Philosophical Quarterly* 47: 178–95.

―― 2001. 'Reply to Noordhof on Mental Causation'. *Philosophical Quarterly* 51: 90–4.

Savellos, E., and Yalcin, U. 1995 (eds.). *Supervenience: New Essays*. Cambridge: Cambridge University Press.

Woodward, J. 2003. *Making Things Happen*. Oxford: Oxford University Press.

Yablo, S. 1992. 'Mental Causation'. *Philosophical Review* 101: 245–80.

2

Mental Causation on the Program Model

Peter Menzies

1. INTRODUCTION

In the late 1980s and early 1990s Philip Pettit collaborated with Frank Jackson in writing an important series of articles in which they proposed an account of causal relevance that they called the program model of causal relevance (Jackson and Pettit 1988, 1990*a*, 1990*b*, 1992*a*, 1992*b*). While Jackson (1996) seems to have moved away from the model as a solution to the problem of intentional causation (he tells me that he still thinks it is the right account of a major kind of causal relevance), Pettit has gone on to articulate and develop the model in interesting ways on his own. He has applied the model to a number of conceptual problems, ranging from the problem of mental causation to the role of equilibrium explanations in the social sciences (Pettit 1992, 1993, 2002). The model has been deservedly influential because of its wide and varied application.

However, the program model has been particularly influential among philosophers, I think, because it seems to offer a solution to a puzzle about causation. On a certain physicalist view about causation, states that instantiate the variables of the laws of physics have a privileged causal status: physical states of this kind are the only states with genuine causal efficacy. Clearly, this view is in tension with the fact that it is common, in everyday life and in the special sciences, to attribute causal efficacy to higher-level states that cannot be identified with any physical states. The attraction of the program model lies in its seeming to provide

Versions of this paper were read at a conference on Mental Causation, organized by the NAMICONA group at the University of Århus, Denmark, in May 2004; and at a workshop on Mental Causation at Macquarie University in August 2004. I'm grateful for the comments of many participants at these conferences, especially David Chalmers, Frank Jackson, Barry Loewer, and David Papineau. I'm also grateful to Philip Pettit for many conversations about causation and mental causation over the years. More generally, I'm deeply indebted to Philip for his encouragement and wise counsel over many years. My work on this chapter was supported by a Discovery Grant from the Australian Research Council.

a vindication of the causal relevance of higher-level states that is compatible with the physicalist view about causation.

In this chapter I shall consider whether the model actually succeeds in its aim of vindicating the causal relevance of higher-level states. I shall take as an illustrative example the application of the model to the problem of mental causation; and I shall focus on the causal role of intentional mental states in order to abstract away from the complex issues surrounding sensory and experiential mental states. I want to consider, in particular, whether the model manages to reconcile the common-sense attribution of causal efficacy to intentional states with the popular view that only physical states are causally efficacious.

My overall conclusion is that the program model does not offer a satisfactory account of the causal relevance of intentional states. After outlining the program model in the next section, I devote the following three sections to giving my reasons for this conclusion. Ultimately, it seems to me that the model fails because trying to reconcile the physicalist view about causation with common-sense views about the causal efficacy of intentional states is like trying to square the circle. The views are simply incompatible, and they cannot both be true. By adopting a certain well-developed treatment of causation, one can see the problem as lying not with the common-sense views about the causal efficacy of intentional states, but with the physicalist view about causation.

2. THE PROGRAM MODEL OF CAUSAL RELEVANCE

To start with, let us consider a schematic description of the model and a simple illustrative example. Let us suppose that a higher-level state S_1 is realized by a lower-level physical state S_2, which is assumed to be causally efficacious in producing some effect E. For example, the fragility of a vase is realized by its molecular structure, which is known to cause the vase to break when dropped. It is reasonable, at least sometimes, to think that the higher-level dispositional state S_1, as well as the lower-order physical state S_2, is causally relevant to the effect E. For example, it is reasonable to assert that the vase's fragility caused it to break if we want to eliminate the idea that the vase's breaking was a random occurrence. The central question which the program model addresses is: How can S_1 be causally relevant to E, given that S_2 is known to produce E by itself? How can the vase's fragility, for instance, play a causal role in its breaking when its molecular base is sufficient to produce this effect? The program model answers these questions by conjecturing that the higher-level state S_1 is causally relevant to the effect E through non-causally ensuring that there is some lower-level physical state—in this case S_2, but some other physical realizer would suffice—that is causally efficacious in producing E. In our simple example, the vase's fragility is causally relevant to the vase's breaking because it ensures that there is some lower-level physical state—as it happens, the vase's molecular structure, but another physical realizer would suffice—which causes the vase to break when dropped.

As its name suggests, the program model draws upon a useful analogy with the way in which a computer program executes a sequence of commands to generate output to describe the relationship between levels. Just as the computer program determines these things by non-causally ensuring that a sequence of physical processes at the mechanical and electronic level is realized, so a higher-level state determines a certain effect by non-causally ensuring that there are lower-level physical states present to produce the effect. Accordingly, the model says that the higher-level state programs for the presence of the productive physical state, and so for the effect it produces.

The example about the causal relevance of a dispositional state is a simple but apt one. For the program model's treatment of the causal relevance of intentional states follows the pattern of this example, as it adopts a functionalist conception of intentional states. On this conception, a subject has an intentional state just when the subject has a lower-level physical state that enters into a distinctive pattern of causal interactions with perceptual states, other intentional states, and behaviour. In other words, a subject has a certain intentional state just when the subject has a lower-level state that realizes the causal role distinctive of that intentional state. In the familiar jargon of functionalism, an intentional state is a causal role state.

However, the causal roles corresponding to intentional states like beliefs and desires are considerably more complex than those involved in simple dispositions like fragility. In this regard, Pettit mentions the collateral and contextual complexity of the causal roles associated with intentional states (Pettit 1993: 29–30). The *collateral complexity* of an intentional state's causal role consists in the fact that it is holistically intertwined with those of many other intentional states in virtue of their typical causal interactions with one another. The *contextual complexity* of an intentional state's causal role consists in the fact that the intentional state may have distal causes and effects in the subject's environment that are constitutive of its content. This kind of complexity is displayed by intentional states involving demonstratives, such as the belief that *that* bird is a parrot or the desire for *that* ice-cream.

In presenting his version of the program model, Pettit is careful to distinguish his functionalist conception of intentional states from another conception that is sometimes, confusingly, called functionalist (Pettit 1993: 24–32). On this other conception, an intentional state is characterized by a distinctive pattern of typical causes and effects, but is not itself that pattern of typical causes and effects. It is not the role state that consists in the having of some or other state realize the causal role but is, in fact, the physical state itself that does the realizing. In the jargon, it is a realizer state rather than a role state. This conception of intentional states is more informatively classified as a version of the identity theory rather than of functionalism. On such a theory, the problem of reconciling the causal efficacy of intentional states with the physicalist view about causation is neatly resolved.

In contrast, Pettit makes it clear that he adopts the more orthodox functionalist conception of intentional states. Indeed, he argues that an identity theory that identifies an intentional state with a physical realizer state rather than a higher-level role state is faced with a serious difficulty (Pettit 1992; 1993: 34). The difficulty stems from the existence of examples of a kind first described by David Lewis (see Menzies 1987). Lewis pointed out that certain dispositions of metals like electrical conductivity, ductility, and opacity are realized by the same physical state—the state of possessing a cloud of free electrons that permeates the metal and holds the atoms in a solid state. In such cases it would be absurd to identify these different dispositions with the same realizer state, since these dispositions differ from one another in their causal properties. For example, the electrical conductivity, rather than the ductility or the opacity, of a piece of metal is causally responsible for the electric shock that a person receives on coming in contact with the metal. Pettit suggests that the same point can be made in connection with intentional states if one is prepared to grant with some theorists (for example, Ramsey, Stich, and Garron 1990) that the different intentional states may be realized by one and the same neural state. If a subject has beliefs that differ in their causal roles but are realized by the same neural state, the beliefs cannot, on pain of inconsistency, be identified with that neural state. I shall consider this kind of situation in more detail in the next section.

On the assumption that intentional states are causal role states, the program model explains their causal relevance in the same way as it does that of dispositional states. Intentional states like a belief and a desire are causally relevant to behaviour by virtue of programming for the existence of lower-level neural states that produce the behaviour. (Neural states are not physical states in the strict sense. But because of their obvious supervenience on the physical, they count as honorary members of the club.) The kind of causal relevance conferred on intentional states by the program model has two notable characteristics. It has *modal resilience*. In other words, the causal relevance that a belief–desire pair bear to some behaviour does not depend on which of its possible neural realizers is actualized. It is actually realized by *this* neural state; but it might have been realized by *that* neural state or some other. It does not matter, because the fact that the pair programs for *some or other* neural realizer is enough to warrant the causal relevance of the belief–desire pair. The kind of causal relevance conferred by the program model has *epistemic resilience* as well. Typically, one takes a belief–desire pair to be causally relevant to the behaviour without knowing how the pair is neurally realized. However, even if one did know the particular neural state that realized a belief–desire pair and did know how the neural state produced the relevant behaviour, that knowledge would not diminish the usefulness of saying that the belief–desire pair was causally relevant to the behaviour. For saying this conveys information about non-actual possible circumstances in which the behaviour would have been produced.

These features of the program model enable Pettit to give an intuitive explanation of the Lewis-type examples that present a difficulty for identity theories that equate dispositions and intentional states with physical realizer states. Thus he argues that even if the conductivity and the opacity of a particular piece of metal are realized by the same cloud of free electrons, the metal's conductivity may be causally relevant to a person's getting an electric shock in a way that its opacity is not. This can happen if conductivity programs for a different set of possible realizers from opacity and if all of conductivity's realizers would produce the electric shock and some of opacity's realizers would not. Likewise, even if a subject has two intentional states that are realized neurally in the same way, it is possible to distinguish one state from the other with respect to causal relevance to behaviour. If the intentional states program for different sets of possible realizers, it can happen that all members of one set produce the behaviour, while some of the members of the other set do not.

To conclude our exposition of the program model let us consider two general disclaimers that Pettit makes about the model. First, he says that the model is neutral on the issue of how the concept of causal efficacy or production is to be understood. It does not presuppose any specific understanding of the concept in terms of objective physical forces, counterfactual dependence, probability increases, or necessary and sufficient conditions. Secondly, it does not assume that a neural state that is a low-level realizer for a higher-level intentional state is absolutely low-level. It may be that it is a higher-level state relative to a still lower-level realizer state.

Notwithstanding these disclaimers, it seems to me that Pettit's application of the program model to intentional states is implicitly committed to the physicalist view about causation mentioned in the introduction. The model gets its traction from the assumption that neural states, in their guise as honorary physical states, have completely unproblematic causal relevance to behaviour. It is because their causal powers are so unproblematic that those of intentional states, conceived as higher-level role states, seem to require justification. The program model is supposed to provide this justification by showing how such intentional states can convey causal information that is not conveyed by their neural realizers. But how satisfactory is this account of the causation of behaviour by intentional states?

3. THE NATURE OF INTENTIONAL STATES

Before I can turn to this question, it is necessary to consider the nature of intentional states in order to appreciate when and how they can cause behaviour and other mental states. My remarks on this enormous subject will, of necessity, be brief. To simplify matters, I will concentrate on the nature of intentional states vis-à-vis their specific role as the causes of behaviour, rather than their role as causes and effects of other mental states.

As we have seen, Pettit takes as a starting-point for his discussion the functionalist conception of intentional states as causal role states. It is important to recognize that this conception gets its intellectual credibility from a framework of assumptions and presuppositions that includes the physicalist view of causation. Suppose you assume that the only states that can cause behaviour are physical states like neural states. Then, if you also assume that intentional states are not identical to physical states, perhaps because they can be multiply realized by neural states, you are left with intentional states that have dubious ontological and causal standing. If the physical neural states do all the causal work, what are intentional states, and what do they do? Within this physicalist framework, it is very natural to try to salvage some ontological standing for intentional states by treating them as causal role states. After all, there should be room in a physicalist ontology not just for a neural state and its causes and effects, but also for the state of there being a neural state with these causes and effects. This treatment has the virtue of allowing for the possibility of multiple realizability, since many neural states can occupy a given causal role. With the ontological standing of intentional states thus secured, the contribution that the program model makes to this overall framework is to offer a vindication of the causal standing of intentional states. The program model, as we have seen, grants that intentional states do not have the causal efficacy of neural states, but it secures their causal relevance to behaviour, at least, by affirming that they bear important causal information through programming for the presence of the neural states that produce the behaviour.

From this sketch, it is evident that the physicalist view of causation plays a pivotal role in this framework of assumptions. This is somewhat problematic for our discussion, since I am going to question this view in the following sections, and so do not want to have it built into the conception of intentional states from the outset. Consequently, I plan to discuss the nature of intentional states, starting from a different point. I shall assume that the correct conception of intentional states is to be settled by reference to folk psychology. Moreover, I am going to assume that folk psychology is a theory that posits intentional states as its central explanatory entities. (For arguments for these assumptions see Churchland 1989: 1–22, 111–28; Fodor 1987: 1–26, 135–54.)

What does this theory say about intentional states? I think it is common ground among philosophers who accept these starting assumptions that intentional states have three crucial characteristics (see Fodor 1987: 10). First, an intentional state has semantic content, which is usually expressed by the proposition embedded in its that-clause. Furthermore, this semantic content is crucial to the identity of the intentional state. Thus, it is the fact that your belief is the belief that *there is beer in the fridge* and your desire is the desire *for beer* that make them the intentional states they are. Secondly, an intentional state has causal powers. For example, your belief that there is beer in the fridge and your desire to drink beer cause you to head to the fridge in the same way that heating metal causes it to expand. Thirdly, intentional states conform to the implicit generalizations of folk psychology. For example, it is a true generalization that if an intentional subject desires X and believes that X is in a nearby location Y, then, *ceteris paribus*, the subject will head towards location Y.

The three characteristics of intentional states are interrelated, I would argue. Intentional states have their causal powers in virtue of their semantic content. Your belief and desire cause you to head to the fridge precisely because they have their specific contents: that is, precisely because your belief is the belief that *there is beer in the fridge* and your desire is the desire *for beer*. Moreover, the implicit generalizations of folk psychology express the causal laws that bestow causal powers on the intentional states; and these generalizations make essential reference to the semantic contents of these states. Thus the generalization above is a generalization which essentially refers to the content of the desire (the desire for X) and the content of the belief (the belief that X is at nearby location Y).

On the face of it, folk psychology is committed to what Fodor has called 'intentional realism': the view that intentional states are real inner states with significant causal powers. However, this is not to say that folk psychology is thereby committed to the language of thought hypothesis. This is a substantive hypothesis about the cognitive architecture of the mind to the effect that intentional states pick out computational relations to internal representations which have syntactic structures that recapitulate the semantic contents of the corresponding intentional states, and thought processes are computational processes involving transitions between such internal representations. Even Fodor admits that the language of thought hypothesis goes well beyond the intentional realism of folk psychology (1987: 135–41). Additional empirical premises are required to get from intentional realism to the language of thought hypothesis. It is, indeed, generally conceded that even if folk psychology is committed to intentional realism, it is silent on the issue of how the intentional states are internally represented in cognitive structures. Folk psychology, taken by itself, does not speak in favour of any particular hypothesis about internal cognitive architecture.

The same point can be made about the underlying neural structures subserving intentional states. Intentional states are the projectable kinds of the generalizations of folk psychology; and these generalizations are neutral on the issue of how intentional states relate to neurology. Indeed, it is reasonable to think that the projectable kinds of folk psychology may cross-cut the projectable kinds of neurology. This point is often expressed as the multiple realizability argument against the identity theory: intentional states are not identical to neural states because any given intentional state can be realized by many possible neural states.

The dialectic around this issue is now very familiar. The identity theorist who accepts the fact of multiple realizability has two options: either she must identify an intentional state with the disjunction of its actual and possible neural realizers; or she must claim that the identity of an intentional state is relativized to kinds, with a different identity for each kind of possible neural realizer. The opponent of the identity theory responds by saying that both options are unsatisfactory. The first option is unsatisfactory as it fails to show how a projectable kind in folk psychology maps on to a projectable kind in neurology: since the possible neural realizers of a given intentional state may be very heterogeneous in nature, there is no reason to think that their disjunction will form a natural, projectable kind in neurology. The second option is unsatisfactory since it does not preserve the projectable kinds of folk psychology, but rather fractures and splinters them into many different subkinds, and thereby fails to capture the explanatory scope of the generalizations of folk psychology.

However this dialectic is resolved, there is another way of making the same point that the projectable kinds of folk psychology are likely to cross-cut those of neurology. The phenomenon of multiple realizability purports to establish this by showing that the realization is a one–many relation. But the point can also be made by noting that realization is a many–one relation; that is to say, the relation is such that many different intentional states may be realized by one and the same neural state. We have seen an analogous phenomenon in Lewis's example of how several dispositional states—the conductivity, ductility, and opacity of a metal—can have a common causal basis—in the cloud of free electrons permeating the metal. Another illustration of the phenomenon is provided by connectionist hypotheses about the cognitive architecture (see Ramsey, Stich and Garron 1990). Connectionists claim that the information encoded in intentional states is not represented in discrete cognitive structures, but is represented in a holistic and distributive manner. In the connectionist framework, intentional states are represented by networks of connected units; and a given network of units with a particular set of weightings on its connections can represent many different intentional states. These are conjectures about cognitive architecture, but the same point would apply with equal, if not greater, force to the way in which intentional states are realized neurally. It is plausible to conjecture that neural realizations of intentional states have a superpositional or overlapping character. This means that complex states of neural networks that realize one intentional state also realize several other intentional states at the same time. If anything like this conjecture is true, it is futile to search for identities between intentional states and discrete neural states, for there are no such identities to be found. And the strategy of taking disjunctions or relativizing identities to subkinds is of no avail in such circumstances.

At this point it might be objected that something must have gone wrong with my argument. It might be asked: Don't eliminativists advance the claim that information is encoded in neural structures differently from the way it is encoded in folk psychology, in order to reject folk psychology and its postulated intentional states? Aren't you using the possibility of such a mismatch to refute the identity theory and to preserve the causal autonomy of intentional states? Why aren't you an eliminativist? The answer to these questions is that both the identity theorist and the eliminativist make a common presupposition; and because I reject this presupposition, I can use the possibility of a mismatch between folk psychology and neurology without lapsing into eliminativism. The common presupposition of these two approaches is that if the projectable kinds of folk psychology—intentional states—are to be scientifically vindicated, it must be possible to map them on to the projectable kinds of neurology. The identity theorist accepts this conditional and also accepts its antecedent, and so insists that intentional states can be mapped on to neural kinds (even if only disjunctive or relativized in form). The eliminativist accepts the conditional, but rejects the consequent, and so rejects the antecedent: since intentional states cannot be mapped on to neural states, they are not capable of scientific vindication. Of course, the presupposed conditional is simply the physicalist view about causation, in a slightly different guise. In the following two sections ?? am going to argue that we should reject this assumption. It has been the source of endless conceptual mischief in the philosophy of mind and elsewhere.

What conclusion about intentional states should we draw from this discussion? First, that folk psychology conceives of them as semantically interpretable states with genuine causal powers. Secondly, it is unlikely, in view of the one–many and many–one nature of the realization relation, that they can be identified with neural realizer states. Any conception of intentional states must, in my opinion, be consistent with these conclusions. It is clear that the functionalist conception of intentional states as causal role states does not respect these conclusions. For this conception presupposes, as we saw earlier, the physicalist view of causation that implies that intentional states, like all other non-physical states, do not have genuine causal efficacy. When grafted on to this view of causation, the program model permits intentional states a kind of ersatz causal power it calls 'causal relevance'. But this ersatz causal power is not the real thing that folk psychology attributes to intentional states. I will elaborate on this claim in the next section. (For other arguments that the functionalist conception of intentional states is incompatible with their having genuine causal powers, see Block 1990.)

Once one gives up the functionalist view, how is one to think of intentional states? Other conceptions are available. For example, it is possible to think of intentional states as primitive, conceptually irreducible entities—as the *sui generis* states of intentional subjects. Of course, it would have to be conceded at the outset that these *sui generis* states are supervenient on the physical: there is no intentional difference between worlds without physical difference. However, this supervenience claim is not a conceptual truth that follows from folk psychology. A pre-scientific philosopher like Aristotle might have had a perfect grasp of folk psychology even though he denied the supervenience claim. The supervenience claim is best seen as a empirical hypothesis, made plausible by the progressive explanatory advances of neurology. It is consistent with the truth of the supervenience claim that intentional states, as *sui generis* states, have causal powers that are independent of those of the physical states on which they supervene.

It is useful to keep in mind a parallel here with the philosophical debate about colour. Physicalists say that the real causes of our colour experiences are physical states. However, since colours themselves cannot, in view of the existence of metamers, be identified with these physical states, they are best understood as dispositions to produce colour experience—dispositions which have those physical states as their causal bases. The unfortunate consequence of this position is that it makes colours causally inert in the production of colour experience. For it is the physical state that is the basis of the disposition, rather than the disposition itself, that causes colour experience. In this regard, the physicalist theory flouts the firm folk judgement that it is the colours themselves that are the causes of colour experience.

John Campbell (1993) has pointed out that there is a way to keep faith with this folk judgement while side-stepping the physicalist's dilemma. It is to think of colours as primitive, conceptually irreducible states; they are *sui generis* states as much as states instantiating primary qualities like shape. As it turns out, they happen to supervene on the physical, but this is an adventitious empirical discovery that does not follow from the folk theory of colour. Moreover, the fact that they supervene on the physical does not mean that they derive their causal powers from the physical, any more than the fact that geological or biological states supervene on the physical means that they derive their causal powers from the physical.

The parallel with intentional states is almost exact. It is open to us to see intentional states as primitive *sui generis* states; it is an adventitious scientific discovery that they supervene on the physical, but this fact does not undermine their causal autonomy, any more than the physical supervenience of biological or the geological states undermines their causal autonomy.

4. THE CAUSAL AUTONOMY OF INTENTIONAL STATES

It is time to spell out in more detail the criticism of the program model made in the last section—the criticism to the effect that it does not provide a sufficiently robust vindication of folk judgements about the causal efficacy of intentional states. (See also Kim 1998: 72–7.) The folk view is that your desire for beer and your belief that there is beer in the fridge cause you to head to the fridge; that your belief–desire pair cause your behaviour in the same full-blooded sense that heating a metal bar causes it to expand; and that your belief and desire have this causal effect in virtue of their semantic content.

The program model fails to capture these intuitions. In the first place, the model says that the real causes of your behaviour are physical neural states rather than your intentional beliefs and desires. To be sure, your beliefs and desires, and your intentional states more generally, are causally relevant to your behaviour, but only in virtue of programming for the presence of the neural states that are the real causes of the behaviour. The program model treats causal relevance as a kind of ersatz causal efficacy. Furthermore, the model states that common sense incorrectly identifies the states that have semantic content with the ones that cause behaviour. For on this model, the states that have semantic content are intentional causal role states, while the states that actually cause behaviour are neural realizer states. The departure from common-sense judgement is minimized by the claim that the intentional states with semantic content are causally relevant to behaviour, even if not causally efficacious in producing it. But once again this falls short of a fully robust vindication of the common-sense judgement that intentional states cause, in some full sense, behaviour in virtue of their semantic content.

The program model is forced into these departures from folk psychology by its adherence to the physicalist view about causation. Thus it assumes that the states that are genuinely efficacious in producing behaviour are physical states; and that the existence of such states makes it superfluous to postulate the existence of other causally efficacious states. Physicalists often try to justify such claims on the basis of a principle that is said to be a well-confirmed empirical generalization: the principle of the causal closure of the physical world. It can be formulated in many different ways, but the following is a convenient and plausible formulation:

> *Principle of causal closure of the physical world*: every physical state that has a cause has a complete physical causal history.

On the assumption that neural states qualify as physical states, the principle can be read as implying that, for any physical behaviour, there is a complete causal chain of neural states leading up to the behaviour. The causal chain is complete in the sense that it is continuous and non-gappy.

Without doubt this principle has a great deal of plausibility. The discoveries of neurology make it reasonable to believe that the causal chains of neural events leading up to behaviour do not have gaps that require completion by mental states. However, this principle does not, by itself, establish the additional physicalist claim that the existence of complete causal chains of neural states *excludes* or *renders superfluous* other causes of behaviour. Another principle is required to justify this claim. Many philosophers have implicitly appealed to some principle such as the following:

> *The exclusion principle*: with the exception of rare cases of overdetermination, no state has more than one complete causal history.

For example, Jaegwon Kim (1998) accepts a similar principle and has used it, together with the causal closure principle, to argue that non-reductive physicalism about the mental leads to epiphenomenalism. Kim's argument, which he calls *the exclusion argument*, is well known. He assumes, for the purposes of *reductio*, that the cause of a person's behaviour is a certain intentional state. But the principle of the causal closure of the physical tells us that there is also a complete causal chain of neural states leading to the behaviour. Yet it is implausible to think in such cases that there are overdetermining sets of causes of behaviour, one set consisting of intentional states and the other set consisting of neural states. Therefore, the exclusion assumption dictates that the intentional state does not cause the behaviour after all, or if it does, it must be identical with some neural cause. Since non-reductive materialists reject the identity of intentional states with neural states, they are forced to conclude that intentional states are epiphenomenal in the causation of behaviour, or so Kim argues.

As I see things, the program model is implicitly committed to something like the exclusion argument and its conclusion that intentional states are not genuinely causally efficacious in producing behaviour. To be sure, it tries to soften this conclusion by claiming that intentional states can nonetheless bear a kind of ersatz causal relation—causal relevance—to behaviour. But to all intents and purposes it accepts the soundness of the argument. In opposition to this, I believe that the exclusion argument is fundamentally mistaken, with the source of its error lying in its acceptance of the exclusion principle.

Elsewhere (Menzies 2003), I have argued that the exclusion principle relies on the mistaken metaphysical view that causation is an absolute, categorical relation. In everyday life and scientific practice, by contrast, causation is conceptualized quite differently: causal relations are picked out by reference to contextually determined models. In particular, I argued that causal relations are regarded as processes that occupy certain counterfactually defined roles, where the important parameters of counterfactual similarity and difference are established by reference to a model. Recognition of these facts, I suggested, opens up the possibility of seeing that there can be different levels of causation. There may be a level at which intentional states cause behaviour by way of distinctive psychological pathways, and a different level at which physical states cause behaviour by way of distinctive neural pathways. Moreover, I argued, these different levels of causation need not be in competition, and need not exclude one another.

Much of my argument depended on advancing a novel semantic framework for counterfactuals and causation. It strikes me now that a better way to make the same points is to use the technically precise structural equations framework for understanding counterfactuals and causation. The use of structural equations to study causation was pioneered by econometricians in the 1930s and 1940s. But the most complete development of the framework is to be found in the work of Judea Pearl (especially his 2000). (Spirtes, Glymour, and Scheines 2000 is also a notable contribution to this tradition.) Several philosophers, including Christopher Hitchcock (2001) and James Woodward (2003), have helped to make this tradition more accessible to other philosophers. I am indebted here to their expository work, especially Hitchcock (2001).

One feature of the structural equations framework should be remarked on straight away: it assumes that the truth conditions of causal claims and judgements are to be understood as relative to a model. It is precisely this feature that makes it useful for my purposes. But many philosophers will find this relativization alien and unattractive. To be sure, some philosophers, such as J. L Mackie (1974), have insisted that causal claims must be understood as relative to a contextually determined field of background conditions. For the most part, however, philosophers have baulked at the thought that causal judgements and statements have relativized truth conditions. Nonetheless, this thought strikes me as very plausible in view of the extent to which causal thinking is steeped in abstraction. The causal schemata by which we interpret the world are irremediably permeated by the kind of abstraction that allows us to attend selectively to some facts while backgrounding others. There seem to be two elements to the kind of abstraction that underlies our causal thinking: generalization and idealization. We generalize by seeing a concrete situation as an instance of a certain kind of system whose behaviour conforms to stable counterfactual-implying generalizations; and we idealize by supposing that these generalizations are *ceteris paribus* generalizations that describe how such systems behave in ideal conditions when they are not subject to interfering influences. In saying that the truth conditions of causal claims are to be understood relative to a model, researchers in the causal modelling tradition can be seen as trying to capture the fact that our causal thinking is permeated by these kinds of abstraction.

In the structural equations framework, a model is usually taken to be an ordered pair $< V, E >$, where V is a set of variables, and E is a set of structural equations. It is implicitly understood that the model is a model of a certain kind of system. The set V contains causally relevant variables that can be used to represent possible states of that kind of system. The structural equations in the set E describe the basic causal mechanisms of that kind of system, with each structural equation corresponding to a discrete causal mechanism. Sometimes, these equations contain an error term to represent other unknown causes; more often than not, they are taken to be *ceteris paribus* generalizations that are true of the systems in question under the assumption that they are not subject to other causal influences.

The variables in the set V are divided into exogenous and endogenous variables. An exogenous variable is one whose values are determined by factors not represented in the model, whereas an endogenous variable is one whose values are determined by the other variables in the model. It is important that these variables can take many values, though in the simple examples we will start with they will take two values, representing the occurrence or non-occurrence of a state or event.

For each variable there is a corresponding structural equation in the set E with that variable on the left-hand side of the equation. The structural equations for the exogenous variables take the simple form $X_i = x_i$, where x_i is the actual value of the variable. The structural equations for the endogenous variables take a more complex form. They state the value of the exogenous variable in question as a function of the values of other variables in the set V:

(1) $Y = f_Y (X_1, X_2, \ldots, X_n)$

This structural equation represents the discrete causal mechanism by which the value of the variable Y is determined by the values of the variables $X_1, X_2, \ldots, X_n$. In virtue of representing this causal mechanism, the structural equation is to be understood as encoding a set of non-backtracking counterfactuals of the form:

If it were the case that $X_1 = x_1, X_2 = x_2, \ldots, X_n = x_n$, then it would be the case that $Y = f_Y(X_1, X_2, \ldots, X_n)$.

For each combination of values for the variables $X_1, X_2, \ldots, X_n$, there is a counterfactual of this form stating the corresponding value of the endogenous variable Y. The counterfactuals are always read off a structural equation with the variables on the right-hand side of the equation appearing in the antecedent and the endogenous variable on the left-hand side appearing in the consequent. Because structural equations encode counterfactuals in this way, they are not symmetric.

A model can be given a simple representation in terms of a directed graph. The variables in the set V are nodes in a graph, which are connected by directed edges or arrows. A directed edge is drawn from X to Y just in case X appears on the right-hand side of the structural equation for Y, or, as it is commonly said, X is *a parent* of Y. A *directed path* from X to Y is a sequence of directed edges connecting X with Y. An exogenous variable is represented in such a graph by a node with no edge directed into it.

An example will help to make these details concrete. Suppose that we are considering what has caused you to open the fridge door and take a beer from the fridge. We can adopt different perspectives to understand your behaviour. From one possible perspective, we can see you as an instance of an intentional system, the causally relevant states of which are intentional states and the laws of which are the laws of rational, intentional psychology. We can capture this perspective in terms of a causal model—let us call it the intentional model I. Let us consider a very simplified version of the model to start with. Let us suppose that the variable set V of this model contains the following variables: $B = 1$ if you believe that there is beer in the fridge, 0 if not; $D = 1$ if you desire beer, 0 if not; $A = 1$ if you take a beer from fridge, 0 if not. Let us suppose that the structural equations of the model can be stated as follows:

(2) $B = 1$
(3) $D = 1$
(4) $A = B \,\&\, D.$

The equations (2) and (3) for the exogenous variables B and D simply specify the actual values of these variables: they tell us that you actually have the belief and desire. The equation (4) for the endogenous variable A represents the basic causal mechanism by which your belief and desire give rise to your behaviour. As such it is to be seen as encoding the following set of counterfactuals:

$$B = 1 \ \& \ D = 1 \ \Box\!\!\rightarrow_I A = 1$$
$$B = 1 \ \& \ D = 0 \ \Box\!\!\rightarrow_I A = 0$$
$$B = 0 \ \& \ D = 1 \ \Box\!\!\rightarrow_I A = 0$$
$$B = 0 \ \& \ D = 0 \ \Box\!\!\rightarrow_I A = 0$$

The subscript I on the counterfactuals represents that these are counterfactuals associated with the model I. The counterfactuals state that you would take a beer from the fridge if you were to desire beer and believe that there is a beer in the fridge; and that you would not take a beer from the fridge otherwise. The causal graph associated with this model is depicted in Figure 2.1.

A system of equations not only encodes counterfactual information, it also enables one to derive other counterfactuals that are true of the system being modelled. In general, the procedure for determining whether a counterfactual 'If it were the case that $X_1 = x_1$, $X_2 = x_2, \ldots, X_n = x_n$, then it would be the case that $Y = y$' is true of the system is this: (i) replace the equation for each of the variables $X_1, X_2, \ldots, X_n$ with the stipulated identities, leaving the equations for the other variables unchanged; (ii) using the structural equations of the model, compute the value for variable Y; and (iii) if the value of Y is equal to y, then the counterfactual is true, and false otherwise. The effect of the first step of this procedure is to create new set of structural equations in which $X_1, X_2, \ldots, X_n$ are exogenous variables. Pearl (2000) suggests that we understand this step as analogous to setting the values of these variables by a kind of idealized intervention in the system that affects the values of these variables and nothing else. Graphically, the interventions break the arrows leading to the variables that have been intervened on. As Woodward (2003) emphasizes, this way of evaluating counterfactuals depends on the fact that the remaining structural equations are invariant, or remain true as generalizations, under this kind of intervention.

To illustrate this procedure, consider what would happen if you did not desire beer. To consider this counterfactual scenario, simply replace the equation (3)

Fig. 2.1.

with $D = 0$; keep the remaining equations (2) and (4) unchanged; and compute the new value for A. It is easy to see that the following counterfactual is true:

$$D = 0 \ \Box\!\!\to_I A = 0$$

Given this general procedure for evaluating counterfactuals, one can characterize a notion of counterfactual dependence, which is central to understanding causation.

> Definition 1. A variable Y *counterfactually depends* upon a variable X in a model $M = < V, E >$ if and only if X and Y belong to the set V, $X = $ x and $Y = $ y, and there exist x$'$ $\neq$ x and y$'$ $\neq$ y such that the result of replacing the equation for X in the set E with $X = $ x$'$ yields $Y = $ y$'$.

This says simply that Y depends counterfactually on X just in case intervening to change the value of X from its actual value will result in a change in the variable Y from its actual value. In the particular example at hand, we can see that whether you take the beer from the fridge counterfactually depends on whether you desire beer:

$$(D = 1 \ \Box\!\!\to_I A = 1) \ \& \ (D = 0 \ \Box\!\!\to_I A = 0)$$

The issue of how counterfactual dependence relates to token-causation is a contested issue within the structural equations framework. Examples of pre-emption and overdetermination make it clear that causation amounts to more than counterfactual dependence between distinct events. Overdetermination raises complex issues, which cannot be discussed in this brief space. Instead, let us consider an example of pre-emption to gauge the kinds of complications that are needed to account for the relationship between causation and counterfactual dependence. Let us suppose that you go to the fridge because of your belief and desire about beer, but you have another belief–desire pair that would have caused you to go the fridge even if you had not had the belief–desire pair about beer: perhaps you desire salami, and you believe there is salami in the fridge. However, your desire for beer is greater than your desire for salami, so the first belief–desire pair pre-empts the second pair from affecting your behaviour. Let us construct a new model—call it I^*—with new variables and structural equations. Let R_1 take the value 1 if you desire beer and believe there is beer in the fridge, and 0 otherwise. Let R_2 take the value 1 if you desire salami and believe there is salami in the fridge, and 0 otherwise. Let P_1 take the value 1 if you intend to reach for the beer when you open the fridge door, and 0 otherwise. Let P_2 take the value 1 if you intend to reach for the salami when you open the fridge door, and 0 otherwise. Let A take the value 1 if you open the fridge door, and 0 otherwise. The structural equations for this model can then be represented as follows:

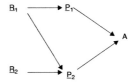

Fig. 2.2.

$$(5) \quad R_1 = 1$$
$$(6) \quad R_2 = 1$$
$$(7) \quad P_1 = R_1$$
$$(8) \quad P_2 = R_1 \mathbin{\&} \sim R_2$$
$$(9) \quad A = P_1 \mathbin{v} P_2$$

The directed graph for the model is depicted in Figure 2.2. Applying the procedure for evaluating counterfactuals to this new set of structural equations, it can be seen that your opening the fridge door counterfactually depends on neither your belief–desire pair about beer nor your belief–desire pair about salami. In fact, it is true that:

$$(R_1 = 1 \ \Box\!\!\mapsto_{I^*} A = 1) \mathbin{\&} (R_1 = 0 \ \Box\!\!\mapsto_{I^*} A = 1)$$
$$(R_2 = 1 \ \Box\!\!\mapsto_{I^*} A = 1) \mathbin{\&} (R_2 = 0 \ \Box\!\!\mapsto_{I^*} A = 1)$$

Yet one wants to be able to say that it was your belief–desire pair about beer, rather than the belief–desire pair about salami, that caused you to open the fridge door.

There are several possible ways of treating such examples of pre-emption in the structural equations framework. But it will be simplest to focus on one easy-to-explain treatment—that proposed by Halpern and Pearl (2001), and expounded in Hitchcock 2001 and Woodward 2003. (For an alternative treatment see Pearl 2000: ch. 10 and Menzies 2004.) The key observation of this treatment is that there are two ways in which R_1 influences A—one corresponding to the directed path that goes through P_1, the other corresponding to the directed path that goes through P_2. So R_1 can have an effect on the value of A by way of the second path through P_2 over and above the effect it has on A by way of the first path through P_1. Nonetheless, it is possible to determine the effect that R_1 has on A along one path by holding fixed the value of the intermediate variable along the other path. By holding fixed or freezing at its actual value the intermediate variable along the other path, one eliminates any influence of R_1 along that path. The following definition is meant to capture the idea that one can isolate the influence of one variable on another along one path by eliminating its influence along other paths.

Definition 2. A directed path from X to Y is *active* in the model M if and only if Y counterfactually depends on X when one holds fixed at their actual values intermediate variables along all other directed paths from X to Y.

Causation is then defined as follows:

Definition 3. An event represented by $X = \text{x}$ *causes* an event represented by $Y = \text{y}$ if and only if (i) $X = \text{x}$ and $Y = \text{y}$ represent distinct occurrent events; and (ii) there is an active directed path from X to Y.

It is easy to see that this treatment ensures that your belief–desire pair about beer, rather than your belief–desire pair about salami, caused you to open the fridge door. For there is an active directed path from R_1 to A, since there is a counterfactual dependence between R_1 and A with the variable P_2 frozen at its actual value 0.

$$(R_1 = 1 \ \& \ P_2 = 0 \ \Box\!\!\rightarrow_{I*} A = 1) \ \& \ (R_1 = 0 \ \& \ P_2 = 0 \ \Box\!\!\rightarrow_{I*} A = 0)$$

But there is no active directed path from R_2 to A, as A does not counterfactually depend on R_1 when P_1 is frozen at its actual value 1:

$$(R_2 = 1 \ \& \ P_1 = 1 \ \Box\!\!\rightarrow_{I*} A = 1) \ \& \ (R_2 = 0 \ \& \ P_1 = 1 \ \Box\!\!\rightarrow_{I*} A = 1)$$

The models we have been exploring are only one kind of model that can be used to understand the causes of your behaviour. Let us consider an alternative model—call it 'the neurological model' N—that employs variables referring to neural states and structural equations concerning the neural mechanisms of your brain. Let us suppose that the exogenous variables of the model are $N_1, \ldots, N_4$, where $N_1 = 1$ and $N_2 = 1$ are neural realizers of the intentional state of desiring beer and $N_3 = 1$ and $N_4 = 1$ are neural realizers of the intentional state of believing that there is beer in the fridge. Let us suppose that we are considering a standard example not involving pre-emption or overdetermination. Then the structural equations of this model might be stated:

(10) $N_1 = 1$
(11) $N_2 = 0$
(12) $N_3 = 1$
(13) $N_4 = 0$
(14) $A = (N_1 \& N_3) \ \text{v} \ (N_1 \& N_4) \ \text{v} \ (N_2 \& N_3) \ \text{v} \ (N_2 \& N_4)$

Of course, any realistic structural equation for the endogenous variable A in the neurological model is likely to be much more complicated than this. Moreover, there is no reason to suppose that it will match up with the corresponding structural equations of the intentional model I in the simple way suggested here. But keeping things simple in this way will mean that no important questions are begged at this stage. It is easy to see that the neurological model N implies that your opening the fridge counterfactually depends on whether you are in the neural state N_3:

$$(N_3 = 1 \ \Box\!\!\rightarrow_N A = 1) \ \& \ (N_3 = 0 \ \Box\!\!\rightarrow_N A = 0).$$

In such a simple example, judgements about causation go hand in hand with judgements about counterfactual dependence. Of course, it is possible to describe more complex causal situations involving pre-emption, for which more complex neurological models would have to be formulated. It is relatively straightforward to see how the definitions of an active directed path and causation could be applied to such situations to track our causal judgements.

This is a good point at which to summarize where we have got to in our discussion. We have looked at two kinds of models that might be invoked to explain the causes of a person's behaviour. The models posit quite different kinds of causes of behaviour and causal processes leading up to behaviour. Intentional models pick out intentional states and processes as causal, whereas neurological models pick out neural states and processes as causal. There is no inconsistency in this result, because the two models involve quite different sets of variables and structural equations. Nonetheless, this result does pose a serious problem for the exclusion assumption. For the multiplicity of causal structures that comes with the existence of different models is not the standard kind of overdetermination covered by an exception clause in the exclusion assumption. For overdetermination examples are like the pre-emption example we have examined in that they are really *intra*-model phenomena. By contrast, the multiplicity of causes and causal processes allowed by different causal modellings is an *inter*-model phenomenon. The most natural conclusion to draw from this result is that the widespread practice of determining causation by reference to models falsifies the exclusion assumption.

There are many questions raised by the practice of causal modelling. One immediate question is: What determines the model in terms of which the causal structure of a given situation is assessed? In one sense, the answer to this question is simple: context determines the relevant model. Terence Horgan has written illuminatingly on the context sensitivity of causal discourse in connection with the exclusion assumption and the problem of mental causation (Horgan 1998, 2001). Much of what he says about the ways in which context fixes the implicit parameters of causal discourse is suggestive of the ways in which context determines the model relevant to a given situation. Horgan argues that the concept of causation is governed by an implicit contextual parameter he calls the level-parameter. This parameter reflects the descriptive/ontological level at which the causal discourse is taking place: in connection with the causation of behaviour, the discourse may be pitched at the microphysical, the neurological, the biological, or the psychological level. Governing each of these levels is a system of laws, often involving determinable properties or variables; the system of laws at a given level generates rich patterns of counterfactual dependence between determinates of the variables; and these patterns of counterfactual dependence determine the causal relations at that level. I suggest that Horgan's claim about the relativity of the causal concept can be interpreted in terms of the view that the concept is relative to a contextually determined model. Models are often small in scale, representing localized phenomena; but large-scale models can also be constructed to represent global phenomena that Horgan might choose to label a level. One virtue of this interpretation is that the treatment of causation provided by the structural equations framework supplies what is missing from Horgan's story—a precise account of the way in which context fixes the truth conditions of counterfactuals and causal claims.

Another virtue of this interpretation is that it enables us to take over Horgan's persuasive diagnosis of the errors involved in the causal exclusion reasoning. Borrowing from David Lewis's (1973) theory of context-sensitive meaning, Horgan explains how subtle unrecognized contextual shifts can generate philosophical confusion. He says that normally the choice of descriptive vocabulary or explanatory framework plays a key role in setting the contextual parameter of causal discourse. But when the context changes, various principles of accommodation come into play. Suppose, for example, you offer an explanation of behaviour in terms of folk-psychological intentional states. This will set the contextual parameter so that an intentional model is presupposed in the context. However, if your conversational partner offers an alternative explanation in terms of neural states, the contextual parameter may change in an unacknowledged way from an intentional to a neural model to accommodate this alternative explanation. Moreover, it may be difficult to reverse the shift in the contextual parameter if the neural model is viewed as providing a more stringent standard for evaluating causal claims. This illustrates a phenomenon noted by Lewis that when a contextual parameter involves a standard that can be raised or lowered, accommodating conversational shifts upwards seems more natural than accommodating them downwards. Horgan diagnoses the error of exclusion reasoning as follows: as we shift from one context to another—for example, from reasoning about causes of behaviour in an intentional model to reasoning about them in a neural model—we accommodate to this shift of standards without recognizing it as such; and when we feel the irreversibility of the shift in standards, we mistakenly think that it indicates some deep metaphysical fact rather than the operation of a simple principle of conversational dynamics.

The practice of causal modelling raises not only descriptive issues to do with which models are *actually* involved in causal reasoning, but also normative issues to do with which models are *best* used for such reasoning. Clearly, our practice recognizes conditions of adequacy on models: not any old model can be used in causal reasoning about a given situation. I do not, however, have anything general to say about these normative issues, except to remark that one obvious crucial condition of adequacy on a causal model is that the structural equations and, more particularly, the counterfactuals it entails should be true.

If intentional models prove to be adequate in the sense of implying only true counterfactuals, it is idle to question the reality of the counterfactual dependences and causal relations disclosed by these models. For they represent real patterns in the world. Perhaps one has to adopt a certain perspective to grasp a model and the pattern of causal relations it describes. Perhaps, for example, an intelligent microbe carried around in the bloodstream of a person could not grasp an intentional model, and so could not discern the pattern of causal relations it picks out. Nonetheless, however perspective-dependent grasping the model is, the pattern of causal relations picked out by the model is as objective and perspective-independent as any can be. Daniel Dennett (1991) makes a similar point about the patterns in observable phenomena. However, the patterns of causal relations I am discussing are patterns revealed not just by observation, but by experimentation and the manipulation of objects and processes. The set of counterfactual dependences implied by the structural equations of a model correspond to sequences of events that do, or would, occur under actual and hypothetical interventions in systems of the kind being modelled.

Some philosophers (e.g. Clark 2001: 53–6) have questioned whether the patterns of counterfactual dependence, even if empirically confirmed, count as indicating causal relations. There are, without any doubt, considerable philo-sophical concerns about the details of how counterfactuals relate to causation. But the concerns expressed by these philosophers usually transcend such mat-ters of detail. They take the form of arguing that counterfactual dependences between intentional states and behaviour do not amount to causation because they do not demonstrate the kind of physical causation evident in the expe-rience of pushing-and-pulling. On this physical conception, genuine causes must exert a physical force on their effects, and intentional states, for one, do not seem capable of exerting such a force on behaviour, however tight the counterfactual connection between them may be. In my view, this position lacks scientific credibility, not just because it employs a physical conception of causation that is imprecise and undeveloped, but because it overlooks the central importance that counterfactuals play in causal reasoning in all the sciences. The structural equations framework formalizes and regiments causal methodologies used extensively in the biomedical, behavioural, and social sci-ences. It provides a technically precise and well-understood framework for evaluating counterfactuals and causal hypotheses. Assuming that the patterns of counterfactual relations entailed by an intentional model are true, then it is fanciful to deny that the relationship between intentional states and behaviour is causal.

5. THE RELATIONSHIP BETWEEN LEVELS
OF CAUSATION

In the last section I have argued that it makes sense to think that intentional states are the causes of behaviour in one kind of causal model, while neural states are the causes of behaviour in a different model. If one thinks of the models involved as describing large-scale patterns of causal relations at different levels of description, this makes sense of philosophical talk of there being different levels to the causation of behaviour. But if anything like this is correct, it follows that the program model is fundamentally mistaken in assigning one kind of causation—causal efficacy—to neural states, but another kind—causal relevance—to intentional states.

In response to this line of argument, it might be conceded that the distinction between kinds of causation is an unfortunate, but entirely dispensable, part of the program model. It is dispensable because the central goal of the program model is not to distinguish kinds of causation, but to show how different levels of causation are related to each other. In particular, the program model aims to show how higher-level causal relations hold in virtue of lower-level causal relations. It cannot be a sheer coincidence that at one level intentional states cause the very same behaviour that is caused by neural states at a different level. Such a coincidence would be literally incredible. It is not a matter of simple coincidence, precisely because the higher-level causal relation between intentional states and behaviour programs for the lower-level causal relation between neural states and behaviour. So, on this line of defence, the program model should be seen as an account of the relationship between causal levels, no matter how causation is understood.

In this section I want to consider whether the program model offers a plausible account of the relationship between causal levels. On this understanding, the program model involves two specific hypotheses: (i) *the linkage hypothesis*—whenever there is a causal relation between an intentional state and behaviour, there is a causal relation between an underlying neural state and the same behaviour; and (ii) *the dependency hypothesis*—first relation holds in virtue of the second. I shall examine the plausibility of the linkage hypothesis by tracing its consequences within the structural equations framework for causation. I shall argue that the hypothesis has absurd consequences that undermine its plausibility and that of the dependency hypothesis, which presupposes it.

At the outset of our discussion I shall make an assumption that will considerably simplify the discussion. I shall suppose that different intentional states cannot be realized by the same neural state. This supposition rules out connectionist-like architectures in which networks of neurons can be in states that realize several intentional states at the same time.

Another preliminary remark is in order. In the last section I claimed that models generate counterfactuals in distinctive ways. To elaborate the argument below, I need to show that the counterfactuals generated have a coherent semantics. Traditionally, philosophers have developed truth conditions for counterfactuals in terms of similarity relations between possible worlds. One classic treatment is David Lewis's (1973) possible world semantics. (Pearl 2000: 238–48 shows how the axioms of Lewis's theory follow from the axioms of his own structural semantics.) One central feature of Lewis's semantics is that it uses a system of nested spheres of possible worlds centred on the actual world. A sphere represents a set of possible worlds that are equally similar to the actual world: the smaller the sphere, the more similar to the actual world are the possible worlds within it.

I propose a modified semantics for the kinds of counterfactuals that differs from Lewis's in that the similarity relation is specified by reference to a contextually determined causal model. Such a causal model determines the relevant respects of similarity to be considered in evaluating a counterfactual. Adapting an idea of Pearl's (2000: 241), I suggest one way in which a causal model might generate an ordering of spheres of worlds:

> Definition 4. $\{S_0, \ldots, S_n\}$ is *a system of spheres ordered by the model M* iff S_0 is the sphere that contains only the actual world; and S_i is a sphere of worlds such that the actual world is transformed into a world in S_i by a maximum number of i interventions in the structural equations of the model M.

Then the truth conditions for counterfactuals are defined in the standard way as follows:

> Definition 5. $P \,\square\!\!\rightarrow_M Q$ is *true in the actual world* relative to a system of spheres ordered by a causal model M iff Q is true in all the P worlds in the smallest P-permitting sphere of the system.

I turn now to consider how the linkage hypothesis can be explicated in terms of the structural equations framework. Let us start with the simplest definition of causation, which states that a counterfactual dependence between distinct events constitutes a causal relation. Let us suppose that we have available an intentional model $I^{\#}$ that captures all the true generalizations of folk psychology. Let us also suppose that there is a neural model $N^{\#}$ that captures all the true generalizations of neurology. The linkage hypothesis states that whenever there is a counterfactual dependence between an intentional state R and a behaviour A in the intentional model, there is a counterfactual dependence between a neural state that realizes R and the behaviour A in the neural model.

However, it is crucial to observe that nothing in the above semantics of counterfactuals would guarantee that this is true. This semantics allows for the possibility of a counterfactual analogue of Simpson's paradox: a situation in which a variable Y counterfactually depends on a variable X, but does not depend on any of the realizations of the values of X. Consider the situation

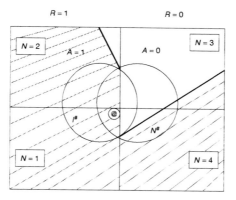

Fig. 2.3.

depicted in Figure 2.3. In this figure the sphere in the centre contains the actual world by itself. The sphere labelled $I^\#$ is the second innermost sphere associated with the model $I^\#$, and the sphere labelled $N^\#$ is the second innermost sphere associated with the model $N^\#$. The other spheres in the systems of spheres ordered by these models are omitted. Note that the overlap between the sphere labelled $I^\#$ and that labelled $N^\#$ contains the actual world. These spheres need not coincide completely, because the two models associated with the spheres generate different comparisons of similarity on the basis of their different sets of variables and structural equations. The column headed by $R = 1$ represents the possible worlds in which $R = 1$ is true; and correspondingly for the column headed by $R = 0$. The partition of the logical space in terms of the four values of a neural variable N represents the fact that $R = 1$ may be realized by $N = 1$ or $N = 2$; and $R = 0$ may be realized by $N = 3$ or $N = 4$. The actual world is one in which it is true that $N = 1$, $R = 1$, and $A = 1$.

The figure depicts the fact that the structural equations of the intentional model are such that there is a counterfactual dependence between R and A.

$$(R = 1 \ \Box\!\!\rightarrow_{I^\#} A = 1) \ \& \ (R = 0 \ \Box\!\!\rightarrow_{I^\#} A = 0)$$

However, the structural equations of the neural model are such that:

$$(N = 1 \ \Box\!\!\rightarrow_{N^\#} A = 1) \ \& \ \sim (N = 3 \ \Box\!\!\rightarrow_{N^\#}$$
$$A = 0) \ \& \ \sim (N = 4 \ \Box\!\!\rightarrow_{N^\#} A = 0)$$
$$(N = 2 \ \Box\!\!\rightarrow_{N^\#} A = 1) \ \& \ \sim (N = 3 \ \Box\!\!\rightarrow_{N^\#}$$
$$A = 0) \ \& \ \sim (N = 4 \ \Box\!\!\rightarrow_{N^\#} A = 0)$$

In other words, A counterfactually depends on R in the intentional model, but it does not counterfactually depend on the neural realizations of the values of R

in the neural model. This kind of situation, which is allowed by the semantics of counterfactuals, would falsify the linkage hypothesis.

What constraint would have to be imposed on the semantics of counterfactuals in order for the linkage hypothesis to hold? It is instructive to formulate such a constraint to see how strong it must be. One such constraint is the following:

> *Mirroring constraint*: (i) Each structural equation in the intentional model for an exogenous variable, $X = x$, must be matched by a structural equation in the neural model of the form $U = u$, where $U = u$ realizes $X = x$; and (ii) each true structural equation for an endogenous variable in the intentional model, $y = f_Y(x_1, \ldots, x_n)$, must be matched by a *set* of true structural equations of the form $v = f_V(u_1, \ldots, u_n)$, where $U = u_1$ realizes $X = x_1, \ldots, U = u_n$ realizes $X = x_n$, and $V = v$ realizes $Y = y$.

If the mirroring constraint is imposed on the semantics for counterfactuals, it can be shown that any counterfactual dependence of the intentional model will be matched by a counterfactual dependence in the neural model. Under these circumstances, the linkage hypothesis will be vindicated.

The mirroring constraint is a remarkably strong empirical assumption. Of course, ultimately it is subject to empirical verification or falsification. But at a glance one can see that it is vastly implausible in view of the phenomenon of multiple realizability. First of all, the constraint implies that, corresponding to the coarse-grained partition of logical space in terms of intentional variables, there is a finer-grained partition in terms of neural variables that appear in the structural equations of the neural model. But how plausible is that? Perhaps, the neural states that realize intentional states do not belong to the projectable natural kinds of neurology. This would certainly be the case if the realizer neural states were very heterogeneous in nature from a neurological point of view. Secondly, the constraint implies that all the realizers of a given intentional state will play exactly the same role in the structural equations of neurology. Again, how plausible is that? The likelihood that the multiple neural realizers are very heterogenous in nature and so do not form a projectable kind in neurology makes it doubtful that this implication will always be met.

However, over and above these particular objections based on the multiple realizability of intentional states, there is the sheer staggering implausibility of supposing that the pattern of similarities and differences that structure the space of possibilities in the intentional model will be matched closely by a corresponding pattern in the neural model. We have seen that on the simple definition of causation, the linkage hypothesis entails that the pattern of counterfactual dependences in one model is mirrored by a corresponding pattern of counterfactual dependences in the other model. But now consider the possibility that the intentional model will model pre-empting and overdetermining causal processes. We have seen in the last section that one treatment of pre-emption relies on much more complex counterfactual relations to establish causal relations. Accordingly, the mirroring constraint would have to be complicated in a multitude of ways to ensure the truth of the linkage hypothesis. It would be a remarkable consequence of the linkage hypothesis, so supported, that one could learn an enormous amount about neurology on the basis of simple inferences from the content and structure of folk psychology. Even the advocates of the language of thought hypothesis, who are careful to present it as a conjecture about cognitive architecture, are not so bold as to say that we can read off the basic laws of neurology from the content and structure of folk psychology.

6. CONCLUSION

I have been concerned in this chapter to cast doubt on the physicalist view of causation to which the program model is implicitly committed. I have suggested that this view ultimately relies on an exclusion assumption to the effect that a set of physical causes of some physical effect excludes or renders superfluous any other set of causes. I have argued that the common practice of establishing causal relations at a given level of description by reference to causal models highlights the falsity of this assumption. Furthermore, I have argued that even if the program model were to relinquish this physicalist view of causation and offer itself as simply an account of the relationship between causal levels, it would have to rely on an implausibly strong empirical assumption about the relationship between levels of causation.

I have argued for these claims by appealing to a substantive treatment of causation within the structural equations framework. Some of the implausible consequences of the program model become visible, I think, only when one examines it through the lens of a substantive theory of causation. Perhaps this theory of causation is incorrect in detail. But some theory along its general lines would suffice for my arguments.

REFERENCES

Block, Ned (1990). 'Can the Mind Change the World?', in George Boolos (ed.) *Meaning and Method: Essays in Honour of Hilary Putnam* (Cambridge: Cambridge University Press), 137–70.

Campbell, John (1993). 'A Simple View of Colours', in John Haldane and Crispin Wright (eds.), *Reality, Representation, and Projection* (New York: Oxford University Press), 257–68.

Clark, Andy (2001). *Mindware: An Introduction to the Philosophy of Cognitive Science*. New York: Oxford University Press.

Churchland, Paul (1989). *A Neurocomputational Perspective*. Cambridge, Mass.: MIT Press.

Dennett, Daniel (1991). 'Real Patterns', *Journal of Philosophy*, 89, 27–51.

Fodor, Jerry (1987). *Psychosemantics: The Problem of Meaning in the Philosophy of Mind.* Cambridge, Mass.: MIT Press.

Halpern, John, and Judea Pearl (2001). *Causes and Explanations: A Structural Model Approach.* Technical Report R-266, Cognitive Systems Laboratory, University of California, Los Angeles.

Hitchcock, Christopher (2001). 'The Intransitivity of Causation Revealed in Equations and Graphs', *Journal of Philosophy*, 98, 273–314.

Horgan, Terence (1998). 'Kim on Mental Causation and Causal Exclusion', *Philosophical Perspectives*, 11, 165–84.

_____ (2001). 'Causal Compatibilism and the Exclusion Problem', *Theoria*, 16, 95–116.

Jackson, Frank (1996). 'Mental Causation: The State of the Art', *Mind*, 105, 377–413.

_____ and Philip Pettit (1988). 'Functionalism and Broad Content', *Mind*, 97, 381–400.

_____ _____ (1990*a*). 'Causation in the Philosophy of Mind', *Philosophy and Phenomenological Research*, 50, 195–214.

_____ _____ (1990*b*). 'Program Explanation: A General Perspective', *Analysis*, 50, 107–17.

_____ _____ (1992*a*). 'In Defence of Explanatory Ecumenism', *Economics and Philosophy*, 8, 1–21.

_____ _____ (1992*b*). 'Structural Explanation and Social Theory', in David Charles and Kathleen Lennon (eds.), *Reductionism and Anti-Reductionism* (Oxford: Oxford University Press), 97–131.

Kim, Jaegwon (1998). *Mind in a Physical World.* Cambridge, Mass.: MIT Press.

Lewis, David (1973). 'Scorekeeping in a Language Game', *Journal of Philosophical Logic*, 8, 339–59.

Mackie, J. L. (1974). *The Cement of the Universe.* Oxford: Clarendon Press.

Menzies, Peter (1987). 'Against Causal Reductionism', *Mind*, 97, 551–74.

_____ (2003). 'The Causal Efficacy of Mental States', in Sven Walter and Heinz-Dieter Heckman (eds.), *Physicalism and Mental Causation* (Charlottesville, Va.: Imprint Academic), 195–224.

_____ (2004). 'Causal Models, Token-Causation and Processes', *Philosophy of Science*, 71, 820–32.

Pearl, Judea (2000). *Causality: Models, Reasoning, and Inference.* Cambridge: Cambridge University Press.

Pettit, Philip (1992). 'The Nature of Naturalism', *Proceedings of Aristotelian Society*, suppl. vol. 66, 245–66.

_____ (1993). *The Common Mind: An Essay on Psychology, Society, and Politics.* Oxford: Oxford University Press.

_____ (2002). *Rules, Reasons, and Norms: Selected Essays.* Oxford: Clarendon Press.

Ramsey, W., S. Stich, and J. Garon (1990). 'Connectionism, Eliminativism and Folk Psychology', *Philosophical Perspectives*, 4, 499–533.

Spirtes, Peter, Clark Glymour, and Richard Scheines (1993). *Causation, Prediction, and Search.* New York: Springer.

Woodward, James (2003). *Making Things Happen: A Theory of Causal Explanation.* Oxford: Oxford University Press.

3

Can Hunter-Gatherers Hear Color?

Susan Hurley and Alva Noë

Philip Pettit (2003) argues that color looks should be explained in terms of manifest powers. He indicates that his view is broadly allied with our own dynamic sensorimotor approach to conscious experience (O'Regan and Noë 2001*a*,*b*,*c*; Hurley 1998; Hurley and Noë 2003; Noë 2004). Pettit finds support for his view in Ivo Kohler's (1964) report of adaptation to color-distorting goggles. However, a potential objection to Pettit's account of color looks derives from synaesthetic color experiences; this objection has also recently been pressed against our position by Jeffrey Gray (2003). Here we review Pettit's account, consider its relationship to our own view, and state the challenge that synaesthesia presents to the perspective that we share with Pettit. We conclude that further work that brings the brain into the picture is needed to deal with Gray's challenge; we undertake this elsewhere (Hurley and Noë, in progress).

Both color and illusion present challenges for any theory of perception—and perhaps especially for accounts, such as Pettit's and ours, that view perception and action as tightly interconnected. As we explain below, 'colored hearing synaesthesia' combines color experience and nonveridicality. Our aim in this chapter is to explore some of the resources for theories like Pettit's and ours to meet this double challenge.

1. PETTIT ON COLOR LOOKS AS MANIFEST POWERS

According to Pettit (2003), a red object looks red because perceiving it *manifestly empowers* in certain ways. That is, it manifestly enables certain responses, e.g. precise discriminatory and tracking responses, and manifestly induces certain

Authorship is fully joint, and names are in alphabetical order. We are grateful for comments and discussion to Dominic ffytche, Jeffrey Gray, Anthony Jack, Erik Myin, Philip Pettit, Hanna Pickard, Kevin O'Regan, David Rosenthal, Simon Saunders, Nicholas Shea, Petra Stoerig, and others on various occasions when we have delivered this and related material. We are also grateful to the McDonnell Centre for Cognitive Neuroscience in Oxford for support of this work in the form of a visiting fellowship for Alva Noë.

related expectancies. This *manifest powers* account of color experience has two distinct elements: the powers element and the manifestness element.

First, obviously, Pettit's account links color experience to the discriminatory powers that perception of the colors enables. Pettit understands powers in terms of both responses and expectancies. That is, for Pettit, the red look of a tomato supervenes on both the ways it enables the perceiver to track it against certain backgrounds and sort it from other objects, and the ways it induces certain expectancies about the sensory consequences of color-relevant changes, such as specific movements or changes of lighting or background.

Second, more subtly, Pettit's account also treats the linkage of color looks to powers as *perceptual* in character. On Pettit's view, the red look of a tomato doesn't supervene *merely* on such powers, but rather on such *manifest powers*. That is, the red look of the tomato supervenes on the *manifest* empowerment of its perceiver in these ways. To look red is to *look empowering* in certain ways, to advertise visually certain empowerments.[1] Note that Pettit's account is not an account of looks in general, but of color looks.

Pettit contrasts the qualia account of color looks with his own manifest powers account as follows. On the qualia view, perceiving a red object manifestly enables certain responses and induces certain expectancies, because the object looks red. By contrast, on the manifest powers view, a red object looks red because perceiving it manifestly enables certain responses and induces certain expectancies. Looks neither cause nor are caused by such manifest empowering, but rather supervene on it. For example, a ball's looking like it is going fast cannot be dissociated from the responses and expectancies that perceiving it manifestly enables. Similarly, for an object to look red cannot be dissociated from certain responses and expectancies that perceiving it manifestly enables.

An essential difference between the qualia view and the manifest powers view is that, on the qualia view, color looks are properties of perceptions that can, in principle at least, vary independently of the manifest powers that perceptions provide. That is, the same set of relations could in principle be realized by perceptions with intrinsically different color looks (see, e.g., Palmer 1999). On the manifest powers view, by contrast, color looks are relational all the way down, rather as a point in space-time is. Space-time points are specified in terms of the structural relations they enter into with fields and matter and other space-time points,[2] not in terms of intrinsic properties that could vary independently of these relations.

Pettit argues that the manifest powers account of color looks will be plausible only if it meets two conditions. First, the set of manifest powers must be *rich* enough to make it difficult to suppose that this set could be dissociated from

---

[1] We return to this point below; it will be important in distinguishing Pettit's view (and ours) from more behaviorist views.
[2] Thanks here to Simon Saunders.

looking red and associated instead, say, with looking green. More generally, the richness of the set of manifest powers on which a color look supervenes should make for a one-to-one mapping between looks and sets of powers; it should rule out that a different look could be associated with just the same set of powers, or that the same look could be associated with a different set of powers. Second, the set of manifest powers must be such as to give looking red its distinctive *unity* (including the unity of veridical and illusory red looks).

Pettit explains how the manifest powers account satisfies the richness requirement. Color perception requires sensitivity to light intensities, to wavelengths, to the ratios of different wavelengths in reflected light, to edge contrasts of such ratios, and to the similarity of such ratios across intervening contrasts and across contexts. These sensitivities enable us to discriminate and track objects by color, to perceive color constancy across variations in illumination, background, movement, and so on, where some but not all of these variations are produced by the subject's own motor activity. Given the complex, varied, demanding responses associated with looking red, Pettit argues, looking green could not have the same signature in the space of manifestly enabled responses. As light varies, for example, moving green objects but not red objects will be trackable against certain backgrounds.[3]

The unity requirement is met, in Pettit's view, by the fact that manifest powers, by their very nature, extend across contexts, in virtue of the expectancies they essentially involve. Nothing would count as the power to *discriminate* an object with respect to color if it did not allow for the ability to track the object as viewing conditions vary—as lighting conditions change, as the object moves, or as one moves in relation to the object. However, to (not just discriminate but) *experience* something as a given shade of red is to expect such color-relevant changes in movement, lighting, and so on to produce certain characteristic changes in patterns of sensation.[4] For something to look red isn't just for it manifestly to enable certain responses, but also for it manifestly to induce certain expectancies about "how the object will show up under a range of possible variations", as Pettit puts it. That is, for something to look red is not just to look response-enabling in certain ways, but to look as if it would look in this or that way under various conditions, to solicit such expectancies visually. As a result of these expectancies, the perceivers may also have further expectations about the discriminating and tracking responses that would be enabled across a range of counterfactual circumstances.

Thus, as Pettit explains, one suite of expectancies unifies looking red across various contexts. However, the truth of these expectancies is not guaranteed by the color look. If those expectancies are false—that is, if they are such as to be disappointed—then the look the object has in this context is illusory; it isn't really red, even though it looks red. Illusory and veridical looks can thus

---

[3] Compare Palmer 1999.   [4] See also Noë 2004.

be unified by expectancies, even though some of those are false for illusory looks. Indeed, illusory looks may persist when the relevant expectancies survive at some level, even though I know intellectually that they are false (for example, in the Mueller–Lyer illusion). We return to Pettit's false expectancy account of illusions below. For reasons explained there, it does not meet the challenge from synaesthesia.

The manifest powers account of color looks thus makes two claims. First, one rich set of manifestly enabled responses and expectancies, or *manifest powers* for short, should not be associated with different color looks. There is a unique mapping from manifest powers to color looks; different color looks should not go with the same manifest powers. In other words, color looks could not be exchanged while corresponding manifest powers are held constant. This claim brings into doubt the possibility of inverted color experiences that the qualia view tolerates.[5] Second, one color look should not be associated with different manifest powers. There is a unique mapping from color looks to manifest powers; different manifest powers should not go with the same color looks. In other words, manifest powers could not be exchanged while associated color looks are held constant.

Pettit invokes Ivo Kohler's (1964) color adaptation results in support of the manifest powers view.[6] The first of the above claims of the manifest powers view, that different color looks should not go with the same manifest powers, predicts the adaptation of color experience to color-distorting goggles that Kohler reports. In Kohler's goggle experiments, which we explain in more detail below, manifest powers (including expectancies) initially disrupted by the goggles are recovered with adaptation, and color looks adapt with them, as the manifest powers view predicts. Kohler's work thus supports the claim that color experience tracks manifest powers.

However, evidence from work with synaesthetic subjects presents a challenge to the manifest powers view. The second of the above claims, that different manifest powers should not go with the same color look, appears to be incompatible with colored hearing synaesthesia, as Gray has argued. We explore this challenge in what follows.

Before moving on, two sidebars. First, what is the right view of the status of the claims made by the manifest powers theory of color looks—and in particular of the claim that there is a one-to-one correlation of manifest powers and color looks? Should this be treated as an a priori claim or as an empirical hypothesis? We don't pursue this question, or probe Pettit's views on it, here. The method we adopt in what follows involves testing the view against empirical considerations about color adaptation and synaesthesia (see also and compare Cole 1990).

---

[5] For related discussions, see Hardin 1997; Cole 1990; Myin 2001.

[6] Cf. Hurley 1998, which invoked Kohler's results in arguing against the input–output picture of perception and action. See also O'Regan and Noë 2001*b*.

Second, a theory about what color looks are is not necessarily a theory about what colors are. A manifest powers account of the experience of color is compatible with a range of different empirical and philosophical theories of the nature of colors. We also leave aside the exploration of this point and related issues.

2. BEHAVIORISM VERSUS THE HUNTING AND GATHERING PERSPECTIVE ON COLOR LOOKS

At a first, superficial glance, Pettit's manifest powers account of color looks may seem to reduce color looks to certain responses to color perception, and hence to be a species of behaviorism. However, this would be an inaccurate understanding of his view. The second element in Pettit's view—the perceptual manifestation requirement—differentiates his view from behaviorism, and makes clear that it is not an attempt at reduction.[7] The experience of redness is not taken to be constituted merely by its behavioral effects or the responses that it enables. Something's looking red is, irreducibly, a fact about how it looks. This second element is also what enables the view to meet the more traditional qualia theory on its own phenomenological ground. Pettit's account suggests that to do justice to what it is like to experience a color, we need to recognize that when we experience an object as colored, we experience it as entering into a suite of saliencies: as standing out from a background so as to look fit to empower us in certain ways.

As we interpret Pettit, the difference between *merely enabling* certain responses and *manifestly enabling* them can be understood partly in terms of the subject's expectations of the sensory consequences of his own potential movements, as well as other possible color-related changes—in Pettit's words, expectations "of how the object will show up under a range of possible variations". Part of what it is for perceiving something manifestly to enable certain responses is for the perception to carry with it an implicit practical understanding, of what the sensory consequences of certain movements would be. The manifestness of the enabling of responses is in part a function of these visually solicited expectancies. The subject can see not just how something looks here and now, but also how it would look if he were to do this or that, and hence what he can do; moreover, these sensory and practical implications of given color looks are all tangled up with, not strictly separable from, the color looks themselves (see also Noë 2004 on the fractal character of color experience).

Consider, for example, Pettit's comparison of color looks with the look of a ball moving towards one's face. Here is the way we would describe the latter

---

[7] See also Hurley 1998: 213, 420–1, and Hurley 2001, as well as O'Regan and Noë 2001*a,b,c* and Noë 2004, for more on the difference between our views and behaviorism.

experience, emphasizing the difference from more behaviorist views; we believe that our dynamic sensorimotor view is here consistent with Pettit's account (though at times his formulations veer in a more behaviorist direction). Seeing the ball enables ducking to avoid it, and does so manifestly. But it looks as if the ball can be avoided by ducking *because* it looks as if ducking would make the situation look different in certain ways. Thus, when a ball looks as if it is moving towards one's face, it looks as if ducking would make the situation look different; as a result, it looks as if ducking would avoid the ball, and thus ducking to avoid the ball is enabled.

We agree with Pettit that there is no visual quale as of a ball about to hit one's face that is independent of the powers that such an experience manifestly enables. In particular, seeing that a ball is about to hit one's face manifestly enables one, by moving in certain ways, to avoid being hit, *because* it manifestly induces expectancies about how things will look if one does. That is, we suggest, the *manifestness* of the enabling of responses by this experience depends on the *expectancies* about the sensory consequences of movement that it manifestly induces. In seeing the ball coming, the perceiver also knows what the sensory consequences of doing this or that will be, and hence knows how to respond for certain purposes.

Thus, for the ball to look as if it is moving towards one's head is not for the ball simply to look as if it affords opportunities for avoidance behavior. Rather, it is for the ball to look to be related to one in such a way that the merest movement of the eyes or head or body would alter, in specific ways, the way it looks. Because the dynamics of the perceiver's relationship to the ball are manifest in the experience, the experience normally does acquire an action-guiding role. However, the relevant dynamics concern the sensory effects of movements, expectations which, in the normal course of things, enable certain responses and bring the consequences of movement under intentional control. What Pettit calls 'expectancies' about the sensory consequences of movement are what we refer to as implicit practical knowledge of sensorimotor dynamics. Such implicit understanding of the sensory effects of movement is part of what it is for the ball to look as if it is moving toward one's head. A knowledge of how to exploit the way things look to guide action is a further ability, which one's perceptual skills enable one to acquire.

We have stressed the way in which Pettit's view differs from behaviorism. A similar point applies to our dynamic sensorimotor view, which is sometimes wrongly assimilated either to behaviorism or to the view that, since perceptual systems evolved to guide action, a visual experience can be understood solely in terms of its role in guiding action and as inextricably linked to ways of acting that are responsive to certain perceptions.

For example, a certain type of objection may be pressed against positions like Pettit's and our own by adherents of a two visual systems view. On this view, visual processing in the dorsal neural pathway or 'how' stream serves to guide action on line and demonstrates direct perception–action linkages. However, dorsal visual processing does not support conscious visual experience. This is supported only by processing in the ventral neural pathway or 'what' stream, along with perceptual judgments and identifications.[8] Neurological and neuropsychological evidence has been interpreted to show that dorsal and ventral functions are dissociable; some patients can use visual information they do not consciously perceive to guide action, while others cannot use visual information they do consciously perceive to guide action. Such dissociations, it can be argued, show that perceptual experience cannot be understood solely in terms of dorsal, action-guiding functions.

However, we do not claim this; nor do we claim that you need to move or act in order to see. This kind of objection is therefore misplaced. We *do* claim that the ability to see is partly constituted by implicit knowledge of the sensory effects of movement, and that an experience is inextricably linked to understanding of the ways in which experience would change were one to act in various ways.[9] This understanding is, of course, very useful in guiding action, but whether it is used in this way is a further question. It may not be so used for a variety of reasons.

If the capacity to move were necessary for experience, then experience by the paralyzed or by those with locked-in syndrome would be ruled out. Our view, by contrast, has no such implications. Someone can know what the sensory consequences of movement would be, even if he cannot in fact move because he is paralyzed. If the ability to use visual information to guide action were necessary for visual experience, then patients with optic ataxia, who cannot use visual experience to guide action, should be blind. Again, our view has no such implication (nor is there any independent reason to believe that optic ataxic patients lack visual experience). Someone can understand what the sensory consequences of certain movements would be, even though she cannot use this knowledge to guide her actual movements. Knowledge of the sensory consequences of movement may be useful (or even necessary[10]), but is not sufficient for the visual guidance of actual movements. That is, lack of knowledge of the sensory consequences of movement isn't the only possible reason why the visual guidance of movement can break down. For example, in principle, some motor plans (but not all) might interact with this knowledge in ways that render it ineffective.

However, a cogent further worry is this: we emphasize the expectancies, or implicit practical knowledge of the sensory consequences of movement, that

---

[8] See Milner and Goodale 1995; cf. Gallese et al. 1999; Jacob and Jeannerod, who advocate a 'weak' and heavily qualified version of the two visual systems theory, e.g. 2003: 102–4, 188 ff., 126, 131–2, 254–5. On the role of dorsal–ventral interactions in visual awareness, see, e.g., Beck et al. 2001.

[9] This account of perception is laid out in O'Regan and Noë 2001*b*. It is developed in Hurley and Noë 2003 and Noë 2004.

[10] See Cole 1991 on Ian Waterman.

perception involves, yet we deny that such knowledge is necessarily available to guide actual movements. But what is implicit practical knowledge of the sensory consequences of movement if not knowledge of how to do certain things; namely, to act in ways that produce certain sensory consequences?[11] In what does the implicit practical knowledge or skill consist, and in what sense is it genuinely implicit practical knowledge, genuinely a skill (as opposed to some other kind of knowledge or understanding), if it cannot be used to guide action?

In a chapter focused on the challenge presented by synaesthesia, we cannot take undertake a full-fledged investigation of how views such as ours and Pettit's should respond to the variety of evidence for the two visual systems view. This needs to be done elsewhere. However, we do have something more to say, in Section 6 below, about the specific challenge the two visual systems view presents to Pettit's false expectancy account of color illusions. At that point we will offer a partial response to the kind of worry expressed in the previous paragraph.

The burden of this section has been to differentiate Pettit's view, and ours, from other views they may be confused with, such as behaviorism, or the view that perceptual experience can be understood solely in terms of its action-guiding functions. In doing so, we have described important common ground between Pettit's manifest powers account of color looks and our dynamic sensorimotor view (although there are differences of emphasis and detail). In what follows we will refer to this shared view of color experience as *the hunting and gathering perspective*, to reflect its emphasis on the characteristic sensorimotor dynamics of color experience. This does not mean that we, or Pettit, identify color experience with hunting and gathering behavior, or with the mere capacity for it. Rather, this perspective emphasizes the essentially dynamic and practical aspects of perceptual experience: the ways in which dynamic, practical interaction between the perceiver and his environment are manifest in perceptual experience, and the understanding on which this depends, in particular, of patterns of dependence of sensation on movement. Normal perceivers can usually use what they see to guide what they do, and this general practical capacity depends on their possession of sensorimotor knowledge, or 'expectancies', as Pettit would put it. In particular, the complex sensitivities that are expressed in color experience enable us to track and discriminate objects—to hunt and to gather—as we move, as objects move, as light and background changes, and so on. The empowerment of hunting and gathering that is manifest in color experience essentially involves understanding of sensorimotor dynamics—as we would say—or—as Pettit would say—expectancies about characteristic ways in which patterns of sensation change with other changes, including movement.

---

[11] For a related point, see Jacob and Jeannerod 2003: 172.

3. COLOR ADAPTATION FOR HUNTER-GATHERERS

As mentioned above, Pettit claims that Kohler's color adaptation results support his manifest powers account of color looks. In this section we explain and probe that claim.

Kohler's subjects wore goggles with vertically divided lenses. The right half of each lens was yellow and the left half was blue, so when subjects looked to the right, the world looked yellowish, and when they looked to the left, the world looked bluish. However, after wearing the goggles for some weeks, the subjects' experience of color adapted: the subjects reported that the world no longer looked yellowish or bluish when they looked to the right or the left, respectively. Thus a white object viewed by an adapted subject with his eyes looking rightward through the yellow halves of the lenses looked white to the subject. It would continue to look white as it moved sideways in front of the lenses or as the subject moved so that it was viewed through the blue halves of the lenses. Moreover, when the subjects removed the goggles after wearing them continuously for 60 days, they experienced color aftereffects: the world now looked bluish when they looked to the right (in the direction that with the goggles had been yellow) and yellowish when they looked to the left (in the direction that with the goggles had been blue). Kohler suggests that eye movement switches between color compensation mechanisms. Others have tried to obtain similar or related results, with mixed success,[12] so it cannot be assumed that these adaptation results are beyond dispute, but for present purposes we will accept them at face value.

Pettit argues that the manifest powers view of color would predict such adaptation, while the qualia view would not.[13] To this extent, Kohler's results support the manifest powers view. Kohler himself comments that, as the goggle wearer's expectations about color looks are revised, his behavior falls into line with his expectations, so that he is no longer distracted when something changes from looking blue to yellow under certain movements, and then color looks themselves fall into line (1964: 113). How the world is expected to look has a role in determining how it does look. However, these suggestions by Kohler about what happens are not entirely clear. Is his suggestion that we are distracted because color looks aren't obeying familiar sensorimotor rules? Does this mean that we learn new sensorimotor rules in the course of adaptation? Why would that yield changed color experiences, rather than restore veridical experiences?

---

[12] See Peppmann and Wieland 1966 (replication claimed to succeed after only 11 days); McCollough 1965 (replication claimed to fail after 75 days); Harrington 1965 (replication claimed to fail after 103 and 146 days).

[13] Though the qualia view isn't strictly inconsistent with adaptation here, it provides no explanation of it, and leaves it looking rather mysterious.

J. J. Gibson's introduction to Kohler (1964) is somewhat clearer on this issue. Gibson explains that the light delivered to the eyes by Kohler's goggles still carries information about colors in the environment to the eyes, but in a transformed form (Kohler 1964: 8–9, 12). This information can be recovered by factoring out the distortion produced by the subjects' movements from the transformed light produced by the goggles, on the assumption that the proper underlying sensorimotor profile of colors reflects constancy rather than variation across sideways eye movements.

Pettit's interpretation of Kohler and Gibson in effect distinguishes the underlying sensorimotor dynamics of colors, which are invariant, from their particular implementation, which can vary and which the goggles change. As we would put it, adaptation is a process of acquiring skillful familiarity with the new implementation of the familiar invariant sensorimotor dynamics of specific colors. This distinction is important in specifying hunter-gatherer accounts of color looks. The sensorimotor expectancies characteristic of particular colors relate ultimately to the underlying invariant patterns of dependency of sensation on movement, and these do not change when the goggles are worn. But their implementation is transformed, and as a result, the perceiver's understanding of them is disrupted until his expectations have adjusted to this new implementation and related it to the underlying invariant patterns.

Our dynamic sensorimotor view also predicts adaptation to Kohler's goggles (see discussions in Hurley 1998; Noë 2004: ch. 4). As we would put it, the sensorimotor skills of color perception consist in practical knowledge of underlying patterns in the way in which sensations vary as the perceiver moves and as other environmental conditions change. Color constancy, on this view, depends on discerning a characteristic underlying, invariant structure in the way in which sensations vary with movement and changes in illumination.[14] Practical knowledge of these underlying patterns and structures enables active hunting and gathering. Part of what color perceivers know is that the world does not in general look a different color from one angle of vision versus another.

When the goggles are first donned, a blue–left, yellow–right pattern appears that is not consistent with the underlying dynamics of color *in its familiar implementation.* That is, the goggles create a conflict between implicit expectations about the underlying dynamics of color and implicit expectations about how it is implemented. The apparent change of color with movement is not just illusory, but is also contrary to the expectations of color perceivers; as a result, it interferes distractingly with the normal role of color constancy in the active exercise of perceptual skills in hunting and gathering. For example, the blue look of something viewed with eyes leftward by the unadapted goggle-wearer involves

---

[14] This suggestion is supported by striking recent work by Philipona, O'Regan, and Coenen on the intrinsic sensorimotor information structure of colors, which is invariant across changes in robotic implementation; see below in Sect. 7.

expectations about the way things will look under movement that turn out to be misleading. The perceiver's practical understanding of the relevant underlying sensorimotor patterns and consequent practical skills are initially disrupted by the goggles.

But this understanding is regained as the subject learns that the underlying patterns are still present in a new implementation. The goggles transform the way the underlying sensorimotor patterns characteristic of color constancy are registered, and adaptation involves acquiring familiarity with this transformed registration. With adaptation, the misleading expectations are replaced by expectations that again reflect the underlying sensorimotor dynamics of color, but in the new implementation. As this understanding is restored, the blue–left, yellow–right appearance fades away, and normal color appearances return.

When the goggles are removed, the implementation changes again: the original implementation is restored, and readaptation is now needed to restore normal color experience. At the level of implementation, expectations change, and then change back again. But these changes are driven by the perceiver's understanding of what is invariant across these transformations, the characteristic underlying sensorimotor dynamics of color looks. Expectations at the level of implementation are brought into line with implicit knowledge of the underlying sensorimotor dynamics of color and expectations that color looks will continue, *in one way or another*, to respect them.

Pettit's manifest powers view and our dynamic sensorimotor view are thus closely allied in predicting and explaining Kohler's color adaptation results. However, it is less obvious how our hunter-gatherer perspective on color looks should handle colored hearing synaesthesia. This presents a challenge to both views, and has indeed been pressed by Jeffrey Gray (2003) as an objection to our view. We first provide some background on synaesthesia, and then explain how synaesthesia challenges the hunting and gathering perspective on color experience that we share with Pettit.

4. SYNAESTHESIA, COLORED HEARING, AND ALIEN COLOR EFFECT

In synaesthesia, perception in one modality induces illusory experience in another modality. Synaesthesia is normally for life: adult synaesthetes have typically been synaesthetic for as long as they can remember, and recall being astonished to realize at some point while growing up that most other people did not have similar synaesthetic experiences, which they had regarded as normal (Motluk 1997). However, synaesthesia can be induced by lesions or drugs, and it can be lost; moreover, there is some evidence that synaesthesia is more common in children and can disappear with age (Harrison and Baron-Cohen 1997a; Cytowic 1997; Marks 1997; Maurer 1997). In one case, when a previously synaesthetic subject became color-blind as a result of brain damage, he also lost his synaesthetic color experiences (Frith and Paulesu 1997). A disproportionate number of synaesthetes are female or left-handed; synaesthetes tend to have excellent memories, but to be bad at mathematics; synaesthesia runs in families, so appears to have a genetic basis (Cytowic 1997; Harrison and Baron-Cohen 1997*b*). There is evidence that synaesthesia can facilitate sorting, remembering, and understanding.

While many varieties of synaesthesia are known, by far the most common is auditory to visual induction. We will concentrate here on so-called colored hearing, in which a specific sound induces experience of a specific color (see Nunn et al. 2002). The color may be experienced as nonlocalized but co-conscious with the sound (Gray et al. 2002), or as bound to the sound itself (Marks 1997), or to a visual image of the word or letter that is also induced by the sound (Frith and Paulesu 1997), or to a generic shape (as opposed to a well-differentiated image or scene) (Cytowic 1997). Synaesthetic colors are not confused with the actual colors of objects, which subjects also perceive reliably (Marks 1997; Frith and Paulesu 1997; Gray et al. 2002). Attempts to create synaesthesia by associative training or to explain it in associative terms have generally been unsuccessful (Marks 1997; Harrison and Baron-Cohen 1997*b*; Gray et al. 2002; but cf. Taylor 1962). Synaesthesia appears not to be merely the metaphorical association of words or letters with colors. For example, in a synaesthetic analogue of standard tests for color-blindness, a synaesthete may immediately see a particular numeral in a pattern of letters because the synaesthetic color of certain letters makes them stand out from the rest, where a nonsynaesthete would see no numeral (Ramachandran and Hubbard 2001*a*,*b*).

In one pattern of colored hearing, the initial letter of a heard word, such as 'k' in 'kick' or in 'knock', induces a specific color. The color is experienced only if the word is heard or silently subvocalized by the subject; reading relevant words without subvocalization or inner speech does not induce synaesthetic colors. Moreover, while heard words trigger the experience of synaesthetic color, the mapping from word sound onto color is mediated by spelling. For example, even though the 'k' in 'knock' sounds like an 'n', hearing 'knock' induces the color associated with 'k': 'kind' and 'knock' may induce one color, 'nice' a different color (Frith and Paulesu 1997; Ramachandran and Hubbard 2003: 55). In a variant of this pattern, experience of the color blue might be induced by the letter 'b'; as a result, hearing the word 'black' would also induce experience of the color blue.

Jeffrey Gray and co-workers refer to the induction of color experiences by incongruent color names as the *alien color effect* (ACE) (Gray et al. 2002; Gray 2003). For example, hearing the word 'red' might induce experience of green, or hearing the word 'white' might induce experience of yellow. They have done experiments on ACE that provide a variation on conventional Stroop effects. Stroop effects are found in normal subjects who are asked to name the color in which words are printed and who show delays when the words are names of colors incongruent with the ink color. For example, normal subjects shown a word printed in green ink tend to be slower in naming the ink color if the word is 'red' than if it is 'fed'. Gray and co-workers categorized synaesthetic subjects according to the percentage of color names affected by ACE, and found that subjects with higher levels of ACE were slower to name ink colors.[15] Delays were comparable to those found in conventional Stroop effects. However, the effects were similar whether subjects were naming the ink colors of color words such as 'red' or merely of strings of letters such as 'XXX' (see also Mattingley et al. 2001). Gray et al. (2002) hypothesize that the delay induced by ACE is mediated by subvocal retrieval of the name of the ink color used, whether to print 'red' or merely 'XXX', which induces an interfering ACE synaesthetic color. This delays the correct naming of the ink color, even though ACE subjects are able to perceive and name ordinary colors reliably, and do not confuse synaesthetic and ordinary colors.

Gray (2003) suggests that synaesthetic colors can be dysfunctional, on the basis of the delay of color naming attributed to interference from ACE. In effect, delays in color naming such as those found in Stroop effects would be generalized by ACE to all color naming where the correct color name is associated with an incongruent synaesthetic color. For example, when an ACE child is asked, 'What color is that bus?', and prepares to answer correctly 'red', an ACE experience of green may be induced, delaying the correct response. As Gray et al. (2002; see also 1997) argue, ACE adds to the evidence against the hypothesis that synaesthesia results from associative processes.

5. THE CHALLENGE FROM SYNAESTHESIA TO THE HUNTER-GATHERER APPROACH TO COLOR

Gray (2003) argues that colored hearing synaesthesia, and ACE in particular, provide fatal counterexamples to any account of color experience in terms of the behavioral functions associated with color perception. While he originally conceived of this objection as an objection to functionalism, Gray applies it to our dynamic sensorimotor account of qualities of experience (Hurley and Noë 2003; see also O'Regan and Noë 2001*a,b,c*; Noë and Hurley 2003). If Gray's

---

[15] This delay was found when ACE subjects were tested outside an fMRI scanner; they responded quickly and made some mistakes (Gray et al. 2002). When tested with a somewhat different experimental design and inside the scanner, ACE subjects took longer to respond, were more careful, and did not make mistakes (Gray et al. 2006). The ACE-related delay found in the first experiment was not found in the scanner experiment. However, the delay result from the first experiment is still robust. Being in a scanner may have induced a significant generalized delay in various ways, which overrode the small ACE-related delay. Thanks here to Dominic ffytche for clarification.

objection does apply to our account, it may be expected to apply also to Pettit's account of color looks, in view of the common ground between them.

However, as Gray formulates his objection, we doubt that it applies to either. His objection bears the traces of its original target: functionalism. We have explained how the hunter-gatherer view of color looks that we share with Pettit differs from behaviorism. For related reasons, it should not be assimilated to functionalism—often regarded as a more sophisticated descendant of behaviorism. The functions of standard versions of functionalism, as Gray emphasizes, mediate between sensory input and behavioral output.[16] By contrast, on the hunter-gatherer perspective we share with Pettit, action and perception are mutually dependent. Our shared perspective emphasizes the understanding of sensorimotor dynamics, and treats the way action is guided by color experience as underwritten by understanding of the way sensation depends on movement. Nevertheless, as we go on to explain, a reformulated objection is in the offing from consideration of synaesthesia, which does apply to the hunter-gather perspective.

The target of Gray's objection is the claim that there is a one-to-one mapping between the ways colors look and the behavioral functions. Yet, Gray urges, that is exactly what we find in colored hearing. Green objects look green to a synaesthetic subject. Yet synaesthetic green also looks green to such subjects. While experience of synaesthetic green is not confused with the perception of a green object, these experiences have the distinctive character of greenness in common.[17] However, the experience of synaesthetic green is associated with very different behavioral functions from those associated with perceiving green objects. For example, a red truck comes round the corner, and Mother says, "Look at that red truck!" Suppose the synaesthetic child *experiences* green because the spoken word "red" is synaesthetically green for this child. What does this situation have in common with one in which the child experiences green because she is looking at an unripe tomato in normal lighting? Not, at any rate, behavioral functions. The experience of synaesthetic green is associated with measurable behavioral effects that are quite different from those of perceiving green objects. For example, experiencing synaesthetic green may delay naming the color of red objects; but it is not associated with the set of hunting and gathering responses that perceiving a green object enables.[18] Same color look, different behavioral functions. Not exactly the same look, of course; different

[16] Hence they are versions of the input–output picture criticized in Hurley 1998. This is explicit in Gray et al. 2006.

[17] Similarly, experience of a green afterimage isn't confused with the perception of a green object, but nevertheless shares the quality of greenness.

[18] This point does not depend on synaesthetic green and normal green being experienced in different contexts. Of course, we can have the same kind of experience in different contexts, just as we can use a word with the same meaning in different contexts. Rather, synaesthetic and normal green have different behavioral functions in the same context.

enough looks to tell the difference between seeing green objects and experiencing synaesthetic green. But nevertheless, looks with the character of greenness in common.

Suppose, for the sake of argument, that we concede this objection to functionalism. Gray was nevertheless wrong to think that the objection as formulated applies to our dynamic sensorimotor view of experience. For the same reason, it does not apply to Pettit's manifest powers account of color looks. Neither view identifies color looks with behavioral functions. To put the point in Pettit's terms, the objection as formulated overlooks the important difference between *mere* hunting and gathering powers, and *manifest* hunting and gathering powers, and the way in which the *manifestness* of empowerment in color looks, as we have argued, depends on 'expectancies' about the characteristic ways in which sensation depends on movement.

However, Gray's objection can be reformulated to take this point into account. Instead of insisting merely that the same color look can go with different behavioral functions, the objector now insists that the *same color look* can go with *different manifest powers and expectancies*, reflecting the subject's understanding of quite different underlying sensorimotor dynamics in the two cases. That is, different manifest powers *and expectancies about the dependence of sensation on movement* are associated with synaesthetic experience of green and with normal perceptual experience of green objects.

This is more worrying for the hunter-gatherer perspective. There is good reason to think not just that the underlying sensorimotor dynamics of normal green and synaesthetic green are quite different, but also that synaesthetic subjects know this, implicitly. Expectancies about the characteristic ways in which sensation depends on movement that are associated with normal perceptual experience of green objects are not associated with experiences of synaesthetic green. For example, the subject understands that sensations depend on eye movements in perceptually experiencing a green object. But there is no reason to suppose that a synaesthetic subject has such expectancies when hearing a particular word that induces experience of synaesthetic green. As she well understands, she can experience synaesthetic green with her eyes shut!

More generally, on the hunter-gatherer view, color looks depend on implicit understanding of the characteristic ways in which sensation changes with movement and other color-relevant conditions; to experience something as green is to experience it in the light of this implicit understanding of changeability. But synaesthetic color looks are not in the same way subject to this sort of changeability; nor are they understood to be. Synaesthetic subjects don't implicitly expect synaesthetic sensations to change as lighting conditions change, or as their eyes move. Synaesthetic color looks do not empower hunting and gathering responses in the way that normal color perception does. But the critical point is that synaesthetic color looks do not mislead in this respect. They do not pretend to manifest such empowerment, or visually solicit expectancies they cannot fulfill.

The sensorimotor knowledge involved in normal perceptual experience of color appears to be irrelevant to synaesthetic color looks.

How can the hunter-gatherer view respond to this line of argument?

6. SAME COLOR LOOKS? A PRELIMINARY RESPONSE

The reformulation of Gray's objection (like the original) turns on the assumption that color experiences and corresponding synaesthetic experiences are qualitatively alike with respect to color. Greenness is what is supposed to be common to perceptual experience of a green object and synaesthetic experience of green induced by a heard word. If color looks differ between normal and synaesthetic experience of color, then the 'same color look, different manifest powers and expectancies' objection does not apply. Is the 'same color look' assumption justified?

First, synaesthetes with colored hearing do not confuse synaesthetic colors with normally perceived colors; synaesthetic color experiences do not misleadingly present themselves as normal perceptual experiences of color. This is not controversial. But nor does it have any tendency to show that these experiences are not experiences of the same color. Many qualitative differences in experience are compatible with sameness with respect to color. Different perceptual experiences of green objects need not be absolutely qualitatively identical in order to have greenness in common. The assumption is that synaesthetic experience has greenness in common with perceptual experience of a green object, not that it is exactly similar. Similarly, the experience of green in an afterimage isn't confused with the perception of a green object but, nevertheless, is reasonably assumed to share the quality of greenness. Green afterimages, green synaesthetic experiences, and normal perceptual experiences seem to have something in common, despite the phenomenal differences between them.

Second, there might seem to be a quite different kind of reason for calling into question the assumed common color quality of experience of synaesthetic green and normal perceptual experience of green: disjunctivism (see Snowdon 1980–1; McDowell 1986). Disjunctivism is an anti-Cartesian view about experience that is motivated by general considerations regarding illusions and knowledge (among other things). Disjunctivists argue that perceptual experiences are genuine relations between perceivers and the objects they experience. The contents of normal perceptual experiences are, in this sense, object-dependent. For this reason, it will never be the case that perceptual experiences and corresponding illusory experiences have the same content, even though they may seem to be indistinguishable. For in the nonveridical case, the object of the experience is missing. But the content of the original experience was dependent on an actual relation to just that object.

As we've said, synaesthetic experiences of color wear their phenomenal differences from normal perceptual experiences of color on their sleeve. They don't even *seem* to be indistinguishable from normal perceptual experience. Disjunctivism isn't needed to get this far. But perhaps it could be employed to argue that not only are synaesthetic and normal experiences of green different in the way they seem to be, but they are even more deeply different: they are not even similar in respect of greenness, since one experience involves a relation to a green object and the other does not. However, we cannot resolve issues about disjunctivism here, and so set this line of response aside.

In what follows we will grant the assumption that synaesthetic experiences and normal color experiences can share color qualities. What other responses to the challenge are available to the hunter-gatherer view?

7. THE FALSE SENSORIMOTOR EXPECTANCY ACCOUNT OF ILLUSORY COLOR LOOKS

A second line of response is suggested by Pettit's appeal to expectancies to unify color looks and to explain color illusions. We are very much in sympathy with this approach, which converges with our own general views. It is worth exploring in detail, in order to understand why in the end it doesn't succeed in meeting the challenge that synaesthesia presents to the hunter-gatherer perspective.

A general strategy to account for perceptual illusions is to appeal to sensorimotor expectancies common to illusory and veridical experiences. Take the veridical case first. When you visually experience a tomato as three-dimensionally extended, you expect that as you move, bits of the tomato will come into view that are concealed from the initial vantage-point. The experience of the whole tomato as three-dimensionally present on the basis of perceptual contact with a single side of the tomato depends on expectations of this sort about the sensory consequences of movement (see Noë 2004).

Now consider misperception. A glimpse of a plastic tomato façade may trigger just the same sensorimotor anticipations as does the glimpse of a genuine tomato. The suggestion is that the non-veridical experience of the tomato façade as three-dimensionally voluminous is grounded on the activation of the same sensorimotor expectancies that would be triggered by an actual tomato. Normally, these expectancies would be activated along with and against the background of a wealth of other cognitive judgments and expectations. For example, most of us know what tomatoes are, and can recognize them on sight; this intellectual skill influences our experience. But it would be a mistake to suppose that the sensorimotor expectancies are themselves a matter of *judgment*. The tomato façade can look three-dimensionally voluminous from a given angle *even when you know* it is only a façade; your sensorimotor anticipations can arise even though you know they will not be fulfilled. Similarly, in the Mueller–Lyer illusion, the lines still look different lengths even when you know that they are the same length; knowledge that the appearance is illusory doesn't make the illusion go away (for discussion, see Jacob and Jeannerod 2003: ch. 4).

Pettit applies this general type of account of nonveridical experiences to color looks. On his manifest powers view, expectancies are critical to explaining how there can be color illusions: how something that is not yellow can look yellow—that is, can look the same color as a yellow object. Perceiving a yellow object does not just empower hunting and gathering, but does so manifestly, which involves generating expectancies about the way in which patterns of sensations would vary with light, background, and movement. These expectancies unify different instances of looking yellow; but they are not necessarily accurate. Sameness of color looks may thus reflect a similar set of expectancies, even if many of these are false for illusory color looks. Something may look yellow here and now, yet may not fulfill the relevant expectancies—may not vary in the expected way with movement, or changes in light or background, say—because it is not actually yellow. Its yellow look would then be revealed to be a trick of the light or an illusion.

Pettit also notes that illusory looks can persist even though we recognize that the expectancies associated with them are false, as in the Mueller–Lyer illusion. He suggests that certain practical expectancies may be hardwired in normal subjects to certain patterns of sensory input, so that our intellectual recognition that the corresponding experiences are misleading does not penetrate our natural responses and expectancies to constitute practical knowledge. Accordingly, the illusions survive recognition that they are illusions.

Whatever one thinks about their "hardwired" character, it seems clear that practical expectancies are often not defeated by intellectual judgments. Nevertheless, there may be reasons to doubt that false practical expectancies can provide a general explanation of persistent illusory looks. These doubts derive from a line of research associated with the two visual systems view, claiming that action resists visual illusions.

For example, one illusion that persists even when you recognize intellectually that it is an illusion is the Titchener circle illusion: disks that are really the same size nevertheless appear to be different sizes, or vice versa, according to the size of surrounding disks. Aglioti et al. (1995) claimed to show that certain sensorimotor skills are unaffected by the Titchener circle illusion: normal subjects adjust their grip to the true size of the disks in reaching for them, rather than to the apparent illusory size of the disks.[19] Implicit practical knowledge of the true properties of the disks governs at least some of the subjects' interactions with the disks, while they are nevertheless subject to the illusion. It would seem that the subjects' implicit expectancies about how it will feel when they move their hands to touch

---

[19] See also Milner and Goodale 1995: 167–8; Jacob and Jeannerod 2003: ch. 4, who also explain similar demonstrations for the Mueller–Lyer illusion.

the disks are correct, yet the illusion persists. If so, then it can be argued that we cannot explain the persistence of illusion here by reference to false sensorimotor expectations, since there do *not* seem to be false sensorimotor expectations.

We offer two responses to the 'action resists illusion' objection, in defense of the false sensorimotor expectancy account of illusory looks.

First, the use of these results *as an argument against the false sensorimotor expectancy account of illusions* is over-ambitious; it does not show what it sets out to show. To see this, recall the context. The false sensorimotor expectancy view of illusions is an aspect of the hunter-gatherer approach that we share with Pettit. As explained above, this does not claim that perceptual experience can be understood solely in terms of its role in guiding action, but gives sensorimotor expectancies a fundamental role. But neither does this approach rely on a narrow set of sensorimotor expectancies associated with a particular type of action to capture a look; rather, an important role of expectancies in Pettit's account (and ours) is to unify looks across diverse contexts and potential actions. But only a broad set of specific expectancies can play this role, including expectancies about the specific ways in which sensation depends on a variety of changes, in movement, lighting, background, and so on. To challenge the false sensorimotor expectancy account of illusions, what would have to resist illusion is a significant part of the relevant broad set of specific manifest powers—of sensorimotor skills and expectancies—and not merely a particular element of it, pertaining, say, to a particular grasping movement.

But the 'action resists illusion' results do not show this. Subjects in the experiment of Aglioti et al. can use what they see to guide certain specific movements correctly, despite the illusion, and with no apparent false expectancies. But this doesn't show that the broad set of sensorimotor powers and expectancies associated with the illusory look of Titchener circles is significantly different from the set associated with similar but veridical looks in a variety of different contexts. For present purposes, the relevant manifest powers comprise a rich, complex set of sensorimotor skills and expectancies, capable of playing a unifying role across different actions and contexts. Though specific actions, such as grasping in specific contexts, may resist a certain visual illusion, other actions in different contexts may not resist that same illusion. And despite the fact that the sensorimotor expectancies associated with a specific action of grasping in a specific context may be accurate, and so not explain the illusion, many other false sensorimotor expectancies from the relevant unifying set of expectancies may still be present, and may explain the illusion. Hunting and gathering powers, including diverse expectancies about how sensation changes with movement, lighting, and background, go far beyond the ability to point or grasp accurately on prompt and the limited expectancies that may be associated with these specific abilities.

However, the more general claim needed to mount the challenge to the false sensorimotor expectancy account would be hard to defend, since illusion-resistant actions tend to be highly specific to certain tasks or contexts.[20] Moreover, such tasks are prompted within constrained experimental set-ups in which the veridical information is used implicitly, not explicitly. An analogy may help to drive the point home. The fact that blind-sight subjects can, when prompted, localize lights they do not see consciously does not mean that they have a full range of dynamic sensorimotor skills and expectancies in acting explicitly on this spatial information; on the contrary, their powers and expectancies in acting on this information are very severely limited. Similarly, the fact that normal subjects can, when prompted, use information (in grasping) that they do not see consciously (given the illusion) does not mean that they have a full range of sensorimotor powers or expectancies in acting on this information.

In sum, the relevant sets of sensorimotor powers and expectancies appealed to in the hunter-gatherer approach to illusions is much broader than the actions and associated expectancies in demonstrations of illusion resistance (cf. Jacob and Jeannerod 2003: 172, whose discussion misses this point). Thus, the latter are not counterexamples.

Our second response, in passing, is that the claim that action resists visual illusions is itself controversial; contrary, or at least heavily qualifying, evidence has been offered.[21] The correct overall interpretation of the mixed evidence is unsettled. However, we cannot do justice to these general issues here, which would require a full-fledged investigation into the evidence for two visual systems and its significance for theories of perceptual experience.

8. WHY THE FALSE SENSORIMOTOR EXPECTANCY ACCOUNT OF ILLUSORY COLOR LOOKS DOES NOT MEET THE CHALLENGE FROM SYNAESTHESIA

We have defended the false sensorimotor expectancy approach to illusion against a general objection from the 'action resists illusion' results. But since our topic here is color looks, we now set aside the question of how successful the false practical expectancy approach is as a general explanation of illusions, in order to focus on how well it handles *illusory color looks* in particular.

It works well when applied to Kohler's color adaptation results. The yellow look of something with eyes rightward for Kohler's goggle-wearer did not persist, but adapted away. Recall the explanation: the illusory yellow look experienced with eyes rightward reflects false expectations about how sensations will vary with certain movements. The underlying sensorimotor dynamics of color looks,

---

[20] Here we are grateful to discussion with Kevin O'Regan.

[21] See, e.g., Franz 2001; see also Glover 2002; Milner and Dyde 2003; Jacob and Jeannerod 2003: ch. 4; recall that Jacob and Jeannerod advocate a version of the two visual systems theory that is, by their own account, 'weak' and heavily qualified; see pp. 102–4, 126, 131–2, 188 ff., 254–5.

associated with perception of color constancy across various changes, has not changed. But its implementation has been transformed by the goggles, so that expectations based on the old implementation are now false. The subject learns that her expectations about rightward, initially yellow-looking objects when she or the objects make certain sideways movements are misleading. These sensorimotor expectancies are not hardwired to certain patterns of retinal input. As the subject's expectations come back into alignment with the underlying sensorimotor dynamics of color, they are relocated to their proper, yellow objects, and so too is the yellow look. The goggles temporarily deprive the subject of some of her sensorimotor understanding of how sensations change with movement, but as she learns through active exploration wearing the goggles that the light coming through the goggles still carries the old sensorimotor patterns for color looks but in a new guise, her expectations adapt, and veridical color looks return. The illusion of rightward yellow survives the subject's intellectual knowledge that she is wearing the goggles, but it does not survive her reacquisition of sensorimotor skills and understanding.

This account of Kohler's results accords well with recent work by Philipona, O'Regan, and Coenen. They analyze patterns of sensorimotor contingency as various colored surfaces are moved in relation to the eyes. Their analysis distinguishes intrinsic or code-independent structures, which are underlying patterns of dynamic sensorimotor contingencies characteristic of specific colors and their relations, from more superficial patterns that depend on the way in which specific inputs or outputs are coded (cf. Ramachandran and Hirstein 1998: 1616, 1623, on labeled lines versus pattern coding). They show that the intrinsic sensorimotor structure of colors captures intensity, hue and saturation, black and white, and pairwise opponency, which are thus independent of specific neural circuitry. In these terms, our claim is that the subject has practical, skill-enabling knowledge of the deep sensorimotor structure of color. This deep structure survives the superficial change in registration imposed by the goggles. When the subject relocates it and regains the relevant skills, his color experiences renormalize also.

However, the false expectancy account does not fare so well in accounting for colored hearing synaesthesia (which Pettit does not discuss). Consider how Pettit's false expectancy account of illusions might characterize one of Gray's ACE synaesthesia subjects:

"The ACE subject's synaesthetic illusion of green when naming red objects is associated with the sensorimotor expectations characteristic of normal perception of green things in hunting and gathering activities (after all, she can also perceive green things). However, these expectations are misleading when they are aroused by the word 'red' or by the naming of red objects: synaesthetic green does not satisfy hunting and gathering expectancies for green. Moreover, the ACE subject realizes this intellectually; after all, she does not confuse normal green and synaesthetic green. But these practical

expectancies are in some way hardwired to 'red', so that her intellectual recognition of their falsity does not penetrate her natural responses to constitute practical knowledge; hence illusory synaesthetic experience of green survives her recognition that it is illusory, and generates delays in color naming."

The problem with this story is that there is little reason to think that synaesthetic subjects do in general have *false* sensorimotor expectancies associated with synaesthetic experiences of green. After all, synaesthetic subjects *don't* expect synaesthetic green to display the characteristic combination of variation and constancy under different lighting and contrast conditions that a green object does. They recognize the difference, practically as well as intellectually, between normal and synaesthetic colors, and they use synaesthetic colors for different practical purposes: for example, as aids to memory.[22] Synaesthetic colors achieve constancy on the cheap, with no need to employ one's practical mastery of the sensorimotor dynamics of normal color: for example, if 'red' is synaesthetically green, it is always synaesthetically green; background, lighting, movement, and so on are irrelevant to its constant greenness. The normal hunting and gathering powers and expectancies associated with perceptual experience of green objects are absent. So there is little reason to think synaesthetic color experience is characterized by false sensorimotor expectancies at all (let alone that they are hardwired).[23]

If color illusions are explained in terms of false sensorimotor expectancies, but synaesthetes do not have such false expectancies, then synaesthetic color illusions cannot be explained in these terms. However, one response to the lack of false sensorimotor expectancies in synaesthetic color experience is to suggest that perhaps synaesthetic color experience should not be regarded as *illusory* in the first place, any more than afterimages are illusory. The reason in this argumentative posture cannot of course be simply that no misleading expectancies are aroused. A view that appeals to false sensorimotor expectancies to explain color illusions cannot respond to a plausible counterexample by claiming that because there are no false sensorimotor expectancies, there is no illusion.

---

[22] " . . . the next time you see her you don't say: 'It's Ethel', so you: 'It's the green blob: therefore, it is Ethel' " (Cytowic 1997: 25).

[23] Not only are the normal hunting and gathering powers and expectancies of perceptual experience of color absent from synaesthetic experience. In addition, the automatic priming powers of synaesthetic color experience are more limited than those of normal color perception, and do not extend to masked priming. Normal colors have priming effects when perceived unconsciously as well as when they are perceived consciously; i.e. normal colors can function as primes in naming and pointing tasks even when they are masked so as not to be consciously experienced (Schmidt 2000, 2002; see also Breitmeyer et al. 2004*a*,*b*). By contrast, synaesthetic colors can function as primes but not as masked primes (Mattingley et al. 2001; Rich and Mattingly 2002). Thus colored hearing does not have all the powers of normal color perception at the unconscious level either. An interesting experiment would compare masked color priming with lack of masked synaesthetic color priming in the same synaesthetic subjects, in effect combining the Schmidt and Mattingley paradigms. As far as we know, this has not been done.

That would beg the question at issue. But without doing that, we can agree that in neither synaesthesia nor afterimages does the color experience misrepresent itself as a perception of color or prompt us to think that an object is colored when it is not. We have no trouble telling these experiences apart from normal perceptual experiences of color. So perhaps there is no real conflict in the case of synaesthesia: no misperception, just different, extra perceptions. In this respect, synaesthesia may be quite different from wearing Kohler's goggles.

Although this point may be correct, it does not resolve the challenge that synaesthesia presents to the hunter-gatherer view of color looks. The challenge does not ultimately depend on whether synaesthetic experience is illusory or not, but merely on the fact that synaesthetic experience of a given color and normal perceptual experience of that color have a color look in common. They share the aspect of, say, greenness, however much they may differ qualitatively in other ways, and even if they are not confused with one another and neither is illusory. The challenge is simple: same color look, different sensorimotor powers and expectancies.

In this case, we cannot respond as we did to the 'action resists illusion' objection, by appealing to a broad set of expectancies to unify a look, even if some elements of that set relating to specific actions in specific contexts may be missing. For in the case of synaesthesia, pretty well the whole set of hunter-gatherer powers and sensorimotor expectancies associated with normal color looks is missing. Not only can synaesthetic colors not actually be used to guide hunting and gathering, but synaesthetic color experience does not generate expectations that sensations will vary with movement, with light, with background, or any of the normal sensorimotor expectations that perceptual experience of color generates. It is truly a hard case for the hunter-gatherer perspective.

9. DOES ACE PROVIDE A WAY OUT?

Recall at this point (as explained in Section 4 above) that synaesthetic experience can produce mild interference with normal color naming. When ACE synaesthetes exercise the skill of naming ordinary colors, their ACE synaesthetic experience appears to interfere and cause delays in naming. This delay is very different from misleading sensorimotor expectancies of the kind we have been appealing to so far. It is very different, for example, from the misleading expectancies of a novice wearer of Kohler's goggles, who expects an object to be discriminable and trackable in certain ways across different angles of view, and who is distracted by unexpected effects of movement.

However, perhaps Gray's ACE results can be used to extend the manifest powers account to include ACE responses to synaesthetic colors. A normal tendency when asked to name a perceived color is to respond by naming the color; perceiving the color enables the naming response to appropriate queries. Even though this naming power is acquired with language learning, once learned, the response tendency may become automatic in some sense. Perhaps the enabling of such automatic naming responses and associated expectancies are part of the correct specification of the manifest powers of color perception on which color looks supervene, along with hunting and gathering powers and expectancies.

Suppose that when an ACE subject is asked to name a red object, she will automatically tend to name green as well as to name red, which creates interference and delay in color naming even though it is inhibited. This would be analogous to the false expectancies that Pettit suggests may explain why illusions persist even when subjects recognize intellectually that they are illusions, in that the automatic naming tendency in the ACE subject persists even though the subject recognizes intellectually that she has been asked to name the color of the red object, which she sees is not green. This automatic ACE tendency is of course not normal; nor can it be completely hardwired, since it is acquired with language learning. However, on this account, the look of synaesthetic green associated with the word 'red' and the naming of red objects would supervene on the automatic tendency to respond with 'green' when asked to name red objects. Even if *someone else* says 'red', the ACE subject experiences green because she has a nonnormal counterfactual 'expectancy' that she would tend to say 'green' if she were asked to name a red object, which she has to inhibit, and which persists although she recognizes that this response would be erroneous. (The expectancy itself isn't false here, even though the inhibited response would be false.) On this suggestion, the look that unites green objects and synaesthetic green supervenes on this automatic tendency to respond 'green' if you are asked for a color name and associated expectations. The tendency, like Pettit's expectancies, extends across actual and counterfactual conditions to provide the unity of the green look of both green objects and the word 'red'.

But this extension of the expectancy account to exploit the tendencies of ACE subjects is not plausible. We emphasize that we do not attribute this extension to Pettit; it is simply one more (unsuccessful) attempt to respond to the challenge presented by synaesthesia. The extension is not plausible, because it discards the sensorimotor powers and expectancies associated with hunting and gathering, which Pettit and we emphasize, to focus on naming powers and associated expectations as the source of the unity of normal green and synaesthetic green. It thus discards the heart of the hunter-gatherer approach to color. But it is not plausible to claim that naming powers and expectations alone unite normal and synaesthetic color looks.

This claim certainly conflicts with the naive view that we learn to attach the same color names to colors that look the same to us. The claim we find implausible in effect says the opposite: that colors look the same to us if perceiving them manifestly empowers us to attach the same names to them and induces associated expectations. However, this claim is not made any more plausible by rejecting a view of color experience as having an autonomous universal structure in favor of a more relativistic view of color experience, as culturally constructed and variable to a greater degree than we may naively assume (see Saunders and van Brakel 1997; cf. Berlin and Kay 1969/91). It may be argued, for example, that color terms are context-dependent in culturally variable ways: one word for 'black' may be applied to night, tattoos, and flying foxes, but not to hair, whales, or fish (Saunders and van Brakel 1997). But if experience of color looks reflects such cultural influences, then synaesthetes should *not* come to experience green when asked to name red objects. Thus, the claim that the ACE subject's naming powers and expectations alone unite synaesthetic and normal green faces a dilemma: it is not plausible *either* on the 'naive' view that we learn to apply color names according to the colors we experience, *or* on the 'sophisticated' view that our color experiences are to some degree culturally determined and relative.

10. WHY DON'T SYNAESTHETIC COLORS ADAPT AWAY?

The question at the heart of the challenge from synaesthesia to the hunter-gatherer perspective on color looks is: why don't synaesthetic color experiences, and ACE experiences in particular, adapt away? If color experiences supervene on manifest hunting and gathering powers and sensorimotor expectancies that are familiar to synaesthetes from their perceptions of normal colors but are missing from their synaesthetic experiences, what explains the similarity of synaesthetic and normal color experience? Synaesthetic color experience is not associated with the powers and expectancies characteristic of normal colors, and synaesthetes know this implicitly; they don't have contrary expectations. So how can a given color quality continue to occupy such disparate sensorimotor roles? Why does the synaesthetic experience persist instead of adapting away? How can hunter-gatherers hear as well as see color?

In fact the challenge raised by our discussion is broader: how can *any* account of color looks explain *both* why color experience does adapt to Kohler's goggles and why it does not adapt in synaesthesia. The hunter-gatherer perspective can explain the Kohler adaptation, but not the lack of it in synaesthesia; other views may have the opposite problem. The trick is to explain why color experience defers to the colors of the world in some cases, such as Kohler's, but not in others, such as synaesthesia.[24]

---

[24] This is a version of the problem of explaining the difference between neural deference and neural dominance, discussed in Hurley and Noë 2003. In work in progress, we extend our 2003 account to synaesthesia.

We suggest that in order to respond to this challenge, it is necessary to go beyond the pure hunter-gatherer perspective—though holding on to its insights—and to consider the ways in which the relevant powers of the dynamic, sensorimotor interaction with the world engage and are constrained by the brain and nervous system. We should resist the assumption that the character of experience must ultimately be explained either *just* in terms of what happens in the brain, or *just* in terms of the active subject's relations to the world. Our dynamic view rejects this inner/outer dichotomization of potential explanans. The sensorimotor dynamics that govern experience are in principle distributed across brain, body, behavior, and environment (though they can be so distributed to different degrees). What is needed to respond to the broader challenge that synaesthesia presents is to bring brain activity and the extended dynamics in which it is embedded within a unified explanatory framework.

REFERENCES

Aglioti, S., Goodale, M. A., and DeSousa, J. F. X. (1995). "Size-contrast illusions deceive the eye but not the hand". *Current Biology* 5: 679–85.

Baron-Cohen, Simon, and Harrison, John E., (1997) (eds.). *Synaesthesia: Classic and Contemporary Readings*. Oxford: Blackwell.

Beck, D., Rees, G., Frith, C., and Lavie, N. (2001). "Neural correlates of change detection and change blindness". *Nature Neuroscience* 4(6): 645–50.

Berlin, B., and Kay, P. (1969/1991). *Universality and Evolution*. Berkeley: University of California Press.

Breitmeyer, B., Ogmen, H., and Chen, J. (2004*a*). "Unconscious priming by color and form: different processes and levels". *Consciousness and Cognition* 13: 138–57.

—— Ro, T., and Singhal, N. (2004*b*). "Unconscious color priming occurs at stimulus—not percept—dependent levels of processing". *Psychological Science* 15(3): 198–202.

Cole, D. (1990). "Functionalism and Inverted Spectra". *Synthese* 82: 207–22.

—— (1991). *Pride and a Daily Marathon*. London: Duckworth.

Cytowic, Richard E. (1997). "Synaesthesia: phenomenology and neuropsychology". In Baron-Cohen and Harrison 1997: 17–39.

Franz, V. H. (2001). "Action does not resist visual illusions". *Trends in Cognitive Sciences* 5(11): 457–9.

Frith, Christopher D., and Paulesu, Eraldo (1997). "The physiological basis of synaesthesia". In Baron-Cohen and Harrison 1997: 123–47.

Gallese, Vittorio, Craighero, Laila, Fadiga, Luciano, and Fogassi, Leonardo (1999). "Perception through action". *Psyche* 5(21); <http://psyche/cs.monash.edu.au/v5/psyche-5–21-gallese.html>.

Glover, Scott (2002). "Visual illusions affect planning but not control". *Trends in Cognitive Sciences* 6(7): 288–92.

Gray, J. A. (2003). "How are qualia coupled to functions?" *Trends in Cognitive Sciences* 7(5): 192–4.

_____ Williams, S., Nunn, J., and Baron-Cohen, S. (1997). "Possible implications of synaesthesia for the hard question of consciousness". In Baron-Cohen and Harrison 1997: 173–81.

_____ Chopping, S., Nunn, J., Parslow, D., Gregory, L., Williams, S., Brammer, M. J., and Baron-Cohen, S. (2002). "Implications of synaesthesia for functionalism: theory and experiments". *Journal of Consciousness Studies* 9(12): 5–31.

_____ Parslow, D. M., Brammer, M. J., Chopping, S., Goparlen, N. V., and ffytche, D. H. (2006). "Evidence against functionalism from neuroimaging of the alien colour effect in synaesthesia". *Cortex* 42: 309–18.

Hardin, C. L. (1997). "Reinverting the Spectrum". In A. Bryne and D. R. Hilbert (eds.), *Readings on Color, i: The Philosophy of Color* (Cambridge, Mass.: MIT Press), 289–301.

Harrington, T. (1965). "Adaptation of humans to colored split-field glasses". *Psychonometric Science* 3: 71–72.

Harrison, John E., and Baron-Cohen, Simon (1997*a*). "Synaesthesia: an introduction". In Baron-Cohen and Harrison 1997: 3–16.

_____ _____ (1997*b*). "Synaesthesia: a review of psychological theories". In Baron-Cohen and Harrison 1997: 109–22.

Hurley, S. L. (1998). *Consciousness in Action.* Cambridge, Mass.: Harvard University Press.

_____ (2001). "Perception and Action: Alternative Views". *Synthese* 129: 3–40.

_____ and Noë, A. (2003). "Neural plasticity and consciousness". *Biology and Philosophy* 18: 131–68.

_____ _____ (in progress). "Synaesthesia and sensorimotor dynamics".

Jacob, P., and Jeannerod, M. (2003). *Ways of Seeing: The Scope and Limits of Visual Cognition.* New York: Oxford University Press.

Kohler, I. (1951). "Über Aufbau und Wandlungen der Wahrnehmungswelt". *Österreichische Akademie der Wissenschaften. Sitzungsberichte, philosophish-historische Klasse* 227: 1–118.

_____ (1964). *The Formation and Transformation of the Perceptual World.* Published as a monograph in *Psychological Issues* vol. 3 (monograph 12). New York: International University Press. [This is a translation of Kohler 1951.]

Marks, Lawrence E. (1997). "On colored hearing synaesthesia: cross-modal translations of sensory dimensions". In Baron-Cohen and Harrison 1997: 49–98.

Mattingley, J. B., Rich, A. N., Yelland, G., and Bradshaw, J. L. (2001). "Unconscious priming eliminates automatic binding of colour and alphanumeric form in synaesthesia". *Nature* 410: 580–2.

Maurer, Daphne (1997). "Neonatal synaesthesia: implications for the processing of speech and faces". In Baron-Cohen and Harrison 1997: 224–42.

McCollough, C. (1965). "The conditioning of color perception". *American Journal of Psychology* 78: 362–78.

McDowell, John (1986). "Singular thought and the extent of inner space". In P. Pettit and J. McDowell (eds.), *Subject, Thought, and Context* (Oxford: Oxford University Press). Also in J. McDowell, *Meaning, Knowledge, and Reality* (Cambridge, Mass.: Harvard University Press, 1998).

Milner, David, and Dyde, Richard (2003). "Why do some perceptual illusions affect visually guided action, when others don't?" *Trends in Cognitive Sciences* 7(1): 10–11.

Milner, David, and Goodale, Melvyn (1995). *The Visual Brain in Action*. Oxford: Oxford University Press.

Motluk, Alison (1997). "Two synaesthetes talking colour". In Baron-Cohen and Harrison 1997: 269–77.

Myin, Erik (2001). "Color and the duplication assumption". *Synthese* 129: 61–77.

Noë, A. (2004). *Action in Perception*. Cambridge, Mass.: MIT Press.

——— and Hurley, S. (2003). "The deferential brain in action: response to Jeffrey Gray". *Trends in Cognitive Sciences* 7(5): 195–6.

——— and O'Regan, K. (2002). "On the brain-basis of visual consciousness: a sensorimotor account". In A. Noë and E. Thompson (eds.), *Vision and Mind: Selected Readings in the Philosophy of Perception* (Cambridge, Mass.: MIT Press), 000–00.

Nunn, J. A., Gregory, L. J., Brammer, M., Williams, S. C. R., Parslow, D. M., Morgan, M. J., Morris, R., Bullmore, E., Baron-Cohen, S., and Gray, J. A. (2002). "Functional magnetic resonance imaging of synesthesia: activation of color vision area V4/V8 by spoken words". *Nature Neuroscience* 5(4): 371–4.

O'Regan, K., and Noë, A. (2001*a*). "Acting out our sensory experience". *Behavioral and Brain Sciences* 24(5): 955–75.

——— ——— (2001*b*). "A sensorimotor account of vision and visual consciousness". *Behavioral and Brain Sciences* 24(5): 883–917.

——— ——— (2001*c*). "What it is like to see: a sensorimotor theory of perceptual experience". *Synthese* 129(1): 79–103.

Palmer, Stephen E. (1999). "Color, consciousness, and the isomorphism constraint". *Behavioral and Brain Sciences* 22(6): 1–21.

Peppmann, P., and Wieland, B. (1966). "Visual distortion with two-colored spectacles". *Perceptual and Motor Skills* 23: 1043–8.

Pettit, P. (2003). "Looks red". *Philosophical Issues* 13(1): 221–52.

Philipona, D., O'Regan, J. K., Coenen, O. (in progress). "On the intrinsic sensorimotor structure of colors". Abstract at <http://webhost/ua.ac.be/assc8/089Phil.html>.

Ramachandran, V. S., and Hirstein, W. (1998). "The perception of phantom limbs". *Brain* 121(9): 1603–30.

——— and Hubbard, E. M. (2001*a*). "Psychophysical investigations into the neural basis of synaesthesia". *Proceedings of the Royal Academy of London* 268: 979–83.

——— ——— (2001*b*). "Synaesthesia—a window into perception, thought and language". *Journal of Consciousness Studies* 8(12): 3–34.

——— ——— (2003). "The phenomenology of synaesthesia". *Journal of Consciousness Studies* 10(8): 49–57.

Rich, A. N., and Mattingley, J. (2002). "Anomalous perception in synaesthesia: a cognitive neuroscience perspective". *Nature Reviews: Neuroscience* 3: 43–52.

Saunders, B. A. C., and van Brakel, J. (1997). "Are there non-trivial constraints on colour categorization?" *Behavioral and Brain Sciences* 20(2): 167–228.

Schmidt, Thomas (2000). "Visual perception without awareness: priming responses by color". In T. Metzinger (ed.), *Neural Correlates of Consciousness* (Cambridge, Mass.: MIT Press), 157–70.

——— (2002). "The finger in flight: real-time motor control by visually masked color stimuli". *Psychological Science* 13(2): 112–18.

Snowdon, Paul (1980–1). "Experience, vision, and causation". *Proceedings of the Aristotelian Society* 81: 175–92. Repr. in A. Noë and E. Thompson (eds.), *Vision and Mind* (Cambridge, Mass.: MIT Press, 2002), 151–66.

Taylor, J. (1962), *The Behavioral Basis of Perception*. London: Yale University Press.

4

Structural Irrationality

T. M. Scanlon

Many normative claims are substantive claims about reasons—claims, for example, about the reasons that a person in certain circumstances has to do or to believe something. But not all normative claims are substantive claims about reasons. In particular, some claims about what it would be irrational for someone to do are normative claims, but not claims about the reasons that person has. Here are some examples.

If a person believes that *p*, then it would be irrational for him to refuse to rely on *p* as a premise in further reasoning, and to reject arguments because they rely on it. To say this is not to say that the person has good reason to accept these arguments. Perhaps what he has most reason to do is to give up his belief that *p*. The claim is only that *as long as he believes that p*, it is irrational of him to refuse to accept such arguments. Similar claims hold in regard to practical reasoning: if a person intends to do *A* at *t*, and believes that in order to do this she must first do *B*, then it is irrational for her not to count this as a reason for doing *B*. This is not to say that she has any reason to do *B*. Perhaps what she has most reason to do is to abandon her intention to do *A*, or to change her mind about whether it is necessary to do *B* in order to do *A* later. But as long as she does not do either of these things, it is irrational for her to deny that she has any reason to do B. Normative claims of this kind involve claims about what a person must, if she is not irrational, treat as a reason, but they make no claims about whether this actually *is* a reason.[1]

I will call claims of this kind *structural* claims about rationality, to distinguish them from *substantive* claims about what is a reason for what. They are structural because they are claims about the relations between an agent's attitudes that must

I am grateful to participants in the discussion at the Common Minds conference for their helpful criticisms and suggestions. For comments on later versions, I am indebted to Luca Ferrero, Pamela Hieronymi, Nadeem Hussain, Niko Kolodny, Derek Parfit, Jay Wallace, and members of my Fall 2003 colloquium for first-year graduate students.

[1] I believe that these are what John Broome has called normative requirements. See, e.g., "Reasons", in R. Jay Wallace, Michael Smith, Samuel Scheffler, and Philip Pettit (eds.), *Reason and Value: Themes from the Moral Philosophy of Joseph Raz* by (Oxford: Oxford University Press, 2004), 28–55.

hold insofar as he or she is not irrational, and the kind of irrationality involved is a matter of conflict between these attitudes. In earlier work, I have suggested that we should restrict the term 'irrational' to instances of what I am here calling structural irrationality.[2] I am not relying on that restriction here. My present thesis is just that some claims about what a person must do insofar as he or she is not irrational are of this kind.

In this Chapter I will first examine in more detail the kind of normativity involved in requirements of structural rationality. I will then consider how these requirements are to be formulated, first in general and then with regard specifically to intentions and to beliefs. Finally, I will consider the implications that my conclusions have for the widely discussed idea that beliefs and desires have different "directions of fit".

1. THE NORMATIVE BASIS OF STRUCTURAL RATIONALITY

What I am here calling structural requirements of rationality are examples of what Philip Pettit calls "programmed regularities that have the status of norms".[3] They are regularities that any being will generally conform to insofar as it is a rational agent, and ones that can serve as the basis for explanations of such a being's behavior. We can explain the fact that a rational agent accepts a certain argument by referring to its beliefs, and we can explain what it does, or declines to do, by reference to what aims or intentions it has adopted, or judged there to be good reasons to adopt. These explanations are what Pettit calls "programming explanations" because the regularities they invoke hold in virtue of lower-level causal regularities guaranteed by the physical states that realize the psychological states in question. To claim that some being is a rational agent is, in part, to claim that it is so constituted, physically, that these regularities will in general hold. It is also to claim that this being is one for which these regularities are norms. I want now to consider in what way such regularities are normative.

The behavior of a rational agent will exhibit (at least to a significant degree) the regularities described by requirements of rationality. But this is not because the agent sees this way of behaving as required by principles that she must be guided by. A rational agent who believes that p does not accept arguments relying on p as a premise *because* she sees this as required by some principle of rationality to which she must conform. Nor does she generally do it "in order not be irrational". Rather, she will be willing to rely on p as a premise simply

---

[2] *T. M. Scanlon, What We Owe to Each Other* (Cambridge, Mass.: Harvard University Press, 1998), 25–30.

[3] See Philip Pettit, "Three Aspects of Rational Explanation", in *Rules, Reasons, and Norms* (Oxford: Oxford University Press, 2002), 177–91, p. 183.

because she believes that *p*. Similarly, a person who believes that doing *A* would advance some end of hers will not see this as counting in favor of *A* because some principle requires her so to count it, or because she must do this in order to avoid irrationality. Rather, insofar as she is rational, she will see the fact that *A* would advance this end as a reason for doing *A* simply because she has the end in question. Ideas of rationality and irrationality belong to a higher-order form of reflective thought that we need not engage in when, for example, we see that we have reason to do what will advance one of our ends.

Nonetheless, a person who violates these requirements can be described correctly by others as irrational, and she can so describe herself. Moreover, irrationality of this sort is a defect, a failure to meet standards that apply to us. John Broome puts this by saying that the requirements I have been discussing are ones that we *ought* to conform to. He says, for example, that "You ought (to intend to M if you intend to E and believe your M-ing is a necessary means to your E-ing)."[4] But how are such 'oughts' to be understood? What kind of normativity do they involve?

One might say, plausibly, that a charge of irrationality is a judgment of functional deficiency, of the same kind as a judgment that a carburetor, or a kidney, is deficient because it does not operate in the appropriate way. This is what Pettit suggests when he writes that "A regularity will count as a norm for a system just in case the satisfaction of that regularity is required for the system to succeed in the role for which it has been designed or selected."[5]

This sounds right, but there is a question as to whether this idea of a norm can account for the normativity involved in charges of irrationality of the kind we are considering. There are other modes of functioning, such as having a capacity and a desire to reproduce, that we have been selected for and which therefore constitute norms for us in the sense that Pettit describes. It may be true in a functional sense that we "ought" to have the capacity to reproduce—that we are functionally defective if we lack this capacity. But these norms, and 'oughts', need have no normative force for an agent who recognizes them. I can recognize that, in this functional sense of the term, members of my species ought to reproduce, without believing that, in any sense that is even remotely action guiding, I myself ought to reproduce.

I said earlier that a person who sees the fact that some action would advance her end as a reason to do it need not reach this conclusion by way of the idea of rationality, or see this action as required by a norm that she is guided by. Nonetheless, a person who sees that she has been irrational will see this as a defect in a sense that goes beyond the functional sense just described. She will see her

---

[4] Broome, "Reasons", 29. Broome means the parentheses to indicate that the ought in question is of "wide scope", and therefore non-detaching. That is to say, from S ought (to intend M if he intends E and believes that p), S intends E, and S believes that p, one cannot infer that S ought to intend M.

[5] Pettit, "Three Aspects", 183.

attitudes as in need of revision—feel some "normative pressure" to revise them. So there is a question about how this kind of normativity is to be understood.

We can approach this question by considering what Pettit goes on to say in the article I have been discussing. He distinguishes there between what he calls normalizing explanations and interpretive explanations, which appeal to the fact that the subject of explanation saw things in a certain way. He observes that normalizing explanations need not be interpretive, and as an example cites decision-theoretic explanations. We might, he says, assign to a subject certain probability and utility functions and explain its behavior by seeing it as maximizing its expected utility (given these functions.) But in order to do this, we need not suppose that the subject reasons in terms of those functions, or even that it is conscious at all. This would be a normalizing explanation (if, for example, we assume that the subject is designed or selected for utility maximization), but not an interpretive one. Utility maximization would be a norm for this subject only in a thin, purely functional sense.

It is also true that beliefs and preferences are attributed to the subject in this example only in a very thin sense. Indeed, one might question whether such a subject can be said to have beliefs or preferences at all. So let us enrich the example by supposing that the subject is a conscious agent and that it is designed or selected not merely to maximize its utility but to do this by reasoning in terms of probability and desirability. If this is so, then it would be a functional defect in the subject not only if it failed to maximize its utility but also if it failed to think about doing so in the proper way—for example, if it failed to see new evidence as a reason to revise its probability assignments in a certain way.

Would this give utility maximization normative force *for an agent* of the kind I have been discussing? For reasons I have already mentioned, the mere fact that the subject was selected to reason in terms of utility maximization would not make it more than a functional defect for it to fail to do so, or to do so in the right way. One way to ground a stronger claim would be to argue that insofar as the agent *sees* itself as reasoning in terms of probability and utility, it must see certain considerations as providing reasons. The claim would be that insofar as this is what it sees itself as doing, it cannot, insofar as it is not irrational, refuse to accept certain considerations as counting in favor of an action, or in favor of a change in belief.

This explanation has two components. First there is the "constitutive" claim that seeing things in a certain way, or reasoning in a certain way, involves seeing certain things as reasons. This is a purely analytical claim. Normativity enters only from the point of view of the person who has these attitudes, and therefore sees the relevant considerations as reasons. The "normative force" we have been trying to explain is just the force of those reasons, for the agent who sees them as reasons.

I want to argue that the normative content of requirements of rationality that I have been discussing has this same character. It lies in the fact that insofar as a subject has beliefs and intentions, it must see these as responsive to its assessment of the reasons for these states; and insofar as it has a certain belief, or intention, it must see this as providing the basis for further reasoning about what to believe and what to do. The relevant norms are thus elements of ("constitutive of") certain attitudes, and the relevant normativity is provided by what the agent sees as reasons.[6] I will now try to argue for this by spelling out in more detail how it might work in the cases of intention and belief.

2. FORMULATING REQUIREMENTS OF STRUCTURAL RATIONALITY

If there are rational requirements governing attitudes such as belief and intention, what is their content? So far, I have stated them as requirements concerning what an agent who has certain attitudes must treat as a reason for certain other attitudes. For example, I have said that insofar as an agent believes that p, he or she must treat the fact that q follows from p as a reason for believing that q, and insofar as an agent intends to do A at t, he or she must treat the fact that doing B is required in order to do A at t as a reason for doing B. These formulations seem to me inadequate in several respects. As a start toward seeing why, we should ask what is meant here by "believing that p" or "intending to do A at t".

Believing that p can involve a number of different things: judging there to be sufficient evidence for the truth of p, being willing to (sincerely) affirm p, and being disposed to rely on p as a premise in further argument—that is to say, disposed to regard the fact that something follows from p as a reason to accept it as true.[7]

Having an intention to A at t can involve similarly diverse elements: judging that one has good reason to A at t, having consciously decided to do A, and being disposed to take one's doing A at t into account in further reasoning by, for example, treating the fact that doing B would facilitate doing A at t as a reason for doing B and treating the fact that doing B would interfere with doing A at t as a reason against doing B.[8]

All of the elements I have mentioned may be present in an ideal case of belief or intention, but they need not all be present every case. Someone might have no view about whether p is supported by the evidence (or even think that it is not), and might be unwilling to affirm that p when asked, yet might regularly

---

[6] In putting the matter this way I am following Niko Kolodny, "Why Be Rational?", *Mind*, 114 (2005), 509–63.

[7] Peter Railton makes a similar point that belief and intention involve "bundles" of attitudes and dispositions which may sometimes come apart. See his "On the Hypothetical and Non-Hypothetical in Reasoning about Belief and Action", in G. Cullity and B. Gaut (eds.), *Ethics and Practical Reason* (Oxford: Oxford University Press, 1997), 70–3.

[8] I will state my argument in terms of "intending to do A", but I believe that the same points could be made in terms of "having E as an end".

rely on p as a premise in theoretical and practical reasoning. We might say of such a person that he believes that p even though he denies it, and, if he judges there to be conclusive evidence against p, that he is irrational in so believing. On the other hand, if a person consistently refused to rely on p as a premise, and rejected arguments relying on it, then it would be plausible to say that he did not really believe that p even though he in fact judged p to be supported by good evidence. (Readiness to affirm p is a swing case. If the person in the example just mentioned were unwilling to affirm that p, this would, I think, count strongly in favor of saying that he did not believe that p. If he affirmed p but was unwilling to rely on it, this would be less clear.)

Similarly, even if a person judges himself to have good reason to do A at t, if he fails to give this factor any weight in further practical reasoning we might well say that he does not really intend to do A at t, even though he claims to have this intention and even though, given his assessment of the reasons for doing A at t, he may be irrational in not having it.

The fact that willingness to give a certain consideration weight in further theoretical or practical deliberation has such a central place in our criteria for attributing beliefs and intentions may lend support to the idea that readiness to reason in this way is "constitutive" of these attitudes, in the sense of being a necessary condition for having them at all. The problem that this raises for my present purposes is that it seems to turn the claim that, insofar as one has these attitudes, their contents must figure in one's subsequent reasoning in the relevant ways, into a tautology rather than a requirement of rationality that it is possible to violate.[9]

This problem could be avoided by identifying believing that p or having an end, E, not with *actually* taking p or E into account in one's subsequent theoretical and practical reasoning but rather with being *disposed* to do so. On this reading, the requirements I have stated would not be tautologies, since a single failure to perform in a certain way does not show that an agent lacks the disposition so to perform. The problem with this interpretation of the requirements is that they cease to be requirements of rationality, since acting contrary to a disposition one has is not necessarily irrational.

So we need to look for a different way to understand the content of these requirements. They specify that *if* an agent fulfills certain conditions, *then* he or she must, on pain of irrationality, have or not have a certain attitude. The question is how these antecedent conditions are to be interpreted. The hypothesis I will pursue in the rest of this Chapter is that these conditions consist in some judgment or commitment on the part of the agent. The first question to be addressed in carrying out this strategy is how this judgment should be interpreted.

---

[9] Christine Korsgaard emphasizes this as a problem for certain attempts to formulate the principle of instrumental rationality. See her "The Normativity of Instrumental Reason", in Cullity and Gaut, (eds.), *Ethics and Practical Reason*, 215–54. I am indebted to her discussion.

One possibility, which I have sometimes invoked, is to interpret this antecedent as what I will call an attitude-directed judgment—a judgment about the adequacy of reasons for holding the attitude in question. So, for example, it might be that an agent who judges there to be conclusive reason to believe that p must, insofar as he or she is not irrational, believe that p. That is to say, he or she must be willing to affirm p, take the fact that q follows from p as a reason for believing q, and so on. Similarly, we could say that an agent who judges him-or herself to have conclusive reason for intending to A at t must, insofar as he or she is not irrational, intend to do A at t—that is to say, must take the fact that doing B is necessary in order to A at t as a reason for doing B, take the fact that doing B would be incompatible with doing A at t as a reason against doing B, and so on.

One problem for this proposal is that the range of possible reasons for *having* a certain attitude may be too broad, because these could include "pragmatic" or "state-given" reasons for having a certain belief or intention.[10] For example, a person might have been promised a large reward for having that attitude or threatened with a terrible punishment for not having it. But these reasons might not provide grounds for giving weight to that belief or intention in further reasoning.

Leaving that problem aside for the moment, the formulations just given do seem to state genuine requirements of rationality. It does seem clearly irrational to have an attitude that one explicitly judges oneself to have conclusive reason not to have. One might say that this irrationality just reflects the fact that belief and intention are what I have called judgment-sensitive attitudes: that is to say, attitudes that, insofar as we are rational, will be responsive to our assessments of the reasons for them.[11] It may be that non-human animals and human infants have beliefs and intentions that are not linked to assessments of reasons in these ways, because they not capable of making judgments about what they have reason to do or to think. But for those us who are capable of making such judgments, these connections hold. For us, belief and intention are attitudes that must, insofar as we are not irrational, be responsive to our assessments of relevant reasons. To say this is not to say that, for us, beliefs and intentions generally arise in response to conscious judgments about reasons. Clearly they do not. (Perceptual beliefs are obvious counterexamples, and there are many others.) To say that belief and intention are judgment-sensitive is only to say that *when we do make judgments about the relevant reasons*, these attitudes will, insofar as we are rational, be responsive to them.

Even accepting that one's beliefs and intentions will, insofar as one is rational, be responsive to one's judgments, questions remain about which judgments in

---

[10] I take the terminology of "state-given" and "object-given" reasons from Derek Parfit. See his "Rationality and Reasons", in Dan Egonsson, Jonas Josefsson, Björn Petersson, and Toni Ronnow-Rasmessen (eds.), *Exploring Practical Philosophy* (Aldershot: Ashgate, 2001), 20–5.
[11] See Scanlon, *What We Owe to Each Other*, 20–4.

particular they are to be responsive to. So far, I have been describing them as attitude-directed judgments, which are explicitly about whether there are compelling reasons for the attitudes in question. This interpretation is what gave rise to the problem I mentioned about pragmatic reasons for having an attitude. But this problem reflects a larger difficulty, which is that judgments explicitly about the reasons for other judgments have a higher-order character that makes them somewhat artificial.

We do sometimes express what appear to be attitude-directed judgments. We might say, for example, that there is (or is not) good reason to believe that there are weapons of mass destruction in Iraq, and we may ask someone what his reason is for intending to take early retirement. But these may just be round-about ways of expressing content-directed judgments or questions, and a special context may be required in order for these attitude-directed formulations to sound natural. More commonly, when a belief or intention arises from a conscious judgment, this judgment is content-directed. In deciding whether to believe that p, we "direct our attention to the world" and ask whether p is true, and a judgment leading to an intention to do A at t is likely to be a judgment about the merits of doing A.

As I have remarked above, the rational requirements we are considering can be explained in a particularly direct way if the judgments that figure in the antecedents of these requirements are understood in attitude-directed form, since it seems clearly irrational to fail to have an attitude that one explicitly judges oneself to have conclusive reason for, or to continue to hold an attitude that one explicitly judges oneself to have conclusive reason against. But if attitude-directed judgments are somewhat artificial, then this explanation may not be one we should rely on. In any event, we should look for a justification that would apply as well to the wider range of normal cases involving content-directed judgments.

There is also a potential problem of illicit generalization. The claim that it is irrational to fail to hold an attitude that one judges to be supported by conclusive reasons (and irrational to continue to hold an attitude that one judges there to be conclusive reasons against) is a perfectly general one. To recognize these as instances of irrationality, one need not inquire into any features of the attitudes in question aside from their judgment sensitivity. I have been inclined to rely on this generality, and to argue on this basis that belief and intention are more similar than commonly supposed. But insofar as charges of irrationality rest on the clash between particular attitudes and more specific content-directed judgments, the basis for these charges may be different for different attitudes. Belief and intention may both be judgment-sensitive attitudes, but the reasons why they are sensitive to particular content-directed judgments are, presumably, different. So we need to look more closely at those reasons.

3. INTERPRETING RATIONAL REQUIREMENTS: INTENTION

Consider first the case of intention. It will be helpful here to distinguish three attitudes: judging oneself to have conclusive (or sufficient) reason to do *A* at *t*, deciding to do *A* at *t*, and taking what is required to do *A* at *t* into account in one's subsequent assessments of one's reasons for doing, or not doing, other things. I do not mean to suggest that every intention arises from a conscious decision. This is certainly far from being the case. But there is such a thing as deciding to do something (forming the intention to do it), and this can come apart from the other attitudes I have listed. One can judge oneself to have sufficient reason to do many different incompatible things, and one of the functions of deciding to do something is the necessary task of selecting among these. Nor is deciding to do something the same as judging oneself to have *conclusive* reason to do it. One can judge that one has conclusive reason to call the travel agent today to book a ticket, or to call the doctor today about the strange lump one has noticed in one's chest, yet not decide to do these things. Speaking for myself, I confess that I often fail to decide to do what I know that I have conclusive reason to do. Doing this is irrational but, sad to say, all too familiar.

So we have identified two points where irrationality is possible (that is to say, two points where there are normative links that can be violated). The first is between judging oneself to have conclusive reason to do *A* at *t* and deciding to do *A* at *t*. The second is between deciding to do *A* at *t* and taking doing *A* at *t* into account in the proper way in one's subsequent reasoning. The task is to explain what kind of normative force the charge of irrationality has at each of these points.

If deciding to do *A* at *t* is something different from judging oneself to have reason, even conclusive reason, to do *A* at *t*, what more does it involve? Speaking metaphorically, one might say that it involves putting doing *A* at *t* on one's agenda, as something that is to structure one's further deliberation. Less metaphorically, it involves a commitment on one's part to think about what to do in a way that is compatible with one's doing *A* at *t*.[12] In particular, it is a

---

[12] It involves adopting a plan to do A in the sense described by Michael Bratman. See his *Intention, Plans, and Practical Reason* (Cambridge, Mass.: Harvard University Press, 1987). In my view, making such a commitment changes what one must, insofar as one is not irrational, see as a reason. But it does not give one a reason that one did not have before. On this see my "Reasons: A Puzzling Duality?", in Wallace et al., 231–46. Nadeem Hussain has pointed out in commenting on this chapter that Bratman holds that what distinguishes intentions and plans from desires is that they are governed by consistency constraints and demands for means–ends coherence (*Intentions, Plans and Practical Reason*, 31). It would therefore be circular, he says, to appeal to commitments (understood as what Bratman calls plans) in order to explain these constraints. Whatever Bratman's strategy may be, mine is not to explain commitment in

commitment to take the fact that doing some action B would facilitate one's doing A at t as a reason for doing B, and to take the fact that doing B would be incompatible with one's doing A at t as a (normally conclusive) reason against doing B. It is irrational for someone who has decided to do A at t (and has not changed his or her mind about this) to refuse to treat the fact that B would facilitate this as a reason for doing B or to refuse to treat the fact that doing B would be incompatible with doing A at t as a reason against doing B. These things are irrational because they involve acting contrary to a commitment that one has made (and not revised).

One can tell a functional story about why there should be such a thing as deciding to do something. We need to be able to do this because, in order to act effectively, we need to be able to structure our decision making in certain ways. We often need to select among alternatives each of which is supported by sufficient, but not compelling reasons. And even when we have compelling reason for a particular alternative, in order to pursue that aim effectively we need to be able to give it a particular standing in our subsequent deliberation.

This functional story explains why there should be such an attitude as deciding to do something, and why it should have the character that it does—why it should involve a certain kind of commitment. It is not yet, however, a full explanation of the irrationality that is involved when a person, having decided to do A at t (without revising that decision) refuses to treat the fact that B would facilitate his doing A at t as a reason for doing B. As I have said, the force of the charge of irrationality, for a person who finds himself in this situation, is not that of realizing that he has a certain functional deficiency. This force, it might be suggested, lies in the clash of attitudes that will be experienced by a person who has made a commitment of the kind described, but finds himself with other attitudes that are incompatible with it. The importance of this clash is brought out by the fact that what is irrational is *denying* that the fact that doing B would facilitate my doing something I have decided to do is a reason to do B. Simply forgetting to do B, or absent mindedly overlooking the fact that one had decided to do A, would undermine the effective pursuit of my aim just as much as denying that I had reason to do what would promote it. But these failings would not be instances of irrationality, because they do not involve the appropriate clash of attitudes.

So we might say that the functional story explains why there should be such an attitude as deciding to do something, and why it should involve a commitment of a certain kind, and that we then have a "constitutive" explanation of why

terms of rational requirements. Rather, it is to explain these requirements in terms of a notion of commitment that I take to be understandable independently: in particular, in terms of the role that such states play in our practical and theoretical thinking.

someone who *has* a particular attitude of that kind and another attitude that it rules out should feel "normative pressure" to revise these attitudes.[13]

This is not the whole story, however. Insofar as the irrationality in question is just a matter of incompatible attitudes, we could avoid it by giving up either of them. But while it is true that refusing to treat the fact that doing *B* is necessary if one is to do *A* at *t* is irrational only so long as one has not abandoned one's decision to do *A*, it may seem that the situations we are concerned with are not entirely symmetrical. If one has decided to do *A* at *t*, rationality may seem to speak more on the side of taking oneself to have a reason to do *B* than on the side of abandoning one's decision to do *A*. If there is this normative asymmetry, then something more is needed to explain it.

Nevertheless, insofar as there is an asymmetry here it is qualified. If the steps necessary to do what one has decided to do turn out to be very costly, then what one has most reason to do may be to reverse that decision. Whether this is so depends on the reasons supporting the decision. What we are concerned with, though, is not what an agent has most reason to do but what he or she must do insofar as he or she is not irrational. For the purposes of answering *this* question, what matters is not the reasons that the agent actually has for doing A but, as Niko Kolodny has argued, the agent's assessment of these reasons.[14] If the agent's judgment is still that, even taking into account the cost of *B* as a necessary means, he has conclusive reason for doing *A*, then (whatever the merits of this judgment) it is irrational for him to resolve the conflict we have been discussing by abandoning his decision to do *A*. (This is the asymmetry we have been considering.) But if this is not his judgment, then abandoning *A* is not irrational (although it may still be inadvisable), and if he holds the opposite assessment, then it would be irrational for him *not* to abandon the decision to do *A*.

Earlier, I distinguished two points at which irrationality may occur (that is to say, two points where there are normative links that can be violated). The first was between judging oneself to have conclusive reason to do *A* at *t* and deciding to do *A* at *t*. The second was between deciding to do *A* at *t* and taking doing *A* at *t* into account in the proper way in one's subsequent reasoning. I have so far been addressing the second of these links. In explaining the irrationality of denying that one has reason to take steps necessary for doing what one has decided to do, I appealed first to a constitutive claim about deciding: because deciding involves seeing oneself as making a certain kind of commitment, an agent who has decided must see a conflict between this decision and his subsequent denial. Then, in order to explain why it is sometimes irrational for an agent to resolve this conflict by abandoning the decision, I had to appeal to the idea that there is a normative link between an agent's decision to do *A* and his assessment of

---

[13] The constitutive claim being just that deciding to do *A* at *t* involves committing oneself to giving one's doing *A* at *t* a certain place in one's subsequent reasoning about what to do.

[14] See Kolodny, "Why Be Rational?"

the reasons for doing A.[15] But this is just the first of the two links that I earlier distinguished. So I must turn to the question of what this link involves, and how it is to be explained.

First, if one judges oneself to have conclusive reason not to do A at t, it is irrational to decide to do A at t, or if one has decided this, not to reverse that decision. This is irrational because deciding to do A at t involves committing oneself to giving the needs of doing A at t a certain positive weight in one's practical thinking—to take one's doing A as something that can provide reason to do or not to do other things. But it is irrational to do this if one judges there to be conclusive reason against doing A at t.

Second, if one even judges oneself not to have sufficient reason to do A at t, it is irrational to give positive weight in one's practical thinking to what is required in order for one to do A at t, since one would then be giving one's doing A at t a weight that one judged it not to have. So, if one judges oneself not to have sufficient reason to do A at t, then it is irrational to decide to do A at t and, if one has so decided, irrational not to reverse this decision.

Finally, if one judges oneself to have conclusive reason to do A at t, is it irrational not to decide to do A at t? Well, perhaps not, if one's not deciding is simply a matter of forgetting, or falling asleep, and not if one believes that A is something one cannot do.[16] Is it, then, at least irrational to *decline* to decide to do A at t, or to decide not to do it even though one believes one could? To do either of these things would be consciously to decline to take account of a consideration (one's doing A at t) that one in fact judges to be significant. There is, however, a temporal factor here that may be important. If t is some time far in the future, one might judge that one has conclusive reason to do A at t, but no reason to take this into account in one's present thinking about what to do. So declining to decide, now, to do A at t would not be, as I just said, consciously to ignore what one judged to be a significant consideration. If one can costlessly defer the decision, then doing so will not be irrational, and it might even be favored by a principle of economy of thought (not encumbering one's deliberation with unnecessary commitments.)

One might summarize this line of thought by saying that even if one judges oneself to have conclusive reason to do A at t, it is irrational to decline to decide (now) to do A at t only if such a decision is needed in order to facilitate one's doing A at t. This might be taken to suggest that declining (now) to decide to do what one judges oneself to have conclusive reason to do later is irrational only

---

[15] In appealing to these two elements I am retracing, in a slightly different way, the steps of Korsgaard's "The Normativity of Instrumental Reason". Her account of the instrumental principle appeals to a constitutive claim about the attitude of "having an end". But she also argues that the normativity of this principle cannot be explained without appeal the normative standing of the agent's end itself.

[16] For this last qualification I am indebted to Alison McIntyre's discussion in, "What's Wrong with Weakness of Will?", *Journal of Philosophy*, 100 (2006), 284–311.

if deciding now to do it would facilitate one's doing it then, and thus that this is irrational only when it is a violation of instrumental rationality. This might seem to threaten a regress, insofar as what we are trying to explain is in part the normative force of requirements of instrumental rationality. In addition, it seems to me artificial to describe one's decision to do something as a means to doing it. I therefore prefer an explanation that appeals only to the bare idea of irrationality as failing to give a consideration the weight in one's thinking that one in fact judges it to have. If matters that are the subject of current deliberation will affect one's doing A at t, then declining to decide (now) to do A at t will involve irrationality of this kind. But if t is so far in the future that nothing in one's current deliberations will bear on it, then in failing to decide, now, to do A at t one will not be failing to give one's doing A then the weight that one judges it to have. So no irrationality will occur.

For an agent, the force of the three normative links between an assessment of the reasons for doing A at t and a decision to do A at t lies in the incompatibility that the agent who violates these links must feel between her various normative attitudes. As I noted previously, however, mere incompatibility of attitudes alone is symmetrical: it can be avoided by giving up either attitude. But it would be irrational for an agent to avoid the incompatibility between judging herself to have compelling reason to do A at t and her not deciding to do this by abandoning the former judgment unless she saw some reason to revise this assessment. And it is difficult to imagine a case in which she could take her failure to decide to do A at t as a consideration bearing on the merits of doing it.

Finally, what I have said here does not assume or imply that a rational agent holds the view that she *ought* to decide to do what she judges herself to have conclusive reason to do, or that he *ought* to give doing the things he has decided to do a certain place in his subsequent reasoning. My claims have been only about what an agent, insofar as he or she is not irrational, will see as reasons.

4. INTERPRETING RATIONAL REQUIREMENTS: BELIEF

Let me turn now to the case of belief. Proceeding in parallel with the case of intention, we might distinguish the following three things that can be true of a person:

1. S judges there to be conclusive evidence for the truth of p.
2. S accepts p as true.
3. S accepts p as a premise in further theoretical and practical reasoning (that is to say, S takes the fact that q follows from p as a reason for accepting q as true.)

In (2), "accepting p as true" is meant to be the theoretical analog of deciding to do A (or adopting A as an aim). As I argued above, to decide to do A is to give doing *A* a certain status in one's practical reasoning, the status of something that provides reasons for doing what will facilitate this. Similarly, the idea here would be that to accept something as true involves giving it the status of something that is to be relied on in further theoretical reasoning by providing reasons for accepting what it entails, and to be relied on as a premise in practical reasoning.

As David Velleman has pointed out, there are various ways in which one can treat something as true. When we imagine that *p*, or accept *p* as a hypothesis or an assumption in order to see what follows from it, we are, in a sense, "treating *p* as true", and at least in the latter case we are showing a disposition to rely on *p* in subsequent reasoning (albeit reasoning of a hypothetical sort.) But, as Velleman says, believing that *p* involves more than this: it "entails regarding *p* as 'really' true".[17] I intend "accepting p as true" to be understood in this stronger sense.

One difference between the cases of belief and intention should be noted at the outset. One important function of deciding to do something is to select among various alternative courses of action each of which one has sufficient reason to do, and to identify the one that is to form the basis of one's subsequent decision making. In the case of belief, when one has incomplete information, one may have to choose which of a set of plausible hypotheses to rely on in deciding what to do. But the result of this kind of selection is not *belief*.

Another difference between the cases of belief and intention is that in the case of belief it may be questioned whether (2) could be true of a person without (3) also being true. Could someone accept that *p* is something that is to be relied on in these ways yet refuse on some occasions so to rely on it? It seems to me that this is possible, but I do not need to argue for this, since it is at least clear that if this were to occur, it would be an instance of structural irrationality of the kind I have been discussing. Being (really) true is sufficient to give something the status it needs to be a premise in further reasoning. So accepting *p* as really true while refusing to accept arguments that employ it as a premise would involve failing to recognize something as having the status in one's reasoning that one has acknowledged it to have.

I will therefore set aside the question of the normative link between (2) and (3) and concentrate on the relation between (1) and (3): between a person's assessment of the evidence for *p* and their willingness to accept arguments that employ *p* as a premise—that is, to take the fact that *q* follows from *p* as reason to accept *q* as true.

Velleman suggests that we should take a link between these as definitive of belief, but the kink he has in mind is dispositional. He writes:

when someone believes a proposition . . . his acceptance of it is regulated in ways designed to promote acceptance of the truth; he comes to accept the proposition, for example,

---

[17] David Velleman, "The Guise of the Good", *Nous*, 26 (1992), 3–26, p. 15. Velleman says that this entails "regarding *p* not only as true but also as correct to regard in this way". I will return to this part of his view.

when evidence indicates it to be true, and he's disposed to continue accepting it until evidence indicates otherwise. Part of what makes someone's attitude toward a proposition an instance of belief rather than assumption or fantasy, then, is that it is regulated in accordance with epistemic principles rather than polemics, heuristics, or hedonics. An attitude's identity as a belief depends on its being regulated in a way designed to make it track the truth."[18]

But this does not seem right. It does not seem necessary, in order for an attitude to count as belief, that the subject is *actually* disposed to regulate it in a way designed to make it track the truth. We may have some beliefs that we are careful to screen off from any critical assessment of the evidence for or against their truth. In so doing, we are irrational (especially if we do so because we suspect that there may be strong evidence against these beliefs.) But we still, I would say, believe these things. Velleman's proposal seems to make this kind of irrationality impossible.

Perhaps one should say that an attitude counts as belief only if the subject recognizes that he *should* regulate it in this way. Lloyd Humberstone makes a similar suggestion. He says that "unless one takes there to be a criterion of success in the case of an attitude toward the proposition that *p*, and, further, takes that criterion to be truth, then whatever else it may be the attitude in question is not that of belief. So unless the attitude-holder has what we might call a controlling background intention that his or her attitudinizing is successful only if its propositional content is true, then the attitude taken is not that of belief."[19]

So, following Humberstone, we could say that a person "accepts *p* as true" in the sense intended in (2) and (3) only if he or she has a controlling intention of this kind. It follows that a person must see this attitude as one that ought to be responsive to what he or she takes to be evidence for the truth of *p*. This provides a link between (1) and (2) that grounds a requirement of structural rationality. If a person regards "acceptance as true" as an attitude that is successful only if *p* is "really" true, then she will regard this attitude as one that should be formed if there is conclusive evidence for the truth of *p* and abandoned if there is conclusive evidence that *p* is false[20]

There is a question here about what might be called the "initial direction" of the controlling intention that Humberstone describes. Velleman proposed that in order for a state to be a belief, the agent had to be disposed to modify it in the light of what he or she took to be evidence of its truth. So he proposed a dispositional link reaching, so to speak, backwards from (2) and (3) to (1). One might take Humberstone to be proposing a link in the same direction, but one consisting of an intention rather than a disposition—an intention to regulate one's belief in the light of one's assessment of the evidence for its truth. This

---

[18] David Velleman, *Nous*, 14.

[19] I. L. Humberstone, "Direction of Fit", *Mind*, 101 (1992), 58–83, p. 73.

[20] As before, I leave aside here the possibility of "state-given" reasons for having a belief.

would provide a link of the right kind between (2) and (1): one that can be violated, but only on pain of irrationality. An agent who accepted *p* as true despite judging that there was conclusive evidence against its being true, or who refused to accept *p* as true although he also judged there to be conclusive evidence in its favor, would be irrational because he would be failing to regulate his acceptance of *p* in the way required by his own "controlling intention".

This is quite plausible. It does, however, depend on a higher-order, attitude-directed intention. One may wonder whether an agent must have such an intention with regard to anything that can be called a belief, even beliefs that one holds in the face of what one sees as contrary evidence. A person who has such a belief seems in some way committed to modifying his belief in the light of evidence, but this commitment may not be best expressed in terms of an attitude-directed intention to do just this.

An alternative account of this link would take Humberstone's controlling intention as facing in the opposite direction: from (2) toward (3). The idea would be that a person accepts *p* as true in the way involved in belief only if he or she intends to rely on *p* in further reasoning about what the world is like, and about what to do. A belief held with this intention is "successful" only if it is appropriate to rely on it in these ways—that is, only if it is true. Although it does not mention grounds or evidence, this intention brings with it a rational requirement linking (2) and (1). It is irrational to take *p* as having the status just described while simultaneously judging there to be conclusive evidence against the truth of *p*. (Similarly, it would be irrational to refuse to accept *p* as a premise in further argument if one judges there to be conclusive evidence for the truth of *p*.) This irrationality consists simply in the conscious holding of attitudes that are directly incompatible. The normative pressure that an agent who is irrational in this way feels to modify his acceptance (or non-acceptance) of *p* comes not from his acceptance of some higher-order intention or "ought" judgment, but simply from the reason-giving force that he attributes to the evidence against (or for) the truth of *p*.

5. CONCLUDING THOUGHTS ABOUT "DIRECTION OF FIT"

The points made in preceding sections about intentions and beliefs have some bearing on the idea that beliefs and desires are distinguished by having different "directions of fit". In this concluding section I want to examine these implications.

I take claims about reasons, such as "I have conclusive reason to *A* at *t*" to be ordinary declarative statements that can be true or false and can be the objects of belief.[21] I have been arguing that a person who believes that she has conclusive

---

[21] I argue for this in "Metaphysics and Morals", *Proceedings and Addresses of the American Philosophical Association*, 77 (2003), 7–22.

reason to do A at t will, insofar as she is not irrational, intend to do A at t and (absent change of mind, irrationality, or incapacity) will do so. It may seem, then, that at least on one understanding of the idea of a "direction of fit", the belief that one has conclusive reason to do A at t has, on my view, two directions of fit. As a belief, it is something that is defective if it does not "fit the world" (that is, if one does not in fact have conclusive reason to do A at t). On the other hand, it is something that "the world must fit" (that is, insofar as one accepts it, and is not irrational, one will undertake to bring it about that one does A at t). My view may therefore seem to be in tension with Michael Smith's arguments that there cannot be a state (what he calls a "besire") that has both "belief-like" and "desire-like" like directions of fit.[22]

The idea of different "directions of fit" can be given either a normative or a more descriptive reading. As Smith first states it in *The Moral Problem*, the idea is presented in what sounds like normative terms: a belief is a state that *must* fit the world, whereas a desire is a state that the world *must* fit. The normative ring of these 'must's is explicit in the passage that Smith quotes from Mark Platts.[23] Platts writes that "falsity is a decisive failing in a belief, and false beliefs should be discarded; beliefs should be changed to fit with the world, not *vice versa*." But, by contrast, "the fact that the indicative content of a desire is not realized in the world is not yet any reason to discard the desire; the world, crudely put, should be changed to fit with our desires, not *vice versa*."

When the distinction is put in this way, it is clear that a state cannot have both directions of fit with respect to the same content. A state cannot be both a belief that p and a desire that p, since a belief that p is defective and should be withdrawn if p is not the case, but this is no fault in a desire that p.[24] But it does not follow that a single state could not have two different directions of fit with respect to different contents: that, say, a desire that p could not be a state that the world must fit (with respect to p) but at the same time a state that is defective, and ought to be revised, if it fails to fit the world in some other respect q (such as that there is reason to bring about p). Indeed, the position that Smith himself goes on to defend in *The Moral Problem* seems to be that desires have essentially this character.

This does not mean, however, that desires have both "directions of fit" as Smith understands this notion, because he goes on to define the idea of a direction of fit in dispositional rather than normative terms. He first defines desires and beliefs in terms of their functional role. "Under this conception", he writes, "we should think of desiring to ϕ as having a certain set of dispositions, the disposition to ψ in conditions C, the disposition to χ in conditions C' and so

---

[22] See Michael Smith, *The Moral Problem* (Oxford: Blackwell, 1994), 118–125.

[23] Ibid. 112. The passage quoted from Platts is from his *Ways of Meaning* (London: Routledge & Kegan Paul, 1979), 256–7.

[24] See Smith, *Moral Problem*, 118.

on, where in order for conditions C and C' to obtain, the subject must have, *inter alia*, certain other desires and also certain means–ends beliefs, beliefs concerning ϕ-ing by ψ-ing, ϕ-ing by χ-ing and so on."[25] The idea, then is that to desire to ϕ is to be disposed to do those things that one takes to be ways of ϕ-ing.

Smith does not give a parallel account of the functional role of belief, but I assume that it might be something like the following: We should think of believing that p as having a certain set of dispositions, such as a disposition to affirm p under certain conditions C, to affirm that q under conditions C' (which include the subject's believing that p entails q), to affirm r under conditions C'' (which include the subjects believing that p entails r), and so on.

I have no objection to this. I have suggested above that believing and intending involve dispositions of the kind Smith describes, from which it follows that on my account intending to do A involves desiring to do A in Smith's broad functional role sense of desiring. On both his account and mine, believing that p involves more than the dispositions just listed. And on my account (and I think Smith might agree) intending does as well.

The additional element of belief that is important on Smith's account is a higher-order disposition to modify the disposition I have listed. He writes that "a belief that p tends to go out of existence in the presence of a perception with the content that not-p". But he holds that a desire that p does not tend to change in this way, and this difference in counterfactual dependence is the difference in "direction of fit".[26] Having stated the notion of "direction of fit" in this dispositional rather than normative form, Smith then uses it as the basis for an extended argument against the possibility of states with both directions of fit—an argument that does not apply only against a state's having both directions of fit with respect to the same content.

This is what might be called a modal separability argument, which Smith states as follows: "[I]t is always at least possible for agents who are in some particular belief-like state not to be in some particular desire-like state; . . . the two can always be pulled apart, at least modally."[27] Smith's main example of separability is a case of someone who believes that a certain action would be morally right but has no desire (no relevant dispositions) to do it. But, in line with the discussion earlier in this chapter, we can put the point more generally, in terms of someone who judges that she has conclusive reason to do A at t, but who fails to be disposed to do A at t or to do the things that she believes are necessary if she is to do this. I have argued at some length that this is possible, so I am here in firm agreement with Smith. There are, however, a few points that I would add.

The first is that the phenomena just described, when they are not the result simply of such things as forgetfulness, or falling asleep, or a blow on the head,

[25] See Smith, *Moral Problem*, 113.   [26] Ibid. 115.   [27] Ibid. 119.

are cases of structural irrationality. Here Smith would, I think, agree. Much of chapter 5 of *The Moral Problem* is devoted to arguing for the claim:

C2 If a person believes that she has a normative reason to ϕ, then she rationally should desire to ψ.[28]

Although Smith and I agree on this claim, the interpretation and defense that I have provided for it differs from the one he offers in *The Moral Problem*.[29] On his interpretation, to believe that one has normative reason to ϕ is to believe that one would desire to ϕ if one were fully rational. Given this interpretation of a belief about one's normative reasons, C2 is then explained via the idea that a rational person's desires will conform to what that person judges to be required by rationality. As Smith says later in a slightly different context, but one that I take to be relevant, "an evaluative belief is simply a belief about what would be desired if we were fully rational, and the new desire is acquired precisely because it is believed to be required for us to be rational".[30] So on his interpretation, the belief that one has reason to ϕ not only is what I have called above "attitude-directed", but also explicitly invokes the agent's notion of what is required in order to be rational.

On my interpretation, by contrast, a judgment about one's reasons for doing *A* is just that—an assessment of the strength of certain reasons. It may entail a belief about what one would believe or do if one were fully rational, but it is a judgment with distinct content. As I made clear above, I allow for the possibility that judgments about what one has conclusive reason to do or believe may be attitude-directed. I began this Chapter with this interpretation in mind, and I think it is appropriate in some cases. But, as I have said, I believe that these are only some of the cases, and that in other cases structural rationality requires one to form certain beliefs and intentions in response to content-directed judgments about the reasons one has. Finally, I have maintained that agents, insofar as they are rational, will form certain beliefs and intentions (that is to say, acquire certain complex dispositions) in response to their judgments about the reasons they have, and that they will see these attitudes as supported, and even required, by the contents of those judgments. But it seems to me that in most cases (I am tempted to say, in normal cases) this process will not involve explicit reference to their ideas of rationality: agents will not form these attitudes because they see them as required by rationality or required in order to avoid irrationality.

I will mention two further points, which may be mainly terminological. The first is that Smith identifies having the dispositions that characterize desire with "having a goal". Thus he says: "[S]ince all there is to being a desire is being a state with the appropriate direction of fit, it follows that having a goal just is

---

[28] See Smith, *Moral Problem*, 148. I assume that Smith is here identifying "desiring to ψ" with having the complex set of dispositions he mentions.
[29] I do not know whether Smith's current view has the features I am here discussing.
[30] Ibid. 160.

desiring."[31] Having the dispositions that on Smith's view amount to a desire that *p* may amount to having a goal in a very thin sense, in which a person has the goal *p* just in case he or she is disposed to promote *p*. But if someone has what I would call an aim, then it is not only true that she is disposed to pursue this aim but also that she is irrational if she fails to take the fact that something will advance that aim as a reason for doing it. Merely having a disposition does not provide a basis for this charge of irrationality, since it is not irrational to fail to act on a disposition one has.

The second point is that it seems to me misleading to use the terms 'belief-like' and 'desire-like' to refer to the kind of states that Smith's modal separability argument claims can always be pulled apart. As I have argued above, our common understanding of belief, like that of practical attitudes such as intention, involves diverse elements. Intending to do *A* at *t* generally involves both judging oneself to have sufficient reason to do *A* at *t* and being disposed to take one's doing *A* at *t* into account in one's thinking about what to do. Having *E* as an aim generally involves both judging *E* to be worth pursuing and being disposed to take this aim into account in thinking about what to do by, for example, taking the fact that doing *B* would advance *E* as a reason for doing *B*. Similarly, believing that *p* generally involves not only judging there to be good evidence for the truth of *p* but also having various dispositions to rely on *p* in further reasoning. In each case, these elements can be "pulled apart": one can judge oneself to have conclusive reason to believe that *p*, yet fail to have the relevant dispositions to rely on *p* in further reasoning, just as one can judge oneself to have conclusive reason to do *A* at *t* yet fail to take the fact that doing *B* is necessary to one's doing *A* at *t* as reason to do *B*.

So the phenomena to which Smith's modal separability argument calls attention occur in the case of belief as well as in that of attitudes like intention and having an aim. What can be "pulled apart" are not "belief-like" states and "desire-like" states but, rather, the distinct components of many states, including both beliefs and intentions.

---

[31] *The Moral Problem*, p. 116.

5

Freedom, Coercion, and Discursive Control

Richard Holton

If moral and political philosophy is to be of any use, it had better be concerned with real people. The focus need not be exclusively on people as they are; but it should surely not extend beyond how they would be under laws as they might be. It is one of the strengths of Philip Pettit's work that it is concerned with real people and the ways that they think: with the commonplace mind.

In this chapter I examine Pettit's recent work on free will.[1] Much of my concern will be to see how his contentions fit with empirical findings about human psychology. Pettit is a compatibilist about free will: he holds that it is compatible with determinism. But he finds fault with existing compatibilist accounts, and then proposes his own amendment. My aim is to challenge his grounds for finding fault, and then to raise some questions about his own positive account.

STANDARD COMPATIBILIST ACCOUNTS AND PETTIT'S CRITICISMS

The standard compatibilist accounts of free will derive from Hobbes. From him and those who followed him we get a very simple picture: roughly, to be free is to act (or perhaps, to be able to act) on one's desires. Elegant and enduring though this account is, it succumbed to the realization that it lets in too much. Addicts, for instance, are paradigms of those who lack free will, yet typically they act on their desires, desires for the objects of their addiction. The Hobbesian account needs to be restricted.

There are two main forms that the restrictions have taken in the subsequent discussion. First, we might restrict the desires upon which the free agent acts. We might, as in Frankfurt's early writings, restrict them to the desires that the agent

Thanks to the audience at the Pettit conference for an excellent discussion; and to Geoff Brennan, Rachana Kamtekar, Rae Langton, Philip Pettit, Michael Ridge, Tim Scanlon, and the referees for Oxford University Press.

[1] Philip Pettit, *A Theory of Freedom* (Cambridge: Polity, 2001).

desires to have. Or we might, as in Frankfurt's later writings, restrict them to the desires with which the agent identifies. In Pettit's terminology such accounts posit *freedom as volition*.

Alternatively, we might think that desires are not enough. We might try to add a cognitive component, to give us what Pettit calls *freedom as rational control*. We might require that free agents perform those actions that they believe to be most valuable, or those that they believe to be best in some more open-ended way. Or, more demandingly, we might require that free agents get (or be able to get) their beliefs *right*. We might require at least that they be *rationally formed*. In addition, we might require that they be *true*: we might require that free agents respond (or be able to respond) to the reasons that they actually have, and not just to those that they believe themselves to have.

Pettit thinks that both these kinds of account are vulnerable to the same fundamental failing: their inability to deal with hostile coercion. Suppose that someone is threatening to do something very nasty to you unless you do as they say; and suppose that you quite rationally yield to their threat. Have you acted freely? It seems that both of these accounts will say that you have. You have acted on your strongest desire, a desire with which you fully identify; and your action is, by hypothesis, rational.[2] This is the conclusion that many compatibilists have drawn: coerced acts are free acts, at least in the sense of 'free' that the compatibilist is after. Yet there are two kinds of intuition that make this conclusion questionable:

(i) *Metaphysical intuitions*: coercion is exactly the kind of case in which we would normally deny that you acted freely, or willingly, or of your own free will.

(ii) *Moral intuitions*: coercion affects moral responsibility. If you do something as a result of the coercion that hurts some third party, then we will ordinarily think of you as less culpable than we would if you had caused that hurt without the coercion. Sometimes, though certainly not always, we might think of you as not culpable at all. Yet moral responsibility standardly requires freedom; so a plausible explanation of why you lack responsibility is that you lack freedom.

Pettit's contention, based upon these sorts of consideration (though he does not distinguish them as I have) is that the standard compatibilist accounts are inadequate. Any plausible compatibilism must entail that coercion removes freedom. Of course, this is a thought with which many writers have agreed. The idea is a mainstay in discussions of political liberty.[3] Pettit's aim is to

---

[2] Actually it is far from clear that we can simply assert that there are cases in which succumbing to coercion is rational; but I shall not pursue the issue.

[3] It is also there in some of the compatibilist literature: that which stresses the idea that free actions are those that are unconstrained. For an influential example, see A.J. Ayer, 'Freedom

bring together this political literature with that of the compatibilists, focused as the latter are on personal responsibility. The claim is that underlying both discussions is a single notion of freedom, one that is intimately linked to moral responsibility. According to this single notion, one is free just in case one is fit to be held responsible. Pettit argues that by linking the two literatures in this way we increase the constraints on an acceptable account of freedom, and thus eliminate accounts that otherwise seem plausible. He proposes an account that adds a condition of *discursive control.*

I shall postpone discussion of Pettit's positive account until the second part of this chapter. In the first I shall focus on his criticisms of the traditional account. For I am sceptical. My suspicion is that the kind of freedom that is typically violated by coercion is very different from the kind of freedom that is violated in the cases that form the mainstay of the compatibilist literature: cases of thought manipulation, automatic action, post-hypnotic suggestion, and the like. And I think that the way in which coercion lessens moral responsibility is very different from the way in which moral responsibility is lessened in those cases. Indeed, I think that the main basis for our metaphysical intuition that coercion compromises freedom is quite different from the main basis of our moral intuition that it reduces responsibility. It is exactly the tendency to think that our metaphysical and moral intuitions about coercion must have a single common source that has impeded understanding. In short, my thesis will be this:

(a) The reason why we think that coercion compromises freedom is because it removes our autonomy, where this is understood as freedom from manipulation by others. If our autonomy is violated, we remain agents, but agents whose actions are being manipulated.

(b) The reasons why we think that coercion lessens moral responsibility are varied, but they typically involve treating the coercion as a justification or excuse; we accept that the agent had control of their action, but we think them justified in doing what they did, or excuse them if not. Whilst the fact that the agent was manipulated has some bearing on their justification or excuse, it is far from the main factor.

In contrast, the notion of free will that the compatibilist is trying to capture is the idea that stands behind agency itself. The person who is moved by post-hypnotic suggestion or brain interference ceases to be an agent at all.[4] The loss of moral

and Necessity', in *Philosophical Essays* (London: Macmillan, 1954), 271–84. Other compatibilists, whilst following a basically Hobbesian line, have tried to provide further conditions that free actions must meet, conditions that coerced actions will fail. Gideon Yaffe argues plausibly that Locke falls into this class (see *Liberty Worth the Name* (Princeton: Princeton University Press, 2000), ch. 1); another example is H. Frankfurt, 'Coercion and Moral Responsibility', in *The Importance of What We Care About* (Cambridge: Cambridge University Press, 1988), 26–46, which I discuss below.

⁴ Or at least, post-hypnotic suggestion as philosophers conceive of it. The reality looks to be far more responsive to the existing attitudes of the subject. See, e.g., A. Barnier and K.

responsibility follows directly from the loss of agenthood; there is no need for justification or excuse, since there is no action to be justified or excused. To make the case, I need to look at coercion in much more detail. I start by examining the issues that surround our metaphysical intuitions.

METAPHYSICAL INTUTIONS

It is a feature of coercion as we ordinarily understand it that it is the result of an action by another agent: you can be coerced by a person, but not by nature. Yet philosophers have been keen to minimize the philosophical importance of the point. Harry Frankfurt writes:

> Only another person can *coerce* us, or interfere with our *social* or *political* freedom, but this is no more than a matter of useful terminology. When a person chooses to act in order to acquire a benefit or in order to escape an injury, the degree to which his choice is autonomous and the degree to which he acts freely do not depend on the origin of the conditions which lead him to choose and to act as he does. A man's will may not be his own even when he is not moved by the will of another.[5]

There is perhaps something right about this as a moral claim: it is hard to see how one could be more justified in bending to the coercion of another agent than to the coercion of the inanimate world.[6] However, as a claim about our intuitions about freedom, I think it is quite wrong. The distinction between how our fellow agents manipulate us and how the inanimate world constrains our actions is far from a mere matter of terminology; it lies at the heart of our ordinary conception of what it is to be autonomous.

I think that there is much intuitive plausibility to this: when we give examples of loss of autonomy, it is common to cite a manipulating agent. But it is hard to disentangle this from our intuition about free will as the compatibilists have tried to characterize it.[7] So I shall approach the issue from a very different direction, one that I think will enable us to keep the two issues apart. My interest will be in our motivational structures.

What are our fundamental motivations? There are the obvious physical ones: food, shelter, sex. But in addition, there is a set of fundamental social motivations,

McConkey, 'Posthypnotic Responding away from the Hypnotic Setting', *Psychological Science*, 9 (1998), 256–62.

   [5] Frankfurt, 'Coercion and Moral Responsibility', 45–6.

   [6] In similar vein, Gary Watson argues that it is hard to justify the restriction of the legal defence of duress to cases in which one is coerced by another agent (rather than some other feature of the world): 'Excusing Addiction', in *Agency and Answerability* (Oxford: Clarendon Press, 2004), 318–50, at p. 344.

   [7] Compare Daniel Dennett's characterization of the Bogeyman as one the metaphors used (in his view misleadingly) to motivate the free will problem: *Elbow Room* (Cambridge, Mass.: MIT Press, 1984), 7–10.

fundamental in the sense that they are almost universal, and that we generally cannot flourish if we fail to achieve them.[8] Although there is much debate over exactly how they should be classified, three command fairly widespread agreement.[9] The first is a desire for *social acceptance*.[10] The second is a desire for *control*: we become depressed and apathetic when we find that we cannot control our environment, either because it is uncontrollable or because we lack the necessary competence.[11] The third, which is the one of relevance for us, is a desire for *self-determination*.

The idea of self-determination has been articulated and explored in the work of Edward Deci and Richard Ryan. They write:

> Some intentional behaviors, we suggest, are initiated and regulated through choice as an expression of oneself, whereas other intentional behaviors are pressured and coerced by intrapsychic and environmental force and thus do not represent true choice. The former behaviors are characterized by autonomous initiation and regulation and are referred to as self-determined; the latter behaviors are characterized by heteronomous initiation and regulation and are referred to as controlled.[12]

True choice, they go on to say, applies only to actions that involve 'an inner endorsement of one's actions, the sense that they emanate from oneself and are one's own'. Philosophical readers will be immediately reminded of Frankfurt.[13] But the idea isn't quite the same. Frankfurt is concerned with the issue of what it is to endorse or, better, to identify with one's *desires*. Deci and Ryan are concerned with the issue of endorsement of one's *actions*. The two are importantly different;

---

[8] They are thus plausibly *needs* as well as desires. For a fuller account of the ways in which desires or needs can be fundamental, see R. Baumeister and M. Leary, 'The Need to Belong: Desire for Interpersonal Attachments as a Fundamental Human Motivation', *Psychological Bulletin*, 117 (1995), 497–529.

[9] For an overview see the Introduction to E. T. Higgins and A. Kruglanski (eds.), *Motivational Science: Social and Personality Perspectives* (Philadelphia: Psychology Press, 2000).

[10] See Baumeister and Leary, 'Need to Belong'. This is what underpins the mechanism of what Pettit and Brennan call 'the intangible hand'. See G. Brennan and P. Pettit, 'Hands Invisible and Intangible', *Synthese*, 94 (1993), 191–225.

[11] The former is the basis of Seligman's notion of learned helplessness; the latter, of Bandura's notion of self-efficacy.

[12] E. Deci and R. Ryan, 'The Support of Autonomy and the Control of Behavior', *Journal of Personality and Social Psychology*, 55 (1987), 1024–37, at p. 1024. In a footnote to this passage they remark that the distinction should be understood as marking the ends of a continuum, rather than a sharp break. Although they talk here of control coming from environmental force, in fact this seems to be entirely other people.

[13] Especially of his later writing where, as Scanlon notes, the stress moves to the issue of identification, and away from that of moral responsibility. See H. Frankfurt, 'Identification and Externality', in *The Importance of What We Care About*, and 'The Faintest Passion', in *Necessity, Volition and Love* (Cambridge: Cambridge University Press, 1999). Scanlon's discussion is in his 'Reasons and Passions', in S. Buss and L. Overton (eds.), *Contours of Agency* (Cambridge, Mass.: MIT Press, 2002), 165–83. For a straightforward presentation of exactly what Frankfurt means by identification (i.e. acceptance, rather than endorsement or caring about), see his reply to Watson in that volume, pp. 160–1.

and here we start to see the connections with our topic of coercion. When I am coerced into some wicked act to protect the life of my child, the desire which moves me—the desire for the well-being of my child—is certainly one that I endorse; the wicked action is not. It is only in Deci and Ryan's sense that the action is not my own.

It is tempting to try to give a philosophical analysis of the rather vague notion that Deci and Ryan are after. But care needs to be taken, for the notion is driven by its empirical explanatory value, rather than by an attempt to articulate an existing ordinary language concept. Its explanatory value turns out to be great. Factors that threaten self-determination, such as rewards, threats, deadlines, and even simple evaluation and surveillance, tend to undermine *intrinsic* motivation—i.e. the motivation to go on with the activity even when the pressures are removed. They also undermine interest, enjoyment, and creativity. They tend to lower the trustingness of those exposed to them, increase their aggression, and make them, in turn, more controlling. Even their health suffers.[14]

Intrapersonal factors appear to have similar effects (though this is less well explored). So, for instance, being told that success in a task is an indicator of high IQ makes university students less motivated to go on with that task once they are given the chance to drop it. Even the self-surveillance provided by the presence of a mirror lowers intrinsic motivation. Deci and Ryan hypothesize that people can pressure themselves in much the same way as they can be pressured by others, and with much the same consequences. They go so far as to conclude:

When behavior is prompted by thoughts such as "I have to . . . " or "I should . . . " (what we call internally controlling events), the behavior is theorized to be less self-determined than when it is characterized by more autonomy-related thoughts such as "I'd find it valuable to . . . " or "I'd be interested in . . . ". Accordingly, we predict that the qualities associated with external controlling events and with external autonomy-supporting events will also be associated with their intrapsychic counterparts.[15]

Here I do voice some philosophical scepticism. It is very hard to believe that when things matter so much to us that we feel we *have to* act on them—whether this be Luther's religious commitments or the commitment that a parent has to a child—we will feel a lack of self-determination.[16] It is not, I suspect, obligation in itself that undermines self-determination; it is, rather, our belief about the *source* of that obligation.

Clearly much of what is at issue in both the interpersonal and the intrapersonal case has to do with manipulation: we do not like being pushed about, not by

[14] For a recent set of studies, see E. Deci and R. Ryan, *Handbook of Self-Determination Research* (Rochester: University of Rochester Press, 2002); for a popular presentation of the approach, see E. Deci, *Why We Do What We Do* (Harmondsworth: Penguin, 1996).

[15] Deci and Ryan, 'Support of Autonomy'.

[16] Frankfurt provides a lengthy discussion of this phenomenon, which he terms 'volitional necessity'. See, e.g., 'Rationality and the Unthinkable', in *The Importance of What We Care About*, and 'On the Necessity of Ideals', in *Necessity, Volition and Love*.

others, and not even by our own demanding selves. Behaviour is perceived as more of a threat to self-determination when it is perceived as more manipulative. In this dimension, all rewards are not the same. Those offered for the performance of specific tasks within an experiment do more to undermine intrinsic motivation than those offered for simple participation: subjects perceive the experimenters as doing more to manipulate them.[17]

This has been a fairly lengthy detour. But I hope that it has succeeded in showing that the idea of self-determination is central to our idea of autonomy, which is one of our ideas of freedom. It is not the idea that compatibilists are trying to get at. But it is, I think, what is compromised in cases of coercion. Indeed, 'compromised' is far too weak a word. For coercion provides as radical a subversion of self-determination as one can imagine. Unlike simple incentives, it typically involves a complete disruption of one's own plans in a most unwelcome way.[18] Coercion doesn't provide another option to be considered alongside what one is already doing; if it is successful, it requires us to abandon what we are doing. And even if we resist it, it will typically hijack our thoughts and our emotional energies. Of course, natural disasters can have many of these features too: they can disrupt our plans in most unwelcome ways. What is special about coercion is that another agent is seeking to manipulate us by deliberately employing such disruption. That is what makes the loss of self-determination so egregious.

My contention is that it is the manipulative feature of coercion that explains our metaphysical intuitions about its effect on freedom. But this does not explain our moral intuitions. First, note that in general whilst we think that loss of self-determination is a bad thing, we don't think that it has an effect on moral responsibility. A person who is in gaol has their self-determination greatly reduced, but we don't think that they are thereby relieved of any moral responsibility. Secondly, and more specifically, it appears that there are cases in which we think that moral responsibility is lessened in much the same way as it is in cases of coercion, even though there is no loss of self-determination.

Imagine the kind of case that gets discussed endlessly in introductory classes on consequentialism: one can only save one's dying child if one robs a pharmacy to get the drugs the child needs. Put aside the question of whether the robbery might be morally justified, and just consider the moral responsibility of someone who goes ahead with it. We would surely think that their responsibility was much reduced (compared, say, with someone who committed a similar robbery to fund their summer vacation). It seems, moreover, that the person who robs the pharmacy to save their child has a similar kind of moral defence to the person who robs a pharmacy because they have been coerced into doing so by somebody

---

[17] E. Deci and R. Ryan, *Intrinsic Motivation and Self-Determination in Human Behavior* (New York: Plenum Press, 1985), 72 ff.

[18] Robert Nozick stresses the idea that coercion presents an unwelcome choice in 'Coercion', in S. Morgenbesser, P. Suppes, and M. White (eds.), *Philosophy, Science and Method* (New York: St Martin's Press, 1969), 440–72, pp. 458 ff.

who will otherwise destroy the drugs their child needs. I do not deny that there are differences between the two cases; we shall return to some of them later. Yet both seem to be of a moral piece, despite the fact that the second involves a violation of self-determination that the first does not.[19]

MORAL INTUITIONS

How, then, should we explain the effects that coercion has on our moral responsibilities? There are three obvious forms that such an explanation might have. At a first pass, we might say:

  (i) a coerced action is not a free action at all;

     or

 (ii) a coerced action is a free action, but one that the agent was justified in performing;

     or

(iii) a coerced action a free action, one that the agent was not justified in performing, but one that we nevertheless excuse.

When I talk here of actions that are not free, I don't mean merely those in which the agent is manipulated. I mean what compatibilists have traditionally meant by lack of freedom. To claim that an action is not free is to say that in some important sense it was not the agent's action at all: perhaps the movement was involuntary, or the agent was pushed, or someone had taken control of their brain. Once we realize that an action falls into this class, the question of moral justification or excuse just doesn't arise.

To take the first explanation is thus to assimilate coerced actions to these sorts of action. This, I take it, is Pettit's project. It is also a path that some more conventional compatibilists have taken. Most notably, Frankfurt has argued that coercion occurs only when 'the victim's desire or motive to avoid the penalty with which he is threatened is . . . so powerful that he cannot prevent it from leading him to submit to the threat'.[20] A threat that doesn't move the victim in this way is mere duress; submission is not excusable.

---

[19] Although it remains controversial, English law now fairly clearly recognizes a defence of 'duress of circumstances' as part of a general defence of necessity. See J. Smith and B. Hogan, *Criminal Law*, 9th edn. (London: Butterworths, 1999), 242–3, 245–52. They comment that whether the defendant is driven by a threat from an aggressor, or by natural circumstances, 'his moral culpability, or lack of it, is exactly the same' (p. 23). The status of a parallel 'defense of situational duress' under US law is less clear; but the Model Penal Code proposes a general defence of necessity at Section 3.02.

[20] Frankfurt, 'Coercion and Moral Responsibility', 39. This is only a necessary condition for it to be coercion. In addition, the agent must have a desire or inclination to resist the desire (ibid. 41).

I do not find this approach compelling. In the first place there are difficulties with the details of Frankfurt's account. What is it to be unable to prevent a desire from leading us to action? A natural way to understand this, and one which Frankfurt's comments suggest, is in terms of his own higher-order account of freedom: one is unable to resist a desire iff, were one to desire to resist it, one would not be able to. But that raises a host of problems that beset any conditional analysis: what, for instance, if one would indeed be able to resist if one were to form the desire to resist, but one was unable to form such a desire?

There are replies that might be made on Frankfurt's behalf to such worries; or we might try to salvage the general approach by proposing another account of what makes a desire irresistible. But I think that there are more fundamental problems with any account that tries to deny that coerced actions are free in the kind of way that compatibilists normally understand freedom. To begin with, note that coercion doesn't remove moral responsibility in all circumstances. This is reflected in the legal defence of duress. Under English law the situation is clear: duress can only be a defence if the threat is one of death or serious personal injury; and it is never a defence for murder.[21] In Blackstone's words: 'A man ought rather to die himself than escape by the murder of an innocent.' I take it that Blackstone is here making a moral claim, as well as a legal one. Phrased in such uncompromising terms, that claim is controversial.[22] However, even those who would reject it would normally accept some kind of principle of proportionality like that included in the American Model Penal Code: for duress to be a defence, the harm threatened against the defendant must be greater than that which the defendant's action can be expected to cause. Killing an innocent is hard to excuse, since it is so hard to see how there could be any circumstances in which the cost of resisting the coercion would be higher.[23]

But this suggests that we expect a certain degree of self-control of agents who yield to coercion. We expect them to be able to assess the gravity of the threat relative to that of the act that they are being pressured to perform. This does not suggest a picture of agents driven by irresistible desires. The point is brought out further by the fact that there is no subjective requirement in the law that a victim of duress should lose their self-control—in contrast to a provocation defence, which requires that they do. One can still rely on a defence of duress if one's response has been as calculated as can be.

All of this in turn suggests that the right way to understand coercion's moral status is in terms of either the second or third models. A coerced action is a

---

[21] A terminological point: the standard legal term is *duress*. In English law there is a defence of *coercion*, but it is, oddly enough, normally restricted to crimes committed by women in the presence of their husbands.

[22] The idea that there can be no defence of duress for homicide is not a feature of the Model Penal Code. It remains, however, a feature of English law, having been recently endorsed by the House of Lords in *Howe*. For discussion, see Smith and Hogan, *Criminal Law*, 231–44.

[23] Ibid. 252.

free action, but it is either justifiable or excusable. To suggest this is in no way original; this has been the approach that most theorists have taken. The main debate has concerned which of the two models is correct: whether the coerced person does a justifiable thing in bowing to the coercion, or an unjustifiable thing that we nevertheless excuse because no reasonable person could be expected to do otherwise.[24] I do not propose to try to resolve this question here. In fact, it is unclear to me whether the two explanations are fully distinct. Very often we are concerned not with whether an action is justifiable *simpliciter*, but with whether it is more or less justifiable: justifiability functions more as a scale than an absolute threshold. Then we can unproblematically say that a coerced action is typically more justifiable than a similar action that is not coerced, and frequently sufficiently justifiable to be excusable.[25]

What matters for my purposes here is independent of this debate though. For whether we understand coercion as providing justification or excuse, we will still think of coerced actions as free, at least as the compatibilists mean that. And in so far as there is a sense in which such actions are not free—in so far as we think of the coercion as removing self-determination—this is a feature that has no direct bearing on their moral status.

There remains, however, a puzzle, one that anyone proposing an excuse or justification account should address. The puzzle concerns the relation between coercion and bribery. If I threaten to take away something which you already have if you do not do as I say, that is coercion. But if I offer to give you something that you do not already have if you will do as I say, that is bribery. Put this way, the two do not sound very different; indeed, there are going to be plenty of cases that come between them (I have promised you something which I threaten to withhold if you do not do as I say). Yet we do not generally think that the presence of a bribe removes the agent's moral responsibility (unless, that is, the agent is in such a state that the bribe removes their ability to think: offering cocaine to an addict for instance); in fact it will often make things worse. What is it about coercion that makes it so different?

There are various features that cases of coercion typically have that cases of bribery typically lack. As we have seen, typically people do not welcome the options presented by coercion, whereas they often welcome those presented by a bribe. And typically those who are coerced are dependent upon the coercer for something that they need, a dependence that the coercer exploits.[26] But these are

---

[24] For some recent discussions, see J. Dressler, 'Exegesis of the Law of Duress: Justifying the Excuse and Searching for its Proper Limits', *Southern California Law Review*, 62 (1989), 331–89; D. Kahan and M. Nussbaum, 'Two Concepts of Emotion in Criminal Law', *Columbia Law Review*, 96 (1996), 269–374; Watson, 'Excusing Addiction'; P. Westen and J. Mangiafico, 'The Criminal Defense of Duress: A Justification, Not an Excuse—And Why it Matters', *Buffalo Law Review*, 6 (2004), 833–950.

[25] The issue is further complicated by whether we take justification to be agent neutral or agent-relative; see Kahan and Nussbaum, 'Two Concepts of Emotion'.

[26] See Frankfurt, 'Coercion and Moral Responsibility', 33.

not essential differences. We do not always welcome a bribe. Knowing that we are weak and are likely to succumb, it makes perfect sense not to want to be led into temptation. Sometimes too, those who offer a bribe exploit a need that only they are in a position to meet. When we have a case of bribery that meets all of these conditions—a *coercive offer*, as Frankfurt terms it—is it still obvious that succumbing to bribery is worse than succumbing to coercion?

I think that it is far from obvious. Consider variants of the case described above involving the parent whose child needs medication. In the coercive case the coercer steals the medication and refuses to return it unless the parent obeys. In the bribery case the parent does not yet have the medication, and the briber offers it if he will obey. As I said above, I think that the two cases are very much of a piece. However, I suspect that we are slightly more prepared to forgive the parent who succumbs to the coercion than the parent who succumbs to the bribe. This is especially so if we think of the case as involving excuse rather than justification. Suppose that what the parent does to get the medication involves something terrible—the killing of an innocent, say—so that we should never think it justified. We might, nevertheless, excuse the act; but we should do so more readily in the case of coercion than bribery.

The heart of the explanation of the difference surely lies in the fact that we think the coerced parent more deeply harmed, and so more readily excused in his response. Of course, the briber is wrong to exploit his position; he should give the medication freely. But the coercer does an additional wrong in taking away the medication in the first place. There are two factors here: the wrongness of the theft, and the difference between losing what one already has and failing to gain what one might have. We can control for the former by imagining a third case. Suppose that the parent has lost the medication. The coercer discovers where it is, but refuses to tell unless the parent obeys. We still, I think, would be more ready to excuse a parent coerced in this way than one who succumbed to the bribe.

I suspect that the explanation for this stems from the fact that we just do have a different attitude towards the loss of that which we already have, as opposed to our failure to gain that which we do not yet have. (The contrast can involve a possession, or something which is not properly thought of in this way, like peace of mind, or good health, or a child.) This attitude is manifested in another well-documented psychological phenomenon: *the endowment effect*. We value things more once we possess them.[27] The experiments that illustrate this effect often involve such patent irrationality that it is easy to think of it as a foible to which no importance should be attached. Thus, asked what they would pay for

---

[27] Closely related phenomena are *loss aversion* (losing something brings more cost than gaining it brings benefit) and the resulting *status quo bias* (subjects have a strong tendency to keep with the *status quo* since losses consequent on change figure more prominently than gains). Loss aversion is one of the underpinnings of Kahneman and Tversky's prospect theory; see D. Kahneman and A. Tversky, *Choices, Values and Frames* (Cambridge: Cambridge University Press, 2000).

a Cornell University mug, the average subject offered around $2.50; but, once given the mug, they were not prepared to give it up for less than $5.[28] Yet, whether or not it is justifiable, this is no trivial tendency. We do think it far worse to deprive someone of their sight than to fail to restore the sight of someone already blind; and we tend to maintain that view even under critical reflection.

Perhaps this is merely an irrational tendency; certainly it has its irrational elements. Perhaps it reflects the importance we attach to the fulfilment of legitimate expectations. Perhaps it reflects some fundamental attachment to the status quo. I do not know where to start in pursuing this difficult question.[29] What matters here, since we are concerned with excuse and not with justification, is that we do tend to think in these ways; and hence we are prepared to offer greater excuse to those who think that they risk suffering a greater loss. I conclude that our different attitudes to bribery and to coercion can be explained within the excuse model.

FREEDOM AS DISCURSIVE CONTROL

I have focused so far on Pettit's negative arguments against the conventional compatibilist account of freedom. In this last section I turn to his positive proposal. Although Pettit is critical of the traditional compatibilist accounts, he does not deny that they provide necessary conditions for freedom. His argument is that they do not provide sufficient conditions. He thinks that they need to be supplemented with a further necessary condition: that of *discursive control*. My aim in this section is to give some consideration to this proposal, especially in the light of the kind of empirical considerations about human psychology that have figured so prominently up till now. Even if we are unconvinced by Pettit's argument against the standard compatibilist accounts, it is very plausible that those accounts do not tell the full story, especially if, as I think, the concept of freedom is a cluster concept. Does Pettit's notion of discursive control shed light on some aspect of the cluster?

Pettit's basic idea is this:

An agent will be a free person so far as they have the ability to discourse and they have the access to discourse that is provided within [discourse friendly] relationships.[30]

There are two parts to this. The first, the *ratiocinative*, concerns the abilities of the agent. In addition to the ability to deliberate, free agents must have the

---

[28] D. Kahneman, J. Knetsch, and R. Thaler, 'Experimental Tests of the Endowment Effect and the Coase Theorem', *Journal of Political Economy*, 98 (1990), 1325–48.

[29] The endowment effect plausibly has some work to do in explaining our different attitudes to doing and allowing. For a stimulating discussion, see T. Horowitz, 'Philosophical Intuitions and Psychological Theory', *Ethics*, 108 (1998), 367–85.

[30] Pettit, *Theory of Freedom*, p. 70.

ability to discourse. The second, the *relational*, concerns the social situation of the agent: free agents must be able to enter into actual discourse, and to do this, they must have others around them with whom they can have discourse-friendly relations. I start with the second.

The Relational Condition

Pablo Neruda writes, in his paean to the Communist Party: 'You have given me the freedom that the lone man lacks.'[31] And certainly that may be right. There are many things that one can do with others that one cannot do on one's own. Moreover, the presence of others need not simply confer greater powers of execution: the ability to move heavy things, maintain a twenty-four-hour vigil, outvote the opposition. Others can also help with the process of thinking. They can provide ideas, or force us to question and clarify our own, or enable us to maintain our commitments when we should otherwise despair.

Nonetheless, it is hard to believe that actually available social relationships are necessary for freedom—does Crusoe really lose his freedom until Friday's arrival? And we might wonder about Pettit's claim that freedom, so conceived, is necessary for moral responsibility—if an interlocutor proposes actions so morally grotesque that everyone refuses to talk to him, do they thereby not only remove his freedom, but also absolve him of moral responsibility? Moreover, even the contention that the presence of others will bring us closer to the truth is far from obviously true. Whilst the jury theorem provides some a priori support for it, the empirical evidence is mixed. In some cases, especially those involving simple concrete questions, groups do better than individuals thinking alone. But in some cases they do worse. Part of this can be explained by the presence of a strong tendency to conformity or compromise.[32] This is especially marked when there is no demonstrable right answer: for instance, if the question posed concerns a difficult issue of value, or of which of various plausible actions should be taken. But even in the case of a simple empirical issue with a demonstrable right answer, there is a strong tendency to convergence. One influential set of experiments by Solomon Asch has led to a large literature. Subjects were asked to judge the relative lengths of lines. The task was easy, and, asked on their own, 95 per cent gave the right answer to each of a series of twelve or so tests. They were

---

[31] Pablo Neruda, 'To my party', from *Canto General* (Berkeley: University of California Press, 1991), 298.

[32] I will not discuss the literature on the tendency to compromise, though there is one experiment whose outcome I feel duty-bound to report: academics showed themselves far more likely to agree to see a student for a single twenty-minute meeting if they had previously refused the (surely, one hopes, unreasonable) request to meet weekly for two hours for the rest of the semester. See H. Harari, D. Mohr, and K. Hosey, 'Faculty Helpfulness to Students: A Comparison of Compliance Techniques', *Personality and Social Psychology Bulletin*, 6 (1980), 373–7. For a review of the literature in this area, see R. Cialdini and M. Trost, 'Social Influence: Social Norms, Conformity and Compliance', in *The Handbook of Social Psychology* (New York: McGraw-Hill, 1998), ii. 151–92, at pp. 177 ff.

then placed in a group of six to eight others, confederates who had been briefed to answer correctly on two initial tests, but then to give wrong but unanimous answers on the remaining ten. The subjects could hear what the others said before they gave their own answers; and their answers were in turn heard by the others. In these circumstances only 24 per cent gave the right answer in each of the tests where the others answered wrongly; 25 per cent got more than two-thirds of them wrong. A number of factors seem to be at work: the desire to win the approval of others (as shown by the fact that answers that cannot be heard by the others conform less); a desire not to seem deviant even to oneself; and the conviction that the others must be right.[33]

These factors are surely politically and morally important: they go some way to explaining how politics is possible in a world of opposed interests. Yet it is hard to see how they are important in an account of freedom. If anything, they seem to involve a subordination of the capacities involved in rational control to wider social goals. Individuals willingly (or perhaps unknowingly) give up certain freedoms in belief and desire for the wider good. So let us turn from the issue of whether the free agents need to have actual social relationships to the issue of whether they need to have the ability to engage in them.

The Ratiocinative Condition

The idea here is that in order to enter into discourse an agent must have various abilities; and it is the possession of these abilities, rather than the process of discourse itself, that is necessary for freedom.[34] What abilities does an agent need to enter into discourse over and above the ability to deliberate? They must, of course, have a language in common with those around them, and the ability to hear and be heard (or to read and be read, or whatever). Those are certainly crucial abilities, although, given the social dimensions of knowledge, they are plausibly required even for rational deliberation. What else is needed that is distinctive to discourse? Pettit is not altogether clear about this, but there is one plausible condition. On Pettit's conception, a discourse-friendly relationship is one in which agents can 'reason together'.[35] To do this, discoursing agents must have the ability to justify their beliefs and their actions to each other; it is only through such justification that legitimate influence can take place.

---

[33] For a review, see Cialdini and Trost, 'Social Influence', 162 ff. There are many other factors that affect the way that dialogue in fact develops, including size of the group, gender, familiarity, and whether we are acting for ourselves or for others. For a general overview, see J. Levine and R. Moreland, 'Small Groups', in *Handbook of Social Psychology*, ii. 415–69.

[34] Compare the distinction that T. M. Scanlon makes between his account of contractarianism, in which actual agreement with others is not required, and the position that he attributes to Habermas, in which it is. See *What We Owe to Each Other* (Cambridge, Mass.: Harvard University Press, 1998) 393 n. 5.

[35] Pettit, *Theory of Freedom*, 69 ff.

If this is right, then the ratiocinative requirement certainly does add a further condition: to be free, agents must be able to justify what they think and do. But this is a highly controversial condition. There is good reason to think that in exercising many capacities we simply don't know what it is that we are responding to, so we are in no position to justify either our beliefs or our actions. Chicken sexing is the standard philosophical example, but a bad one: it appears that most chicken-sexers do know which features they are picking up on when they form their beliefs.[36] Human sexing is a better example, at least when we have just the face to go on. Most of us are extremely fast and accurate at telling someone's sex by looking at their face. How do we do it? It turns out that we are sensitive to many cues: for instance, the shape of the nose, especially the bridge, is crucially important. Similarly, we are good at telling someone's age from their face, and here we go mainly not by wrinkles as we might expect, but by overall shape and colour distribution.[37] In both cases we have little clue about what we are doing until we are told. Many other capacities, including learned capacities, are similar. Gary Klein gives a large number of examples involving soldiers, sailors, fire-fighters, doctors, and neo-natal nurses.[38] In many cases we are simply unable to justify our judgements and decisions. Experienced fire-fighters have a gut feeling when a burning building is particularly dangerous; experienced nurses just know when a premature baby has started to develop an infection. Of course, there are cues that these people are picking up on; they are not doing it by magic. But they do not know what those cues are. Moreover, often the attempt to justify them, or to make them using publicly justifiable criteria, actually corrupts our judgement.[39]

One response to this line of worry is to stress that we are dealing with an ideal: in fact people are unable to justify their beliefs and decisions, but ideally they should be able to. But for this line to work, we need some reason to think that it is an ideal, and none has been offered. A second, more plausible response is to say that the kind of judgements we are considering are justified, but that they are justified not by citing the evidence upon which they are based, but by

---

[36] I. Biederman and M. Shiffrar, 'Sexing Day-old Chicks: A Case Study and Expert Systems Analysis of a Difficult Perceptual Learning Task', *Journal of Experimental Psychology: Human Learning, Memory, and Cognition*, 13 (1987), 640–5.

[37] For a nice presentation on both sex and age discrimination, see V. Bruce and A. Young, *In the Eye of the Beholder: The Science of Face Perception* (Oxford: Oxford University Press, 1998).

[38] G. Klein, *Sources of Power* (Cambridge, Mass.: MIT Press, 1998).

[39] See also T. Wilson and J. Schooler, 'Thinking Too Much: Introspection can Reduce the Quality of Preferences and Decisions', *Journal of Personality and Social Psychology*, 60 (1991), 189–92. Ordinary subjects, asked to rank samples of strawberry jam in terms of quality, gave rankings that were close to those of expert tasters until they were told to use explicit criteria, at which point their rankings diverged substantially. Klein gives many examples of cases in which subjects do far worse when asked to make decisions by running through an explicit checklist of factors rather than on the basis of a single overall judgement. The distorting effects of the checklist approach will be familiar to those who have been instructed, by various regulatory bodies, to assign marks to undergraduate essays by summing the marks assigned to supposedly relevant factors: understanding, clarity, structure, breadth of reading, originality, etc.

citing the experience and past performance of the agents who make them. The judgements of the experienced fire-fighter and experienced neo-natal nurse are justified by pointing to the skills they have learned that are manifested in their past successes. That response seems exactly right for these sorts of cases, cases in which the agent has expertise in discerning some hard-discerned empirical fact. But it is less plausible when it is some difficult moral problem that is at issue. At least when we are dealing with adult agents, we are far less happy with the idea that a moral expert can justify a judgement solely on the basis of their track record. Perhaps there are some thick moral concepts for whose application we are rightly prepared to defer to those who have shown they can apply them without being able to justify their application: being sexist, for instance. But it is far less plausible that we would accept a relatively abstract moral principle—'Sexism is wrong'—to be justified on the basis of a testimony of a competent moral judge.[40]

However, rather than being an objection to Pettit's account, this points to a defence. For the idea is perhaps that in presenting *moral* conclusions, we need to be able to give justifications. We do not need to be able to justify every application of a thick moral concept along the way. But we do need to be able to justify the more abstract principles upon which any conclusion rests. The idea might be filled out in various ways. We might, for instance, think that justification affects our cognitive or epistemic standing with respect to a principle: a person must be able to justify a moral principle in order to understand it, or in order to know it. That strikes me as a rather implausible version of the requirement. We would need to know why the power of testimony to confer knowledge was so much more restricted here than elsewhere. A more plausible approach is to think that the requirement is itself a moral one: whilst we might be able to gain knowledge of moral principles entirely on another's testimony, we have a moral obligation to understand the basis of that knowledge.

I am not sure what to think of such a putative moral requirement. I am confident that there was a time when it would have been broadly rejected: a time when accepting God's testimony, or that of his representatives on Earth, without needing to understand the reasoning, was the paradigmatic moral position. But it does seem far more plausible that it is a component of Enlightenment moral thinking.[41] Yet it surely stands in need of some justification. Even if it can be

---

[40] The example comes from Karen Jones, 'Second-hand Moral Knowledge', *Journal of Philosophy*, 96 (1999), 55–78. I think that she is clearly right that, in the application of thick moral concepts like 'sexist', we should be prepared to defer to the testimony of those who are more skilled at applying them; they do, after all, contain a considerable descriptive component. What I question is whether the same is true of more abstract principles (an issue which Jones raises, but on which she does not come to a conclusion).

[41] As I read it, it is one of the elements of the position presented in Kant's *What is Enlightenment?*, in *The Cambridge Edition of the Works of Immanuel Kant: Practical Philosophy*, ed. M. Gregor (Cambridge: Cambridge University Press, 1996), 11–22. The thought there is not simply that one need not be afraid to think things through for oneself, but that there is a moral requirement to do so.

purged of the threat of regress which it obviously invites (can *all* of our moral principles be justified?), we need to be assured that it does not rest on the same kind of foundationalist instincts that have been successfully challenged elsewhere.

Obviously this is a large issue, one that cannot be pursued here. Let me instead conclude by returning to the subject at issue, that of freedom. I have developed the idea of the ratiocinative condition as requiring that we be able to justify our beliefs and decisions; and I have suggested that if this idea has any plausibility, it is as a moral requirement that we be able to justify our moral reasoning. How does this tie in with the issue of freedom? Pettit's proposal is that meeting the requirement is a necessary condition on being free. I think that there is some plausibility to the idea that being free requires a kind of moral ability. But I am doubtful that Pettit would accept it. For it takes us back to the idea of freedom as a kind of rational control, one of the targets of Pettit's criticisms.[42] Perhaps, then, I have misinterpreted the ratiocinative condition; at the least, I hope that I have shown where one natural development leads.

[42] The most striking presentation of this version of the idea is in Susan Wolf's paper 'Sanity and the Metaphysics of Responsibility', in F. Schoeman (ed.), *Responsibility, Character and the Emotions* (Cambridge: Cambridge University Press, 1988), 46–62. There, though, the focus is on the idea that certain moral capacities are necessary for moral responsibility, rather than that they are needed for freedom itself. Note too that Wolf does not endorse any particular moral requirement that one be able to justify one's moral reasoning.

6

Conversability and Deliberation

John Ferejohn

1. INTRODUCTION

Suppose that Congress is to decide whether to enact a statutory scheme, such as, for example, establishing a cabinet department for Homeland Security. Presumably the reasons in favor of the statute would be more or less directed to considerations of welfare or public safety. But the new department may be authorized to behave in ways that may sometimes infringe some people's rights. Whether or not such an agency should be set up and authorized to suspend rights would seem to be a matter of balancing the advancement of a shared interest in public safety against the particular rights violations that such advancement may entail. And, presumably, the appropriate balance should somehow be responsive to arguments, both on behalf of those whose rights are likely to be suspended as well as from those who think that public safety may be inadequately protected.

Philip Pettit has termed this requirement of responsiveness to argument, "conversability".[1] The idea is that if a government is to coerce a person or group, those affected are owed a coherent justification that makes sense of the policy that was adopted in terms they can accept:[2] a justification that displays the policy as rationally related to public objectives—objectives actually held by the government that is claiming to take authorized action on behalf of the public of which they are part. So, conversability presents the government as a kind of intelligent entity capable of responding to reasons of public interest. Indeed, it

---

[1] The comments on this chapter are based on the following paper: Philip Pettit, "Groups with Minds of their Own", <http://socpol.anu.edu.au/pdf-files/W12.pdf>. Pettit has developed these ideas in a number of other papers, some of which appear on the same website and others of which are in various stages of the publication process. While his ideas have developed from what is described here, as far as I know, the notion of conversability itself has not changed.

[2] He might also require that the reasons offered as justification were the reasons that the policy was adopted. I am not sure. This additional demand seems to preclude some kinds of public deliberation in policy making whereby the reasons and the policies co-evolve.

seems to present the people themselves, as a collective entity, as having coherent purposes that may be intelligently pursued.

Conversability is a demanding test of a government—indeed, it is demanding for individuals—but Pettit is not alone in embracing it. Many other legal theorists, social critics, and ordinary people hold something like conversability as well: at least as a normative aspiration, collective decisions ought to be justifiable as aiming at the maximization of welfare, for example, or as furthering some other well-defined public purposes. In other words, legislation ought to be explicable as a result of intentional action by a unified agent.

For example, notions of collective intention figure in various ways in theories of legal interpretation. One idea is that a legal interpreter ought to give weight to the intention of the legislature that enacted the statute, however that is to be discovered. This idea presupposes that the legislature is capable of directing its action rationally by formulating an intention to pursue some objective and deploying the means available to it in a more or less effective manner. The point of intentional determination is to authorize a court, an agency, or a private party to take certain actions in cases where the legislature failed to authorize them in its statute.[3]

A somewhat more vivid attribution of collective intention is found in the language used by the American Supreme Court. The members of the Court, itself a multi-member body, write opinions that refer to what "we" or "this Court" decided when referring to decisions a century old and with which the opinion writer might well be in profound disagreement.[4] Members of the Court have typically taken the precedents established by the Court as "their" settled view for purposes of deciding a current case The idea, at least for the Supreme Court, is that previous decisions establish a continuing policy of the Court itself that is presumptively binding on the current members in sufficiently similar cases that may arise.[5] Thus, the Court is presumed able not only to act intentionally at a moment in time, but also to act as a rational unified agent over long time periods, and is expected to explain or excuse departures from that regular practice.

The notion of collective intention is more controversial when it comes to the legislature, at least if that intention is to extend over time. It seems to conflict with some notions of parliamentary or popular sovereignty, according to which a legislature (or an electorate) may not be bound by its predecessors. With rare and thin exceptions, the notion of precedent does not carry much force in

---

[3] I suppose that rationality is a somewhat stronger notion than intentionality for the purposes of this essay. Later on, the notions of integrity and then coherence are employed in a related manner. That is, I suppose that some amount of coherence, or equivalently integrity, is necessary for ascriptions of intentionality, and that intentionality is necessary for rationality.

[4] While the notion of the Court, as a multi-member body, acting as an intentional agent, may be familiar, it is no less mysterious, in the terms of this chapter, than the idea of a legislature acting in that way.

[5] The notion of "binding" in this sentence is normative: the precedent gives reasons for deciding the current case in a certain way, absent very strong opposing reasons.

ordinary legislatures.[6] If legislative action is constrained in this way, it may be impossible to regard the actions of a legislature as intentional. But some idea of collective intention seems required to make sense of the idea that the legislature or government does in fact undertake commitments to certain policies, and that the existence of these commitments matters to how the government or the legislator conducts, or should conduct, itself over time.[7]

Indeed, some have argued that some notion of intent might be implicit in the idea of legality or law. Ronald Dworkin, for example, thinks that law ought to exhibit integrity, by which he means that it ought to be possible to understand law as a pattern of actions taken by a rational individual. The idea is that when the law is to be deployed against someone, that person is owed a coherent justification what shows that the application is required to secure some accepted public purpose. The idea that each affected person is owed a coherent explanation for law's imposition provides a means by which that person could, in principle, demand the revision of the policy itself.[8]

2. COLLECTIVE INTENTION

Can we require a legislature or a multi-member court to act intentionally as a unified rational agent? Some think that such a duty could be sensible only if such coherence can actually be achieved, at least partially, without violating other duties such as a duty to count votes equally. Obviously, there are both theoretical and empirical reasons to doubt that the statutes produced by a legislature, or the decisions issued by a multi-member court, will automatically exhibit such coherence. I have no reason to challenge these arguments here. Indeed, in what follows I shall confine myself to studying majoritarian decision procedures, which are notoriously prone to incoherence at least on some (common) configurations of member preferences.[9]

---

[6] Those who watched the Clinton impeachment proceedings will remember, however, that members of both House and Senate referred to precedent when it came to arguing in favor of this or that set of meanings for terms such as "high crimes" and "misdemeanors". And in fact, the rulings of the presiding officers of both bodies are codified in volumes of precedents. But the import of such precedents seems much less in the case of House and Senate precedent than in the case of the Courts. After all, they concern only how each chamber will treat the actions of its own members, and not how binding statutes will be applied to all persons.

[7] Modern governments not only generally honor contractual commitments made by their predecessors, but they also take steps to ensure that they are treated as legal persons in various other ways. Typically, this takes the form of granting statutory rights to sue the government on various specified grounds. Obviously governments have an interest in entering into contracts, and this interest extends to their successors. But the "contractual" domain is a limited exception to the general rule that governments are not bound by their predecessors. And indeed, statutes that permit suits against government are always subject to repeal.

[8] This seems to be Pettit's idea of contestability.

[9] Preferences for distributive legislation famously yield cyclic preferences as long as there are at least two programs that can receive allocations.

It is important to note that there is little reason to hope that preference configurations that produce incoherent or cyclic preferences will rarely arise. For example, if preferences are drawn randomly from the set of all possible preferences, then, as long as the number of alternatives is moderately large, the probability of incoherent group choice will be near 1. Thus, if coherent group intentions are to be produced, they will have to be brought about either by restricting the proposals that can be voted against each other, or through operation of processes that, somehow, restrict the diversity of voting patterns that can arise in the group. Pettit's idea of conversability can be understood in this second way.

Pettit argues that not every assemblage of people is able to act conversably. Rather, only certain kinds of groups—he calls them "social integrates"—can aspire to, and succeed at, acting intentionally. These groups have special features that make them capable of acting as rational agents. Because of these special features, they are able to have certain kinds of mental states, such as beliefs and desires, and to choose actions based on those states in the way any rational agent would. What these features are exactly is not clear, but calling these groups social "integrates" suggests, at a minimum, that there are processes at work within them which somehow harmonize or integrate the judgments of individual group members sufficiently to permit the development of something like a collective will. I interpret this as saying that social integrates will exhibit less diverse preferences than other kinds of groups, and that this reduced diversity will be sufficient to permit them to act more or less as unified or rational actors would.

Pettit thinks that there is nothing mysterious in positing this much group mentality. He thinks that there is no need to require that a group have a physical brain to house its beliefs, desires, and intentions. Collective mental states could be seen instead as supervening on certain of the mental attitudes of the group's members.[10] For this to be possible, the group's members must have appropriate kinds of individual attitudes and dispositions toward the group: the disposition to regard group intentions as their own in some sense—to identify with the group's "attitudes" in a certain way.[11] And they must have a disposition to take measures to see to it not only that the group tends to form intentions and guide

---

[10] Most of the work on group intentions is focused on two-person groups, and emphasizes that group intentions are related to certain individual intentions—"we" intentions—that are interconnected in highly reflexive ways. Part of Pettit's contribution is to argue that such interconnected "we" intentions can form and remain stable in rather large and complex organizations. I think that this claim needs a lot more argument than Pettit offers, but I am generally sympathetic to it. Indeed, my objection to Pettit's position is that I don't see the sharp line between the political party (which he thinks can bear intentionality) and the legislature (which he thinks cannot do so).

[11] Group beliefs need not depend on individual beliefs in any very simple way. For a group member to say that "we believe x" does not imply that she as an individual believes x. The group's beliefs may be formed in some more complex way. Members of a jury, for example, might say that "we do not believe that A is guilty" if they mean that the group has not agreed that the state's burden of proof has been met. But the same individuals may individually believe that A is guilty.

its actions in ways that rationality demands, but also that their own plans and intentions are responsive to the group's projects.

In effect, then, Pettit thinks that the prospect of a group being conversable depends on group characteristics. Only groups with the capacity to act more or less as unified agents can be subject to a requirement of conversability. He doesn't specifically address the issue of whether either law or government policy ought to satisfy the requirement of conversability. Indeed, he seems to doubt that highly heterogeneous entities such as electorates, legislatures, or governments are even capable of acting in this way.[12] His core examples are instead:

> groups where it is a matter of internal aspiration that members find common grounds by which to justify whatever line they collectively take. Think of the political movement that has to work out a policy program; or the association that has to decide on the terms of its constitution; or the church that has to give an account of itself in the public forum; or the learned academy that seeks a voice in the larger world of politics and journalism.[13]

These groups have in common a sense of shared purpose and a shared willingness to compromise privately held views to achieve this purpose or else to get others to agree to modify it. It is hard to see modern governments or electorates as possessing anything like this degree of unity.

But suppose it is thought instead that conversability is a duty owed to those affected by an infringement of a person's interests, then it ought especially to apply to governmental and legal actors. This is not to deny Pettit's idea that only certain kinds of groups are actually capable of meeting the demands of conversability. Perhaps such obligations fall only on representatives or agents of the collectivity. When a collectivity's law is unjust, officials do wrong to enforce it. But even if officials do not enforce wrongful acts, it is the act of the collectivity itself that is wrong or unjust. Perhaps, then, members of the collectivity, and not just its agents, have some duties to prevent the enactment of bad laws.

That is the idea I want to pursue. I shall explore the idea that members of a group may have duties to help it achieve coherence by reflecting deliberatively on how they should cast their votes, taking account of how those votes are to be counted. Specifically, members of collective bodies may have duties to choose how to vote in light of the possible coherence of the resulting policies that will be produced. They may have duties, that is, to adjust their votes (and perhaps their desires or beliefs as well) in the course of deliberation, in order to make the

---

[12] Perhaps the most hope he could have for a conversable democratic government is that it adopt the British practice of having government controlled by a single majority party. Insofar as British political parties are capable of acting as social integrates, British legislation may be seen as the product of rational action. But that would be possible only so long as that party retains its majority. There would be little hope of coherent policy over longer time periods in which parties would alternate in office. If this is his view, I think he would also have to have doubts about electoral reforms, such as proportional representation, that would diminish the prospect of single party control of government.

[13] Pettit, "Groups with Minds of their Own", 7.

pattern of their collective decisions cohere. The question then is what demands are placed on legislators by the aim of coherence.

3. A FRAMEWORK

Theories of social choice are usually framed as theories of either preference or information aggregation. Either decision-making institutions are to aggregate preferences to produce social choices, or else decision-making institutions combine privately observed information into collective judgments. For purposes of understanding deliberative processes, these settings seem opaque to many of the sorts of considerations that might lead people to alter their views in the course of collective deliberation. So, the model I employ here is a model of judgment aggregation, where the judgments of the individual group members are not based on private information, but are normative judgments about what the group ought to do or say.[14] These judgments may reflect private considerations, but, I assume, they do not reflect privately observed information that is considered relevant to the group decision.[15] Rather, judgments are normative expressions in favor of a group doing or saying a certain thing.

A simple example, which Philip Pettit has called the "discursive dilemma", will form the basis for my discussion. It can be interpreted as an example of either practical or theoretical reasoning. There are three voters, each of whom is to decide whether to pursue an end, whether some available means will be effective in realizing that end, and whether or not to actually intend the means. The preference pattern shown in Table 6.1 illustrates the discursive dilemma.

[14] The distinction I am aiming at is this: if group members are making their own judgments about some event—whether a criminal defendant is guilty of an alleged crime, for example—they are making their own best judgment as to whether the event occurred or not. Those judgments may be based on private information that is available to each one, and they are in any case the private judgments of the individual jurors as to whether the accused is guilty or not. These judgments may be aggregated into a group decision, and there is some justification for aggregating judgments of these kinds by the use of majority. The judgments I am concerned with are different: they are individual judgments as to what the group should do. They are in that sense public judgments, or judgments as to what "we" should do. It is well known that in the Condorcet circumstances, an individual's private judgment can conflict with what he thinks the group ought to do. He can, personally, think that the accused is innocent based on his own private information, but also believe that the group should judge him to be guilty (if, for example, all of the other group members believe he is guilty). In that case, the individual should revise his private belief to reflect the information conveyed by the guilty judgments made by the others. When it comes to public judgments, we do not have the same kind of justification for aggregation, and there may be no reason to revise one's own public judgment in light of the public judgments made by others. There is no dispersed information to be combined; there are just diverse normative judgments as to what should be done.

[15] A member might judge, for example, that the group should do x rather than y because things are better for her if x is chosen. Indeed, private regarding judgments might often be considered relevant to the action a group should take. If a proposed plan of collective action imposes heavy costs or duties on some group members, that fact might be relevant to a group's decision as to what it ought to do.

Table 6.1.

Voter	Intend end	Means effective	Intend means
1	Y	N	N
2	N	Y	N
3	Y	Y	Y
Collective judgments	Y	Y	Y/N

The dilemma is this: reasoning as individuals, a majority of members have no reason to intend the means, and so a majority would not have reason to intend the means. But, reasoning as a group, as a majority thinks the end desirable, and a majority thinks the means effective, the group has reason to form the intention to purse the means. The dilemma shows that, faced with this pattern of judgments, the group cannot, at the same time, present itself as a rational agent and respect the rational judgments of its members.[16]

One way to think about this example—a way that I resist—is to see the pattern of judgments by the individuals as expressive of their real or true beliefs about what the group ought to do. I shall take these judgments instead as tentative or initial beliefs about the group's proper course of action, rather than preferences. The point of group deliberation is to deliberate to final judgments, and not to aggregate the judgments that the individual group members happen to begin with.

Examples of this kind were first noticed by Kornhauser and Sager, and described in a series of articles about decision making on multi-judge courts.[17] They argued in those articles that this preference pattern, which they labeled the "doctrinal paradox", has actually been observed in multi-judge courts, and that, this, empirically, has led to some curious judicial reasoning. Table 6.2 illustrates one of their examples from the area of contract law. Contract law doctrine says

Table 6.2.

Judge	Valid contract	Breach	Plaintiff wins
1	Y	N	N
2	N	Y	N
3	Y	Y	Y
Collective judgments	Y	Y	Y/N

[16] The structure of the dilemma can be stated a bit more formally. Let c_i be a set of members required or decisive for a group to affirm premise i and label the collection of such sets C_i. Then, a discursive dilemma occurs when $\cap c_i$ is not contained in C_R, the collection of sets decisive for the result. For majority rule, it is clear that $\cap c_i$ may not be decisive if there is more than one premise, or if the smallest decisive set is less than the set of all members.

[17] Lewis Kornhauser and Lawrence Sager, "Unpacking the Court", *Yale Law Journal* 82 (1986), 82–117.

that the plaintiff in a contract dispute prevails only if there is a valid contract and that contract has been breached. Perhaps there are yet other necessary conditions as well, but those will be ignored here.

The pattern of judgments by the three judges generates the paradox: a majority of judges, reasoning individually, would decide against the plaintiff, but a majority of judges thinks that there was a valid contract and another majority thinks that it was breached. Clearly, there are several ways to deal with the decision.[18] One way is simply to have the group's judgment determined by a vote among the members, and so in this case to decide for the defendant. A second way is to determine the group's judgment on the premises—which Pettit calls premise-based decision making—and then if both of these judgments are positive have the court give a judgment for the plaintiff. Groups that have the capacity to act conversably might choose to commit themselves to the premise-driven strategy.[19]

In the example in Table 6.2, the premises are distinguished from the result somewhat artificially—by a conventional legal doctrine. But even when this structure is accepted, group members may feel more confident that there was a breach than that there was a valid contract. Or they might feel quite sure that there was both a contract and a breach, but still be unsure as to whether the plaintiff should prevail. In other words, they may have doubts about the doctrinal structure that appears to require that conclusion. A judge might think, for example, that there were mitigating circumstances that excuse the defendant from performing, even though the premises are both affirmed.[20] If this is right, a group committed to acting as a rational agent may wish to commit only

---

[18] The examples of the discursive dilemma in the paper all concern what are called conjunctive dilemmas. A person or group should decide in favor of some action only if it agrees to each of a series of premise judgments. A disjunctive dilemma arises when the group or person should decide in favor of some action only if it agrees to at least one of a series of premise judgments. The two kinds are formally equivalent in a natural sense. It might be claimed, implausibly I think, that in general, disjunctive dilemmas are more likely to be found in legislatures, and conjunctive ones in courts. The reason for the claim would be this: we expect legislatures to exhibit legitimate heterogeneity of interests and judgments, and so develop norms of legislative deliberation that permit agreement to a decision on any of a number of possibly incompatible grounds. Cass Sunstein has called such agreements "incompletely theorized". I don't deny that such agreements may be legitimate in legislatures, but I think that courts may sometimes adopt such agreements too. The Supreme Court's practice of issuing multiple opinions is an example. My reason for confining attention to the conjunctive case is merely one of convenience.

[19] Actually, any group might make a prior decision to commit to premise-based decision making; but this seems an unlikely choice. Suppose that the probability of discursive dilemma preference configurations is p. Then, if a group were to commit to deciding in the preference-based way, with probability $1 - p$, the outcome would be the same as a judgment-based decision. And with probability p, the outcome will differ from the judgment-based outcome and be inferior to it for a majority. This does not prove that such a commitment would never be made—that depends on how the outcomes are evaluated.

[20] This issue can be incorporated in this framework by including another column specifying whether each judge accepts the "logic" that if the premises are accepted, then the conclusion is to be agreed to. Or the additional premises that may be regarded as mitigating the plaintiff's obligations might be included as additional columns.

to deciding consistently, but not necessarily to premise-based decision making. But even with this weaker idea, the group is committed to making its choices on premises and outcomes coherent, perhaps by adjusting premise rather than outcome judgments. Pettit himself recognizes this kind of discursive consistency as reasoning by *modus tolens*.

Pettit's suggestions seem to me to be at once too modest and at the same time too mysterious. They are too modest in that, as argued earlier, we are not really free to limit the demand for coherence to (possibly small) homogeneous and well-integrated groups, or to groups externally charged to make coherent decisions. The requirement of conversability ought to fall on any group which takes actions that infringe on the interests of others, no matter what the characteristics of that group. Rather, conversability seems required in order to treat other peoples' interests appropriately.

Pettit's proposals are mysterious in that he recommends that the group itself somehow adopt a policy or commitment either to premise-driven reasoning or to some close variant of it, but doesn't really say why group members would agree to adopt such a policy. He might argue that premise-based reasoning (or its *modus tolens* cousin) is the only way to achieve coherence. That seems wrong. Otherwise, he needs an explanation as to why a social integrate would agree to adopt his procedure even when a majority of its members retain conflicting judgments as to what result ought to be reached (as in the examples). Why would a group remain committed to the majoritarian resolution of premise judgments when confronted with the dilemma?

In the example, such a commitment produces a win for the plaintiff, but only because of a self-imposed prohibition not to consider a vote on the result itself. But why prohibit that vote, and not prohibit a vote on one of the premises? Had the court decided to respect their individual judgments as to the result, and ruled for the defendant, it might well have refused to consider that there were majorities in favor of each of the doctrinal elements. Or it might say that judgments on doctrinal elements require unanimity, or at least a super-majority—that without consensus, the court cannot reach a conclusion those issues—but that justice requires a decisive or simple majoritarian procedure on the result. Failure to employ majority rule regarding the result is to put a thumb on the scale in favor of one or the other party.

In the conjunctive case (where agreement on all premises is required for a positive decision) result-based decision making could be seen as introducing a "bias" against group action. The only kind of (conjunctive) discursive dilemma that can arise is one in which the premise judgments are all positive, yet the group decides not to take a positive action. But the opposite interpretation seems as plausible: that premise-based reasoning supports "too many" positive decisions. Either it is "too easy" for a group to decide in a premise-based way in favor of an action, or it is "too hard" to take an action by a conclusion-oriented vote on the action. But the latter interpretation seems to me less plausible: when the premise-based judgments are as in Table 6.2, only a minority of judges believe that the defendant should win; why should their views outweigh those of the majority? It seems to me more natural for a group using a premise-based procedure to require super-majorities for agreeing to at least some of the premises.[21] In the three-person examples considered here, only procedures of this kind would demand unanimous consent on one or more premises.

I want to try another path. I want to say that because a group's decisions (on premises and conclusions) supervene on individual judgments, group members share responsibility for the pattern of outcomes—for final decisions as well as for premise judgments—and that this shared responsibility can be traced back to the actions of individual group members. The idea is that individual judgments about premises, as well as about the result, are normative recommendations as to how the group should act. And these individual expressions have a systematic relation to what the group ends up doing. Of course, that relation will sometimes be very weak—because the individual member in fact has either very common or very unusual preferences within the group, or because the group is so large that no member can be expected to have much actual chance of influencing its choices. Nevertheless, it seems to me that individuals can be held responsible for their effect on group action in some sense.

4. DELIBERATIVE ETHICS: PURE AND IMPURE DELIBERATION

So the question is: how ought deliberation to proceed in the circumstance described in Table 6.2? Can we devise or imagine a deliberative ethics to address this situation. The key idea is that, in collective decision making, the members bear responsibility for what the group does. Obviously this is true at the level of the group, as the group's decisions supervene on the judgments of the members. But, more strongly, individuals or subsets of individuals bear individual responsibility for their judgments insofar as, holding the actions of the others fixed, a change in these judgments would produce a change in the group's actions. Because the decision procedure permits certain members or subgroups to determine the outcome in various circumstances, individuals might plausibly be accountable for such choices.

There are a few observations that should be made about the structure of preferences in the discursive dilemma. First, we have already noted that in the conjunctive case the only kind of dilemma that can arise is one in which the results vote is negative while the premise-based votes are all positive. One interpretation of this is that under results voting the "status quo" (where the plaintiff loses)

---

[21] At least in the conjunctive case. In the case of a disjunctive dilemma we might, for formally equivalent reasons, be inclined to permit minority agreement to premises to have decisional weight.

is privileged relative to the premise-based outcome. Obviously, the status quo "bias" would be even greater had the affirmation of more premises been required for an affirmative premise-based vote. This implies that one way to resolve the dilemma—increasing the required majority for assent to the premises—might be unattractive, in that it would simply confer a bias in favor of the status quo to the premise-driven outcome as well.

Second, in this example, each member is "pivotal" to the pattern of outcomes: there is a way in which she could change her votes so that the pattern of outcomes would become coherent. Judge 1, for example, might decide that there was no valid contract: the result would then stay the same, but the premise judgments would no longer support an affirmative decision. Or she could decide that a breach occurred, which would lead her to change her result judgment to affirmative, so that, again, the pattern of outcomes would be coherent. It must be pointed out, though, that it is easy to construct discursive dilemmas so that no group member is pivotal. Suppose, for example, the rows in Table 6.2 were each to represent the judgments of three judges on a nine-person court. Then no judge is pivotal to any decision. Thus the deliberative principles that should govern this case cannot depend on pivotality in any obvious way.[22]

I want to distinguish two models of deliberation: pure and impure. In pure deliberation, the group deliberates about all of its judgments in a symmetric way, giving no priority to judgments about one issue over another. The aim is to produce a coherent, acceptable pattern of outcomes, and in this process each of the group's judgments is on the table for reconsideration. There may be substantive reasons why it is more difficult to adjust some judgments than others—some beliefs, for example, may be tethered to empirical evidence—but such considerations are invisible at the formal level of pure deliberation. And in any case, each of the judgments that must be made in these examples is a normative judgment that is not determined by factual considerations. The court needs to decide whether a given situation constitutes a contract, with all the attendant obligations to perform, or not. And similarly as to whether a certain action was a breach of a valid contract. There is no reason why judgments on these matters could not be shaped by considerations such as whether or not the defendant has acted wrongly all things considered. In other words, doctrinal structure is determined as cases are decided.

Impure deliberation has the group determine its judgment on some matters, and only then consider adjusting its later judgments. In Table 6.2, the court

---

[22] No single member is pivotal in the resultant decision; the displayed judgment profile at that decision is unanimous. Yet some subgroups can sensibly be thought pivotal, and therefore collectively responsible for that choice. This suggests a deliberative principle: a pattern of judgments is deliberatively stable if no subgroup of the members would be willing to change its premise or result judgments, assuming that those outside the group hold their judgments fixed. I don't follow this path, as I prefer to see the sense in which individuals may be assigned responsibility as in persons, and not as in members of a subgroup.

might decide to fix its collective judgment, irrevocably, on the first question of whether a valid contract exists, and then deliberate on the remaining issues without revisiting that judgment. I think it is clear enough why I call procedures of this kind impure. There is a sense in which there has been an artificial closing of debate on an issue, and a sense that the discursive dilemma has been arbitrarily broken, and not resolved.

Impure procedures may be adopted for reasons of practicality, or perhaps for some other reason relating to the formation of group intention. Members of a group deciding over time may feel bound by their prior decisions, for example. Allegiance to precedent is an example of an impure procedure: judges take issues decided in prior cases as fixed, and not normally open to reconsideration in a present case.[23] Or a group may parcel out its decision tasks to subgroups, and each subgroup may feel bound to honor the determinations of the others. The current example doesn't exhibit this idea, but one could imagine an appellate court stipulating facts established at trial as an example of this sort. So there seem to be a wide variety of impure procedures. We shall start by analyzing one such procedure that is, in fact, a variant of Pettit's models.

Impure Deliberation

Suppose that the court is to decide the case by taking two votes: first, on whether there was a valid contract, and second, on whether or not there was a breach. And then, following the premise-based procedure, the final result is determined by the premises accepted by the court; so the court procedure guarantees a coherent pattern of outcomes. The preferences are as given in Table 6.2. How would the court, configured in this way, decide the case? One way to answer this is to assume that the judges are sequentially rational in expressing their personal judgments, which means that at every point in which a judge needs to make a decision, that decision must be best for her from that point on. The judges are free to alter their initial judgments about preferences or results in light of earlier deliberations, so we need to specify the ways in which they may do this. For a start, let us assume that the judges are each more committed to their views as to how the case ought to be decided than they are to their judgments about the premises.

At the final decision node (when deciding on breach) each judge will need to decide how to vote on breach, recognizing that that vote may affect her own judgment as to the appropriate outcome and could affect how the case will come out. She will know how the court has decided on the contract issue. So, if the court has agree that the contract is valid, we can see that judges 1 and 2 now have reason to vote against breach. Judge 2, for example, would see that either her

---

[23] Of course, judges have devised ways to soften this procedural disposition by "distinguishing" a current case from prior ones, or even by overruling an existing precedent.

vote would make no difference to how the case would come out or else it would be pivotal to the outcome. If she were to vote for a breach, and her vote turned out to be pivotal, this would lead to a positive outcome, which is not the result she thinks is warranted. This means that following a positive determination that there is a contract, judge 2 has reason to alter her views as to whether was a breach or not. At the stage of deciding whether there is a contract, each judge would foresee the pattern of breach voting, and therefore that the court will decide that there has been no breach. So, no matter how the judges vote at the first stage, the case will be decided for the defendant. In other words, there is no deliberative "pressure" on their judgments about contract; they may freely vote their original convictions on this issue.

So, if the court adopts Pettit's premise-based procedure, and its members are result oriented and sequentially rational in the way assumed here, the outcome would be both in favor of the defendant and coherent: the plaintiff would fail to recover, and there would be a coherent explanation for that result. Note that had the votes occurred in the reverse order, the result would have been the same in this respect, though the voting pattern—and therefore the explanation offered to the parties—would have been different.

In this example there is of course no need to consider the question of coherence independently of the decision itself—Pettit's premise-based procedure, applied sequentially, guarantees that the result will cohere. But the outcome is the opposite of what Pettit hypothesizes under premise-based voting. This is not surprising, in that we assumed that judges guide their voting on premises in order to try to reach an appropriate final outcome. Had they been more confident in their views about the premises, perhaps none would change her views on premises, and the result would have been for the plaintiff, as in Pettit's analysis. Of course, some judges would have implicitly altered their original views as to the appropriate outcome of the case: in this case, judges 1 and 2 would have voted in ways that foreseeably produced the positive result. Therefore, depending on whether or not judges are result- or premise-oriented, sequential deliberation can produce changes in explicit or implicit prior judgments.

Indeed, if judges are result-oriented, they may decide to adopt Pettit's *modus tolens* procedure and simply vote on the result and on all but one of the premises, leaving the judgment on the final premise to be decided implicitly. Suppose, for example, that the first decision for the court is whether there was a valid contract, and the second is which party should prevail. In other words, the court does not explicitly take up the matter of breach, but leaves that to be settled implicitly. Consider the final vote on the result. Suppose that the court has already decided that the contract is valid. Then, judges 1 and 2 are free to vote their initial (negative) judgments as to the result, and the plaintiff loses. This of course implies that there was no breach, and each judge is assumed to have made a judgment on that issue that would support the result. This implies that judge 2 must be presumed to think that there was no breach, counter to her initial judgment on that matter. Again, the plaintiff loses, and there is a coherent explanation; but that explanation is different from the one produced for Pettit's *modus ponens* procedure.

While I don't have space to worry out the argument in detail, there is a theorem here that would have a statement roughly like this: in the conjunctive case, if the pattern of initial judgments produces a discursive dilemma, sequentially rational result-oriented players (in the sense given above) will always produce a coherent pattern of premise judgments supporting a negative result, irrespective of the order of voting. No discursive dilemma will be observed. The argument would go as follows: assume that there are k premises and n voters, that the underlying or prior judgments form a discursive dilemma, and that the premises are voted on first. Then, at a final node following a sequence of positive premise votes, for each person who prefers a negative result, voting against accepting the last premise weakly dominates voting for it, and, by assumption, this set of people forms a majority.[24] Thus the outcome is negative, and there is a coherent justification for it.[25] If the result itself was voted as one of the first k votes, it would fail, as there is no premise-based reason not to vote initial outcome preferences in the first k votes. And on every one of the k − 1 premise votes the judges are free to vote their initial judgments. Only the last premise judgment is to be implicitly fixed in a way that supports previous votes.

What if we assume that the judges are premise- rather than result-oriented, in the sense of being more confident in their premise judgments than in their views about the outcome? Obviously, on the first vote the judges would each vote her initial premise judgment; there is as yet no reason not to do so. But how should they vote on the second vote; on the outcome? In this case premise-oriented judges would vote in ways that support their initial premise judgments on the issue of breach. This implies that judge 2 has reason to vote for a positive outcome, since only that vote would permit her to support her initial premise judgment on breach.

It may seem that a particular idea of sequential rationality is playing too determinative a role in these examples. If that is the concern, there may be a reason to consider a different notion of sequential rationality, or, if you prefer, a different set of deliberative dispositions. One that might be proposed is the idea that once a group has made a decision on any of the issues, each member of the group ought to take that judgment for her own from that

---

[24] A strategy, x, weakly dominates another strategy, y, for a player, if the result of playing x always leaves the player at least as well off as playing y, and better off in some circumstances.

[25] I think that something like this could be established for indefinite procedures of the following kind: voting terminates whenever a result and a coherent pattern of premise votes are reached. Otherwise, it continues in a fixed order. The resulting extensive form is infinite, but has a simple Markovian structure. As long as the voters are (at least a little) impatient, I believe that there will be an equilibrium in which the game terminates after one round of voting, that it will not "reveal" a discursive dilemma, and that in the conjunctive case the result will be negative.

point forward, rather than applying the "backwards induction" notion given above. For example, consider the structure in which the court decides first on whether there is a contract, and then on whether there was a breach. Then, at the final node, following a group decision that there is a valid contract, judge 2 would now accept that judgment as her own and opt for deciding in favor of breach, and therefore endorse a finding against the defendant. On this principle of sequential rationality, the dilemma would again disappear: the premise judgments would both be positive and would agree with the positive result judgment. This might be a reason to adopt, as an ethical maxim, "accept prior group judgments as one's own in further deliberations". And such a disposition seems to support Pettit's ideas about how premise-based procedures would work.

But if members act on this maxim, the result is as arbitrary (or path-dependent) as before, in that it depends wholly on the order in which the group has taken up the issues. If, for example, the result had been voted on first (as in Pettit's *modus tolens* procedure), judge 3 would have had reason to adjust her views on one of the two premises in a negative way, as she would accept the negative results judgment as her own. Because of this arbitrariness, there is reason to consider a less structured decision-making context in which the agents are able to readjust any of their votes in light of the consequences of those votes. This idea is more in line with some ideas about deliberation, where the deliberators may reconsider and perhaps change their expressed preferences in light of the calculated effects of those expressions.

In any case, the deliberative practices described here may be troubling if one thinks that the judges are voting deceptively, concealing their own best judgments (on the premises) in order to produce an appearance of coherence. Perhaps this kind of voting is unacceptable in itself, even if the judge has no invidious reason for voting in this way. Perhaps that is reason to adopt an alternative maxim, one that is implicit in Pettit's work: that judges ought to stick with their initial premise judgments, and adopt the result that is required to vindicate those judgments. If they are unwilling to adhere to these initial judgments, they ought to rearrange the sequence of votes so that the result vote is taken earlier, as in the *modus tolens* procedure, and then adopt the following maxim: stick with initial judgments on every vote that is taken. But is it reasonable to suppose that judges could agree on which votes are to be taken prior to deliberating? And why should they privilege their initial judgments in this way, independently of how deliberations proceed? Perhaps it is better simply to abandon fixed sequences and try to see how pure deliberation might proceed.

Pure Deliberation

I shall assume, therefore, that judges place a value on producing a coherent pattern of results as well as on getting a good result: they want their premise judgments to support their final decision, and will see the failure of this coherence as a reason to continue deliberating. We can start by partitioning the set, X, of outcomes into the following subsets. Let YC be the set of voting patterns that would produce a yes on the result and a coherent set of premise judgments, NC a negative result with coherent preference judgments, YI yes vote with an incoherent set of premise judgments, and NI a no vote with incoherent judgments. So NI is the set of initial discursive dilemma preferences. We have already remarked that in the conjunctive case described in Table 6.2 YI is empty, so we need consider only three subsets. We may suppose that the judges have initial rankings of the elements in X, and that these rankings may be revised or adjusted in deliberation.

Now let's say that an outcome $x \varepsilon X$ is deliberatively unstable if someone may alter her judgments in such a way as to achieve a preferred outcome or a coherent voting pattern supporting the same outcome. The first thing to notice is that the pattern of initial judgments in Table 6.2 is deliberatively unstable. Judge 1 could alter her judgment on contract from Y to N and thereby produce a coherent pattern of judgments in support of the negative result. Or she could change her views about breach from N to Y as well as her view about the final result from N to Y to produce a coherent judgment pattern in support of a positive result.

Indeed, this seems to be a general result for three judges and any number of premises: every judgment pattern in NI is unstable. The argument would go like this: for any $x \varepsilon$ NI, there is at least one individual who is voting Y on a premise and N on the outcome and whose vote is pivotal on the premise. If she changes from Y to N on the premise, the resulting pattern is in NC, which is the better result for her. But the case of three voters is special in that for any profile in NI, there is always at least one player who is pivotal. If each of the rows in Table 6.2 were to represent three judges, none would be pivotal, and the pattern in Table 6.2 would be stable. For this reason it makes sense to require each judge to express her judgment on a question on the assumption that she is pivotal to deciding it. The presumption of pivotality is, in this setting, a device for focusing responsibility and organizing deliberation. It does not say what to do, but it says that individuals—judges in this case—ought to formulate their votes on the assumption that it makes a difference how they do so. And in particular, it makes a difference to how the court is able to present itself to those subject to its decisions.

So now we may consider the case where each of the rows in Table 6.2 represents three judges: no single member can change her ballot in a way that would alter the outcome on any vote, so no one is in fact pivotal to the outcome. But if the judges each vote conditional on pivotality, each judge with preferences in row 1 would reason that, conditional on pivotality, she has reason to alter her vote on contract from Y to N. If each judge in row 1 were to reason in this way, the pattern would shift from NI to NC, a result that each prefers. Thus, if deliberations were to reach the profile in Table 6.2, there is reason for each of the row 1 judges to decide that there has not been a valid contract.[26]

So now we show that (as long as there are only two possible outcomes) there are always deliberatively stable outcomes. There are two cases to consider. Assume that there is a majority that supports a positive vote on the outcome, and that x is a profile in which all of them vote Y on it. Clearly, each of these judges will have made positive judgments on each premise and, as they are a majority, x ε YC. Thus, each of these judges is getting her first best outcome, and can have no reason to alter her view. Now suppose that a majority prefers N on the outcome vote, and that each of them votes that way in the profile x. Clearly, each must have a negative judgment on at least one premise, and x may be contained in either NI or NC. If x ε NC, it is deliberatively stable, since a majority of the judges are getting the outcome they think best. If x ε NI, construct x' by having each member who votes N on the result also vote N on the first premise so that x' is in NC and is, by construction, deliberatively stable.

It is clear from this argument that there will usually be many deliberatively stable profiles, and so, in a sense, the court faces a kind of coordination problem in settling on one rather than another. Each of the different stable profiles reflects a different way in which judges adjust their views on the premises and outcomes. And, as the investigation here remains at a formal or nonsubstantive level, there seems to be no natural way to narrow this set of possible deliberative results. In specific cases there may well be substantive reasons for the court to choose one deliberatively stable profile over another. Moreover, we have said nothing about the dynamics of the deliberative process, and it is possible that institutional details of procedure might play a role here in making it more or less likely that certain stable profiles will be reached.[27]

Is there anything objectionable about the idea of members seeing all of their judgments, on premises as well as on results, as being in play during the deliberative process? Each of these judgments is a judgment as to what the group ought to do and, from a formal perspective, they are more or less symmetrical. Of course, there may be substantive reasons to insist that one judgment has priority over the others. One of them might be dictated by considerations of morality. Or perhaps some judgment is aimed at fitting external facts, so should be guided by considerations of accuracy in ways that make it difficult to defend adjusting it to achieve coherence. These are substantive issues, and perhaps controversial ones, that would themselves be the subject of deliberation.

---

[26] If not all of those switches are required, there is a kind of "bargaining" issue within the subgroup; but this consideration seems to fall outside the ethical perspective that I am trying to develop. All that could be said in that situation is that someone in a subgroup should reconsider how to vote, but which person that is would not be determinate.

[27] I am thinking here of the institutionally specific ways in which courts assemble majorities.

5. TOWARD LEGISLATIVE DELIBERATION

Legislating seems different from judging, in that it is more concerned with making new rules than applying existing ones.[28] Legislating seems more usually to involve substantive, rather than formal or doctrinal, issues in deciding what to do. How could a legislature, unguided by considerations of doctrine, seek to form and enact intentions? Without preexisting doctrine as a guide, a legislature seems free to reason about a decision in any way that it likes. It may individuate premises if its members agree, for example, and try to decide the outcome based on how premise judgments get made. It could, indeed, decide just how those premise judgments ought to relate to the choice of policy. Should the policy be adopted if all premise judgments come out in favor? If most of them do? An answer to questions of this sort obviously cannot be decided at this level of abstraction, but must depend on the substance of the issue and the nature of considerations that might count for or against it. This is too much to take up here.

But we can consider a modest departure from the stylized judicial setting considered in the previous section to analyze a slightly more complex example of Pettit's discursive dilemma, one that I discussed briefly in the introduction. We will ignore the fact that legislation is normally produced by bodies of elected representatives and binds citizens generally. Insofar as representatives may be held accountable in elections, the demand for conversability may be somewhat less than in the judicial case. But elections are blunt instruments, so I think that there is still good reason to require a coherent explanation for new laws.

So imagine that the legislature is faced with an external security threat and is considering setting up a new agency with powers to interfere with certain rights or interests. We may envision two substantive issues: Is the security threat serious enough to warrant the new agency? And, assuming that the threat is serious, are its proposed powers safely lodged in the agency? But now there is a third, formal issue: if it is determined that the threat is serious and that the powers are safely instituted, should the legislature regard that as a sufficient reason to enact the law?

The situation in Table 6.3 is an example of Pettit's discursive dilemma, but in this example the legislature is also able to decide whether or not it should be bound

[28] This is meant only as a rough distinction, as it is clear enough that courts often engage in rule making, if only implicitly. But it is possible to argue that the notion of parliamentary sovereignty, which is said to be the foundation of some legal systems, may force a sharp distinction between two kinds of institutions. Courts may be said to be "bound" by doctrine in some way; but if a legislature were to be bound in this way, it would not be sovereign. I sidestep this kind of issue in the following, assuming that the issue of conversability or coherence is addressed by the legislature itself at the moment of decision, and is not imposed upon it by a previous legislature, or court, or any other entity.

Table 6.3.

	Serious threat (S)?	Safely instituted (SI)?	S&SI → enact?	Enact law?
A	Y	N	Y	N
B	N	Y	Y	N
C	Y	Y	N	N

by its decisions on the substantive premises. In effect, it can choose to adopt a "doctrinal" structure to guide its decisions in order to ensure that they cohere in the way that conversability requires. And here we see that while a majority favors this idea, member C opposes it. So the dilemma now has the additional twist that the members may vote in favor of something like conversability as a principle, affirm both substantive premises, but refuse nevertheless to enact the law itself. In this case none of the legislators, based on their own judgments and reasoning with respect to all three issues, favors enacting the law. If we confine our attention to the substantive issues in the first and second columns, the example is the same as that in Table 6.2: a majority thinks that there is a serious threat to security, and a majority thinks that the agency can be trusted to make appropriate judgments about rights, but a majority opposes the legislation.

This seems to be a case in which Pettit's proposal for premise-based decision making might be attractive. One can imagine the legislature deciding in this case to follow the premise based recommendations and enact the new law, notwithstanding the unanimous opposition to it, if it were to come to a vote. But, based on the analysis of the judicial case, we know that if the members are result-oriented—if they are more confident in their own independently derived conclusions than they are in the aggregative results of voting—they would vote sequentially in a way that would produce a negative result with a coherent explanation.

It could be objected that to be results oriented in this way is somehow to express distrust in the operation of the deliberative process in the legislature. Result-oriented members refuse to take seriously the results of the deliberations about premises. Indeed, their failure to take these deliberations seriously is expressed in their willingness to change their views on premises to get a result they see as best. Perhaps it is true that legislative deliberations are less likely to produce reliable judgments about the premises that may support a decision than about the decision itself. The premises that may go into supporting a decision may be more or less freely chosen by the legislature itself without preexisting doctrinal or logical restrictions. And evidentiary standards in legislatures are at best vague in comparison to those in courts. But when it comes to deciding on the outcome of something—a decision that may impose costs and benefits on constituents—legislatures normally recognize that they may be held accountable, electorally or morally. So there may be less reason for legislators to agree to be bound by its premise judgments in this circumstance. Perhaps that justifies C's vote against such binding in Table 6.3. Perhaps, when it comes to legislatures rather than courts, the accountability for results is all the discipline that can plausibly be imposed. And if that is right, the things for which they will most likely be held accountable for are decisions that have impacts on citizens: that is, votes on results, and not on premises.

In any case, there is no a priori reason to assume that legislators will always be more inclined to trust their own individual deliberative capacities to reason to the best result over the legislators' collective capacity to "reason together". One can imagine circumstances in which a legislature deploys its internal procedures to decide on premises that either naturally or conventionally seem necessary for a particular decision, in a way that its members have confidence in judgment on premises. If that were to occur for some issue, the members might freely decide that they had sufficient faith in their collective premise judgments to be willing to let the outcome be decided in the way that Pettit supposes: by reference to the pattern of collective premise judgments.

6. SOME CONCLUDING REMARKS: STATUTES AS PARTIAL PLANS

Suppose, finally, that a collective body must make a decision based partly on past findings or decisions. Last year the legislature voted to begin a new program for funding prescription drugs, based presumably on whatever reasons were before it at the time, and now it must decide whether to appropriate funds for the program. It seems wrong to think of this decision as one that stands free in time; rather, it is part of a longer legislative project. Michael Bratman argues that when thinking about what to do, people have reason to adopt what he calls "partial plans", which specify perhaps some goal that is to be reached but which do not, at the beginning, contain a lot of detail as to how that goal will actually be pursued.[29] Rather, they make some initial decisions that are necessary or at least supportive of attaining the goal, leaving until later the taking of additional decisions that may be necessary. The partial plan has an intentional aspect—the person has a goal that she intends to reach, and to do this will require planning: arranging her activities in ways that bring that end into being. The partial plan gives her reasons for taking or not taking various actions as time goes on, by filling in or completing the plan, and not taking actions inconsistent with it. Insofar as she responds to these reasons by choosing actions that enable her to achieve her goal, the plan plays a role in coordinating her actions over time.

---

[29] Michael Bratman, *Intention, Plans, and Practical Reason* (Cambridge, Mass.: Harvard University Press, 1987; paperback edn. 1990; reissued 1999 by CSLI Publications); idem, *Faces of Intention: Selected Essays on Intention and Agency* (Cambridge: Cambridge University Press, 1999).

As far as I can see, groups have, if anything, even more need for planning than individuals. The coordination problems they face are more extensive and difficult. They often face problems of explanation and justification when defending their actions to those who may be affected by them, either inside or outside the group. And, as a matter of fact, it seems that groups often do develop policies that look pretty much like Bratman's partial plans. Moreover, those policies are often defended and adjusted in view of the various purposes they may serve. So group plans seem to exhibit the kind of premise-based structure that Pettit describes. Legislative statutes seem especially apt examples: statutes typically embody certain purposes (even if these are only vaguely specified, and even if those purposes are in some tension with one another); they are incompletely specified; and they give reasons for the members of the legislature and for others (judges, bureaucrats, ordinary people) to arrange their lives in ways that those purposes can be advanced.

The legislature may of course refuse to fund the program. And this may be justifiable if somehow circumstances have changed in certain ways. Perhaps the need for the program has been shown to be less than had been thought, or that its costs have increased. These could count as reasons for rejecting the partial plan. But ordinarily, without some new and unexpected information, we would expect, and the members would expect as well, that there would be reason to fund the program. But suppose there has been no such new information. We could represent this issue as one in which premise-based findings had been made in a previous session of the legislature, and the question facing the legislature now is whether to do what the premise judgments together point to or, instead, for the members to decide whether to fund the program based on their own prior premise judgments. Specifically, suppose that the members decide in the premise-based way to enact the program based on their premise judgments in Table 6.4.

Are the members now somehow obliged to proceed to fund the program even though, as before, a majority would have preferred not to, given their prior judgments on the premises? It seems plausible that the legislature at the funding stage ought to take its prior determinations as fixed, and not ordinarily revisable without new and surprising information. To do otherwise is to make the vote on enactment a form of posturing or position taking. So if the legislators decided to enact the program, they ought to be willing to fund it without reopening the original issue. There are, of course, reasons against adopting this general

Table 6.4.

	Need program	Costs bearable	Enact program	Fund program
A	Y	N	N	N
B	N	Y	N	N
C	Y	Y	Y	Y

policy too. There is something arbitrary about it, in that the group is somehow forcing itself to take certain issues as fixed or settled and then make decisions automatically based on those prior decisions. This is not to say that there are never reasons to reopen old decisions or to overturn established policies. Courts, after all, sometimes decide not to honor a precedent or even to overturn it. And sometimes in the course of planning, we come to see that the end we have been pursuing is not really worth the sacrifices it demands of us. But these events must be fairly rare in the lives of well-ordered people or collectivities, and must normally, it seems, be based on some real change in circumstances.

Indeed, there is something to be said for the idea that funding raises the issue of trading off spending money on this program rather than another, and so ought not to be determined automatically by a previous decision to enact the program.[30] One can imagine the legislators deciding to enact the program based on their collective premise judgments, but then deciding later as individual members not to fund it. Perhaps the issue of cost, which was relevant at the earlier stage, is simply too powerful a consideration for member A to permit her to vote to fund the program at the end. So, while premise-oriented decision making may be attractive at the enactment stage, when it comes to funding, the members ought to be willing to stand before their constituents as free deliberators who will be held responsible for the consequences of their acts. If this is right, enacting the program cannot be taken as a precedent for any kind for funding: it is an answer to a completely different question from that asked at the time of funding. Indeed, if the members vote automatically in the premise-oriented way on enactment, they have done no more than repeat their earlier findings on premises. Nothing new has been decided.

'For these reasons, it seems that the profile in Table 6.4 represents a real and sometimes difficult political circumstance. It seems to raise the issue of whether Bratman's planning views are viable for legislation. Or better, if one assumes as I do that the planning view is more or less required by conversability, it raises the issue of whether members ought to vote in the automatic, premise-oriented way that Pettit suggests on the enactment vote, or whether they should act in the result-oriented way that they will on the funding vote. Even though the enactment vote has no immediate consequence, and even though members may not therefore be held accountable for it by their constituents, a positive outcome on that vote is required for implementation of the program. To support the program at this stage, knowing that there will not be support for funding, is to behave in an incoherent manner, and not as a planner. As there is no new information that is learned between these stages, the planning view urges that the stages ought to be decided in a consistent manner. Therefore, members have reason to deliberate in the result-oriented way on enactment if that is how they are inclined to decide on funding.

---

[30] Also, members of Congress often seem to find it politically advantageous to treat the enactment decision as having no obligating consequences at all; as an opportunity to express costless support for a popular idea.

7

Pettit's Molecule

Jeremy Waldron

1. MISGIVINGS

The most striking thing in Philip Pettit's political philosophy is his attempt to replace the standard liberal conception of negative freedom with a conception of freedom as non-domination, which he associates with the republican rather than the liberal tradition of political thought. Since I first read Pettit's book *Republicanism: A Theory of Freedom and Government*,[1] I have had my doubts about this contrast, and about the appeal of the Pettit's conception. But I never could quite put my finger on these misgivings. Now I think I can.

2. RIVAL CONCEPTIONS OF FREEDOM

Let us begin with a brief summary of each conception. What I refer to as negative liberty involves a definition of freedom as the absence of external interference with a person's actions, specifically the absence of human interference. "I am normally said to be free", says Isaiah Berlin, "to the degree to which no man or body of men interferes with my activity."

[L]iberty in this sense is simply the area within which a man can act unobstructed by others. If I am prevented by others from doing what I could otherwise do, I am to that degree unfree.... The criterion of oppression is the part that I believe to be played by other human beings, directly or indirectly, with or without the intention of doing so, in frustrating my wishes.[2]

---

[1] Philip Pettit, *Republicanism: A Theory of Freedom and Government* (Oxford: Oxford University Press, 1999).
[2] Isaiah Berlin, "Two Concepts of Liberty", in his *Four Essays on Liberty* (Oxford: Oxford University Press, 1969), 118–72, p. 122.

We are accustomed to regarding Thomas Hobbes as the high priest of negative freedom[3] and chapter 21 of *Leviathan* as the *locus classicus* of the position:

Liberty, or Freedome, signifieth (properly) the absence of Opposition; (by Opposition, I mean externall Impediments of motion;) . . . For whatsoever is so tied, or environed, as it cannot move but within a certain space, which space is determined by the opposition of some external body, we say it hath not Liberty to go further.[4]

Our custom is to call this *the* negative conception of freedom or, to use Berlin's terms "[t]he notion of negative freedom". However, strictly speaking, "negative freedom" is the name of a family of positions, distinguished from one another by (among other things) what they recognize as interference. Some define interference as physical restraint only, and they exclude coercion by threats, while other conceptions regard threats too as a form of interference.[5] Some define interference as deliberate human restraint; others are willing to include inadvertent restraint or restraint as a by-product of other intentional actions, individually or en masse.[6] But these various conceptions have in common something that Jeremy Bentham pointed out in a passage that Pettit quotes:[7] freedom is treated as a *negative* concept, since it is taken to connote the absence of something and to be non-committal on what is affirmatively supposed to exist—in the way of free decision making—in the space that is left when interference and obstructions are cleared away.

Positive freedom, too, must be regarded as a label for a *type* of position, and the point is even clearer there. There is no one view that counts as *the* conception of positive freedom. On the contrary, there are all sorts of different positive accounts of what truly free decision making consists in—Rousseau's conception, Hegel's conception, Raz's, St Paul's, and so on.[8] Diverse though

---

[3] As we proceed, we may want to modify this characterization. One of the interesting things about Hobbes's approach is that evidently he does not think liberty is really all that important—it's much less important than security, he argues. And what he thinks is unimportant is precisely *liberty defined in the negative way* that we are all familiar with. The stridency of his insistence on the negative conception is thus not correlated with any sense that liberty is the key to normative political philosophy. See below, n. 44 and accompanying text.

[4] Thomas Hobbes, *Leviathan*, rev. edn., ed. Richard Tuck (Cambridge: Cambridge University Press, 1996), 145.

[5] As Pettit points out (*Republicanism*, 37), Hobbes toys with both these conceptions: on the one hand he says that "Feare, and Liberty are consistent: . . . [a]nd generally all actions which men doe in Common-wealths, for feare of the law, are actions, which the doers had liberty to omit" (Hobbes, *Leviathan*, 146); on the other hand, he says that men have "made Artificiall chains, called Civill Laws", adding that it is "[i]n relation to these Bonds only . . . that I am to speak now, of the Liberty of Subjects" (*Leviathan*, 147).

[6] Cf. F. A. Hayek, *The Constitution of Liberty* (London: Routledge & Kegan Paul, 1960), 133 ff.

[7] Pettit, *Republicanism*, 44.

[8] Jean-Jacques Rousseau, *The Social Contract* (bk. I, ch. 8), in *Rousseau: The Social Contract and Other Later Political Writings*, ed. Victor Gourevitch (Cambridge: Cambridge University Press, 1997), 53–4; G. W. F. Hegel, *Elements of the Philosophy of Right*, (sect. 149 and "addition"), ed. Allen Wood (Cambridge: Cambridge University Press, 1997), 192–3; Joseph Raz, *The Morality of Freedom* (Oxford: Clarendon Press, 1986), 369 ff.; Rom. 7: 15–18.

they are, Philip Pettit insists that what *he* opposes to negative liberty is not one of these positive conceptions.[9] His conception has little or nothing to say about the phenomenology or moral quality of "truly free" decision making. It is closer to the negative conception—actually closer, I am going to argue, than Pettit wants us to believe—but certainly closer even on his own account, because it is concerned with what goes on *outside* the agent, in his relation with others, not with what goes on inside, when the agent is said to be free or unfree.

According to Pettit, a person is free when he is not dominated by another. Freedom, he thinks, is a relational matter: it is a matter of dependence and independence as relations between persons. Freedom is not having to live "at the mercy of another . . . in a manner that leaves you vulnerable to some ill that the other is in a position arbitrarily to impose", like a wife at the mercy of a brutal husband or a worker cowed by his employer.[10] And whether or not I am independent of another is a matter of the power that the other has, which gives him a capacity to interfere with me, whether he actually exercises that capacity or not. For I may well defer to what I take to be another's wishes or interests simply because I perceive that he *can* coerce me; I don't need to wait until he actually does. If I defer to him in this way, I am surely as subservient, as much a slave to him, as I would be if I were responding directly to his force or his threats. So that's the first distinctive thing about the Pettit conception—the emphasis on capacity. I shall call this "the capacity point". And the second distinctive feature of Pettit's conception is that he is not interested in the capacity to interfere *tout court*. He is interested in the capacity to interfere *arbitrarily*, and much of his exposition of the non-domination conception has to do with the elucidation of this term "arbitrariness". (Briefly, interference is arbitrary, according to Pettit, when it is exercised without reference to the interests or opinions of the person affected by it.[11]) I shall call this "the arbitrariness point".

It is worth noting, as a point of initial interest, that there seems to be no particular reason why these two features should go together. One could imagine a conception of liberty which restricted the interference in which it was interested to *arbitrary* interference: one could say, as a modification of the Berlin position, that liberty is the area within which a man can act without being *arbitrarily* obstructed by others, and that only if he is *arbitrarily* prevented by others from doing what he could otherwise do, is he to that extent unfree. No doubt this would be a very considerable modification of the traditional non-interference view. But it wouldn't necessarily bring the capacity point along with it. Similarly, one could pursue the capacity point without committing oneself to the arbitrariness point. One could say that a person is unfree when another has the capacity to interfere with him, whether that is a capacity for arbitrary or for non-arbitrary interference. To establish a link between the two ideas, we have to focus our attention on a third notion, which in most cases comes along with the other two but is logically independent of them: we may say that one person, Q, has the capacity to interfere with another person, P, only if there are two or more choices available to Q so far as possible impact on P is concerned, and Q is in a position to choose among those two or more options.[12] If this is an implication of the very idea of a capacity to interfere, then it seems to follow that capacity to interfere implies the prospect of arbitrary interference. For if Q can choose among these options as he pleases, without regard to the interests of P, it follows that he can act arbitrarily so far as P is concerned. In fact, however, a capacity to interfere need not always involve choices of this kind. And even when it does, the choices may be such that choosing among them is necessarily non-arbitrary: Q may face two choices impacting on P, both of which are for P's interest but only one of which may be chosen. In these ways, then, the capacity point and the arbitrariness point can still come apart.

This is not necessarily a criticism. There is no particular reason why the different features of a conception of freedom have to be related to one another or cast light on one another. It is interesting, however, that in the case of many positive conceptions of liberty, which also involve a distinction between arbitrary and non-arbitrary interference, there *is* a tighter relation between the constituent elements of the conception than we find in Pettit's case. Characteristically, a positive theory of freedom will specify a mode of decision making which counts as truly free decision making; and in some conceptions there will also be a suggestion that certain justified external constraints and interferences do not count as derogations from freedom when they are imposed on an agent. In these conceptions of positive liberty, the connection is that properly justified interferences—interferences which are non-arbitrary in the relevant sense—interfere only with *fake* exercises of freedom, not with true exercises of freedom (as distinguished by the other part of the theory). So I may be "forced to be free", in Rousseau's phrase,[13] by certain forms of non-arbitrary interference, which impact only upon my lower self or my bestial self, not upon the self that really chooses in the manner in which true choice ought to be exercised. But this is a digression. In general, my worry that the capacity point and the arbitrariness point come apart opens up Pettit's conception only to charges of eclecticism, and at worst that's a technical misdemeanor.

3. HISTORY: HOBBES, BENTHAM, AND THE REPUBLICANS

In mitigation of whatever misdemeanor is involved, Pettit will remind us that the non-domination conception, with its two distinctive but conceptually quite

---

[12] I owe this suggestion to Robert Goodin.
[13] Rousseau, *Social Contract* (bk. I, ch. 7), p. 53.

separate features, is not something he has constructed on his own, but something he has resurrected out of an older political tradition—the tradition of republican thought. He may plead that he has had to take that tradition more or less as he found it, eclecticism or no. In other words, Pettit is not *advising* us to associate an interest in arbitrariness with a quite separate interest in the importance of capacities for interference, as though this were a novel suggestion; he is rather reminding us that these two things have in fact been associated in this older political tradition. In their battles against slavery, in their resistance to monarchy, and in their opposition to various other forms of subservience, republican theorists found it politically convenient to package together these different concerns and present them in combination under the label of "liberty".[14] And—Pettit is suggesting—this might be something that is worthwhile for us to do as well.

That is fair enough. But now I want to pursue a slightly different point about the historical pedigree of these various conceptions of liberty. Pettit suggests that the conception of liberty he is promoting must be understood as emerging out of a particular historical tradition of republican struggle and resistance, and he believes that we can advance our understanding of liberal traditions of negative liberty in this light as well. The idea is that negative liberty emerges as part of a particular series of political campaigns and that republican liberty emerges as part of a different series of political campaigns. But I actually doubt whether this is the best way to understand a given conception of liberty. Is it really the case that the great political theorists we study formed their conceptions of freedom purely to advance a political agenda? I guess that Pettit can speak for the civic republicans, but what he says in his book about the other tradition—about the negative liberty conceptions of classic liberal theorists like Thomas Hobbes or Jeremy Bentham—strikes me as reductive, and a little misleading, historically as well as philosophically. Hobbes's aim, says Pettit, was to support authoritarianism and discredit republican opposition to absolutism, and that was why he developed a negative conception.[15] To this end, he says, Hobbes wanted a concept of liberty that would allow him to say that there was as little freedom under republican laws as under laws made by a monarch: all law restricts liberty. And Jeremy Bentham, he says, was worried that a republican conception of liberty as non-domination would require the emancipation of women and servants; since Bentham did

---

[14] See also Quentin Skinner, *Liberty before Liberalism* (Cambridge: Cambridge University Press, 1997) for further elaboration of republican conceptions of liberty.

[15] Philip Pettit, *A Theory of Freedom: From the Psychology to the Politics of Agency* (New York: Oxford University Press, 2001), 145: "Hobbes was an absolutist about the state, believing that only a government with the absolute power of a Leviathan, as he described it, could hope to ensure peace in a time of religious and civil strife. In the attempt to defend that state—an anathema to contemporary republicans—he defined political freedom in a wholly new way and used the definition to argue that people could be just as free under Leviathan as under a republic." See also Pettit, *Republicanism*, 38: "[Hobbes's] own ultimate end was the defence of authoritarian government, and it served his purposes well to be able to argue that no set of laws was particularly associated with liberty."

not want to be branded as a radical, he tried to suppress that conception and go back to the Hobbesian tradition.[16] I disagree with both claims as theorems in the history of ideas. My bristling at them is partly my usual response to Cambridge-style reductivism in the history of political philosophy, whereby Peter Laslett, Quentin Skinner, and some of their followers have tried to bully students into treating works of political philosophy as nothing but politically motivated pamphlets, and into treating analytic or philosophical argument as nothing more than ad hoc and politically motivated rhetorical maneuvers. (I have fought that hard in the case of John Locke, for example.[17]) But I think that this sort of reductivism is particularly off the mark in the present cases. In that of Thomas Hobbes, it underestimates the strand of Galilean science and analysis in his work, a strand which was not appropriated just for political reasons, and which is highly relevant to what Hobbes was doing in and around the concept of freedom.[18] And similarly in the case of Bentham. Both thinkers were convinced—rightly or wrongly in the case of Hobbes, rightly without doubt in the case of Bentham—that contemporary thought about law and politics (that of Hobbes's republican contemporaries; that of Blackstone and the common lawyers in the case of Bentham) was a hopeless muddle, which needed analytic redemption. And it needed analytic redemption not just—or even mainly—to avoid untoward political consequences, but to advance the scientific enterprise of getting some clarity in these murky areas of rhetoric.

Even in terms of the debate between Hobbes and his republican contemporaries, Pettit's characterization is misleading. Hobbes did not in fact use the negative conception to argue that there was no difference in the extent of liberty under different regimes. The conception cannot support this conclusion, and Hobbes himself acknowledges that the degree of liberty may be variable. If we define liberty, with Hobbes, as the silence of the laws, then patently the laws may be more or less silent. Hobbes certainly wanted to warn us that when the laws are silent in a given area, that may mean that other threats to liberty—e.g. the aggression of private men—will rampage unabated. But he is not asserting any thesis of a constant quantum of liberty taking public and private interferences

---

[16] Pettit, *A Theory of Freedom*, 148: "What is much more likely to have influenced Bentham and [William] Paley, however, is this. . . . If they said that the state should provide for the freedom of people in general and took freedom in the sense of non-domination, then they would have to argue in an impossibly radical vein that contemporary family and master–servant law should be overthrown; according to that law, after all, women and servants were inherently subject to their masters and incapable of enjoying non-domination. Their solution to that problem was to give up the ideal of non-domination in favour of the ideal of non-interference." The evidence that Pettit adduces is evidence for attributing this motivation to Paley; but he provides no evidence for attributing it to Bentham, who seems to be tarred here simply by association.

[17] See Jeremy Waldron, *God, Locke, and Equality: Christian Foundations of Locke's Political Thought* (Cambridge: Cambridge University Press, 2002), 11–12, 50–2.

[18] See the discussion of Hobbes's approach to science in David Johnston, *The Rhetoric of Leviathan: Thomas Hobbes and the Politics of Cultural Transformation* (Princeton: Princeton University Press, 1986).

into account. The laws *may* speak when they need not, and Hobbes is willing to concede to his critics that what we want is "few lawes, few things forbidden, and those the sorts of things without which there would be no Peace".[19] For the purposes of this criterion, he says, it does not matter whether you are dealing with a monarchy or a democracy.[20]

It is true, as Pettit says, that Hobbes writes in *Leviathan* that a citizen has no more liberty in a republic like Lucca than a subject has under despotism in Constantinople. But this Lucca/Constantinople equivalence is not advanced as a general proposition. The context is a discussion of what it means to say that a city is free, which has to do with its external relations with other states. The ancient republics were free, Hobbes concedes, in the sense that they were not subject to regular interference by other states (though this meant of course that they were constantly at war), and so was Constantinople. But we cannot infer from that—"infer" is Hobbes's word, and it makes the relativity to context explicit—"that a particular man has more Libertie, or Immunitie from the service of the Commonwealth there, than in Constantinople".[21]

Pettit notes that, nevertheless, republicans like Harrington did contest even this limited version of the Lucca/Constantinople equivalence. Harrington did so mainly on the ground of lack of political participation: the man allegedly constrained by the laws of Lucca has had a voice in making them, whereas the man in Constantinople has not.[22] But it is significant that *this* is actually a part of the republican heritage that Pettit wants to distance himself from.[23] (He wants to be free to defend non-participatory modes of political decision making for the modern world, like American-style judicial review of legislation,[24] and he does not want his republicanism to prevent him from denigrating democratic decision making by association with what he says is "the ultimate form of arbitrariness: the tyranny of the majority".[25]) In other words, Pettit picks and chooses among various aspects of the republican heritage. And in the end, ironically, just like Hobbes, Pettit thinks that participation in lawmaking is an anachronistic hangover from the liberty of the ancients, and that it is not part and parcel of a useful modern conception of liberty as non-domination.

Let me also say something about Jeremy Bentham. I don't believe that there is any evidence for Pettit's suggestion that Bentham was attracted to negative liberty mainly because he "saw in it a way of conceiving of freedom that would

---

[19] Thomas Hobbes, *On the Citizen* (ch. 10, sect. 8), ed. Richard Tuck and Michael Silverthorne (Cambridge: Cambridge University Press, 1998), 121.

[20] "If they understand liberty to mean few lawes, few things forbidden, and those the sorts of things without which there would be no Peace; then I deny that there is more liberty in Democracy than in a Monarchy. For Monarchy can rightly coexist with such liberty as well as Democracy" (ibid.).

[21] Hobbes, *Leviathan* (ch. 21), p. 149.   [22] See Pettit, *Republicanism*, 39.

[23] Ibid. 27, 180 ff.   [24] Ibid. 180–3.

[25] Ibid. 8. I am not sure what "ultimate" is supposed to mean here: the most oppressive form of arbitrariness, or the most likely, or a paradigm case of arbitrariness, or what?

allow even dominated agents like women and servants—so far as they did not suffer actual interference—to count as free".[26] In fact the negative definition of freedom is an integral part of the philosophical construction with which Bentham confronted what he regarded (rightly) as the sloppy thinking and the equivocations of William Blackstone and other theorists of English common law. Bentham's position—that all law restricts liberty, and that there is on that account a presumption (albeit an easily defeasible presumption) against it—is bound up with the detail of his jurisprudence, on the one hand, and of his utilitarianism, on the other. So far as the jurisprudence is concerned, Bentham tells us that law is a kind of command, issued by a sovereign and backed up by a threat. It is a paradigm case of interference by one person (or assemblage of persons) in the action of another, and when we are subject to law, we are to that extent unfree. Does this mean that our unfreedom is always *pro tanto* an evil? Well, it is not surprising that Bentham held that it was, since, characteristically, interference prevents us from doing what we want, and it is axiomatic in Bentham's utilitarian moral theory that the frustration of a want is always *pro tanto* an evil, though of course not a conclusive one. Another way of putting this is to say that the emphasis on non-interference in Bentham's conception of freedom is key to his theory of responsible lawmaking:

There is always a reason against every coercive law—a reason which, in default of any opposing reason, will always be sufficient in itself: and that reason is, that such a law is an attack upon liberty. He who proposes a coercive law ought to be ready to prove, not only that there is a specific reason in favour of it, but that this reason is of more weight than the general reason against every such law.[27]

I suppose that Bentham could have made something like this point about the need for care in lawmaking without associating the word "liberty" with the *prima facie* objectionable feature of every law. He could just have said that law frustrates wants, and reserved the word "liberty" to apply only to those actions that will be permitted by justified laws and not to the actions that justified laws prohibit.[28] But if one thinks—I am actually not sure whether Bentham believed this or not—that there is something specially bad (though of course, again, not

---

[26] See Pettit, *Republicanism*, 272.

[27] Jeremy Bentham, *"Principles of the Civil Code"*, in his book, *The Theory of Legislation*, ed. C. K. Ogden (London: Kegan Paul, Trench, Trubner & Co., 1931), 94.

[28] Bentham's own objection to this is mainly fulmination: "The proposition that every law is contrary to liberty, though as clear as evidence can make it, is not generally acknowledged. On the contrary, those among the friends of liberty who are more ardent than enlightened, make it a duty of conscience to combat this truth. And how? They pervert language; they refuse to employ the word *liberty* in its common acceptation; they speak a tongue peculiar to themselves. This is the definition they give of liberty: *Liberty consists in the right of doing every thing which is not injurious to another*. But is this the ordinary sense of the word? Is not the liberty to do evil liberty? If not, what is it? What word can we use in speaking of it? Do we not say that liberty should be taken away from idiots, and bad men, because they abuse it? According to this definition, I can never know whether I have the liberty to do an action, until I have examined all its consequences?" (ibid., 94–5).

conclusively bad) about frustrating active desires, i.e. desires that people would otherwise act on themselves, then one might want to have *some* special term (e.g. "loberty") for what is stake when society stops people *doing* something they want as opposed to just not satisfying some want. And the thing about loberty is that it would be important for us to be able to deploy it in our calculations about whether a proposed law is justified or whether an action we propose to prohibit is wrong: we would add up how much loberty the proposed law frustrates and how much loberty it protects, and we would add in any other relevant preferences on both sides, and do our calculation. Maybe we would embody the results of our calculation in a Pettit-style conception of *liberty*. But "loberty" could not do the work we need done in the calculation unless its use was non-committal on the question of the justifiability or arbitrariness of the restrictions under consideration.

4. MORALIZED CONCEPTIONS OF LIBERTY

I believe that what I said in the last paragraph indicates the possibility of a serious difficulty in Pettit's account. No doubt liberty becomes a nicer concept—more inspiring, more morally respectable—when it is used only to oppose arbitrary interference, and when it protects only responsible actions. (It is very distasteful to have to talk about the liberty of a rapist or a murderer, which is what we have to do on Bentham's usage.) But though it may be nicer, it is not necessarily as serviceable. There is work to be done in justifying (or debating the justification of) our laws and principles that requires something like a non-moralized view of liberty (whatever we call it). So it is not enough for Pettit to show (if he can) that the non-domination conception is more attractive. He would also have to show that there is no work to be done—under something like the heading of liberty—that would require the other conception.

To elaborate this, let me back up a little bit. I said at the outset that Pettit's conception of freedom is distinguished by two features: (i) his emphasis on capacity for interference, as opposed to interference itself, and (ii) his emphasis on arbitrary interference, rather than interference of all sorts. We will focus on (ii) for the purposes of the argument I am about to make. Interference is arbitrary, according to Pettit, when it is exercised without reference to the interests or opinions of the person affected by it.[29]

On the face of it, Pettit's point (ii) seems quite different from the sort of moralized definitions that Bentham was attacking—"Liberty consists in the power of doing every thing which does not hurt another" or "Being unrestrained in doing evil is not liberty". The definitions that Bentham was targeting have the consequence that interference with P is not excluded when it prevents P from

---

[29] Pettit, *Republicanism*, 55.

harming Q's interests, or when it prevents P from doing wrong; whereas Pettit's definition has the consequence that interference with P is not arbitrary when it is attuned affirmatively to P's interests and opinions. These positions—Pettit's and the position attacked by Bentham—look as though they should come apart, that is, in cases where P has an interest in doing wrong or in harming Q. In fact, Pettit wants to block this move. He says that non-arbitrary interference with P tracks *some* of P's interests (his "relevant" interests) and not others:

I may have an interest in the state imposing certain taxes or in punishing certain offenders.... But I may still not want the state to impose taxes on me—I may want to be an exception—or I may think that I ought not to be punished in the appropriate manner, even though I have been convicted of an offence. In such a case, my relevant interests and ideas will be those that are shared in common with others, not those that treat me as exceptional, since the state is meant to serve others as well as me. And so in these cases the interference of the state in taxing or punishing me will not be conducted on an arbitrary basis and will not represent domination.[30]

This need not amount to a collapse of the interest-regarding definition of non-arbitrariness into a morality-regarding definition of non-arbitrariness (for there may be moral cases where there is a conflict of interests or where the relevant interest are not shared[31],) but it is close. And one wonders why Pettit thought it more helpful to *introduce* the notion of non-arbitrariness with reference to tracking P's own interest, and then tack on this maneuver (confining the point to relevant shared interest), rather than to say up front that his notion of non-arbitrariness is moralized or partly moralized. I suspect that he wanted to do this in order to avoid the association with various theories of positive liberty which do this explicitly, even notoriously: I mean theories like Rousseau's which imply that there is nothing objectionable about forcing someone to act freely in the service of the general will.[32]

So we have a partly moralized definition of non-arbitrariness in Pettit's account. To figure out which interferences are arbitrary and which are not, someone has to figure out a way of determining which are the appropriately relevant and shared interests in cases like the taxpayer case and in cases like the punishment case that Pettit mentioned. I suspect that this is a role for a complete social theory, but never mind. The point is this. Is there a need for anything like a concept of liberty to be deployed *in these calculations*? If there is, then it cannot be the partly moralized one that Pettit has introduced us to, on pain of circularity. For we understand *that* concept only when we have already done the calculations to figure out which individual interests are "relevant" and which are

---

[30] Pettit, *Republicanism*, 55–6.

[31] Does Pettit want to say that interference in the service of the right solution to these cases would be arbitrary, since it forces P to sacrifice his interest to Q's, even though this is what morality requires? I am not sure what the answer is.

[32] Rousseau, *Social Contract* (bk. I, ch. 7), p. 53.

not. So, if there is a liberty element—for example, if we want to say that an interference is not arbitrary if it helps to sustain a proper distribution of people being able to do what they want—it will have to be something different from Pettit's approach.

This is a point that has sometimes been made in discussions of the justification of property. All property rights restrict liberty, say Bentham and Hart, for example;[33] and they mean negative liberty in the elementary sense of being able to act without interference. G. A. Cohen elaborated the point as follows in an attack on libertarian defenses of capitalism:

> Let us suppose that I wish to take Mr. Morgan's yacht, and go for a spin. If I try to, then it is probable that its owner, aided by law-enforcing others, will stop me. I cannot do this thing that I wish to do, because others will interfere. But liberty, Narveson reasonably said, is "doing what we wish without the interference of others." It follows that I lack a liberty here. Patently the point is generalisable. Private property always limits liberty, as in the Morgan example.[34]

A common response to this is to say that, since using someone else's property is wrong, being forcibly prevented from using someone else's property is not really an affront to liberty.[35] But if we are taking that approach, we must *already* have decided what are the best arrangements to make about property. That is, the moralization of our concept of liberty presupposes that we have *already* settled the issue of the justifiability of alternative property systems. And we must have done this without appealing to the value of liberty! Accordingly, by building the morality of a given property system into the concept of freedom, the moralizing approach precludes the use of that concept as a basis for arguing about property. If when we use the words "free" and "unfree", we are already assuming that it is wrong for P to use something that belongs to Q, we cannot appeal to freedom to explain why Q's ownership of the resource is justified. We cannot even extol our property system as the basis of a free society, for such a boast would be nothing more than tautological. Since most theorists of property do not want to deprive themselves of the concept of freedom as a resource in moral argument, insisting

---

[33] Hart used the point (which he attributed to Sidgwick) in a critique of John Rawls: he doubted whether Rawls's principle of "equal liberty" could be made consistent with private property, "since to own anything privately is to have liberty to use it in ways denied to others" (H. L. A. Hart, "Rawls on Liberty and its Priority", in Norman Daniels (ed.), *Reading Rawls: Critical Studies on Rawls' A Theory of Justice* (Stanford, Calif.: Stanford University Press, 1989), 234.) See also Bentham, "*Principles*," 93: "in the nature of things, the law cannot grant a benefit to one, without imposing, at the same time, some burden upon another.... How confer upon me the right of property in a piece of land? By imposing upon all others an obligation not to touch its produce.... It is impossible to create rights, to impose obligations, to protect the person, life, reputation, property, subsistence, liberty itself, except at the expense of liberty."

[34] G. A. Cohen, "Capitalism, Freedom and the Proletariat", in A. Ryan (ed.), *The Idea of Freedom: Essays in Honour of Isaiah Berlin* (Oxford University Press, 1979), 11–12.

[35] As Cohen imagines the response, "[p]erhaps what is intended by 'doing what we wish without the interference of others' is 'doing what we wish without the *unjustified* interference of others'" (ibid. 12).

that the enforcement of property rules does not count as a restriction on freedom must be a mistake.[36]

Well, similarly, Pettit must be sure that he does not need anything like the concept of freedom to distinguish arbitrary from non-arbitrary interference. If he does, then we might have to conclude that he has not really substituted liberty as non-domination for traditional conceptions of negative liberty, but at best added it to the traditional repertoire as an extra layer.

5. A CATEGORY MISTAKE?

I want to turn now to the relation between conceptions of freedom that focus on the capacity to interfere and conceptions of freedom that focus on interference. My initial misgiving about the contrast between Pettit's conception and traditional liberal conceptions of negative freedom was that the contrast rested on a sort of category mistake, because it does not contrast a concern about interference with something different, but rather contrasts a simple concern about interference with a more complicated idea that already assumes a concern about interference. Negative liberty, we have said, is defined as the absence of interference; and domination is defined as the absence of the potential for arbitrary interference. The conceptions are surely different, but it is hard to resist the impression that the second is just a more complicated version of the first.[37]

I suspect that the real difference between the two has to do with the point about arbitrariness, particularly the point that I pursued in the second paragraph of Section 4 above. If we follow that point, Pettit's theory does look like a genuine competitor to the liberal tradition of negative liberty; but it starts to look like a Rousseauian positive liberty conception, which is not necessarily what Pettit wants.

But is that the only difference, the only distinctive thing about Pettit's account? What about the specific point about capacity—the claim that freedom as non-domination is not concerned with actual interferences but with the potential for interference, because people might respond (or be driven to respond) slavishly to the potential even if it is never exercised? Is this sufficient to characterize Pettit's account as a completely different kind of conception?

I think not, for two reasons. First, Pettit exaggerates the extent to which the bare potential for interference is a concern quite apart from the prospect of its exercise. Take the extreme case in which P knows that Q has the capacity to

---

[36] This is adapted from Jeremy Waldron, "Homelessness and the Issue of Freedom", *UCLA Law Review*, 39 (1991), 304–8.

[37] Cf. the review of Pettit's *Republicanism* by Roger Boesche, *Political Theory*, 26 (1998), 863: "At best Pettit is splitting hairs. I can only conclude that his whole ideal of freedom as non-domination is simply one variant of liberalism, a conclusion that certainly deflates and diminishes the central argument of the book."

interfere with P's choices (by force or threats) but P is certain that Q will never exercise the capacity. Is Q's capacity a matter of concern? Well, it is unlikely to be matter of concern to P, given P's certainty that it will never be exercised; and if it is a concern to us on P's behalf, it is only to the extent that we think that P might be wrong in this assessment. In other words, it is the prospect of interference, not the mere potential, that is important, and it is important precisely in terms of the magnitude of the prospect. The interference itself, in other words, is front and center-stage in this calculation. All we are doing, with the capacity idea, is figuring out the probability of its occurrence.

Secondly, it is wrong to suppose that the negative freedom tradition has no interest in any probability of interference, short of its actual occurrence. The negative freedom tradition may not refer to the potential for interference as unfreedom; but that is not the same as a lack of concern. We may be alarmed by the probability of unfreedom, without saying that the probability is unfreedom. And in fact, negative libertarians have characteristically been concerned about concentrations of power, etc. in society, even in advance of its exercise.

6. ATOMS AND MOLECULES

There is more to be said about this alleged contrast between a conception that emphasizes interference and a conception that emphasizes the potential for interference. But to say it, I need to drift way from Pettit's work for a moment and talk more generally about the way we construct our theories of freedom.

It is fairly clear that, whatever your conception of freedom, a given person can be free in respect of some of his choices and not others, or at some times and not others, and in respect of some areas of his life and not others. Moreover once we reflect on that, we see how people may vary in these regards. The members of a given society may differ in the areas of choice in which they are free, or in the extent of freedom that they have in these areas. Accordingly, there may be a difference between what we say *freedom* is, what we say being *a free person* amounts to, and what a society has to be like before we are willing to label it *a free society*. We have to reconcile our theory of what it is to be a free person with the fact that inevitably everybody is going to be free in some respects and not in others, and we have to say something about the extent and distribution of freedom, or perhaps the distribution of the property of being a free person, before we can talk about a free society. I don't mean that our theories have to reconcile themselves tamely to harsh reality in this regard. They may still be critical of the extent of unfreedom in the lives of individuals and in the spread across society. All I mean is that there is nothing automatic about moving from a theory of what freedom is to a normative theory which tells us what criticisms and suggestions to make about the array of freedoms and unfreedoms in individual lives and in society at large.

This is what I am referring to in my title when I talked about Pettit's molecule. There are atoms and molecules in a theory of freedom. On one plausible approach to theorizing about negative liberty, one might say that we begin at the atomic level—the level of individual actions. We say that a person, P, is free to perform an action of type A at time t_1 when there is nothing in the way of external human interference stopping, blocking, or obstructing that performance. (I'm talking now just as though we were developing a negative theory, in the traditional liberal sense—leaving it open for a few moments how this relates to Pettit's conception.) With this as our starting point, we might begin to build up layers in our theory: molecules out of the atoms of negative liberty.

Notice that although we are at the atomic level, our conception at this stage is not unanalyzable. It has structure: there are references to action, interference, and so on.[38] And there will be controversy, too, at this level—rival conceptions of the negative starting point. I have already mentioned some of these: How important is the element of intention in interference? How do we fit coercion by threat into the model of interference, when the threat does not involve any actual restraint? And so on. When we answer these questions, then we have the atomic wherewithal to begin building our molecules.

One initial question is whether we invest negative freedom with value at the atomic level. Is interference with an action something to be avoided, other things equal? I suggested earlier that Bentham might think the answer was "Yes",[39] and I am inclined to think that Berlin would say that the answer was "No", waiting for us to produce a molecule like "free man" rather than "free action" before attributing moral significance to the concept.[40] But if the answer is "Yes", then other things might follow—depending on what we say about the atomic structure. If we say that deliberately interfering with someone's action is *prima facie* wrong, do we commit ourselves to any judgment about reckless or inadvertent interference? It depends on why we are concerned about interference. If we are concerned primarily with the predicament of the person who is interfered with, it makes no sense to condemn intentional interference, yet remain indifferent to negligent or reckless interference (unless we think that what the interferee suffers from is some sense that he has been deliberately targeted by another). But if we think that the real problem is the depravity of the interfering mentality, we will not be disposed to condemn inadvertent interference. All this is pretty obvious; and there will be versions of it all the way up as we proceed to the molecular level.

A more important point for our reading of Pettit's conception is that for those who are concerned about interference as such, or for those who (in the light of some molecular conception) end up being concerned about *some* interference, there will be a whole set of further ancillary issues about preventing interference,

---

[38] See above, text accompanying n. 2.   [39] See text accompanying n. 27–8 above.
[40] See text accompanying n. 45 below.

prophylactics against interference, investigating interference, punishing it, and so on. I have already objected to Pettit's assertion that the negative liberty tradition has no interest in these matters, no interest—that is to say—in doing anything about the *potential* for interference or aggregates of power that *threaten* interference, etc. And this is the place to say it again: the capacity feature of Pettit's conception simply indicates one layer in the building up of molecular theory of freedom out of the atoms of a concern about interference. It does not make it a different kind of theory.

So far we have remained pretty close to the atomic level. But now I want to consider the way in which we build much grander molecules for our libertarian theories. We started from P's freedom or lack of freedom to perform a certain kind of act, A, at a particular time. By some sort of simple aggregation, we might also want to talk about P's freedom in regard to a whole range of act-types or a whole series of times. I am not saying that we can necessarily assign numbers here—there are great difficulties (which Hillel Steiner has bravely explored[41]) in quantifying liberty. One obvious difficulty is that we do not begin with a determinate number of act-types as a quotient for determining what percentage of freedom or unfreedom there is in a given person's situation at any moment, let alone over time. Still, there are various things we can say: we can identify a set of actions which we know this person particularly wants to perform or that people in general tend to want to perform, and ask how many of those are blocked in a particular case. And it may be possible to make some sort of ordinal comparisons between persons or in the life of the same person over time: I was free to perform this action yesterday, but I am not free to perform it today, and nothing else has changed, so I am less free; or P's situation with regard to external interference with action is exactly the same as Q's except that P is prevented from performing A, so in that sense P is less free.

On this sort of account, whether a person is free is a matter of degree. And freedom is something that a person might want to maximize in his life, or at any given period of it. But we might also want to have a conception of "free person" which is binary, by indicating some sort of threshold of freedom that a person needs or ought to be accorded.[42] Thomas Hobbes had his doubt about this: "[A]ccording to [the] proper, and generally received meaning of the word, A Free-Man, is he that, in those things which by his strength and wit he is able to do, is not hindred to doe what he has a will to."[43] But there can be no such person, according to Hobbes: everyone is hindered in some of the things he wants to do, either by the laws or by aggression by others in the absence of laws. There are no free men, and there cannot be any free men. All there are, are degrees of

---

[41] See Hillel Steiner, *An Essay on Rights* (Oxford: Basil Blackwell, 1994), ch. 2.
[42] Cf. Stanley Benn and William Weinstein, "Being Free to Act, and Being a Free Man", *Mind*, 80 (1971), 194.
[43] Hobbes, *Leviathan* (ch. 21), p. 146.

freedom, depending in civil society on "the silence of the laws" together with some determination of whether the silence is operating in areas where people are vulnerable to other sorts of interference which the laws might possibly restrain.[44]

But there are other ways of doing it. Isaiah Berlin suggests that we think in terms of "a certain minimum", such that if freedom diminishes beyond that minimum for a person he may be said to be effectively "enslaved".[45] He attributed this view to Locke, Mill, Constant, and de Tocqueville, all of whom, he said, held that:

> there ought to exist a certain minimum area of personal freedom which must on no account be violated; for if it is overstepped, the individual will find himself in an area too narrow even for that minimum development of his natural faculties which alone makes it possible to pursue, and even to conceive, the various ends which men hold good or right or sacred. . . . We must preserve a minimum area of our personal freedom if we are not to "degrade or deny our nature".[46]

I guess that the minimum might be specified quasi-quantitatively, but as this passage suggests, it is more likely to involve specific types of freedom, along the lines of Rawls's identification of certain basic liberties, in *A Theory of Justice*, as key to self-respect.

Notice—and this is important for our discussion—that it is with regard to this minimum that the theory of negative freedom becomes insistently normative. Berlin is not committed to the proposition that *any* diminution of negative liberty—i.e. any restraint on action—is, as such, a bad thing. True, his talk about trading off liberty for other values does refer to a loss when liberty is traded off, and that may indicate that he thinks (as Bentham thought) that every loss of liberty is *prima facie* bad, though the value is weak and overridable.[47] But liberty only becomes a passion and principle and anything like a moral absolute at what I have called the molecular level, where Berlin is attempting to specify the quantum of liberty that must be regarded as a moral minimum. Notice also that in order to explain this principle of the moral necessity of securing a certain minimum freedom, Berlin reaches out way beyond the austere confines of negative freedom as such and talks about self-development, etc. As the theory becomes molecular, rather than atomic, it starts to engage with other values, beyond those involved in the simple specification of negative liberty at the atomic level.

The other molecular construction that is required is some specification of what we mean by a free society, or (if we don't want to use that phrase) some sense of the appropriate distribution of liberty across persons. Again, one might use a

---

[44] Hence my suggestion in n. 3 above, that Hobbes turns out to be not really interested in freedom as he defines it.

[45] Berlin, "Two Concepts of Liberty", 122.

[46] Ibid. 124–6 . (1ptThe phrase quoted at the end of this excerpt is from Benjamin Constant.)

[47] This is the passage—ibid. 125—where we find Berlin's famous insistence, with implicit reference to Bishop Butler, that "Everything is what it is: liberty is liberty, not equality or fairness or justice or culture, or human happiness or a quiet conscience."

simple maximizing principle: we want to increase the total or average amount of free action in the society, or diminish the total amount of interference. However, this sort of simple aggregative approach will usually be implausible, and we will find ourselves pressed on the question of distribution:[48] not how much liberty overall, but how free is each person, compared with each other person? Here the liberal tradition has tended to associate negative liberty very firmly with a principle of equality.[49] Though sometimes we talk loosely of an opposition between equality and liberty, they are more like function and argument: talk of equality invites the question "Equality of what?" and "Liberty" is one plausible answer; and talk of liberty invites the question "Liberty for whom?" and "Liberty for all, equally" is one plausible answer. Pettit is right to insist that equality and liberty are natural associates, though quite wrong—in my opinion—to argue that this is true only of his non-domination conception and not of the negative conception of liberty.[50] I think that Pettit wants to say that maximizing non-interference does not necessarily equalize negative liberty.[51] That is true; but there is no reason why a liberty-egalitarian should even start off down the maximization road, no reason why such a person should ever talk in terms of maximization at all.

Certainly the liberal tradition is full of egalitarian talk about liberty. The clearest case is that of Kant. Freedom, says Kant, is "the only original right belonging to every human being by virtue of his humanity".[52] He means negative freedom ("independence from the constraint of another's will"), but it is negative freedom universalized, i.e. "[f]reedom . . . insofar as it can co-exist with the freedom of every other in accordance with a universal law".[53] So once again, what is moralized, what is made the subject of a principle, is not the absence of constraint per se, but the absence of constraint accorded to everybody on equal terms. The value kicks in at the molecular as opposed to the atomic level. There is a clear and deliberate echo of the Kantian position in Rawls's theory too: "Each person has an equal right to a fully adequate scheme of equal basic liberties which is compatible with a similar scheme of liberties for all."[54] Though Rawls's first principle of justice uses a negative conception to determine

---

[48] See Jeremy Waldron, "The Primacy of Justice", *Legal Theory*, 4 (2003), 272–80.

[49] See also Ronald Dworkin, *Sovereign Virtue: The Theory and Practice of Equality* (Cambridge. Mass.: Harvard University Press, 2000), ch. 3.

[50] Pettit, *Republicanism*, 111.   [51] Ibid.

[52] Immanuel Kant, *The Metaphysics of Morals*, in *Practical Philosophy*, ed. Mary Gregor (Cambridge: Cambridge University Press, 1991), 393 (vi. 237 of the Prussian Academy Edition of Kant's *Works*).

[53] Ibid.

[54] John Rawls, "The Basic Liberties and their Priority", in S. McMurrin (ed.), *Liberty, Equality and Law: Selected Tanner Lectures on Moral Philosophy* (Salt Lake City: University of Utah Press, 1987), 5. The earlier formulation in John Rawls, *A Theory of Justice* (Cambridge, Mass.: Harvard University Press, 1971), 250, was: "Each person is to have an equal right to *the most extensive* total system of basic liberties compatible with a similar system for all" (my emphasis). Rawls defends the change in "Basic Liberties", 46–9.

whether a person is free or unfree in regard to the types of action it privileges, the principle itself privileges not negative liberty as such, but a certain distribution of it. This is a very clear example of what I mean by the distinction between atomic and molecular arguments about freedom.

Now I want to connect these comments back to what I said in Section 4 about moralized concepts of liberty. There are two ways in which a conception of liberty may be moralized. (1) It may be moralized with reference to morality in general, so we would say that being free from interference with one's vicious or depraved or wrongful action is not true liberty. (2) Or it may be moralized specifically with regard to issues about liberty itself: that is we may say (in Kantian fashion) that acting in a way that prevents similar action by others is not true liberty, because it is not universalizable. Put (1) aside. Noting the variations between full moralization and partial moralization, I have said all I want to say about that in Section 4: it's a version of positive liberty. But think about (2). If we say that the only liberty worth protecting is the equal liberty of a free society or, in Kantian terms, liberty that is compatible with the similar liberty of others under a universal law, then we are invoking the term "freedom" twice in our account. (a) We invoke it first to specify the raw material for the sorting and disciplining process that equalization and universalization involve. And (b), we invoke it to refer to some demand for non-interference that is privileged on account of the success of the sorting and disciplining process that equalization and universalization involve. Now we may reserve the terms "liberty" and "freedom" for the second usage (b), but we will certainly need something like them for (a) as well. If we do use "liberty" or "freedom" in sense (a), it doesn't follow that we are saying that there is value in negative liberty quite apart from its distribution. We may understand perfectly well a point that I have stressed several times in this section—that it is an open question (I mean a question open for normative argument) whether value is accorded to negative liberty as such, or to the property of being a free man, or to liberty as properly distributed, or whatever. But even if we are determined to withhold the element of value until we are in command of sense (b), we still need sense (a) of liberty. And we still need to have a theory of it, so that we can keep track of what it is that we have been doing in our construction of (b).

For this reason, and for the other reasons I have stated, I think it wise not to simply throw out the negative liberty conception, particularly for the sake of a concept of freedom as non-domination which seems to have been, in various ways, constructed on the basis of it.

8

Contestatory Citizenship; Deliberative Denizenship

John Braithwaite

RETHINKING DEMOCRACY

Political philosophy is construed as having a relevance problem to a world where power has become pluralized, governance networked. We cannot assume that the Westphalian project of progressively centralizing power in the hands of the state at the expense of other centres of power such as the church, granting the state a monopoly over the use of armed force, continues to be a project with explanatory force. Philip Pettit's political philosophy of republican dispersal of power and contestatory democracy to secure freedom as non-domination is a serviceable framework for coming to grips with pluralized governance through networks. At the same time, Pettit's doubts about the feasibility of citizens being empowered with a direct voice in a deliberative democracy can be revised in accordance with the realities of networked governance as developed by Clifford Shearing and his co-authors. At the nodes of governance that make networked governance buzz, deliberative democracy is a feasible ideal. The ideal articulated here is of a circle of expanding circles of deliberative democratic contestation. There is deliberative accountability within each circle and contestatory accountability from other circles in a circle of checks and balances. The nodal governance of crime is used to illustrate the feasibility of this blend of contestatory and deliberative democracy for securing freedom as non-domination against arbitrary power.

The structure of the chapter will be to argue first that governance has become more networked, making central state planning the governance technology of a time past and nodal governance of growing importance. These facts render most political philosophy anachronistic. Then it will be argued that Philip Pettit's republicanism provides an analytic repertoire that can escape this irrelevance. Particularly important is his idea of the republic as a contestatory democracy. Yet Pettit's philosophy needs adaptation to the possibility of crafting nodes of governance for the deliberative democracy of what Shearing calls 'denizens'. The nodal governance of security is then used to illustrate these ideas. The conclusion argues that while contestatory citizenship must remain central to Pettit's republican project, deliberative denizenship becomes more central to securing freedom as non-domination.

BEYOND WESTPHALIAN POLITICAL PHILOSOPHY

Political philosophy naturally became a Westphalian tradition since the 1648 Peace of Westphalia reconfigured the world into sovereign territorial nation-states. This was a world in which nation-states were the sites of most of the politics that mattered. Today nation-states remain extremely important sites of governance. But it is no longer true that they are the sites of most of the politics and governance that matter most. Political philosophy, like much of the discipline of political science, continues to act as if this were still true. Therein lies its relevance problem to a world in which governance has pluralized rather radically. Of course, many plural forms of governance of people's lives beyond nation-states have been with us for a long time—sub-national levels of government at the province, county, or city level, schools, families—and have been long accommodated by at least some strands of political theory such as feminist philosophy. Some of these long-standing non-state sites, notably religious institutions, actually declined as centres of governance that mattered in the West during the Westphalian era, though Islamic religious institutions may do more governing of people's lives than they did when colonial regimes suppressed them.

The biggest real changes in the governance of the world over the past century are a result of the growth of private corporations. A century ago most of the most consequential actions in the world were actions of individuals, with state action being the second big category. Today, in contrast, when important things are done in the world, whether for good or for ill, they are more likely to be the actions of corporations than of individuals. Ronald Burt has shown (in Coleman 1982: 12) that during the century from the 1870s to the 1970s the percentage of front-page space in the *New York Times* devoted to individual persons fell continuously, and the proportion devoted to corporate actors rose continuously. By the end of the Second World War three times as much of the front page was devoted to corporate actors compared to persons. In the middle of the nineteenth century, fewer than 20 per cent of participants in New York State Court of Appeals cases were corporations; in 1923 for the first time the number of corporate participants exceeded the number of individuals (N. Grossman, cited in Coleman 1982: 11).

In the nineteenth century most of the people of the world had no experience whatsoever of being governed by private corporations, even allowing for the fact of the governance of substantial parts of the world by the British and Dutch East

Indies companies. Even in Europe in the late nineteenth century, the number and size of private corporations were small; the state-owned Prussian Railways was still the business in Europe that employed the largest number of workers. In the United States, where incorporation arose earlier and more vigorously than elsewhere, there had been only 335 incorporations by 1800 (Davis 1961: p. vii). But for the next two centuries the growth curve for the number of people who worked for corporations exceeded that of people in state employment. Today the largest transnational corporations have incomes higher than the GDPs of the majority of the world's states. For the first time in the mid-1990s, the majority of the 100 largest 'economies' in the world were corporations (Anderson and Cavanagh 1996).

The corporatization of the world has had profound effects on the competing source of power to the business corporation—states. Corporate governance colonized state governance. From the 1980s we saw corporatization within Western governments. Monolithic state bureaucracies were divided into separately managed corporatized operating units (Hood et al. 1998: ch. 9). The New Public Management in the UK and Europe, and 'reinventing government' in the USA, were about managing government in the image of business management—less control by hierarchy, more government by contract, more 'partnerships' with a plurality of business corporations. In the 1980s it was common for these developments to be referred to as privatization and deregulation, but actually privatization was associated with building new state regulatory capabilities. For example, when nations privatized telecommunications, they almost invariably established a new telecoms regulatory authority. So a more apt description is Osborne and Gaebler's (1992) of movement to a state that does less rowing but more steering—less direct provision and more regulation of privatized provision of formerly governmental services. In addition, there has been a shift in the way states regulate from direct command and control to regulated self-regulation. This means that not only has state provision been privatized, but front-line regulation of the quality of that provision is instituionalized as self-audit, with states auditing the quality of the self-audits. From the perspective of the consumer of formerly governmental telecommunications services, not only is the provider a private company, but if she has a complaint about the service that she tries to take to the state, she will be told in the first instance to call the company's complaints line, and if she gets no satisfaction there, to take it to the industry-funded Telecommunications Ombudsman. Iteratively across many domains of privatized or contracted-out government, this leaves us with a world of radically pluralized nodes of governance.

In addition to government that is delegated down or partnered sideways, a lot has been delegated upwards to international organizations. So the standards that shape the quality of our telecommunications service are mostly set by the International Telecommunication Union in Geneva. Our food standards are established by the Codex Alimentarius Commission in Rome. Many of our pharmaceuticals standards have been set by a joint collaboration of the Japanese, European, and US industries and their regulators called the International Conference on Harmonization. For decades many of the world's air safety standards were written by the Boeing Corporation in Seattle, or, if not by them, then by the US Federal Aviation Administration in Washington. Our ship safety laws have been written by the International Maritime Organisation in London. Our motor vehicle safety standards come from Working Party 29 of the Economic Commission for Europe. In the most thorough study of the law of product standards globally, Harm Schepel (2005: 414) concludes by inverting a well-known quote from Habermas on how deliberation in civil society can generate impulses for national law making: 'National legal systems are but the "impulse-generating periphery" of global standardisation [by mostly private standard-setters].'

THE END OF THE REPUBLIC OF CENTRAL PLANS

The bottom line is that governmental capabilities have been pluralized in many different directions. This means that states no longer do indicative planning. To the extent that they still do strategic planning, they do it taking account of the strategic plans of a galaxy of pluralized nodes of governmental power beyond themselves. But really governments no longer plan so much as seek to mobilize networks of power to get things done. This is why networked governance is such a major theoretical theme in contemporary political science (Rhodes 1997; Bevir and Rhodes 2003), why Foucault's decentred views of governmentality have influenced all of the social sciences (Burchall et al. 1991), why sociologists theorize 'circuits of power' (Clegg 1989), why international relations theorists see international law and other global decision making being transacted by trans-governmental networks (Slaughter 1997).

Empirically, Braithwaite and Drahos (2000) found that while the governments of states, especially the USA, are important, the networks that assert global power are not primarily trans-governmental. NGOs, professional associations, and even intellectuals are frequently important within those networks, but more fundamentally the influence of business often shapes network action more profoundly than does the influence of states. An informal node of decision making often enrols the governmental heads of power in the network. So with the network that remade the global information order through TRIPS (the Trade Related Intellectual Property agreement of the World Trade Organization), two Washington legal entrepreneurs persuaded the CEOs of Pfizer and IBM that linking intellectual property to the trade regime would be in their interests. They organized a committee of sixteen US CEOs as a node of governance that enrolled the President of the United States, the European Commission, the government of Japan, and international trade secretariats to network for them (Drahos with Braithwaite 2003).

THE RISE OF NETWORKED GOVERNANCE

The most ambitious retheorizing of state and society in these terms has been Manuel Castells' (1996, 1997, 1998) three-volume magnum opus on *The Rise of the Network Society*. For Castells (1996: 500), 'Networks constitute the new social morphology of our societies . . . the power of flows takes precedence over the flows of power.' By this he means that the way to dominate others in such a society is to harness the right networks to your project of domination. This, for example, is how comparatively powerless Washington legal entrepreneurs managed to enrol a network that resulted in HIV–AIDS drugs being rendered unaffordable for the people of Africa. Castells (1997: 355) sees it as 'indeed a tragic irony that when most countries in the world finally fought their way to access the institutions of liberal democracy (in my view, the foundation of all political democracy), these institutions are so distant from the structure and processes that really matter that they appear to most people as a sarcastic grimace in the new face of history'. Networks with 'resistance identities', like Al-Qaeda, loom large in Castells's analysis. Five and six years before the wars in Afghanistan and Iraq he wrote: 'States can shoot, but because the profile of their enemies, and the whereabouts of their challengers, are increasingly unclear, they tend to shoot randomly, with the probability that they may shoot themselves in the process' (Castells 1997: 359).

Because our historical vision has become so used to orderly battalions, colourful banners, and scripted proclamations of social change, we are at a loss when confronted with the subtle pervasiveness of incremental changes of symbols processed through multiform networks, away from the halls of power. It is in these back alleys of society, whether in alternative electronic networks or in grassrooted networks of communal resistance, that I have sensed the embryos of a new society, labored in the fields of history by the power of identity. (Castells 1997: 362)

REVIVAL OF NODAL GOVERNANCE

Clifford Shearing with various colleagues has developed the theme of nodal governance in a way that has been greatly influenced by Pettit's republicanism (Brogden and Shearing 1997; Shearing and Wood 2003). Because a network society is more fluid, complex, and indeterminate than older structures of government like parties and ministries, understanding how governance unfolds is more challenging. This challenge has increased the appeal of nodal governance as a way of thinking about possibilities for strategic regulatory action. The question becomes what are the nodes where networks can be organized, where the levers at the disposal of one network can be tied in to the levers available to another network, or a number of them. A node is a place where resources, ideas, deliberative capability, and leadership are available to make networked governance buzz. These nodes are the focus of attention in this theoretical tradition, because synoptic understanding of how whole networks and sets of networks operate is beyond our grasp. What we may be able to grasp is whether there are effects when nodal governance is mobilized to bind networks together. This is an old idea in Eastern philosophy. Sima Qian around 89 BC quotes the following exchange with Confucius:

'Do you think me a learned, well-read man?'
'Certainly,' replied Zi-gong. 'Aren't you?'
'Not at all,' said Confucius. 'I have simply grasped one thread which links up the rest.' (Quoted in Castells 1996: 1)

Each strand of a web of controls that seeks to govern some persons or some phenomenon may be weak. We may have a dim understanding of this complex web of governance. Yet, if we learn to pull the right strand at the right time, we may find that the entire fabric of the web of controls tightens to become quite strong. Conversely, we can learn that if we pull the wrong strand at the wrong time, the entire fabric of control can unravel. From a republican point of view, we should be interested in how to cause the unravelling of webs of control that dominate citizens in an arbitrary way and how to secure webs of control that prevent domination. This will be accomplished by strategic deliberation at strategic nodes of networked governance.

PETTIT'S CONTESTATORY DEMOCRACY

Philip Pettit's work is less vulnerable than most in political philosophy to the discipline's relevance problem in a post-Westphalian world. Pettit is concerned not just with the micro of individual and the macro of state action. He is also philosophically engaged with the meaning of the meso of collective action at various intermediate levels, and more recently with supra-state collective action (Pettit 2002). His republican ideal of freedom as non-domination is obviously as relevant to non-state as to state domination and protection from it. Instead of being focused in a traditional state-constitutionalist way on the separation of powers between legislature, judiciary, and executive, Pettit's (1997: 177) theory is oriented to the 'dispersion of power'. This way of specifying a key condition for republican governance is well designed to be as applicable to concentrations of corporate power as to concentrations of state power. That said, Pettit's work is overwhelmingly in the Westphalian tradition of political philosophy.

Pettit does not see democracy narrowly as the means whereby a society as a whole asserts its collective will—its own autonomous will as opposed to that of a dictator or a colonial overlord. He sees this as an important side of democracy—the side that makes it important to have referenda at times and to elect the legislatures that enact the laws that protect against arbitrary exercise of power. This is the (indirect) 'authorial' role that democracy requires the people to have. But Pettit also emphasizes the 'editorial' role of the people, which he describes as the 'contestatory' side of democracy. For Pettit, contestability is more important than consent in preventing exercises of power that are arbitrary (Pettit 1997: 184–5). For contestation to be possible, decision making must be open enough for there to be potential for public reason to contest it, and there must be many channels of contestation—writing to an MP, complaint to an ombudsman, judicial appeals, rights to take to the streets in protest, and so on. Because Pettit rejects democracy as a purely electoral ideal, he disagrees with hand-wringers who see in every global decision-making forum an erosion of national electoral sovereignty. If a global institution, say a UN human rights agency, effectively contests a national form of domination, then that national polity has more channels open for public reason to contest its power. Hence, democracy may be enlarged rather than reduced by it.

Petitt's republicanism is in better shape than a unidimensional electoral conception of democracy for application to a world of networked governance. You can't elect a network; you can't have written constitutions for all the nodes of governance that matter. We cannot ensure that networked power is a product of popular will. The contestatory dimension of democracy is more useful for a world of nodal governance of networks. We can ensure that networked power is required to survive popular contestation by setting up multiple nodes of popular contestation at strategic intersections of networks. Before challenging the supremacy of electoral democracy with contestatory democracy, Pettit is rather dismissive of the feasibility of the ideal of direct deliberative democracy. We are no longer in the village, the New England town, or ancient Athens. The scale and institutional complexity of a mass society with a sophisticated division of labour means that direct participatory democracy, even in the most important domains of governance, is for Pettit an impossible ideal.

Just as the realities of plurally networked governance make electoral democracy a less serviceable ideal than contestatory democracy, so the realities of nodal governance should cause us to return to a rediscovered serviceability of deliberative democracy at the nodes that count. It is the contestatory ideal that accounts for the importance of democratic citizens joining together at a node of governance to contest networked power that they believe oppresses them. Once those citizens are assembled at that place, even if it is in cyberspace, deliberative democracy is the ideal that can most fruitfully be deployed to enrich freedom as non-domination. I presume here that giving direct democratic voice to people affected by a decision is the best way to respect the autonomy and empower the public reason of citizens wherever it is institutionally feasible and affordable to do so.

CONTESTED DENIZENSHIP

Clifford Shearing and Jennifer Wood (2003) have resurrected a distinction between citizens (in the discourse of state governance) and denizens (in that of nodal governance). 'Denizen' is a pre-Westphalian term that has disappeared from the latest edition of the on-line *Oxford English Dictionary* (<http://dictionary.oed.com>) but is still to be found in the previous edition. For Shearing and Wood (2003) a denizen is a habitual, even if temporary, visitor to a place, who has rights and responsibilities in the governance that occurs in that place. This is consistent with a 1655 attribution of the online *OED* that 'The Charter of London . . . is the birth-right of its own Denisons, not Strangers.' Denizens were often frequent travellers to a place where they were not native-born. Genoan merchants who frequented the Genoan Guild in Bruges or London would be described as denizens of those places. So the *OED* refers from 1632 to 'An authenticke Bull, charter or patent of denizonship or borgeousship of Rome'. But by 1871, the triumph of Westphalianism seems to have devalued the currency of denizenship: 'Denizenship is a mongrel state, not worth preserving when the process of obtaining naturalization is so simple.'

Consider national and nodal governance of armed conflict. Citizens of Israel who are concerned about their state's conduct in Palestine can mobilize electoral democracy, voting against their current national leadership. They can engage with contestatory democracy by attending peace rallies, signing petitions, etc. Or they can strategically engage with the networked governance of armed conflict by initiating or joining a node of second-track diplomacy in Geneva which has key participants from the crucial networks of stakeholders in the conflict. As that node of governance develops an alternative peace plan to the US state's Roadmap, the number of participants around the table in Geneva is sufficiently small for the democracy of the node to be directly deliberative. Contestatory democracy from citizens of Israel can take them to the node of second-track diplomacy; deliberative democracy can inform their participation in the public reasoning at that node. When that node delivers up a draft peace plan, contestatory democrats will come out to criticize the plan from many directions. Then good democratic practice involves inviting those critics into a widened circle of democratic deliberation at the node. In summary, we have three stages of contestatory citizenship with deliberative denizenship:

1. In a world of networked governance, democratic citizenship contests domination most effectively at strategic nodes of deliberative governance.

2. The decisions of that node of deliberative governance should be contested by citizens who did not participate in it.

3. The circle of deliberation should be widened by inviting in the most vigorous and contentious contestors.

THE NODAL GOVERNANCE OF CRIME

Pettit sees criminal justice and crime as peculiarly important to both securing and threatening dominion. Shearing and Wood (2003) discuss local Peace Committees in South Africa as one strategy of nodal governance to respond to crime and other insecurities. Here I will develop the theme of contestatory citizenship and deliberative denizenship with respect to restorative justice conferences—an approach from the same family of nodal approaches as the Peace Committees. Restorative justice is conceived as a horizontal process of democratic deliberation that is integrated into external processes of accountability to courts and the rule of law. This integration of direct democracy and the rule of a representative democracy's laws is an opportunity to enrich thinking about the relationship between responsibility and accountability in a democracy. Responsibility is conceived here as an obligation to do some right thing, accountability as being answerable to give a public account of some thing. The restorative justice ideal of responsibility is active responsibility as a virtue, the virtue of taking responsibility, as opposed to passive responsibility we are held to. The restorative justice method for engendering active responsibility is to widen circles of accountability. This is conceived as part of a civic republican institutional design of *a circle of widening circles of deliberative accountability.*

When responsibility is taken, and accounts accepted as sufficient to acquit that responsibility, justice is done. From a restorative justice perspective, justice is always unfinished business until an account has been accepted by the stakeholders in the injustice. Even when the state intervenes to hold someone passively responsible by imprisonment after they fail to take sufficient active responsibility for their wrongdoing, there should be no giving up on active responsibility. Responsibility may be admitted and acquitted on release from prison. Victims, with the family of the offender and other stakeholders, may accept the offender's account at that time with considerable benefit to all if they choose to be involved. Injustice on all sides may still be hurting at the time of release, so justice can still heal then. Deeper democracy, on this account, is one where the institutional preference is for responsibility that is active rather than passive, bottom-up rather than top-down, but where failure of bottom-up responsibility results in a form of state accountability that never gives up on restoring bottom-up, deliberative accountability.

THE CONCEPT OF RESTORATIVE JUSTICE

Restorative justice is a process designed to involve, to the extent possible, those who have a stake in an injustice to identify collectively and address harms, needs and obligations in order to heal and put things as right as possible (adapted from Zehr with Gohar 2003: 40). It involves an attempt to help solve problems by moving emotions from anger to reconciliation and repair. The idea is that because crime hurts, justice should heal. Restorative justice has much in common with other Alternative Dispute Resolution ideologies like mediation. But there are important differences. Restorative justice facilitators are not morally 'neutral' about mediating 'conflicts'. Restorative justice is about righting the wrongs of injustices. A restorative justice conference to confront domestic violence is not morally neutral about violence as merely a conflict between two people. Most mediation is between two parties to a conflict; restorative justice views it as morally important to give an opportunity for all those who see themselves as key stakeholders in an alleged injustice to participate in the deliberation about what to do. So the predominant structural form of restorative justice is deliberation among people seated in a circle, as opposed to two people negotiating across a table. Empirically, the outcomes from a plurality of stakeholders sitting in the restorative justice circle tend to be different from those from dyads assisted by professional mediators. Some think they are often better outcomes (Braithwaite 2002).

I have argued (Braithwaite 2002) that criminologists know quite a lot now about what can be done to prevent crime. The challenge is to get societies to be rationally interested in investing in those things rather than investing in prisons and retribution. Restorative justice is seen as a strategy of nodal governance with the potential to supply that motivation. To take a banal example, in areas where natural surveillance is not effective, burglar alarms work in preventing burglary. The best opportunity for targeting police crime prevention work on this is when a person has just been burgled. In a restorative justice conference, both the convicted burglar and the police can offer good technical advice on how to do this. It is also the best time to motivate the investment, because the police can explain to the victim that the single best predictor of future burglary victimization is having been a victim of burglary in the past three months. We will see below that restorative justice is much more successful in persuading offenders to actually complete rehabilitative programmes that work—like anger management and drug rehabilitation programmes. This is because the direct participatory justice of the stakeholders in the circle delivers superior commitment to complete agreements than the hierarchical justice of court orders. The legal citizenship obligations of a representative democracy's justice are less effective than the participatory obligations engendered among the denizens of a place.

Restorative justice is a nodal governance strategy for connecting crime prevention to where the resources are in police bureaucracies—responding to crimes once they have occurred. In strategic cases, I argue (Braithwaite 2002), these nodes of deliberative governance can and do initiate major reforms to the law, to public policy, and to the policy making of large private corporations. One of the referees for this chapter is doubtful at this point. She or he ponders:

There is a big difference between neighborhood watch committees, which seem to me "clean" examples of associative democracy, and restorative conferences which are, I think, as much concerned with emotional reconciliation as with any matter of policy making or enforcement. Although technically public, restorative conferences are very largely personal and they seem to have no intrinsic connection with democracy or representative government.

I have argued that the empirical evidence runs the other way (Braithwaite 2002: 215–16). Citizens are less motivated to attend neighbourhood watch meetings than they are to attend restorative justice conferences. Neighbourhood watch is seen as a form of community policing in decline, while restorative justice is growing. One reason is that neighbourhood watch meetings discuss more depersonalized security concerns than restorative circles. Restorative justice offers people an opportunity to make the personal political. Mothers can and do take the police to task for using excessive violence against their sons in restorative justice conferences in a way they never could in a court of law or through electoral politics. What we cannot claim, however, is that this frequently leads to changes in police policy. While there are many isolated examples where restorative justice processes have led to significant changes in national laws and national policies, the contemporary state of restorative justice is so far failing to realize its promise as a deliberative process that bubbles up policy change. Truth and reconciliation processes following armed conflicts are restorative justice processes that have stronger claims in that regard (see Braithwaite 2002: ch. 6). So do restorative circles to confront injustices such as bullying in schools, which have stronger claims for influencing education policy. In all this, we must remember that it can be more important to reform policy in a police district or an education district (or even a single school) than nationally. In a world of corporate power, it can be more important for restorative justice to change the culture of a single large corporation on an issue like sexual harassment than to have an elected representative speak on the matter in the parliament.

RESTORATIVE JUSTICE: DEMOCRATICALLY EXPERIMENTAL[1] BUT UNACCOUNTABLE?

Many of the concerns about restorative justice rest on a belief in the virtues of hierarchical accountability. Roche (2003) concludes from his survey of

---

[1] Dorf and Sabel 1998. Research and development on restorative justice has also been experimental in a scientific sense. The Centre for Restorative Justice at the Australian National University in 1995 commenced a randomized control trial on 1,300 criminal cases randomly assigned to court versus a restorative justice conference. Research/practitioner groups from Indiana, Pennsylvania, and the UK subsequently visited the Canberra experiment and then conducted a number of follow-up randomized controlled trials in their own jurisdictions. Preliminary evaluation results as of 2002 are summarized in Braithwaite 2002 and Strang and Sherman 2005.

accountability in twenty-five restorative justice programmes across six nations that while hierarchical accountability to prosecutors and courts that sit above restorative justice circles do useful work, horizontal deliberative accountability of one actor in the restorative justice circle to others in the circle does more work in practice. One of Roche's examples concerns accountability of the police for excessive use of force during arrest, or for coercing an innocent person to confess, which is more likely to be forthcoming within the circle from a citizen who pleads with the circle about such unfair treatment. In a court case, such a citizen will be silenced unless she is called as a witness relevant to the conduct of the offender, as opposed to the conduct of the police. As Dolinko (2003) has pointed out, in the case of an innocent offender coerced into a guilty plea, he will find it impossible 'to discuss with the victim what he's done and how to repair the harm he's caused when he knows quite well he has in fact done nothing and has caused no harm. And even if his participation in a conference could somehow be secured, the conference will hardly be a success—the putative offender will simply insist "I'm innocent; they're framing me; I didn't do anything to you and there is nothing for me to 'restore' or 'repair'!" ' Again, the accountability mechanism that is doing the work here is horizontal deliberative accountability in the restorative justice circle, for an account of how we could repair harm to a victim when we have not inflicted any harm upon them.

In criminal cases, Roche (2003) argues that there are some simple reasons why empirically it turns out that deliberative accountability in the circle does more of the work of accountability than accountability to higher-level institutions like directorates of public prosecutions and courts. One is timeliness. An obligation to give an account that occurs in the circle in the process of making a decision elicits immediate responses from other stakeholders: 'That's no excuse.' 'Is that all you are proposing to do?' 'What about the emotional havoc this has heaped upon your mother?' Such contestation of accounts inside the process of deliberation more often than not attracts an immediate response: 'What I want to say to mum is that I recognize that. I am so sorry, mum. I will never cause you that pain again. You know my plans to be a better son from now on.' This example of giving an account is not chosen casually. It is meant to illustrate Strang's (2002) empirical conclusion that emotional reparation like this turns out to be more important to accountability being accepted in the circle, even to victims of violent crime, than material reparation. Immediate face-to-face accountability therefore not only has the virtue of timeliness; it also has the virtue of authenticity of emotional communication in the giving of accounts.

Authenticity of emotional communication also builds commitment to follow through on accountability. One of the puzzles to those who have not experienced the emotional power that can be generated in a restorative justice conference for serious crime is why compliance is more likely to happen with a victim-compensation agreement or community service agreed as a voluntary, non-enforcible outcome of a conference than with the legally enforcible order of a court. One reason is that the emotional dynamic of the offender discussing with a victim the pain she has suffered builds commitment when the offender promises to do something to try to heal that hurt. But, second, commitment to follow through is built among other stakeholders in the circle. An offender promises to attend an anger management programme. His mother says he was ordered to an anger management programme last time he offended. An uncle is moved to say: 'This time I'll take responsibility for making sure he goes. I'll pick him up every Tuesday night to get him there.' Then the uncle becomes a signatory of a conference agreement that says that this particular responsibility belongs to him. Roche (2003: 159) found the most elaborated version of this kind of commitment building in two American programmes that institutionalized a 'celebration circle' that reconvened the stakeholders when all the undertakings in the agreement were successfully completed. As a matter of research evidence, we cannot be sure which of the foregoing mechanisms is most important to the superior accountability that restorative justice delivers. What we can now be reasonably sure of is that it does deliver it. In a meta-analysis of thirty-two restorative justice evaluations by the Canadian Department of Justice, the biggest, most statistically robust, effect size was that completion of restorative justice agreements was higher than compliance with orders/agreements in control groups (Latimer, Dowden, and Muise 2001). A subsequent review by Poulson (2003: 187–9) combined data from several studies to show that both offenders and victims were significantly more likely to perceive offenders to be 'held accountable' in restorative justice cases compared to controls that went to court.

Now let us return to juxtaposing the immediate deliberative accountability in the circle to the delay of hierarchical accountability. The biggest problem with hierarchical accountability is precisely that it *is* hierarchical. By this I mean that an infinite regress of accountability is required. If guardians of accountability are arranged in a hierarchy as in the left-hand side of Figure 8.1, we have a problem when the top guardian is corrupt. And unfortunately criminal justice institutions such as police departments, and indeed whole states, are like fish; they rot from the head down. The only solution to the corruption of nth-order guardians is to add an $n + 1$th-order guardian. But if we arrange guardians of accounts in a circle (Fig. 8.1, right-hand side), each guardian can be a check on every other guardian. We can escape from the infinite regress of hierarchical accountability. The more separated public and private powers there are in a polity, the richer the checking of one guardian by many other guardians can be (Braithwaite 1997). So abuse of power by a restorative justice conference might be checked by a prosecutor, while abuse of power by the prosecutor might be checked by a court, the media, human rights NGOs, or indeed by a restorative justice circle reporting a complaint about the prosecutor to a court, an ombudsman, or a human rights commission.

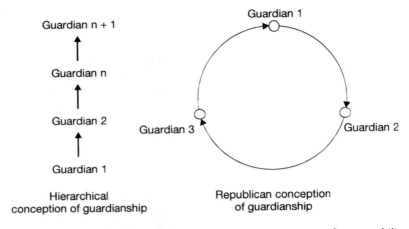

Fig. 8.1. Formal models of hierarchical and republican conceptions of accountability.

Deliberative accountability among a group of denizens who meet face to face has its own pathologies—like groupthink (JkernJanis 1971). So we actually need a prudent mix of deliberative accountability within the circle and accountability from a separate source of power that is external to the circle. What Figure 8.1 argues is that we can still get that mix of internal deliberative accountability and external accountability to separated powers by organizing circles of deliberative accountability in a circle. The republican ideal is for all nodes of governance in a separation of powers to become more deliberative in their decision making. This means a more deliberative parliament (Uhr 1998), more deliberative courts (Sunstein 1988), and more deliberative regulatory agencies (Braithwaite 2002). So we end up with a checking and balancing circle of deliberative circles.

Parker and I (Braithwaite and Parker 1999) have argued that restorative justice circles should be checked by the rule of law, and the rule of law should be permeable to messages bubbling up from the rule of the people as articulated in restorative justice circles. This is Roche's (2003) conclusion as well—deliberative accountability and external accountability have different effects;[2] while deliberative accountability is cheaper and more contextually grounded, and can therefore do most of the hard work of practical accountability, external accountability is also needed, particularly because of the superior linkage it can offer to a rule of laws enacted by democratically elected governments.

---

[2] E.g. Roche (2003: 216) finds that horizontal accountability more often leads to interventions to 'prevent overly harsh outcomes', while vertical accountability more often leads to interventions to prevent outcomes that are 'too lenient'. Put another way, horizontal accountability works best for checking upper limits on punishment, vertical accountability for checking lower limits on punishment.

ACTIVE AND PASSIVE RESPONSIBILITY

Roche and I (Braithwaite and Roche 2000) have suggested that restorative responsibility might be conceived as that form of responsibility most likely to promote restoration—of victims, offenders, and communities. Given that framework, following Bovens (1998), we find a useful distinction between active and passive responsibility. Then we show that the active–passive responsibility distinction usefully maps on to distinctions between active and passive deterrence, active and passive rehabilitation, and active versus passive incapacitation. We argue that the active versions of deterrence, rehabilitation, and incapacitation are likely to be more effective than their passive versions. While these consequentialist considerations are important in motivating a restorative justice jurisprudence which is a jurisprudence of active responsibility, this part of the argument will not concern us here except in one respect.

This respect is that an important part of a mechanism by which active responsibility delivers active deterrence, active rehabilitation, and active incapacitation is that the circle from which accounts are requested is widened. In our development of these ideas with business regulatory agencies in Australia, we would ask for a conference with those causally responsible for an offence within the company. That conference would often break down when these corporate executives would refuse to accept responsibility and say 'See you in court'. Instead of proceeding to litigation, however, what we would do is widen the circle. The regulator would ask for another conference with the boss of those directly responsible joining the circle. Inviting the boss to give an account would sometimes backfire even more badly, because the boss might be an even tougher nut than her subordinates. Then our idea was to widen the circle even further. In one case with this approach while I was a part-time commissioner with our national antitrust and consumer protection agency, we widened the circle right up to the Chairman of the Board. The Chairman could be moved by shame about the corporate offence and by a simple appeal to his sense of moral responsibility. He fired his CEO (not very restorative!), participated in an agreement where generous compensation was paid to victims, impressive internal compliance measures were put in place to prevent recurrence of the offence, and a program of industry-wide compliance reform was led by the company. The idea is that we can keep widening the circle of accountability; at each step there are extra people with extra capacities to prevent recurrence of injustice and to right the wrongs of past injustice. With active deterrence, we keep widening the circle beyond hard targets who are not deterrable until we reach a responsible target who can be deterred by shame. With active rehabilitation of a homeless young offender, we widen the circle beyond a nuclear family who will not have him back until we find a more distant relative or family friend, perhaps in another city, who will take him into their home.

John Braithwaite

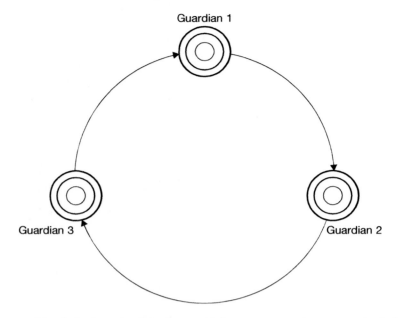

Fig. 8.2. The ideal of a circle of checking and balancing separated powers, each of which is potentially a widening circle

In Figure 8.1 we ended up with a checking and balancing circle of deliberative circles. Now we have added the further idea that the circles should be iteratively widened to remedy responsibility and accountability failures. So the ideal is a circle of widening circles of deliberative accountability (Figure 8.2).

Mark Bovens (1998: 27) first distinguished active from passive responsibility. Elaborating Bovens's conception somewhat, passive responsibility is something we hold wrongdoers to; we hold someone responsible for something they did in the past. Active responsibility means *taking* responsibility for putting something right into the future. One can be actively responsible for righting a wrong in the future without being causally responsible for the wrong in the past. Family members of an offender might offer to work with the offender to help repair the damage that a victim of crime has suffered, for example. Restorative justice is partly about community building, by encouraging citizens who are not offenders to assist in righting wrongs that offenders have caused. One virtue of the active responsibility of an offender's loved ones is that it nurtures active responsibility on the part of the offender. Restorative justice is about creating a space in which offenders are most likely to take responsibility. Conventional Western criminal justice is about creating spaces in which offenders will be held responsible in proportion to their culpability.

HOW DOES THE RESTORATIVE JUSTICE ACCOUNT OF RESPONSIBILITY DEEPEN DEMOCRACY?

The first respect in which the account of responsibility/accountability sketched here is claimed to deepen democracy is that there is a shift in the balance of how responsibility is exacted, from responsibility as a coercive imposition of states upon citizens to responsibility as something that autonomous citizens take after listening to a democratic conversation about harms done, dues owed. Second, the principal stakeholders in a directly democratic conversation about an injustice—offenders and victims in the case of a crime—can directly veto any allocation of responsibility they view as unjust. Then, however, these principals must put the determination of responsibility into the hands of the less participatory but more authoritative process for allocating responsibility in the mainstream legal system. That is, principals should retain their right to adjudication of responsibility according to rules of law enacted by a democratic state. Without abandoning this old democratic right, restorative justice should mean a new right to the option of directly participatory democracy over responsibility allocations. Citizens are simultaneously accorded citizenship rights to accountability of the rule of the law and denizenship rights to deliberation at a node of governance that directly affects their lives.

Third, even when the state takes over authorization for responsibility allocations, there should be further opportunities at each stage of state intervention (police, prosecution, court, prison, parole, etc.) for citizens to take responsibility back into the realm of direct stakeholder democracy. State accountability is reformed to enable responsibility to become something that autonomous citizens freely choose, as opposed to something the state enforces upon them. Every time accountability for justice obliges the state to "steal a conflict" (Christie 1977) from the direct control of stakeholders in that conflict, it should also create a path where denizens can take it back so long as they agree to provide an account to the state of how they use the new opportunity to take responsibility for any serious injustice.

Hence, on this theory, responsibility for injustice is thrown back to the realm of a direct democracy of denizens, qualified by accountability to the state to ensure that fundamental principles of the rule of law are not fudged. Yet that state accountability is itself being qualified by an exhaustive commitment to keep throwing the game back from external to internal accountability in the circle of stakeholders. Democracy is enriched when the justice of the people and the justice of the law each become more vulnerable to the other (Braithwaite and Parker 1999). Democracy can be enriched by the set of preferences for responsibility being active rather than passive, bottom-up rather than top-down, accountable both deliberatively and externally rather than just deliberatively among stakeholders or just externally to a state agency. Together these preferences make restorative justice a more deeply democratic practice of justice both in terms of citizen participation and in terms of accountability to a rule of law that is an accomplishment of the people. Not only is it a practice that takes democratic accountability more seriously than does a rule of law that we are held to by grey men in white wigs. It is also a practice that takes responsibility more seriously because it never settles for passive responsibility, but always struggles to turn passive back into active responsibility owned by wrongdoers and other stakeholders. To settle for passive responsibility, cursed by the criminal as a rope breaks his neck, is to settle for a muted responsibility and a muted democratic conversation about justice.

ELECTORAL, CONTESTATORY, AND DELIBERATIVE DEMOCRACY

This extended consideration of restorative justice shows the feasibility of a major shift in a significant institutional arena from decision making by hierarchical state institutions to deliberative decision making by stakeholders in civil society partnering the state. Elsewhere I have attempted to show how these principles can be applied more widely to tort and contract law, corporate decision making, education, economic policy, and rebuilding democracy following a war, among other arenas (Braithwaite 2002). In some societies—for example, New Zealand, Norway, and Austria—the scale of this displacement with criminal justice is now substantial. In a world in which the real decisions that affect crime and security and any number of other important matters are less in the hands of states than in private–public networked governance by denizens of the place where the crime happens, nodal governance wherein democracy is deliberative makes more and more sense.

Contestatory democracy is what triggers nodal deliberative governance—the victim of crime complains of being offended against, an environmental NGO calls a conference to solve a pollution problem, a parent calls a school conference to discuss a bullying problem in the school, an Afghan warlord calls a conference to confront international peacekeepers who, he alleges, is harassing his men.

Contestatory democracy also plays the role that Pettit saw as its primary one—that of contesting the decisions dished up by electoral democracy. None of the revisionism of contestatory citizenship and deliberative denizenship denies the importance of electoral democracy. Indeed, in a world of pluralized governance, we need electoral democracy at many levels—city government, state government, European Union, United Nations, annual meetings of corporations to elect directors, annual meetings of NGOs and professional associations to elect officeholders. It is just that in a world of networked governance, perfect electoral democracy at all these levels would be a thin set of reeds to protect against domination. Pluralized electoral democracy still leaves us with a shallow democracy unless we also invest in the kind of contestatory democracy of citizens advocated by Pettit, complemented by deliberative democracy of denizens at strategic nodes of governance, as advanced by Shearing and Wood (2003). A rich democracy gives us frequent opportunities to *vote* for people who represent our interests and many nodes of governance that give us an opportunity to *contest* power and *deliberate* in our own voice at that node of governance. Controlling domination does not require that we all spend our evenings in meetings, just that enough of us assume the responsibilities of denizenship when we see injustices that are not being righted. It requires a learning democracy, in which enough of us learn to care enough to engage, learn to be democratic through early experiences of deliberation in schools and families. Controlling domination requires that we learn how to convene nodes of governance at the strategic intersections of networks that can regulate abuse.

CONCLUSION

The crime example has illustrated that statist governance working on its own is not very effective in responding justly and effectively to a problem like crime. In contemporary conditions the effective governance of security is networked. Among its requirements is that denizens of a place forge nodes of governance that work to prevent the niches of criminal opportunity that emerge in that place. I have contended that there is evidence that deliberative denizenship sometimes works to secure our property and our persons from violence. This is a pragmatic participatory politics favoured by growing ranks of hard-headed state police, not a deliberative democracy confined to romantic dreamers of radical politics. But it is not enough. We also need a state with awesome powers to shoot at, interrogate, and incarcerate those who threaten our security. Here the classic form of Pettit's republicanism comes into its own. Pettit gives an account of why such frightening state powers are tolerable, but only if they are contested by active citizens of a democracy, and only if their exercise is non-arbitrary, constrained by a rule of law. A state with a Guantanamo Bay cannot be a republic.

Yes, freedom as non-domination requires contestatory citizenship. But our case study also shows that it requires deliberative denizenship. Let us assume that Castells is right—that while states still matter a lot, governance is becoming less statist, more networked, across the spectrum of all issues of public concern, not just crime. If so, deliberative denizenship that seizes opportunities for nodal governance will become increasingly central to institutions of republican governance. An emergent role for contestatory citizenship will then be to contest down to the decisions of the denizens of places as well as up to the rules and rulers of states.

REFERENCES

Anderson, S., and J. Cavanagh (1996). The Top 200: The Rise of Global Corporate Power. Washington, DC: Institute for Policy Studies.

Bevir, M., and R. Rhodes, (2003). Interpreting British Governance. London: Routledge.

Bovens, Mark (1998). The Quest for Responsibility. Cambridge: Cambridge University Press.

Braithwaite, John (1997). 'On Speaking Softly and Carrying Sticks: Neglected Dimensions of Republican Separation of Powers'. University of Toronto Law Journal 47: 1–57.

____ (2002). Restorative Justice and Responsive Regulation. New York: Oxford University Press.

____ and Peter Drahos (2000). Global Business Regulation. Melbourne: Cambridge University Press.

____ and Declan Roche (2000). 'Responsibility and Restorative Justice'. In M. Schiff and G. Bazemore (eds.), Restorative Community Justice (Cincinnati, Oh.: Anderson).

____ and Christine Parker (1999). 'Restorative Justice is Republican Justice'. In Lode Walgrave and Gordon Bazemore (eds.), Restoring Juvenile Justice: An Exploration of the Restorative Justice Paradigm for Reforming Juvenile Justice. Monsey, NY: Criminal Justice Press.

Brogden, Michael, and Clifford Shearing (1997). Policing for a New South Africa. London: Routledge.

Burchall, G., C. Gordon, and P. Miller (1991) (eds.) The Foucault Effect: Studies in Governmentality. London: Harvester Wheatsheaf.

Castells, Manuel (1996). The Information Age: Economy, Society and Culture, I: The Rise of the Network Society. Oxford: Blackwell.

____ (1997). The Information Age: Economy, Society and Culture, II: The Power of Identity. Oxford: Blackwell.

____ (1998). The Information Age: Economy, Society and Culture, III: End of Millennium. Oxford: Blackwell.

Christie, Nils (1977). 'Conflicts as Property'. British Journal of Criminology 17: 1–26.

Clegg, Stewart (1989). Frameworks of Power. London: Sage.

Coleman, James S. (1982). The Asymmetric Society. Syracuse, NY: Syracuse University Press.

Davis, John P. (1961). Corporations: A Study of the Origin and Development of Great Business Combinations and their Relation to the Authority of the State. New York: Capricorn Books.

Dolinko, David (2003). 'Restorative Justice and the Justification of Punishment'. Utah Law Review 2003(1): 319–42.

Dorf, M., and C. Sabel, (1998). 'A Constitution of Democratic Experimentalism'. Columbia Law Review 98: 267–473.

Drahos, Peter, with John Braithwaite (2003). Information Feudalism. London: Earthscan.

Hood, Christopher, Colin Scott, Oliver James, George Jones, and Tony Travers (1998). *Regulation Inside Government: Waste-Watchers, Quality Police, and Sleaze-Busters.* Oxford: Oxford University Press.

Janis, Irving (1971). 'Groupthink among Policy Makers'. In N. Sanford and C. Comstock (eds.), Sanctions for Evil (San Francisco: Jossey-Bass).

Latimer, Jeff, Craig Dowden, and Danielle Muise (2001). The Effectiveness of Restorative Justice Practices: A Meta-Analysis. Ottawa: Department of Justice, Canada.

Osborne, D., and T. Gaebler (1992). Reinventing Government: How the Entrepreneurial Spirit is Transforming the Public Sector. Reading, Mass.: Addison Wesley.

Pettit, Philip (1997). Republicanism: A Theory of Freedom and Government. Oxford: Oxford University Press.

——(2002). 'Two-Dimensional Democracy and the International Domain'. Presentation to New York University Law School, 4 October.

Poulson, Barton (2003). 'A Third Voice: A Review of Empirical Research on the Psychological Outcomes of Restorative Justice'. Utah Law Review 2003: 167–203.

Rhodes, R. (1997). Understanding Governance. Buckingham: Open University Press.

Roche, Declan (2003). Accountability in Restorative Justice. Oxford: Oxford University Press.

Schepel, Harm (2005). The Constitution of Private Governance: Product Standards in the Regulation of Integrating Markets. Oxford: Hart.

Shearing, Clifford, and Jennifer Wood (2003). 'Nodal Governance, Democracy and the New "Denizens": Challenging the Westphalian Ideal'. Journal of Law and Society 30: 400–19.

Slaughter, Anne-Marie (1997). 'The Real New World Order'. Foreign Affairs 76: 183–97.

Strang, Heather (2002). Repair or Revenge: Victims and Restorative Justice. Oxford: Oxford University Press.

——and Lawrence Sherman (2005). 'Effects of face-to-face restorative justice on repeat offending and victim satisfaction', Campbell Collaboration Review, <www.campbellcollaroation.org>.

Sunstein, Cass (1988). 'Beyond the Republican Revival'. *Yale Law Journal 97*: 1539–90.

Uhr, John (1998). Deliberative Democracy in Australia: The Changing Face of Parliament. Melbourne: Cambridge University Press.

Zehr, Howard, with Ali Gohar (2003). The Little Book of Restorative Justice. Peshawar: Uni-Graphics.

9

Crime, Responsibility, and Institutional Design

Nicola Lacey

In this chapter, I address certain aspects of two questions to which Philip Pettit's work has made an important contribution. First, given both our normative commitments and our understanding of human psychology and the social world, how can we best design institutions of criminal justice? Second, what role does the concept of human responsibility play in the legitimation of criminalizing power, and how do normative and social analyses of responsibility interact in contributing to our understanding of this question? In selecting these topics, I have been guided not merely by my own research interests, but by what I see as one of the greatest strengths of Pettit's work: his astute grasp not only of normative and conceptual questions in moral and political philosophy, but also of the relevance of empirical facts bearing on, and the institutional conditions of existence of, normatively desirable political arrangements. In normative philosophy, the temptations of elaborate and elegant theory construction, of the development of beautiful utopian visions, provide a substantial incentive to ignore inconvenient obstacles thrown up by the recalcitrant empirical world. It is a sign of the strength and maturity of Pettit's work that he insists that philosophers must nonetheless interest themselves in what we might call 'the feasibility question': can the ideas we find morally attractive be realized in the world as we know it? And if not, can the underlying conditions be changed? It is this willingness to confront the complex questions of social infrastructure implicit in any attempt to realize normative ideas which marks Pettit's philosophy as peculiarly relevant to the social sciences.

Another distinctive feature of Pettit's work is its consistent assumption that persistent themes and arguments in the history of ideas—whether it be the insights derived from a rational choice analysis, from a functionalist sociology, from discourse analysis, or from analytic philosophy—will turn out to have

With thanks to Bob Goodin, Julian Le Grand, and Geoffrey Brennan for perceptive comments on an earlier draft of this paper, and to David Soskice for helpful discussion of its argument.

some core of sense or insight which can be distilled and put to use in a genuinely synthesized approach. In what follows, I shall do my best to echo this intellectual breadth, and indeed generosity, which lends so much to Pettit's contribution.

My chapter falls into two main sections. In the first section, I take up certain questions of institutional design, and in particular Pettit's argument about the possibility of designing incentive systems which deal effectively with 'knaves'—those whose motivations are selfish or oppositional to system values—without destroying the intrinsic motivations of 'knights'—those disposed to comply in any event.[1] I argue that Pettit's suggested three-level 'managing strategy' of screening, compliance-enhancing sanctions, and escalating penalties for repeat offenders requires some refinement if it is to serve as a general framework in the criminal justice sphere.[2] To illustrate the direction in which revision is needed, I examine Pettit's hypothesis, made on the basis of a combined functional and rational choice framework, about the tendency for levels of punishment to escalate in democratic societies. This hypothesis, I argue, is flawed; and the reasons why this is so illuminate the further factors which we would need to grasp before we could fully understand the conditions under which the managing strategy might be effective. This part of the discussion attempts to shed light on the relationship between the different disciplines whose insights contribute to our understanding of social institutions such as criminal justice. In the second section of the chapter, pursuing the question of how Pettit's framework might be revised, I step sideward to consider an apparently very different question relevant to criminal justice institutions: the concept of human responsibility. In this section, I argue that the institutionalization in criminal justice systems of a concept of responsibility itself makes a distinctive contribution to resolving the problem of how to address the subjects of a regulatory institution as 'knaves' without destroying their 'knightly' motivations.

1. REGULATING THROUGH CRIMINALIZATION: QUESTIONS OF INSTITUTIONAL DESIGN

Criminal law and criminal justice are at some level systems of public regulation. Of course, they are also understood in intrinsic and symbolic terms: as systems which express or reflect certain core ideals, values, or standards which hold a particular place in a political society's conception of itself. Moreover, as Pettit acknowledges, these affective and symbolic aspects of criminal justice have the

---

[1] The term 'knaves' is that used by Pettit: see *Rules, Reasons, and Norms* (Oxford: Clarendon Press, 2002), 276–7. The contrast with 'knights' was developed by Julian Le Grand, in *Motivation, Agency, and Public Policy* (Oxford: Oxford University Press 2003).

[2] See Philip Pettit, *Republicanism: A Theory of Freedom and Government* (Oxford: Clarendon Press, 1999), ch. 7; idem, 'Institutional Design and Rational Choice', in Robert Goodin (ed.), *The Theory of Institutional Design* (Cambridge: Cambridge University Press, 1996), 54–89.

capacity to obstruct the development of rational criminal justice policy[3]—a point to which we shall return below. However, it would be perverse as a matter of social interpretation to deny that states use criminal justice systems to pursue certain regulatory goals and to undertake regulatory tasks. To the extent that this is true, it is appropriate to interrogate criminal law systems not only in terms of their normative credentials but also in terms of their capacity to combine respect for important moral norms with the effective pursuit of regulatory goals. And one key question here is how a system geared in part to the imposition of penal sanctions can effectively draw on the more altruistic or intrinsic, stably law-abiding motivations. Can a criminal law system treat people as knaves, threatening them with punishment as its main communicative strategy, while also fostering social trust and people's motivations as 'knights'—as subjects committed to the standards which criminal law purports to uphold?[4]

This is an area in which Pettit's work has generated important insights. Here, Pettit draws together issues arising within both rational choice and functionalist social explanations and brings them to bear on normative questions in a highly productive way. In a bold move designed to align the rational choice assumption of human egocentricity with the folk-psychological insight that people often behave altruistically, Pettit suggests that this common sense can indeed be reconciled with rational choice:

[W]hile people may generally deliberate in culturally acceptable, not particularly self-regarding mode, still they may well have the following dispositions: first to intervene in any decisions where that pattern of deliberation begins to compromise their self-interest and, in particular, to ring alarm bells; second, having intervened in that way, to revise their deliberative routine so as to guard against the threatening compromise; and third, having made that revision, to return to automatic pilot and once again to put explicitly egocentric considerations out of play. We can say, in a phrase, that people are virtually self-interested even when they actually deliberate in other ways: their self-interest is in the wings, waiting to be called on stage should the relevant alarm bells ring.[5]

It is this capacity for self-interest to be relegated to 'the wings' which opens up a space for Pettit's suggested resolution of the difficulty of designing institutions so as to foster 'knightly' motivations while keeping 'knavish' ones within our regulatory sights. The approach, he argues, should be a 'managing strategy' in relation to self-interest (and the concomitant issue of free-riding), and it should have three levels. Our preferred strategy should be to screen out decision-makers or actors most likely to be influenced by selfish motivations. Where this fails, our second strategy should be to focus on sanctions which reinforce, rather than

---

[3] Pettit, *Rules, Reasons, and Norms*, 171–2, 278.

[4] This dilemma is not, of course, exclusive to criminal justice systems. It is confronted by a range of normative systems which attempt to balance the regulatory potential of threatened sanctions with that of the internalization of norms. The way in which Christian religious doctrines, for example, address their subjects comes to mind.

[5] Pettit, *Rules, Reasons, and Norms*, 168–9.

destroy, 'knightly' or virtuous motivations oriented to compliance. And our strategy of last resort should be to escalate our sanctioning levels in response to repeat offenders.[6] In Pettit's work with John Braithwaite, a similar approach is put to specific use in relation to criminal justice, in which the implication is argued to be a preference for restorative and reintegrative sanctions over punitive and exclusionary ones, for symbolic penalties such as apologies over material sanctions, and for the resort to coercive and disintegrative penalties such as imprisonment as a last resort for the most recalcitrant and serious recidivists.[7]

Let us consider the implications of Pettit's overall propositions about the managing strategy for criminal justice. At first sight, the screening option looks unfeasible: criminal regulation, after all, speaks to all those with basic capacities within a particular territory, and though screening issues certainly arise in relation to the selection of decision-makers at all stages of the criminal process, it appears to have no application to the subjects of regulation. Yet this superficial impression is misleading. For it is premissed on the idea that the regulation of crime is achieved first and foremost through criminal justice and penal processes. In fact, both common sense and research evidence suggest otherwise: compliance with the norms of criminal law is secured largely by the voluntary internalization of those norms, rather than by the threat of punishment. And this internalization—the very process which keeps self-interest 'virtual', safely in the wings—is itself fostered more effectively by institutions of parenting, education, and so on than by the mere announcement of norms of criminal law.[8] More generally, the ability of a social order to keep 'in the wings' the self-interest which would tempt subjects to break the criminal law has, as Braithwaite and Pettit make clear, centrally to do with giving subjects a full stake in the social order and with avoiding structural social exclusion. Hence all aspects of social policy geared to the effective inclusion of, and respect for, citizens—education, housing, social welfare, health—might be seen as part of the screening processes which should constitute our normatively preferred strategy for reducing or preventing crime.

Pettit's second suggested principle of the managing strategy—designing sanctions which themselves either foster or at least do not destroy voluntary motivations oriented to compliance—has at first sight more obvious and straightforward implications for criminal justice, and many of these are indeed discussed in his and John Braithwaite's important work developing a republican theory of criminal justice.[9] A preference for symbolic and reintegrative

  [6] Ibid. 277–8.

  [7] John Braithwaite and Philip Pettit, *Not Just Deserts* (Oxford: Oxford University Press, 1990). See also John Braithwaite, *Crime, Shame and Reintegration* (Cambridge: Cambridge University Press, 1989); idem, *Restorative Justice and Responsive Regulation* (Oxford: Oxford University Press, 2002).

  [8] See my 'Criminalisation as Regulation', in Christine Parker, Colin Scott, John Braithwaite, and Nicola Lacey (eds.), *Regulating Law* (Oxford: Oxford University Press, 2004).

  [9] Braithwaite and Pettit, *Not Just Deserts*.

punishments such as apologies, restorative settlements, or community service over socially exclusionary and stigmatizing penalties such as imprisonment are immediate and obvious implications of this second principle. And at the third level of the managing strategy, too, the institutional upshot is both obvious and plausible: increase the severity with which repeat offenders are dealt with, in order to reinforce the relevant compliance motivations more strongly in the case of those with the strongest interest in acting as free-riders, as evidenced by their previous behaviour.

Notwithstanding these relatively straightforward implications from theory to institutional design, however, and true to his commitment to explore or at least bear in mind the feasibility condition, Pettit concedes that the managing strategy may be hard to implement, particularly in relation to criminal justice and to the second level of the strategy. His argument is as follows. At the level of social interpretation, we should acknowledge that criminal punishment in many societies is not merely an instrumental strategy geared to crime reduction but, rather, has an emotional dimension which speaks to the outraged and vengeful feelings prompted by serious crime. Punishment, we might say, has an inevitably retributive aspect. In this context, it may be hard consistently to implement, or rather to find sufficient stable political support for implementing, moderate sanctions which are supportive of non-egocentric motivations for compliance. In this context, Pettit hypothesizes that:

> if criminal sanctions fail to be punitive in the measure demanded under local criteria of satisfaction, then they will increase towards the point where they are. Even if the sanctioning is working for the reduction of crime in a very efficient way, there will be an outrageous offence, sooner or later, which would not have occurred under more punitive sanctioning; this will be given media publicity and will give rise thereby to public outrage; politicians will have to respond to the outrage in soundbites and headlines; and, short of jeopardising their electoral standing, the only way they can do this will be by calling for tougher sentences. Thus there will be a mechanism in place whereby the functionality of vengeful sanctioning in placating public outrage will make such a level of sentencing a resilient feature of relevant societies.[10]

At first sight, this looks like a powerful explanation of the current criminal justice climate in the United States and, to a somewhat lesser extent, countries like the United Kingdom and Australia. Indeed, Pettit's thumbnail sketch here has much in common with the influential analysis of the new politics of law and order—the punitive 'culture of control'—recently offered by David Garland.[11] Yet some basic precepts of comparative social inquiry should make us wary of going along with this institutional generalization. To start with, there is a difficulty about explaining the point of departure of the hypothesis—punishment below 'local criteria of satisfaction' in a democratic society—if its other assumptions

---

[10] Pettit, *Rules, Reasons, and Norms*, 172.
[11] David Garland, *The Culture of Control* (Oxford: Oxford University Press, 2001).

are true. Yet more importantly, as a matter of fact, a considerable number of contemporary societies with the sorts of electoral systems which Pettit highlights as part of the formative context for his hypothesis have avoided any such ratcheting-up of penal severity. Further, the relative levels of, for example, draconian penalties such as long terms of imprisonment and capital punishments vary hugely even among countries of relatively similar levels of economic development and with relatively similar democratic systems of government. And these differences are not easily explained in terms of other relevant variables such as crime rates. In other words, 'local criteria of satisfaction' vary widely across relatively similar societies. This suggests that these 'local criteria' should not be taken as an exogenous variable in a theory of criminal justice. The vastly different levels of punishment in contemporary societies, relative to levels of recorded crime, prompts therefore some serious inquiry into how the institutional capacity to deliver moderate criminal justice policies is formed. Furthermore, we have some spectacular and well-documented historical case-studies where democratically elected governments have been able to implement reductive or moderating penal policies, and these case-studies include countries like the UK which have, at other times, exemplified the ratcheting-up problem which Pettit identifies.[12]

My suggestion, therefore, is that here Pettit gives up too easily on his own commitment to exploring the institutional conditions of existence of normative ideas. Even leaving aside the questionable assertion that the spiral of severity will inevitably be prompted by 'an outrageous offence . . . which would not have occurred under more punitive sanctioning'—a counterfactual which would be almost impossible to establish empirically except under extremely stringent policy conditions, such as widespread incapacitative incarceration—there is reason to think that Pettit has stopped short of asking some crucially important empirical and institutional questions which are raised by his own hypothesis. For there is a hugely interesting social science and comparative question here, and one which has important implications for the achievability of our normative goals. What makes some societies able to resist this ratcheting-up of penal severity, and how might those conditions be inculcated in societies which have so far proved unable to resist it?[13] In analysing these questions, it is evident that a wide array of features

---

[12] See Andrew Rutherford, *Prisons and the Process of Justice: The Reductionist Challenge* (London: Heinemann, 1984); David Downes, *Contrasts in Tolerance* (Oxford: Oxford University Press, 1988); and my 'Historicizing Contrasts in Tolerance', in T. Newburn and P. Rock (eds.), *The Politics of Crime Control* (Oxford: Oxford University Press, 2006), 197–226.

[13] To point out the relevance of these questions to Pettit's line of analysis is not, of course, to assert that their resolution is necessarily a project of his particular genre of social theory; rather, it is to assert that such social theory ought at a minimum to identify and flag up such questions. The difficulty of addressing them is reflected in the fact that even criminologists have often failed to get to grips with them: see my 'Principles, Politics and Criminal Justice', in Lucia Zedner and Andrew Ashworth (eds.), *Theoretical Foundations of Penal Policy: Essays in Honour of Roger Hood* (Oxford: Clarendon Press, 2003), and Lucia Zedner, 'Dangers of Dystopias in Penal Theory', *Oxford Journal of Legal Studies* 22 (2002), 341–66. For honourable exceptions to the failure to

of social and political structure such as electoral systems and levels of social and economic inequality and exclusion will be relevant.[14] It seems unlikely, as Pettit himself indicates, that these concrete questions can be analysed on the basis of a narrowly rational choice model of criminal justice. Rather, we would need a sophisticated model which attends to the ways in which symbolic features of crime and punishment and, crucially, the power relations which characterize what we might call the 'law and order environment' in particular societies affect the formation of citizens' preferences, values, and attachments. This implies that the question of institutional design which Pettit, very properly, highlights can only be tackled through a multi-disciplinary analysis of the interlocking relationships between criminal justice and other social institutions in a particular social and historical context. Only through this more contextualized analysis can the true potential for the managing strategy be assessed. Though philosophers and social theorists cannot be expected to pursue these multi-disciplinary and empirical questions, they should at a minimum flag them up when venturing general hypotheses of the kind which has been under discussion in the last few pages.

2. CRIMINAL RESPONSIBILITY: SQUARING THE MOTIVATIONAL CIRCLE?

I now want to pursue the question of what hypotheses we can usefully make about criminal justice regulation at a general socio-theoretic level by moving on to consider the apparently very different question of responsibility for crime. Here I want to focus on the relationship between the normative idea of criminal responsibility and the practical resolution of the motivational dilemma implicit in criminal justice which we considered in the last section: the problem of fostering knightly motivations while threatening sanctions premissed on knavish ones. Further, I want to draw out a connection between this relationship and another question analysed by Pettit: the question of how both functional and rational choice explanations contribute to our understanding of the resilience of certain features of institutions over time, drawing on both paradigms to explain why something forms part of a stable institutional equilibrium.

While the centrality of the notion of human responsibility to the design and practice of modern criminal law is more or less taken as given among lawyers

---

address key comparative questions, see F. Adler, *Nations Not Obsessed by Crime* (Littleton, Colo.: F. B. Rothman 1983); David Downes, *Contrasts in Tolerance* (Oxford: Oxford University Press, 1988); Michael Tonry, 'Symbol, Substance and Severity in Western Penal Policies', *Punishment and Society*, 3 (2001), 517; and James Q. Whitman, *Harsh Justice: Criminal Punishment and the Widening Divide between America and Europe* (Oxford: Oxford University Press, 2003).

[14] For an overall approach to comparative political economy, based on an analysis of institutional foundations of comparative advantage, which is suggestive of the sort of account which I am arguing needs to be provided in relation to criminal justice, see Peter A. Hall and David Soskice (eds.), *Varieties of Capitalism* (Oxford: Oxford University Press, 2001).

and philosophers, views of just what this notion entails differ. Largely as a result of the influential work of H. L. A. Hart,[15] the dominant normative view of criminal responsibility in late twentieth- and early twenty-first-century criminal law theory focuses on the question of human capacity. On this view, human responsibility is premissed on a set of volitional and cognitive capacities: only those of us who have certain capacities for self-control and understanding count as full subjects of criminal law, and we are not accounted responsible for our actions unless these capacities were properly engaged at the time of acting. The concrete implications of this general view of criminal responsibility are, however, a matter of controversy among capacity theorists. For some, the capacity view entails a focus on human choice which issues in a strong commitment to 'subjective' principles of criminal responsibility: we should be held responsible only for those actions which we choose to do in the sense that we are in fact aware of all the relevant circumstances and/or consequences, we know what we are doing, we act intentionally or recklessly (in the sense of foreseeing the possible consequences of our actions and going ahead regardless). For others—including Hart himself—the capacity view should be understood not in these subjective, psychological terms, but rather in terms of a normative vision of fair opportunity. The nub of the issue is whether a person had a genuine opportunity to do otherwise than he or she in fact did. If she did not, then it would not be fair for the state to pursue its general justifying aims of punishment—deterrent, incapacitative, rehabilitative, or otherwise—at her expense. Notice that on this version of the capacity theory, the conditions of criminal responsibility may consist not merely in 'subjective' mental states such as knowledge, intent, or foresight, but also in 'objective' attitudes such as negligence—a failure to reach a reasonable standard of care or behaviour. So long as the defendant had the general capacity to attain the reasonable standard, such objective forms of responsibility condition do not offend the fair opportunity version of the capacity theory. On either version of the capacity approach, however, there is an assumption either of freedom of the will or of the compatibility of attributions of responsibility with the truth of determinism.

From the 1980s onwards, a second, apparently philosophically opposed conception of the conditions of criminal responsibility began to surface, or rather resurface, in criminal law theory. This conception focused not so much on capacity as on character or disposition, and it found its philosophical roots not so much in Enlightenment philosophy as in the writings of Aristotle and, in some versions, Spinoza.[16] On the most plausible version of this view, the core of criminal responsibility is a judgment that the defendant's action is a full expression of 'bad character' not in a global sense but rather in the sense that

[15] H. L. A. Hart, *Punishment and Responsibility* (Oxford: Clarendon Press, 1968).
[16] The variants of this position are further elaborated and discussed in my *State Punishment* (London: Routledge, 1988), ch. 3.

the conduct in question constitutes an unambiguous rejection of, or hostility to, the relevant norm of criminal law. It is this law-breaking attitude or disposition expressed in conduct which encapsulates the idea of responsibility; and it is the absence of such an attitude or disposition which we refer to when we talk in a certain way about criminal defences. The person who has stolen under duress or killed under provocation has acted, we might say, 'out of character': this is a shorthand for the judgment that the conduct does not express a rejection of the norms of criminal law. Notice that this conception of responsibility gives a more central place to motivation than does the capacity theory, though it can also give a distinctive place to negligence liability.[17]

As an interpretation of how criminal justice systems operate the idea of responsibility for crime, and indeed from a normative perspective which concerns itself with what I earlier called the feasibility condition, this second, dispositional approach has certain recommendations, at least as compared with the subjectivist, choice-based version of the capacity theory. For the real ability of a trial process to investigate subjective capacity is institutionally circumscribed in obvious and unavoidable ways. Moreover, a stringent version of even the fair opportunity version of the capacity theory threatens to confront judges and juries with some virtually unanswerable counterfactual questions: if understood literally, how could we ever be satisfied beyond reasonable doubt that a defendant 'could have done otherwise then they did'? By contrast, the question 'What attitude did the defendant's conduct manifest?' seems a more straightforward question—and indeed one which resonates with the fair opportunity version of the capacity theory. Yet, within a modernist moral framework which accords importance to notions of freedom and agency, the immediately obvious riposte to the 'dispositional' conception of responsibility is that if we are not 'responsible' in the 'capacity' sense for our dispositions, then it can hardly be fair to hold us responsible for their manifestation. This, certainly, is a decisive objection to any holistic version of character responsibility which focuses on a global judgment of the defendant's character as expressed in the allegedly criminal conduct. But the more limited, dispositional approach, which focuses specifically on the attitude disclosed by the conduct in question, does not meet this objection except in the sense that any theory of human responsibility must confront the question of the compatibility of judgments of responsibility with the facts of determinism. After all, what more can we ask of a system of criminal law than that it respond to us according not only to what we do but also to the attitudes which our actions

---

[17] In this, its upshot is similar to that of the fair-opportunity version of the capacity theory, but is arrived at by a somewhat different route. While under the fair-opportunity theory the justification for negligence liability is founded in the defendant's capacity to conform her conduct to a reasonable standard, which implies responsibility for that conduct, on the dispositional view, the careless attitude itself, which is expressed in and characterizes the relevant conduct, is the object of responsibility. The dispositional view, in other words, takes a less dualistic view of human action than either version of the capacity view.

disclose? In these terms, the dispositional approach to responsibility appears as a useful supplement to—even a practical way of thinking about—a moderate version of the fair-opportunity theory.

Philip Pettit's approach to the question of responsibility, and in particular to the question of what meaning and importance we should give to the idea that someone 'could have done otherwise', gives further assistance in seeing how both capacity and dispositional or attitudinal dimensions interact in our understanding of what it is to be responsible for our conduct. The key point here is to look at criminal responsibility not in abstract, metaphysical, or conceptual terms, but rather in the context of a particular social practice—such as that of criminalization—in which the sub-practice of attributing responsibility to individuals (and, in some instances, corporations or groups) plays a central practical and normative role. From Pettit's point of view, capacity does indeed play a key role in the agent-centred understanding of responsibility.[18] However, capacity is relevant at a relatively high level of generality, rather than at the specific level of judging capacity in relation to any particular act. This amounts to a reinterpretation of the idea that a person 'could have done otherwise'—a reinterpretation which overcomes the feasibility problem noted above. As Pettit puts it:

Rather than assuming that that remark is meant to direct us just to something about the way the action was generated within the person, it suggests that the intended interpretation bears on the sort of agent that X more generally is . . . When we say of an agent that he or she could have done otherwise . . . we are presupposing the relevance of certain background standards and, in the case where the agent fails to meet those standards, we are saying that this failure was not typical. The agent could have done otherwise, we remark, intending to convey the thought that he or she is capable of better. The actual choice made may have fallen away from those standards, but this should not be taken as indicative of the sort of agent in question: it should be put down to the influence of a more or less incidental factor.[19]

Hence the ascription of criminal responsibility, though sensitive to manifested attitude or disposition, falls short of any global assessment of a defendant's character, while it depends on an assumption about the agent's *general* capacity to conform to the norms of criminal law. At an abstract level, incapacity of a radical kind—insanity, say—might lead to a judgment that the agent is not responsible (though it will be likely to invoke an alternative, non-agency-based rationale for social intervention). But notice that it is only at this general, background level that the question of whether an agent 'could have done otherwise' comes into play.

For Pettit, the relevant capacity at play here is the general capacity of the agent to track certain social standards, and the ascription of responsibility in institutions

---

[18] Pettit, *Rules, Reasons, and Norms*, 262–4.   [19] Ibid. 262–3.

such as criminal justice further depends on a background practice within which agents hold themselves out to each other as tracking certain shared standards. Agents are, as Pettit puts it, 'disposed to act in those ways that . . . are in line with the standards' because they are more generally disposed to track standards identified in a certain way—for example, because they are part of criminal law—whether or not they would have been so disposed otherwise. This relates closely to the dispositional or attitudinal reading of the 'character' approach to responsibility sketched above. Rather than being focused entirely on capacity, our interpretation of each other's conduct at the concrete level has, in Pettit's view, primarily to do with how we interpret conduct in terms of what attitude in relation to tracking relevant standards we understand it as manifesting. In our assessments of responsibility, therefore, though we respond primarily to the act, we interpret it in the light of something more general about the agent him- or herself. What justifies the further practice of praising or blaming responsible agents, on Pettit's view, is the common knowledge background which is part of this interpretive practice. As he puts it:

agents represent themselves to others as tracking certain standards, where this representation is overt: it is a matter of common knowledge among the parties involved that this is what is happening . . . [I]f agents overtly represent themselves to others as tracking certain standards, despite its being a matter of common knowledge that others will therefore form and act on corresponding expectations, then they presumably acquiesce—again, as a matter of common knowledge—in others holding them to those expectations: this must be a matter of presumption so long as they do not reject reciprocity and community with the others involved. They license others to feel aggrieved about any failure on their part to satisfy the standards, and they license them to feel gratified by any success. They give others permission to blame them for failure and to praise them for success; they invite those responses by the way in which they represent themselves.[20]

Pettit therefore locates both the idea of human freedom and that of human responsibility firmly within a social ontology. Humans, he argues, are distinctly 'conversable' subjects, subjects who exist in a world of reason and discourse. And this, Pettit argues, entails that they 'must be disposed to track, on pain of not really counting as conversable subjects . . . those standards that people must fulfil under intuitively favourable conditions'.[21] These are essentially conditions of rationality and responsiveness to rational argument. Responsibility, praising, and blaming, on this view, are social practices premised on certain reciprocal attitudes which find their basis in the facts not only of human psychology but also of social infrastructure. As a general proposition, this seems plausible. As we have already seen, however, there are important questions to be asked about the extent to which criminal justice systems can be theorized exclusively in terms of this sort of rational discourse model—questions which, as we shall see

---

[20] Pettit, *Rules, Reasons, and Norms*, 266.   [21] Ibid.

below, become yet more pressing under conditions of social conflict or value heterogeneity.[22]

My suggestion, then, is that an account of responsibility something like Pettit's points us in the direction of a reconciliation of the contributions of dispositional and capacity-based conditions in the construction of criminal responsibility: particular attributions of responsibility focus on manifested disposition or attitude, but such attributions take place against a background assumption of capacity. It is a reconciliation, what is more, which gives a key role to the institutional and psychological circumstances under which practices of responsibility attribution go forward. This, I would argue, is more likely to produce a conception of criminal responsibility which combines normative attractiveness with feasibility. In other words, it provides a normative ideal of responsibility which we would have some hope of operationalizing in the practice of criminal law—both at the level of the design of its doctrines and in terms of their implementation in the prosecution, trial, and penal processes. To argue this, however, is not yet to provide an account of precisely what normative and practical work the idea of responsibility is performing in modern criminal justice systems.

Most commentators on post-Enlightenment systems of criminal law in both continental Europe and the common law systems of the modern world identify the commitment to a principle of responsibility as one of the identifying marks of criminal justice. In fact, in many systems, not all offences do require proof of a significant degree of responsibility or 'mens rea' such as intent or recklessness. Yet it is nonetheless argued that the assertion that liability and punishment must, at least in the case of more serious or stigmatizing offences, be premised on a finding by the state of normative responsibility on the part of the offender constitutes a hallmark of criminal as opposed to civil law regulation—and of legal regulation as opposed to the imposition of arbitrary power. What explains this ideological dominance and practical resilience of the principle of responsibility in modern criminal justice systems? There is certainly something to be explained here. The requirement to prove responsibility is, after all, costly; and it is not obviously functional to instrumental goals of the criminal process such as crime reduction.

In tackling this explanatory question, criminal law theory tends to be on less substantial ground than in either its identification of the ideological salience of the priniciple of responsibility or its analysis of the contours of the concept. The general assumption is that the ideas of moral agency and responsibility which became philosophically dominant in the wake of the Enlightenment somehow found their way into criminal law, presumably via the efforts of enlightened reformers facilitated by liberal-minded governments. As I have argued at length

---

[22] For a thoroughgoing attempt so to theorize criminal justice, see R. A. Duff, *Trials and Punishments* (Cambridge: Cambridge University Press, 1986), and idem, *Punishment, Communication, and Community* (Oxford: Oxford University Press, 2001).

elsewhere,[23] this is an unsatisfactory assumption from both a socio-theoretic and a historical point of view, not least because the available evidence shows that the reception of the notions of criminal responsibility which we take for granted today was a slow and uneven one, at least in common law systems. In these systems, principles of responsibility found their way into criminal law by a more indirect and precarious route than was the case in the civilian systems in which modernization was effected through decisive codification. In the light of this evidence, I argued, it would be more productive to analyse the emergence of an attachment to proof of responsibility in functional terms. On this account, the finding of individual responsibility gradually became crucial to the legitimation of criminalizing power and to the co-ordination of the expectations and knowledge necessary for its operation under increasingly democratic conditions and in the context of value pluralism and the huge expansion and diversification of criminal norms.[24]

As Pettit points out, however, such functional explanations suffer from an obvious deficit. As he puts it:

typically functionalists have nothing to say on why the functionality of the pattern should explain its presence. They cannot invoke a designer in most plausible cases. And neither, by contrast with the biological case, can they usually invoke a history of selection that would have favoured social formations with the pattern over formations without it. The required mechanism, whether of design or selection, is missing.[25]

Hence, just as it seems implausible to think of the emergence of the principle of responsibility in exclusively rational choice terms—by what mechanism could the necessary constellation of individually rational decisions have been co-ordinated towards the identified result?—a functional explanation does little to fill this particular gap. But, Pettit suggests, there is a solution to this puzzle, and one which allows us to regard rational choice and functional accounts as complementary. For, he argues, if we see functional and rational choice explanations as geared primarily to making sense of the fact that certain features of social institutions are relatively stable or resilient over time, the missing mechanism problem disappears: 'an institution might be resilient in the required sense without ever having been designed and without having been the product of a history of selection.'[26]

On the face of it, this argument is unsatisfactory, because it leaves the resilience of the relevant institution unexplained: it merely pushes the explanatory question from the issue of origins on to that of persistence. Yet I would agree with Pettit that his tempting conclusion can indeed be sustained on the basis of a synthesis between functional and rational choice explanations. Pursuing his insight that resilience is a key object of analysis for social theory, the argument might go like

---

[23] Nicola Lacey, 'Criminal Responsibility and Modernity', *Journal of Political Philosophy*, 9 (2001), 249.

[24] Nicola Lacey, 'In Search of the Responsible Subject', *Modern Law Review*, 64 (2001), 350.

[25] Pettit, *Rules, Reasons, and Norms*, 170.   [26] Ibid. 170

this: *given* a certain spread of institutions and interests, as well as the facts of human psychology, relevant environment, and so on, hypotheses about 'social functions' may be seen as generalizations about why it is in a critical mass of relevant actors' interests to support the relevant institution, hence creating a stable equilibrium. This, of course, provides us with only the most abstract of hypotheses, which must then be filled in with a wealth of empirical and institutional texture. The implications of the failure to move down to this more concrete level are well illustrated by our earlier discussion of Pettit's hypothesis about the ratcheting-up of punishment levels under conditions of democracy.[27]

Returning, then, to our question about the role of responsibility in modern criminal justice systems, what might such a contextualized analysis look like? One pervasive problem of institutional design, and a problem not unrelated to the question of how we make institutions incentive- and discourse-compatible—fostering existing compliance-oriented motivations and aligning regulatory incentive systems with broader social norms—is the problem of securing legitimacy in the eyes of the subjects of regulation. In other words, if we are to pursue the second plank of the managing strategy, which consists in shoring up or being careful not to disrupt pre-existing, compliance-oriented motivations, one hugely important pre-condition will be convincing people that they are being treated fairly and with respect. This is a particular challenge for criminal justice under modern, democratic conditions. It is a challenge, because the impact of criminal punishment in most societies is vividly patterned along socio-economic, ethnic, and indeed gender lines, thus raising a *prima facie* question of fairness. And it is a challenge because criminal justice's means are so coercive, and its method of addressing us as 'knaves' threatens to undermine our 'knightly' motivations.

Pettit's suggested resolution of this sort of problem, if I have understood his argument properly, depends in part on his attitude-based account of the emergence of stable norms supported by both self-interested and communally oriented approval and criticism.[28] Under conditions in which not only punitive sanctions but also informal sanctions such as withdrawal of trust and esteem move in similar directions, the second plank of the managing strategy—fostering

---

[27] The development and testing of such hypotheses consists, of course, in a many-staged process of building up further layers of contextualization in order to see if the assumptions hold, and generating further research questions as one goes. In this context, Geoffrey Brennan has made the intriguing—and disturbing—suggestion that in so far as a dispositional conception of criminal responsibility is institutionalized, bringing with it the assumption that repeat offenders are stably and perhaps implacably hostile to the norms of criminal law, and hence that—as suggested by the third level of Pettit's managing strategy—harsher punishments may be necessary and indeed justified, this might engender just the sorts of exclusionary, us/them attitudes to offenders which might underpin an insistent electoral demand for higher overall penalty levels. While this would certainly lend theoretical support to Pettit's 'ratcheting-up' hypothesis, in the light of the comparative data referred to above, the argument would need to be tested through an empirical/interpretive project of tracing relevant differences between conceptions of criminal responsibility in societies with different degrees of popular demand for penal severity.

[28] Pettit, *Rules, Reasons, and Norms*, 280–2.

voluntary compliance while coercively sanctioning deviance—will be relatively easy to deliver. Here, however, I would argue once again that there is a deficit in Pettit's recognition of the feasibility condition—a deficit which becomes clear in the light of certain empirical facts about many contemporary criminal justice systems. In essence, his argument works well under conditions of relative normative homogeneity. But the environment which modern criminal justice systems inhabit is typically that of heterogeneity. The heterogeneity which confronts contemporary criminal justice is of two relevant kinds. First, there is the heterogeneity of the norms of criminal law themselves—a heterogeneity which has undermined any content-based understanding of the rationale of criminal law such as that which informed, for example, Blackstone's *Commentaries* in the mid-eighteenth century.[29] Second, and yet more importantly, there is the heterogeneity consequent not only on moral pluralism within societies—something which has arguably gained significance in the late modern world—but also on a more historically pervasive fact: that, given the distribution of wealth and other forms of political and social advantage, compliance with criminal law is not even roughly equally in the *ex ante* interests of all groups within the population. For these reasons among others, offending behaviour, particularly in areas such as property crime, will not have a univocal impact on offenders' access to goods such as trust and esteem. For competing normative systems coexist with criminal law, and these too produce symbolic and normative, as well as material, goods for those subject to them.

Here, I would argue, it is worth complicating the analytic framework in the way suggested by Julian Le Grand's recent work on institutional design and public policy.[30] Le Grand's suggestion is that the analysis of institutional design should attend not merely to the motivational 'knights/knaves', egoism/altruism axis, but also to a further axis which focuses on the assumed capacities of the subjects of regulation. This axis he characterizes in terms of 'queens'—self-determining, choosing agents—and 'pawns'—passive objects of social policy. In criminal law terms, the resilience of a commitment to the principle of responsibility represents an assumption that the subjects of regulation are 'queens' in Le Grand's terms. My suggestion is that the insistence on a responsibility condition may, under modern conditions, be playing a key indirect regulatory role by legitimating a punitive, coercive, knave-oriented, last-resort strategy.[31]

Recall the conditions of heterogeneity sketched above: criminal regulation today confronts heterogeneity both in terms of levels of popular commitment to the full range of criminal law norms and in terms of the substance of those norms themselves. Bear in mind also that we live in a social and political culture in which being treated as a responsible agent is regarded as a cornerstone—a necessary

---

[29] See my 'In Search of the Responsible Subject' and 'Criminalisation as Regulation'.
[30] Le Grand, *Motivation, Agency, and Public Policy*.
[31] For a more detailed elaboration of this argument, see my 'Criminalisation as Regulation'.

though certainly not a sufficient condition—of being treated with respect. In such a world, the commitment to pursuing the regulatory goals of the criminal justice system only on the 'fair terms', as Hart puts it, that only those found to be fully responsible be punished, may be a hugely important legitimating device. Indeed, in terms of contribution to criminal law's legitimation, it seems likely to be as important as—possibly even more important than—the overlap between criminal law and shared social norms which gives rise to the esteem-based motivational compliance reinforcement on which Pettit prefers to concentrate. In a world in which the widespread internalization of social norms cannot always be relied upon to reinforce 'knightly' behaviour, we have to resort to knave-oriented systems of punishment; we avoid the implication that the state is demeaning its subjects by addressing them as knaves by further resort to the principle that only those who are genuinely responsible for their offences will be treated, in final analysis, as knaves. The general lesson here is a simple one: how we approach our regulatory subjects in terms of our attitude to their capacities—queens versus pawns—may have implications for how effectively we are able to structure or marshall their motivations—to address them as knights as well as knaves.

3. CONCLUDING THOUGHTS

This paper has strayed over a wide range of normative and social questions, and I cannot claim to have dealt fully with any one of them. Rather, my ambition was to suggest ways in which Philip Pettit's work both has contributed and might further contribute to our analysis of the normative basis of, and the institutional possibilities for, criminal justice systems in the real world. First, I suggested that Pettit's three-level 'managing strategy', geared to designing regulatory institutions so as to maximize compliance-oriented motivations while keeping open the possibility of punitive sanctioning, though fruitful in terms of thinking at an abstract level about the proper shape of criminal justice systems, needs to be tempered by a more detailed grasp of social history and institutional context. Here I suggested that differing levels of tolerance and penal moderation across superficially similar societies raises serious questions for social theory, and requires that social theorists either pitch their hypotheses at somewhat lower levels of generalization or at least flag up the need to test their hypotheses comparatively. Second, I suggested that his agent-centred approach to responsibility, located within a sophisticated social ontology, helps to unravel some apparent knots in contemporary criminal law theory, and opens the way to an understanding of human responsibility which could generate notions of criminal responsibility which are both normatively attractive and capable of being put into operation in criminal processes much as they exist. Finally, I suggested that hypotheses about the resolution of the motivational dilemma in institutional design so clearly identified by Pettit, though usefully informed by assumptions about the compatibility of different incentive systems within an institution, need also to build in considerations of how the regulatory subject is addressed, and what his or her capacities are assumed by the regulatory system to be. My argument here was that, in a pluralistic and divided society, there are real limits to the extent to which careful institutional design can overcome the problems of legitimacy and co-ordination faced by criminal justice systems. How such systems address their subjects—as responsible agents rather than passive objects of policy manipulation—may, however, be one way of at least mitigating the difficulties posed by unequal power relations, conflicts of interest, and disagreements of value which characterize the environment of criminal justice in the late modern world.

10

Disenfranchised Silence

Rae Langton

1. SILENCE

1.1 Approving Silence

Silence can sometimes be eloquent. Conversations consist not only in what is said but also in what is not said—the cold silence, the disapproving silence, the appreciative silence, the reverent silence, the baffled silence. Of particular interest is the approving silence, or the consenting silence, and this will be my topic here.

It is sometimes supposed that the silent witness is, through silence, an approving party to what he observes. The biblical prophet was held to be party to iniquity if he did not protest against it: 'When I [the Lord] say unto the wicked, O wicked man, thou shalt surely die; *if thou dost not speak* to warn the wicked from his way, that wicked man shall die in his iniquity; but his blood will I require at thine hand' (Ezek. 33: 8; italics added). On this way of thinking, ordinary German citizens were party, through their silence, to Nazi atrocities. More recently, anyone who did not march or express protest was held party to the war in Iraq. Activist websites and chain e-mails around the globe urged us to 'Remember: *silence is consent!*'—by which means they hoped to goad readers into voicing disapproval, voicing refusal to consent to war. Actually, the goading would be pointless if silence really were, in this context, consent: the goading presupposes that I *am* silent, and that I do *not* consent. If I were not silent, I would not need goading; if I did consent, goading would be useless. So the instruction to 'Remember: *silence is consent!*' is a pragmatic self-defeater if ever there was one. Its target is not the warmonger, but the too-passive pacifist.

There is point to the reminder, though; the point being that silence can be interpreted as consent and approval even if I do not intend it as such. To take what will be a salient example from Philip Pettit: in Maoist China, no one at any level of society was in a position 'to criticize Mao with impunity', but silence was interpreted by the authorities as approval, 'dreamy adulation in the faces of the masses'.[1] It is not just in Maoist China that silence was interpreted in unintended ways. Such wishful misinterpretation is a common feature of political life, and of personal life as well. Grim examples of the latter are the subject of other activist websites, run by equally liberal-minded folk, this time urging the opposite message—'Remember: *silence is not consent!*'—this time hoping to encourage potential date-rapists to see that a woman may not mean 'yes' until she says so.

Suppose silence really could, sometimes, be a way of approving or consenting. There would be something interesting in the idea that a silence could be a speech act, an illocution of approval or consent. Approval and consent are not quite the same, of course: someone may consent to courses of action of which she disapproves, and refuse consent to courses of action of which she approves. Approval is about whether something has value; consent is about whether something is to be done. If committee work is anything to go by, participants in consensus often find themselves having to disapprove, yet consent; and (more rarely) to approve, yet refuse consent. These subtleties are important, but they will not particularly matter for my present task.[2] How plausible is it that a silence could be an illocution of approval, or consent? Paradigm cases of illocution, as described by J. L. Austin, were never silences, but utterances, spoken or written; but Austin did allow that in hurling a tomato one can make a protest, and in tapping a stick one can make a threat; so he did allow that certain non-utterances can have illocutionary force.[3] If tomato hurlings and stick tappings can have illocutionary force, why not silences?

Sometimes a silence is officially counted as an illocution of consent, by default, and what makes it so is the presence of certain explicit directives or conventions: parliamentary debate that concludes with 'unless there are any objections'; marriage ceremonies that require objectors to 'speak now or forever hold their peace'; 'opt-out' rules regarding privacy and consumer data sharing, trade union membership, organ donorship, even marriage—' "[A] virgin should not be given in marriage except after her permission." The people asked, "O Allah's Apostle! How can we know her permission?" [The prophet] said, "Her silence (indicates

---

[1] Philip Pettit, 'Enfranchising Silence: An Argument for Freedom of Speech', in Tom Campbell and Wojciech Sadurski (eds.), *Freedom of Communication* (Aldershot: Dartmouth, 1994), 45–55; repr. in Pettit, *Rules, Reasons, and Norms* (Oxford: Oxford University Press, 2002), 366–77. Page numbers in what follows are to the latter, and the Maoist China example is introduced at p. 374, drawing on Jung Chang's *Wild Swans* (London: HarperCollins, 1991).

[2] The difference won't particularly matter here since I suspect that for Pettit consent and approval go together, as illustrated in his point, to be discussed, about the role of approving silence in building consensus; the upshot is that in conditions of freedom of speech, and absent any obvious, independent reason to the contrary, silence is approval *and* consent.

[3] J. L. Austin, *How to Do Things with Words* (London: Oxford University Press, 1962). I imagine an illocution of approval to be verdictive, in Austin's terms; and an illocution of consent to be commissive.

her permission)." '[4] In such cases, whether silence is counted as consent is an explicit, formal, and (hopefully) predictable matter. The distinct question of whether silence *should* be counted as consent varies, it seems to me, with the kind of case: for privacy and consumer data sharing, the answer should probably be 'no'; for trade union membership, 'yes'; for organ donorship, 'yes'; for marriage, 'yes' as far as potential objectors are concerned, 'no' as far as potential brides are concerned. That, at any rate, is how my list would go, though it would need argument, and the justifications might be variable: the special importance of autonomy, when it comes to consumers and brides-to-be; the special importance of political representation, when it comes to union membership; and so on. If the patterns for default consent look, on the face of it, rather variable, what prospect is there for a more general condition under which silence speaks approval—and why, if there is, should we want it?

Philip Pettit proposes that there is indeed a condition, a significant one, under which silence is eloquent of approval: it is that of free speech itself. And this 'enfranchisement' of silence is something we should want, since it has many benefits for social discourse, social consensus, and the regulation of society via attitude—in short, it has vital benefits for citizenship. I shall argue that Pettit's proposal has considerable interest, from both a conceptual and a political point of view (1.2–1.3): but I shall want to ask whether the enfranchisement of silence does indeed have free speech as its condition, whether free speech is construed as a negative republican liberty (2.1 and 2.2) or as a positive liberty (2.3). There are certain grounds for hope, especially for the latter, and one purpose of this essay is to flag the potential, in this context, of a positive liberty conception of free speech. However, my conclusion is, in the end, a critical one: free speech does not, I think, enfranchise silence. I shall argue that the expression of disapproval is often voluntary, and sometimes costly; and this means the expression of disapproval may be masked (3.1). Moreover, disapproval *itself* is sometimes voluntary, and sometimes costly: and this means that disapproval may be stifled (3.2). This is particularly clear when (though not only when) one considers relationships that are oppressive or dependent. Some of my argument (3.2) thus takes issue with Pettit's views about the involuntary and cost-free character of the moral sentiments, and hence has implications for his broader views about how social life is regulated by attitude. My main purpose, though, is to put a small question-mark against the hope that the enfranchisement of silence is so readily achieved; and a large question-mark against the hope that we have already achieved it.

---

[4] Sahih Al-Bukhari, 7.67, from a website on Islamic marriage law, which includes the comment: 'Virgins need not speak up to declare that they want a marriage; simply not speaking out against the marriage (her silence) is sufficient consent for a virgin'; and a further citation: 'Malik related to me . . . that the Messenger of Allah, SAAWS, said, "a virgin must be asked for her consent for herself, and her consent is her silence" ' (<http://muttaqun.com/wali.html>).

1.2 The Condition of Enfranchised Silence: Freedom

Pettit proposes that the condition under which silence speaks approval is the condition of free speech itself. When we have free speech, 'the silent observer gets as close as makes no difference to the position of meaning or communicating by her silence that she approves of what she observes . . . silence in the presence of freedom of speech is itself capable of becoming a form of meaning and communication . . . silence is enfranchised.'[5] So he writes in a paper whose title subject is this enfranchisement of silence. If you are free to speak, and you don't speak, then your silence means something. If you are not free to speak, because speaking gets you gaoled or worse, your silence means nothing. Silence goes blank. In Maoist China, a speaker could not use her words to protest with impunity; and while the resulting silence was taken as approval, it was not approval. Silence can only mean approval when it is given under conditions of freedom.

Note that Pettit's interest is not in formal conventions or directives which make silence 'count' as consent; he is interested in real consent, where saying nothing is legitimately taken as agreement precisely because the person intends it so, and can exploit the knowledge that her silence will be so taken. Under conditions of genuine freedom of speech, silence is rightly interpretable as approval, because approval is what it is indeed intended to be.

When speech is free, if you disapprove, you can express your disapproval without fear; which is why silence's default meaning, in such conditions, is approval. Pettit allows, however, that in certain contexts silence can be disapproving: the stony silence, for example, of someone who simply sits, after a lecture, while all those around are voluble in their congratulations. The speaker is free to speak his disapproval, but need not speak it to convey it. This silence is not approval, since there is an 'obvious, independent reason' why the speaker remains silent, given that speech is expected. But silence does have its default setting, he thinks: in conditions of free speech, absent other obvious reasons for silence, approval is what silence gets to mean.[6]

---

[5] Pettit, 'Enfranchising Silence', 372.

[6] Actually, he thinks some other conditions must be met too. In addition to (i) the condition that 'there is no obvious, independent reason why the person should remain silent', it is required (ii) 'that the stimulus is a public act that is significant for others, and (iii) 'that the subject matter involved falls in the domain of free speech' ('Enfranchising Silence', 372). The first two of these I discuss later on. The third I do not, partly because I don't think it affects my argument materially, and partly because I'm not sure I understand what it amounts to: I don't see why speech being outside the domain of free speech (e.g. libel?) should *ipso facto* thwart the possibility of responding to such speech (one can sometimes respond to libel). Perhaps Pettit has the special cases of 'silencing' speech in mind, e.g. hate speech or pornography, that are arguably self-entrenching and hard to protest about.

1.3 The Point of Enfranchised Silence: Citizenship

This capacity of silence to mean approval matters a great deal, says Pettit, because it assists social discourse, social agreement, and social identity. Eloquent silence matters to one's standing as a participant in political life; it matters to citizenship.

The ability to mean approval by her silence enables someone to have a conversational presence in the life of her community, even if she does not speak. Freedom of speech not only empowers a citizen to speak, but empowers her to the extent that she cannot remain speechless, even when silent.

The second benefit concerns interpersonal consensus. Where there is consensus, people not only believe the same things, but believe that they each believe them; and given that in a large community not everyone can vocalize their beliefs, the evidence of consensus will rest on the significance of silence in communicating assent. This, in turn, is crucial to a citizen's social identity.

Unless we are each in a position, without fear of delusion, to identify what we all think in a group, and what it is commonly believed that we all think, then none of us is in a position to identify in a significant and sensible way with that group. We are deprived of perhaps our most important connection to the life of the community.

The third benefit concerns the 'intangible hand' whereby we are capable of controlling one another's behaviour, not through overt actions, not through words of praise or censure, but by the mere manifestation of our attitudes of approval and disapproval. This connects with an important theme in Pettit's philosophy: the capacity we have as a group to police ourselves out of collective predicaments. It is sometimes complained, he says, that uncooperative predicaments cannot be resolved by appealing to people's approval of co-operation and disapproval of non-cooperation. After all, even if we did know that strategic approval and disapproval would help make others co-operate, if we are not spontaneously co-operative to start with, 'why go to the trouble of approving or disapproving?' This complaint is misconceived, thinks Pettit. The formation of attitudes of approval and disapproval is spontaneous, and cost-free: it 'is not intentional, and involves no trouble for the agent'; in these respects, attitudes are unlike overt actions of praise or blame. And this is where eloquent silence plays a role. Free speech, with its consequent enfranchisement of silence, allows free play of attitude, and imputation of attitude. Free speech allows attitude to be manifest to others, and to be attributable by others. If silence is unable to convey the attitude of the subject, as it could not in Maoist China, then attitude is unable to exercise this vital control over others.[7]

---

[7] The quotations regarding the second and third benefit are from Pettit, 'Enfranchising Silence', 376.

Three reasons, then, for thinking it matters that silence be given a voice: even when silent, the citizen can be an active presence in the conversation of the community; she can be an active party to the emergence of consensus; and she can be an active regulator of the behaviour of her fellow citizens.

2. FREE SPEECH

2.1 Free Speech as Republican Negative Liberty

The enfranchisement of silence gives us additional reason for thinking that free speech itself matters, according to Pettit: the enfranchisement of silence constitutes a neglected, independent argument for freedom of speech, since it is in the presence of freedom of speech that silence attains its significant voice.[8]

On Pettit's account, freedom of speech is a negative liberty, freedom from interference, but it is not the bare absence of interference. You have not got freedom of speech until you have *resilient* non-interference. What Pettit proposes here is a special instance of the republican ideal of freedom that he develops elsewhere, the ideal of freedom as non-domination. You are dominated when someone has the *capacity* to interfere, on an arbitrary basis, in certain choices that you are in a position to make: choices, for example, about whether to speak, and what to say. You do not have freedom of speech if you merely happen not to be interfered with, but others still have the capacity to interfere. On this account, while freedom of speech is essentially a negative liberty, it has something positive about it, as does every republican freedom, for 'it needs something more than the absence of interference: it requires security against interference'.[9]

Now, I find this a very interesting proposal, from a conceptual point of view, and from a political point of view as well; and I shall take a few moments to say why, before proceeding to further business. There is a nice paradoxical flavour to the central idea of the *silencing of silence*, and how republican freedom aims to prevent it. What is this silenced silence: how could silence be made silent, if it is already silence? In speech act terms, there is no paradox: the idea is that something that could have had illocutionary force is deprived of that force. Something that could have meant approval, in the presence of genuine freedom, has gone blank. I am tempted to describe this as the *illocutionary disablement* of silence. To illustrate illocutionary disablement, imagine an actor who seeks

---

[8] A further point of interest about this argument is that it appears to offer a justification for free speech that is not obviously intrinsic and not obviously instrumental either: free speech matters not (only) in itself, but because it enfranchises silence; yet this enfranchisement is not (only) an effect of free speech, but something enabled by it, in the way that voting is illocutionarily enabled by relevant voting laws (not, or not just, caused by such laws). In Kantian terms, it is perhaps a conditioned value, but not an instrumental one.

[9] Philip Pettit, *Republicanism: A Theory of Freedom and Government* (Oxford: Oxford University Press, 1997), 51.

genuinely to warn his audience with his words, 'Fire! Fire! I mean it! Look at the smoke!', and who cannot warn, since those are precisely the words the play requires him to utter at that juncture. Imagine a woman who writes a book of protest against the pornography industry and finds it being sold as pornography. Imagine a woman who says 'no' to sex, yet finds her 'no' failing to count as a refusal. These are cases where something that could have had illocutionary force is deprived of that force. And there is, perhaps, a similar disablement in the phenomenon of silenced silence.[10]

A different point of interest is the potential of Pettit's account to accommodate feminist concerns about the tyranny of freedom of speech, when that freedom threatens women. Freedom of speech may be a negative liberty, but it is not an absolute freedom. Pettit allows, for example, that if the free speech of pornographers sufficiently undermines women's freedoms—for example, through legitimating harassment and sexual violence—that may argue for restricting pornographic speech.[11] This is all the more so, given that the republican conception of liberty has implications relevant to the feminist case. When we are considering whether women's freedoms are undermined by something, it is women's *resilient* freedoms that matter. We must consider not just whether women in fact suffer the forms of interference that are rape, or harassment, but whether women are *secure* from that interference: not just whether women are safe, but whether women are resiliently safe. Many women do suffer rape; many, thankfully, happen not to. But how many of the latter are *secure* in that freedom? Republican liberty requires more than non-interference: it requires *resilient* non-interference. So it may well require substantial measures in defending women's freedom from sexual violence, even to the point of restricting the speech of pornographers. This I take to be an important feature of Pettit's proposal, and one that merits further reflection.

There are reasons, then, for finding Pettit's proposal an interesting one. These virtues notwithstanding, I suspect it is mistaken. I shall not, for present purposes, take issue with the claims about the benefits of enfranchised silence—the benefits of silent conversational participation in one's community, silent contribution to consensus, and silent control of others' behaviour through manifestation of attitude (though I confess I see the latter as a more likely force for ill than for good). I shall take issue with his argument that freedom of speech enfranchises silence; in particular, with his idea that in conditions of freedom of speech, silence acquires the default force of approval.

[10] Rae Langton, 'Speech Acts and Unspeakable Acts', *Philosophy and Public Affairs* 22 (1993), 305–30. I am tempted to describe 'silenced silences' this way, but perhaps I should resist: my examples involve tokens where the speaker intends some illocution but her speech 'misfires', but it doesn't seem accurate to describe Pettit's silenced silences as 'misfires'. I leave this for further reflection.

[11] Pettit, 'Enfranchising Silence', 368. Pettit himself points out in this connection the relevance of republican freedom to the pursuit of resilient liberty for women.

2.2 Does Negative Free Speech Enfranchise Silence?

For Pettit, free speech is a certain negative liberty, a freedom from interference; and his claim is not simply that freedom of speech is necessary for enfranchising silence, but that it is necessary and sufficient for enfranchising silence, provided certain other conditions are in place. He asks us to imagine a small community in which free speech is well and truly established: 'no-one is exposed to the danger of interference, because a protective field of law and custom guards against interference, and it is common knowledge in the community that this is so.'[12] Suppose now that in this community someone performs a 'public' act, i.e. an act that is not only of significance to the agent herself:

> The freedom of speech enjoyed by those who observe her in that performance means that they may be expected to complain or criticize in the event of believing that the action is not for the best. But the freedom of speech also means that, if they say nothing, then, absent any obvious alternative reason why they should remain quiet in the face of such a stimulus, they may be presumed by the agent, and by the others involved, not to disapprove of what has been done; they may be presumed, in effect, to approve of the behaviour. . . . [T]he silent observer [communicates] by her silence that she approves; she acquiesces in their recognizing that she acquiesces in this way; and she acquiesces in the fact of that recognition leading them to form the relevant belief.[13]

This enfranchisement of silence depends on the condition of freedom of speech, together with the additional conditions that the stimulus is public, i.e. significant to (and perhaps observable by) others, and that there is no obvious, independent reason why the person should remain silent. But under these conditions—and such conditions 'are going to be run of the mill in a community where freedom of speech is established'—approval is indeed what silence gets to mean.

In questioning this, I want to consider some silences that are not approval or consent, though they may be taken as such. I want to see what light they shed on Pettit's connected claims that free speech enfranchises silence, and that free speech is to be understood as a republican freedom. One could perhaps take examples from the literature on sexual violence, where the results of reading silence as default consent are particularly troubling. But I shall allow readers to draw their own conclusions on that subject, and offer instead a down-to-earth story about some ordinary employment conditions in a fairly enlightened Western democracy; for it will do just as well, I think, to illustrate my concerns.

Undercover journalist Polly Toynbee took a job as a 'dinner lady' at a Lambeth primary school, with an image of 'the sort of job cosy mums did for a bit of extra pin money', lounging around at the hatch, 'doling out dollops of food while chatting cheerily'. The reality was a kitchen with no dishwashing machines, and staff who tackled their back-breaking, messy tasks at a punishing speed. 'Why

---

[12] Pettit 'Enfranchising Silence', 370.   [13] Ibid. 372.

so hard and fast, non-stop, harder than seemed necessary . . . with no obvious supervisory whips at our backs?' The answer came after the four-minute lunch break, a deluge of new work, as vanloads of unwashed dishes arrived from all the surrounding primary schools, whose kitchens had been closed to save money. Only a maniacal work pace, set by the ferociously determined workers, allowed the tasks of so many kitchens to be done by one. Toynbee reflects on the workers' attitude:

Maggie and Wilma . . . worked together in perfect harmony, understood one another's every move, mood and gesture, and they were fond of each other. They both said the work was impossible, unbearable, under timed and underpaid. . . . Why did Maggie and Wilma stay? They liked the school, the staff, the head, and one another. More than that, it was as if the very harshness of the work bound them together in a daily challenge to keep going. . . . Work can become a compulsive activity, even when you hate your employer. The familiar if harsh rhythms of sheer physical labour, the perfectionism of keeping that kitchen running clean, tidy, and well-organised, the sheer difficulty of the daily task, seemed in a perverse way to tie them to the place. . . . Besides, the friendship and understanding between them kept them together. These are sentiments on which companies trade relentlessly.[14]

Elsewhere in her book Toynbee comments on the uncomplainingness of the job-seekers she encountered, 'waiting, waiting, filling forms and waiting again in grim and shabby lobbies all over the city [of London] . . . unnaturally patient, with no expectation of good treatment and no disappointment or surprise when things turn out badly.'[15] Maggie and Wilma don't complain about their conditions; job-seekers don't complain about the wasted time and money they spend on the trail of interviews that don't exist. Is their silence approval? Of course it isn't. But then perhaps these are not conditions in which there is freedom of speech, or not, at any rate, the right sort of freedom of speech.

When Pettit describes the conditions in which free speech prevails, he contrasts the conditions of Maoist China with those of a small, idealized speech community, and with those of real-life liberal democracies. There is, he says, 'a great contrast' between the situation in China and the 'imperfect but certainly superior situation in most Western democracies'.[16] The implication is that here free speech prevails, that here, unlike China, the conditions of the idealized speech community are realized, if imperfectly. The implication is that in Western democracies silence is more or less enfranchised, as it was not in Maoist China. We can agree with Pettit that there is indeed 'a great contrast' between the situation in Maoist China and the situation on our own doorsteps. And it is indeed a difference that has to do with freedom of speech. There, dissidents were clapped in gaol. Here they are

[14] Polly Toynbee, *Hard Work: Life in Low Pay Britain* (London: Bloomsbury, 2003), 100, 109. Toynbee was partly inspired by Barbara Ehrenreich, *Nickel and Dimed: On (Not) Getting by in America* (New York: Metropolitan Books, 2001).
[15] Toynbee, *Hard Work*, 97.
[16] Pettit, 'Enfranchising Silence', 374.

not, as a rule; here we have laws protecting speech and expression. But we can wonder: while speech is more free here, *is it free enough to enfranchise silence*? And if it is not, *what would it take* to make it so?

Maggie and Wilma will not be gaoled if they speak out against their conditions: in this, the law protects their freedom to speak. The next question is whether they will suffer other forms of 'interference' if they speak out. Pettit takes interference to be something done intentionally, by an agent who intends to worsen someone's choice situation.[17] And Maggie and Wilma do risk interference: vulnerable as they are, they risk losing their jobs if they complain. Complaint might be construed as conflicting with the expectations of the job itself—the 'Always Happy! Never Sad!' smiley-face posters pinned up around the work place by their superiors (shades of Maoist propaganda posters there!); and—should they take complaint further afield—the contracts whose small print required workers not to talk to the press. It seems legitimate, surely, to fire someone who is not doing the job they agreed to do.

Suppose though, that as a matter of contingent fact, Maggie and Wilma would not be fired if they were to complain. The next question is whether they are *secure* in this liberty: is their freedom a *resilient* one? For their freedom to be resilient, they need robust non-interference. Free speech as a republican negative liberty will perhaps require laws giving them a certain security of employment, without which they would be subject to ongoing risk of interference. This strengthening of employment rights would be a more substantial outcome than one antecedently expects from a negative freedom of speech; but perhaps none the worse for that.

Let us, in imagination, give Maggie and Wilma whatever they need for republican freedom of speech: give them whatever they need to speak freely, secure from interference, secure from the penalizing actions of someone who finds their speech unwelcome, and 'intends to restrict their choice situation'; let us give them whatever they need for genuine freedom of speech, understood as a republican, negative freedom from interference. Our question remains: is their silence then enfranchised? When Maggie and Wilma observe a particular 'public act' that impinges on their lives, such as the decision to close the other school kitchens, and when they are silent in the face of that decision, do they get 'as close as makes no difference' to the position of 'meaning or communicating' by their silence that they approve of what they observe? No. Mind you, it would be unsurprising to find their employers construing that silence as approval, and for reasons very similar to the reasons Pettit discusses: Maggie and Wilma would be free to speak; they would not be penalized for speaking; and there would be no other obvious explanation for their silence. Their silence is not approval, all the same.

Maggie and Wilma still have many reasons for silence. One is that it can seem pointless to express disapproval when the current option seems, more or less, the

---

[17] Pettit, *Republicanism*, 52–3.

only option. The workers for this company were desperate mothers, trapped in a low-wage cycle by responsibilities to their children, low-paid because they were without adequate child care to allow training time, and without adequate child care because they were low-paid. Wilma lived nearby, and could not manage other hours or travel because of her family responsibilities. Without the leverage of alternative options, complaining would have no good consequences, and she knows it. Yet her silence is not her approval. Freedom of speech does not fix this problem — or not, at any rate, free speech construed as a negative liberty, i.e. free speech construed as freedom, even resilient freedom, from non-interference.

2.3 Does Positive Free Speech Enfranchise Silence?

It is worth asking whether it would help towards the enfranchisement of silence if we were to understand freedom of speech as something more: if we were to understand free speech as, let us say, a *positive* liberty. Now, I have to confess a general suspicion of 'positive liberty', mostly because it is so hard to pin down. Sometimes positive liberty is the idea of active participation in political life; sometimes it is the idea of self-mastery; sometimes it is the idea of a freedom enjoyed by your true, transcendental self, not your everyday empirical self; sometimes, applied to speech, it is the idea of not only saying words but having your words believed; sometimes it is the idea of not only having freedom from interference, but having the material resources required to exercise that freedom.[18] The only thing these have in common, as far as I can see, is that positive liberty is 'something more than' negative liberty, but there seems little agreement about what that 'something' might be.

Well, let us pin it down, by fiat if nothing else. Let us take it to be the last idea on the list: positive liberty involves, in addition to freedom to speak without interference, the basic material resources needed to exercise that freedom. If free speech is construed as merely a negative liberty, the gaoled dissident lacks it, but the illiterate peasant may have it. If free speech is construed as a positive liberty, you don't have free speech until you have some minimal resources to exercise it; the dissident and the peasant might both be unfree. Someone who is illiterate is not in a good position to exercise freedom of speech: positive free speech may involve literacy as well as non-interference.[19] Someone who is living in abject

---

[18] At least the first three construals appear in Isaiah Berlin, 'Two Concepts of Liberty', in *Four Essays on Liberty* (Oxford: Oxford University Press, 1968); I think the others appear, together with that of 'self-mastery', in Ronald Dworkin, 'Liberty and Pornography', *New York Review of Books*, 15 Aug. 1991, 12–15; also published as 'Two Concepts of Liberty' in *Isaiah Berlin: A Celebration*, eds. Edna and Avishai Margalit (Chicago: University of Chicago Press, 1991), 100–9.

[19] On this way of thinking, it is hypocritical for the USA to refuse its United Nations dues, protesting that the UN helps nations that have insufficient respect for free speech, when that refusal effectively steals funds from UN literacy programs, thereby perpetuating, on a grander scale, the silence of illiteracy.

poverty is not in a good position to exercise freedom of speech either: positive free speech may involve some basic economic resources. Someone who systematically suffers illocutionary disablement is not in a good position to exercise free speech either: positive free speech may involve protection of the background linguistic condition which Jennifer Hornsby calls *reciprocity*—roughly, the capacity hearers have to recognize the communicative illocutions that speakers intend, without which, arguably, one cannot really speak.[20]

Pretty clearly, free speech as a positive liberty is an improvement on free speech as a negative liberty, even republican style, at least when it comes to improving things for enfranchisement. An illiterate peasant who does not complain about his situation, however robustly free from interference his complaining, does not thereby manifest his approval; but his silence is somewhat more likely to be approval if he has not only the freedom from interference, but also the resources, to speak. Suppose Wilma and Maggie were not only protected from interference · (being fired if they complain), but also had more in the way of the material resources to exercise their speech meaningfully. If they had all this, and still they did not complain, their silence too is somewhat more likely to be approval. I shall not, here, take a stand on whether freedom of speech can be plausibly extended as a positive liberty; but if we are interested in what it would take to enfranchise silence, it is worth thinking about whether free speech as a positive liberty is more likely to do the job.

3. ATTITUDE

3.1 The Expression of Attitude: Still Voluntary and Costly

Free speech as positive liberty is an improvement on free speech as negative liberty, if we are after the enfranchisement of silence: an improvement, I have said, but still, I fear, insufficient. It will never, I think, be legitimate to take a shortcut to consensus by assuming that silence is consent, however desirable that would be.

Expressing disapproval is sometimes costly; and the costs are not removed merely when interference is removed and basic resources supplied. Given that expression of attitude is voluntary (as Pettit agrees), when costs of expression are high, there will be times when speakers choose not to voice their disapproval, even when allowed resources to speak and when protected from interference. Think of all the little reasons for not complaining, reasons that have nothing to

---

[20] Whether illocutionary disablement represents a negative or a positive liberty violation is open to debate; I myself elsewhere describe it in negative liberty terms, since I think it results from interference, at least in the relevant examples of silenced protest and refusal; Hornsby, on the other hand describes it in positive liberty terms. See Langton, 'Speech Acts and Unspeakable Acts'; 'Pornography: A Liberal's Unfinished Business', *Canadian Journal of Law and Jurisprudence*, special issue on legal theory (1999), ed. Wilfrid Waluchow, 109–33; Jennifer Hornsby and Rae Langton, 'Free Speech and Illocution', *Journal of Legal Theory* 4 (1998), 21–37.

do with fear of punishment or not having the resources to complain. Maggie and Wilma do not complain, partly because they take pride in their ability to do well a nigh-impossible job. And they do not complain, because there is something good about their situation, something they themselves have created: a partnership where they work in harmony, instinctive understanding, and deep affection. In conditions of perfect freedom, can we be sure they would take their complaint to their employer? I have my doubts.

Whatever one supposes about this example, it is clear that pride and affection can often be incentives for masking one's disapproval, whether in congenial or oppressive circumstances. Pride can stop you complaining when you don't want to reveal that something has got under your skin. Affection can stop you complaining when you think that complaint would hurt the one you like or love. It might be queried whether these are relevant; after all, they are rather personal aspects of one's speech situation, rather different from the observation of 'public acts' that interests Pettit. Well, I want to say that such motives are indeed relevant, and place another reminder, should reminder be needed, about how the personal can be political. Over the centuries when women did not, much, complain of their subordination, one suspects that fear of gaol was an insignificant silencer of disapproval, compared to the motives of affection for spouse and children, together with the invisibility of alternative arrangements. Yet the upshot is in certain respects parallel to the situation Pettit decries in China: the subordination of an entire class of people, whose silence was interpreted as approval, and therefore vindication, of subordination.

Pettit wants a situation in which there is 'free play' for manifestation of attitude, through enfranchised silence, without which the 'intangible hand' is unable to do its good work of regulating social behaviour; and he thinks that freedom of speech, republican style, will provide it. I have suggested that it will not, neither as negative liberty, nor as positive: while free speech removes some costs to speech, it by no means removes them all. There will remain complex and non-obvious incentives for masking one's disapproval. Free speech makes the play of attitude more free, perhaps, than it would otherwise be; but not free enough to let silence count as approval.

3.2 The Possession of Attitude: Likewise Voluntary and Costly

Recall the features which, in Pettit's opinion, enable attitude to regulate behaviour, in the right conditions. Attitudes of approval and disapproval are, he thinks, formed involuntarily; and forming them costs the agent nothing. Expressions of the attitude, on the other hand, are voluntary, and may cost something. If expressing disapproval costs the dissident his freedom, he can voluntarily inhibit what he would otherwise express. That was the point of Pettit's argument: if we remove the costs of expression, by protecting speech, we remove the incentive to voluntarily inhibiting expression; so attitude will helpfully manifest itself. The presence of other costs undermines the force of the argument, as I just tried to show; but it may have further implications too, reaching beyond expression to the attitudes themselves. Consider that what goes for constraints on expression of attitude might go for attitude too. *Expressing* a disapproving attitude can of course be costly; but merely *possessing* a disapproving attitude can be costly too. There is room for doubt about Pettit's assumption that attitude is an involuntary and cost-free matter.

Disapproval is sometimes costly. In many circumstances, including oppressive circumstances, there are costs, not just in expressing, but in *having* the disapproving attitude. There are costs involved in having to hide what one thinks. Hugging one's disapproval all to one's self is a miserable business: there is misery in the disapproval, and misery in the hiding too. In relationships of one-sided dependence, disapproval by the dependant is an ongoing liability, presenting an ongoing risk of accidental disclosure, and consequent danger to one's happiness or security. Feeling disapproval would be a liability for the Chinese dissidents; and for dependants in oppressive personal relationships; and for the kitchen workers. Disapproval of their working conditions would be a cost to Wilma and Maggie, wasting time and energy, and undermining all the modest joys they have managed to create. Even in non-oppressive contexts, disapproval has its costs: disapproval hurts the disapprover as well as the disapproved. Disapproval of someone you like or love can be uncomfortable, even when unmanifested; it can undermine friendships and undermine otherwise happy marriages. Contrary to Pettit's assumption, disapproval is not cost-free.

Because disapproval sometimes has costs to the disapprover, as well as the disapproved, it would be useful for the disapprover to be able to control it. And we *can* control our disapproval. Disapproval is voluntary, at least to some extent. To be sure, we cannot always decide, just like that, not to disapprove; but we can take measures to make ourselves less disapproving. A sour-puss can learn to lighten up. Someone with an over-ready disposition to disapprove can change it—learn to look for the silver linings instead of the clouds, look for the half-full glass instead of the half-empty one, look for the good in people as well as the bad.[21] And just as an over-ready disposition to disapprove can be altered, so too can an *accurate* disposition to disapprove, when such change would be useful. The dissident in China cannot only mask disapproval, but stifle it, through habits of selective attention to the good, inattention to the bad. The same familiar mechanisms enable Maggie and Wilma not only to *show* less disapproval, but to *feel* less disapproval than their situation warrants. When disapproval is uncomfortable, or threatens something we value, we can squash it or mimimize it: spouses stifle their irritation at the other's idea of what 'fair

---

[21] See e.g. Martin Seligman, *Learned Optimism* (New York: Knopf, 1990) on cognitive therapy's methods of training people out of habits of negative evaluation (whether of their own actions or the actions of others).

share' of the housework means; friends think better of each other than they deserve; children try to squash their disapproval of broccoli; parents try to squash their disapproval of their children's disapproval.[22] Making the best of one's situation is a talent one can cultivate, an admirable talent in many ways, even if it occasionally allows ill-doing to escape the disapproval it deserves.

The expression of disapproval is voluntary and sometimes costly, as Pettit assumes; disapproval itself is likewise voluntary and sometimes costly, contrary to what Pettit assumes. If this is so, we are further still from the conditions in which freedom of speech enfranchises silence, if by that is meant a situation that permits a default interpretation of silence as approval. Recall, we were far enough beforehand: conditions of free speech are not enough to guarantee expression of disapproval when disapproval is felt, because other costs may yet motivate its masking.

Now there is still greater distance: for these other costs—threats to security, to friendship, or to happiness—present reasons not only for masking disapproval, but for stifling it, so that people who might otherwise disapprove do not. Can their silence, in such circumstances, be read as approval? No. Employees, friends, spouses, who have taught themselves to make the best of things, and not to waste their energies on useless inward complainings—these are not best read as approving their situation either, particularly if we are after the sort of approval that is ground for consensus.

4. CONCLUSION

Freedom of speech does not, I think, enfranchise silence. It is not true that in conditions of free speech 'the silent observer gets as close as making no difference to the position of meaning or communicating by her silence that she approves of what she observes'. Life is too complicated, I suspect, for there to be any general condition under which silence would count as approval, notwithstanding the potential benefits to citizenship that such enfranchisement might bring. To be sure, silence can be made to count as approval for various purposes, whether for parliamentary debate, or for opt-out arrangements regarding privacy, union membership, organ donation, and the like. But we should not hope for a uniform pattern under which silence appropriately counts as approval or consent: and by 'should not hope' I mean we should neither expect it, nor value it.

Free speech as a negative liberty is not sufficient to enfranchise silence, not even free speech as a *republican* negative liberty—distinctive and promising as that notion is. Free speech as a positive liberty does somewhat better, I think; it presents a possibility worth exploring, if (the above scepticism notwithstanding)

---

[22] For a study of the domestic work-related attitudes of new parents (of varying ideologies), and some apparent correlations between marital success and the stifling of disapproval (especially, but not only, by exhausted wives) see Jay Belsky and John Kelly, *The Transition to Parenthood: How a First Child Changes a Marriage* (London: Ebury Press, 1994), 139–52.

a general condition for the enfranchisement of silence still seems a goal worth pursuing. However, even positive freedom of speech is insufficient for the task, I have suggested. Since expression of disapproval could still have costs, there could be reasons for choosing to mask one's disapproval. And since disapproval itself could still have costs, there could be reasons for choosing to stifle one's disapproval. Free speech is compatible with silence that is masked disapproval, and with silence that is stifled disapproval—neither of which is appropriately interpreted as approval. So free speech does not enfranchise silence.

There is one last thing to say. Recall that, in the example which Pettit took as his inspiration, the Chinese authorities wrongly interpreted the silence of the masses as approval, a 'dreamy adulation' of Chairman Mao. Observe that their interpretation *assumed* the enfranchisement of silence. The assumption was based on a self-serving delusion that the conditions for such enfranchisement were satisfied.

The example shows the dangers of assuming too much. Silence here is doubly disenfranchised, since there is an *incapacity* and also a *twisting*: silence is incapable of being approval; and it is twisted into, interpreted as, approval. Silence is incapable of being approval, given the absence of free speech; yet it is made to count as approval, not as a blank. To have one's words twisted into their opposite can be worse, perhaps, than to say nothing; likewise, to have one's silent disapproval twisted into approval can be worse, perhaps, than to have one's silence a neutral blank. Whether or not it is something worse, it is certainly something extra. Pettit's main interest is in the former silencing of silence: the incapacity of a silence to be genuine approval. I am equally interested in the latter silencing of silence: the way a silence can get twisted. The source of the former disenfranchisement, the incapacity, is (in Pettit's view) the *absence of free speech*; and that has been our chief topic here. The source of the second disenfranchisement, the twisting, is the very *assumption of enfranchisement*. The authorities assumed, wrongly, that the conditions for enfranchisement were met: that is why they took silence as approval. This illustrates the dangers of assuming too readily that the conditions for enfranchisement are present.

The same moral, albeit in a lighter tone, applies to Pettit's own argument. There are dangers in an assumption that Western liberal democracies bring the conditions under which silence is genuine approval. Silence might not be approval, even in conditions of resilient freedom of speech; and it would be disastrous if it were twisted into approval when it is not. There are, sadly, no shortcuts to consensus. If you want to know what people think, there is probably no substitute for asking; and even then, in the most open of circumstances, you still might not find out. Silence is not, other things being equal, consent. Pettit's example supplies, in the end, a double warning: if enfranchised silence has its enemies, they include not only the absence of free speech but the presence of a too sanguine assumption that silence is already enfranchised.

Joining the Dots

Philip Pettit

The contributors to this volume cover a wide swathe of territory and address a variety of questions. My essay is written under the stimulus of their chapters, and with great appreciation for the attention given to my own work; but it is not structured as a set of topic-by-topic replies. Rather, at the insistence of the editors, I have written a broad overview of where I am inclined to stand in the areas covered by the contributors, as well as in adjacent territory, commenting as occasion arises on various observations and criticisms that they make. The essay, in consequence, is a free-standing piece designed to give a brief restatement of claims to which the chapters relate.

But though the observations and criticisms of my commentators are covered only as occasion arises, the restatement I offer is shaped in great part by their contributions. I set up my views in a way that enables me to deal with criticisms and to situate the concessions I make—sometimes these are just a matter of saying, "Agreed, you're right"—in the most illuminating manner possible. The result is that I sometimes reformulate those views substantially, and fill in gaps not covered in previous writing; examples include my discussions of program explanation, reasoning as distinct from rationality, freedom as non-domination, and "proxy" democratic control. I hope that the statement provided will serve as a clear, free-standing account of the views covered. In any case it will help to show how, in my mind, they connect with one another; it may serve to join the dots.

The essay is in nine sections:

   I. Physicalism, causality, and control
  II. Intentionality, reasoning, and free will
 III. Rules, response-dependence, and values
  IV. Phenomenal consciousness
   V. Conversability and morality

The editors of this volume have been staunch and selfless in their efforts to get it together. My gratitude overflows. I am particularly grateful to Michael Smith who, as a colleague in Princeton, carried a somewhat larger share of the burden.

The first section deals with matters of background metaphysics, documenting my commitment to physicalism, to the program story about lower- and higher-level causation, and to the idea of virtual as distinct from active control. The second deals with topics central to the philosophy of mind, covering intentional causation, reasoning, free will, and free thought. The third section elaborates a view on the rule-following that reasoning presupposes and outlines the response-dependent theory of basic concepts—in particular, evaluative concepts—suggested by this view. The fourth section returns to matters of mind, associated in particular with phenomenal consciousness. The fifth moves on to issues of interpersonal relationships, emphasizing the capacity of people to reason with one another, and the importance, even within a broadly consequentialist framework, of the associated value of respect. The sixth covers matters in social ontology, arguing that though people fit the image of more or less rational, reasoning agents, they may still depend on one another non-causally for the capacity to reason, and they may be capable of constructing autonomous collective agents. The seventh section moves on to politics, arguing for the central value of freedom as non-domination, connecting this with the republican tradition, and indicating the basis for policymaking that it provides. The eighth section explores the complementary, republican ideal of a democracy that gives the corporate people editorial as well as authorial control and that opens up the possibility of non-arbitrary government. And the ninth section identifies some unifying themes.

1. PHYSICALISM, CAUSALITY, AND CONTROL

Physicalism

I accept the truth of physicalism or materialism or naturalism, as it is variously called, and this forms an important part of the background to many of the positions with which I align myself and to many of the views discussed in this volume. Physicalists hold that everything in existence is constituted in some way out of physical materials and that all the laws and regularities that hold in the actual world are fixed by physical laws and regularities. 'Physical' might just be taken to mean 'microphysical' or 'subatomic'; taking it in this way would avoid some troublesome ambiguities (Pettit 1993*b*, 1994, 1995*b*).[1] But an alternative

---

[1] One problem with my preferred route is that anti-physicalists have begun to speculate on the psychic or proto-psychic character that some microphysical entities may have. I find the idea outlandish, I confess, despite the flair with which it is presented, e.g., in Chalmers 1996.

and equally acceptable approach would identify it by ostension as the category of stuff exemplified by such and such examples.

However 'physical' is understood, the account given of physicalism means that a minimal physical duplicate of the actual world—a physical duplicate to which nothing is independently added—would be a duplicate *simpliciter*, a duplicate in every respect (Jackson 1998). This is to say that the non-physical character of the actual world is fixed superveniently on the physical. Short of an independent addition, there is no possibility of a change in the non-physical way the world is without a change in its physical makeup; fix the way it is physically, and you will have fixed the way it is in every respect.

Physicalism is only a hypothesis, since it is a contingent truth that the actual world has the character described. It is an economical and attractive hypothesis, however, and it has the advantage of sharpening the challenge for philosophy to try to reconcile the world as we know it in common experience and assumption with the world as it is described in science (Pettit 2004*d*). Physicalism is a worst-case scenario from the point of view of trying to vindicate our everyday presuppositions about macrophysical and psychological causality, about free will and personal responsibility, about the objectivity of the good and the right, and about a host of like phenomena. If such phenomena can be saved under the physicalist assumption—saved, at least up to certain limits—then that is interesting and good news; what can be saved under this assumption is safe as safe can be.

One component that has helped to make physicalism seem more credible and congenial to me is the program model of causal relevance and efficacy that Frank Jackson and I have defended both jointly and separately (Jackson, Pettit, and Smith 2004: part 1). It is addressed in their chapter by Cynthia and Graham Macdonald, and is part of the target in Peter Menzies's critique of my views on mental causation, as well as being relevant to some other chapters. In this first section I try to lay out the elements in the model; to introduce some clarifications that seem to me to be in the spirit of the approach; and thereby to guard myself against points made in those commentaries. Towards the end of the discussion I turn to related issues, involving causal explanation more generally and the possibility of virtual as distinct from active, causal control; some concepts introduced there, in particular that of virtual control, are important in later discussions.

Causal Events and Causally Relevant Properties

With any event that we regard as a cause or causal factor in relation to an effect, we assume that there is a sense in which it produces or at least influences that effect. There are many theories as to what production or influence involves. Some say that real or kosher production requires some unanalyzable 'oomph' or 'bif', others that production can be analyzed in terms of a set of formal conditions of counterfactual dependency, others again that it is a relationship we conceptualize on a pragmatic basis, as whatever it is that makes it possible, or might make it possible, to bring about the effect by manipulating the cause. I have a certain sympathy for the pragmatic approach, but want to abstract from differences between the different accounts of causal productivity and influence—causal efficacy—in presenting the program model. I shall simply assume that we have an understanding of what it is for one event to have an influence on the appearance of another.

Take a cause, then, that produces or influences a certain effect. Apart from assuming that the cause is efficacious in some sense, we also naturally assume that it is in virtue of some of its properties, and not of others, that it is efficacious in producing that type of effect. Consider the event that we describe as the failure of the electricity in my house. The event that produced that effect may be variously described, depending on which properties are highlighted, but some of those properties will clearly be relevant to the production, others not. The property of having been reported in my letter to a friend won't be a causally relevant property, for example; the property of having been a bolt of lightning that struck my house will. That event produced the failure of the electricity in virtue of being a bolt of lightning, we will naturally say, but not in virtue of having been reported in my letter.

What makes the one property causally relevant, the other not? We can work with a straightforward, if rough-hewn, notion of relevance. The bolt of lightning that struck my house would have done the damage envisaged, or been likely to do it, even under considerable variation in other factors: say, variation in the exact time at which it occurred, in the height of the building, in whether various electrical circuits were closed or open, or in whether it was raining or not raining. The presence of the property of being a bolt of lightning that struck my house was more or less sufficient—sufficient across these or those variations—for the realization of the effect.[2] The presence of the property of having been described in my letter, however, would not have been sufficient in the same way to ensure that the electricity failed. There is no salient set of variations across which it would have continued to control for the effect.[3]

---

[2] What of the relevance, then, of the property of being a-bolt-of-lightning-where-two-plus-two-equals-four? I assume that some background assumptions about economy will enable us to identify at any level the minimal property—the property, shorn of redundant aspects—that should count as relevant.

[3] Different theories of causal production or influence will give different glosses on the sufficiency idea used in this paragraph. Some will take the causally relevant property just to indicate production or influence, others to constitute it, others to do one or the other of the two. That the presence of the property suffices for the appearance of the effect is consistent with any of these relationships. As I abstract from the nature of production or influence, so I abstract from the issue that comes up here. The issue can be put in the form of a Euthyphro-like question. Is a property causally relevant in certain cases because it is present when there is a productive connection present? Or is the productive connection present in those cases because the programming property is present? Or can it sometimes be one way, sometimes the other, giving us two more specific senses of causal relevance?

The Nesting of Relevant Properties

We have put in place the notion of a causally efficacious event and the idea that some of its properties may be relevant to the production of that type of effect, others not. One further point to put in the picture now is that the properties of an event that are causally relevant to its producing or influencing a certain type of effect may be nested in a sort of hierarchy. That an event is of type A, instantiating the A-property, may be relevant to its producing an effect of type X to the extent that the continuing presence of the A-property would suffice, across salient variations, for the continued efficacy of the event in producing or helping to produce the X-type event. Yet the following may also be true. The event is of type *a*, where the A-type may be realized at a more specific level by an *a*- or *b*- or *c*-type—I take the notion of realization as primitive—and where it controls for the production of an X across those variations. Yet the *a*-type may also be causally relevant, since the preservation of this property too may suffice, across a salient range of variations in its realizers, for the production of the effect; indeed, the same may be true of the *b*-type and *c*-type too.

Let the event remain of type A, and regardless of how it varies in its realizers, including in whether it is realized by *a* or *b* or *c*, it will produce an X. But equally, let the event remain of type *a* and regardless of how it varies in its realizers, it will produce an X. There is no inconsistency between these claims. The type A property will have a more general causal relevance, in the sense of sufficing for the X across the set of variations in realizers over which *a* suffices, and some other variations as well: it will suffice, even if A is realized by *b* or *c*. The type *a* property will have more specific causal relevance, in the sense of sufficing across only the narrower range of variations.

Suppose that the bolt of lightning that caused the electricity to fail in my house was an electrical discharge of magnitude *m*. Both properties, so we can now see, may have been causally relevant to its causing the electrical failure. Even as the bolt varies in the precise electrical discharge involved, taking the value *m* or any of a range of other values, it will still cause the electricity to fail. Even as the electrical discharge of magnitude *m* varies in finer-grained respects, it will still cause the electricity to fail. But the cases where its being a discharge of that magnitude remains relevant are all cases where its being a bolt of lightning remains relevant. And not vice versa. The one factor is relevant across a more general range than the other.

Programming

Not only do causes produce effects, then; and not only do they do so in virtue of some of their properties, not in virtue of others. What is also true is that the properties that are causally relevant in that way may be nested in relation to one another, with more general properties figuring at the higher end and more specific ones at the lower. At this point we can introduce the notion of programming. A property that is causally relevant to the appearance of a certain type of effect will program for that production in the following sense. It will be capable of being realized across a range of variations in the realizing event: this, as the bolt of lightning may be realized across variations in the magnitude of the electrical discharge. No matter how it is realized, however, the realizing event will produce or help to produce—or be likely to produce or help to produce—the type of effect at issue: this, in the way that the different electrical discharges that may constitute a bolt of lightning will each tend to produce the electrical failure. And, finally, it is a realizer of that property, a particular bolt of lightning, with a particular magnitude, which actually does produce or help to produce the effect.

Where a causal event produces a certain type of effect, a causally relevant property programs for the production of that type of effect. Or, as we can also say, the instantiation of the property, the fact that the property is instantiated, programs for the appearance of that type of event. Let the property be realized and, one way or another, the effect will tend to materialize too; there will be an event present, maybe of this more specific character, maybe of that, which brings it about or helps to bring it about.

Should we say that the instance or token of the property—the event that realizes the property—programs for the effect? Not if we think of that event as a particular, since this is likely to lead us into thinking of programming as itself a particular-to-particular connection. Peter Menzies is misled about my view, for example, when he suggests—admitting that I do not exactly say as much—that the program model assigns causal efficacy to the instances of some properties, and causal relevance to others. Property-instances, and only property-instances, have causal efficacy; properties, and only properties, have causal relevance.

Once we have the notion of programming in place, we can invoke it to address a more or less familiar problem to which physicalism gives rise. This is the problem of explaining how there can be higher-level as well as lower-level causality; in particular, how there can be causality of any kind—say, macrophysical or psychological or sociological causality—that deserves recognition, side by side with the microphysical interaction that physicalists must treat as in some sense basic.

The problem of higher-level causality, as I understand it, is the problem of how properties at different levels can be causally relevant. One property is higher in level than another if the realization of properties of that type is superveniently determined by the realization of properties of the other type. There will be no variation in the higher properties, at least given the assumed context, without variation in the lower: fix the lower pattern, and the higher one will be fixed for free. The property of being colored is higher in level, for example, than the property of being red or yellow or blue; fix the pattern in the particular colors, and you will fix the pattern in what is colored and what is not.

The problem with higher- and lower-level causes of the same type of effect is that it has often seemed hard to explain how they can both be causally related to the effect. The fact that the twirling cape is colored may program for the disturbance in the bull—perhaps any colored cape would do the job—but so does the fact that it is red. So what are we to say about how such different causes combine? They don't combine as simultaneous partial contributors, or as temporally ordered contributors, or as independently sufficient, overdetermining causal factors. So how exactly do they work together?

The programming idea gives us an answer. Whenever a property programs for the production of an event, it will display higher-level causality so far as there is a lower-level property that realizes the higher level, in the usual pattern of supervenience, and that lower-level property programs at a more specific level for the production. Whenever a type A property programs for the production of an X, it will involve higher-level causality so far as there is a type a or b or c property that realizes that higher-level property, and the a or b or c property programs at a more specific level for the production. Thus, when the bolt of lightning programmed for the damage to the electricity supply in my house, so did an electrical discharge of a determinate magnitude. And those programmers related to one another as higher-level to lower-level factors: more general to more specific programming properties.

This gives us a picture, then, of how causally relevant properties may be organized in a programming architecture. Each property at any level will be causally relevant in the sense of programming for the production of the effect. And the properties that program down different levels will do so in progressively more specific ways. The higher-level, general property will program via the programming of the lower-level, more specific property, and there will be no question of any conflict between the two modes of determination.

As we consider this hierarchy, it is natural to ask whether in every case of causal production or influence, there is some lowest-level property that represents the most specific programmer, and whether it should not count, then, as the ultimate source of causal relevance, the real basis for the causal efficacy of the event. This line of thought may become particularly attractive as we envisage the possibility that the lowest-level property may program for the production or influence of the cause only over very trivial variations in spatial and temporal location, or in the composition of the subject of the event. For all that I suppose, however, there need be nothing special about even this last, programming property, if indeed there is a last property to be identified.[4]

---

[4] Different accounts of what production or influence involves—different stories about what is involved in one event's occasioning another—may motivate an asymmetrical view of that property, but as I said earlier, I am abstracting here from such accounts; I am spelling out the sorts of things that will hold, or so it seems to me, no matter what account is given of the causal, particular-to-particular relationship. Admitting that this goes against what I say, Peter Menzies supposes in most of his chapter that I do commit myself to a physical view of 'real' causation.

There is bound to be one sense, of course, in which the most specific programmer for a given type of event is basic; it will direct us to the laws—the microphysical laws, presumptively—in virtue of which all other laws obtain, as physicalism postulates. But there need be nothing special or different about such maximally specific programmers, apart from the fact that they come at the bottom of the program architecture. They need not be productive properties, for example, in a sense that would put them in contrast to higher-level properties; in a sense that would involve the transfer of a basic causal 'oomph' or 'bif'. Like the higher-level programmers, they may direct us to a condition that suffices in one and the same sense for production.

Co-programming without Co-instantiation

The account given of the program model up to this point supposes that the causally relevant properties that are organized in a programming hierarchy—the properties that are co-programmers of the same process—are co-instantiated; there is just one event constituted by their instantiation, and it is the common bearer of all of those properties. The type A event just is the type *a* event, the bolt of lightning just is the electrical discharge of such and such a magnitude, the twirling of the colored cape just is the twirling of the red cape, and so on. This feature of the cases means that not only can we speak of each of the properties as being relevant to the production, but we can say that the event which produces the effect is an instance of any one of the properties we care to mention; this is a standard way of individuating events. The cause of the effect is the single event that instantiates all those different properties at once.

These core cases fit the model of causal efficacy and relevance put forward by Cynthia and Graham Macdonald in their chapter, and in earlier work. They have insisted for some time on the importance of the co-instantiation that the cases exemplify. Such co-instantiation, as we should now be able to see, is quite consistent with what I think of as the program architecture. When we are concerned with properties related in this way, then, contrary to their view, the differences between our approaches are not particularly significant.[5]

What I now want to show, however, is that the main elements in the program architecture remain in place even when we depart from the core cases and allow that two or more properties may each program for the production of a certain type of effect, yet not be properties of one and the same event. Take the simple,

---

[5] They say that the properties of an event divide into constitutive and merely characterizing properties, and suggest that it is the physical property of a mental event, not its mental property, that is going to be constitutive of it. I agree that the physical property will realize the mental, given the context, and will be a more specific programmer. But I don't see why there need be a principled difference between the properties of any other kind. It is we without our particular interests who will treat one property or another as more important, and that will depend on the context and purpose of our talk.

perhaps physically oversimplified, example with which Frank Jackson and I first introduced the notion. The water in a closed, glass flask is boiling, so the mean molecular motion is such and such. One of the molecules has a momentum and position such that it breaks a molecular bond in the flask. And hence the flask itself cracks.

Intuitively, the property of the mass of molecules that consists in its being at boiling temperature programmed for the production of the breaking. There are many different ways in which the boiling may be realized at the lower level, with different numbers of molecules, and different distributions of position and momentum. No matter what the mode of realization, however, there is very likely to be one molecule with a momentum and position sufficient to break a molecular bond in the glass. And it is just such a likely molecule that actually breaks the bond and cracks the flask.

In this case, then, the property of an aggregate event—the boiling—programs for the production of something—the cracking of the flask—though the production of that effect is achieved not by the aggregate event itself but rather by a component event: the vibration of the culpable molecule. A property of the component event—the momentum–position property—programs at the same time, but in a more specific manner, for the production of that very same effect. And the more general programmer programs for the effect via the programming of the more specific programmer. The program architecture still holds.

It is important to see that the program model may be extended to more complex cases like this. I think that the model helps to make sense of how we can have mental or intentional causation at the same time as physical causation, and social causation at the same time as intentional causation, where intentional properties are higher in level than physical ones, and social properties are higher in level than intentional ones. And in many of these cases it would require procrustean efforts of reconstrual to be able to argue that all the relevant programming properties are co-instantiated. Just think of the examples that we will have to handle. We will need to be able to explain how someone's overall set of beliefs and desires can lead the agent to take a particular initiative, where that initiative is prompted by a very particular neural state and programmed for by properties of that state. And we will need to be able to explain how a rise in unemployment programs for a rise in crime, or a pattern of urbanization programs for the appearance of a more secular culture, when the increased crime or secularization is the work of only a subset of those involved in the unemployment or the urbanization. If we are to make use of the program model in dealing with cases like this, then it is important that we loosen up the model so that it applies, not just where co-programmers are co-instantiated, but in the more complex cases akin to that exemplified by the boiling flask.

How is the instantiation of a general programming property going to relate to the instantiation of a more specific property, if the instantiating particulars are not identical; if they are not the same event? The obvious answer, as the

Macdonalds suggest, might seem to be that the first event causes the second; causation is the obvious relation to posit between distinct events. But this line would undermine the capacity of the program model to explain the architecture of causation at different levels; it would have higher-level events exercise causal influence over lower-level ones. Happily, however, there is a different and more attractive approach available.

Let us agree that co-programming properties cannot involve events that are wholly distinct, on pain of undermining the story about higher-level causality. But this does not mean that the events involved have to be identical. Non-identical events will not be distinct if one is a change in a whole, for example, the other a change in a part of that whole. And this is precisely the sort of picture supported by the examples at which I gesture here, and in particular by the example of the water flask.

The event that realizes the more general programming property involves the mass of water molecules, and the event that realizes the more specific programming property involves a part of that whole: the particular molecule that does the damage. The instance of the property of the whole—the boiling of the mass of molecules—will be one event, the instance of the property of the part—the vibration of the efficacious molecule—will be another; they will be non-identical. But they will still not be distinct events. This appears in the fact that the change in the whole cannot cause the change in the part; the change in the whole is partly constituted by the change in the part: it is superveniently determined by the changes of motion in that and the other parts. Co-programming properties have to be properties of non-distinct events. This means that they have to be properties of one and the same event, as in the core cases, or properties that relate like the properties of a whole to the properties of a part, as in the more complex cases.[6]

The Variety of Causes, Explainers, and Controllers

Although the programming architecture is constant across different cases, there are a variety ways in which properties may program for an event, relating as

[6] But while co-programming properties cannot involve distinct events, it is worth drawing attention to a case where something parallel to programming remains in place, even while the events involved are distinct (R. Miller 1978; James 1984; Pettit 1993*a*: ch. 5). Take the traditional claim that the structure of national alliances in Europe about the turn of the century ensured that, one way or another, there would be a great war. The idea in this claim is not just that that structure of alliances helped to bring about certain diplomatic exchanges, and that these exchanges led in turn to war. It is that the structure was such that no matter what exchanges took place in its wake—and no matter how they were prompted, whether by an assassination such as that in Sarajevo or otherwise—they were very likely to lead to eventual war. In this case the instantiation of the alliance property is quite distinct from the instantiation of the exchange property, so that there is no question of their relating as co-programmers; the first is a factor distinct from the second and leads causally to it. But there is an analogue to the way a property can program for an effect in the fact that while the first factor might have led to different exchanges under different scenarios and prompts, any of the exchanges it was likely to trigger would lead eventually to war.

more general and more specific programmers. And this is so, whether or not the programming properties are co-instantiated in the same identical event or in non-identical but still non-distinct events. The more general property may be a disjunction of more specific properties, as when we say that the regularity of a shape programs for a certain effect at a general level, and the triangularity at a more specific level; regularity is taken here as a disjunction of triangularity, rectangularity, circularity, and so on. Again, the more general property may be given by an existential quantification, the more specific by a property involving a name, as when we say that someone's doing something programs for an effect at a general level, and John's doing it programs for the effect at a more specific level. Or the more general property may be a dispositional or a functional property, the more specific the property that realizes that disposition or function; the fragility of the glass may program in a general way for its breaking under a certain pressure, the molecular structure that realizes that fragility may program for it at a more specific level. And so on.

Given the potential variety of programming properties, it should not be surprising that the property invoked in a program explanation of an event need not always be the sort of property that we would routinely regard as having causal relevance, telling us something about how the event came about. The breaking of a fragile glass is just the breaking of a glass under a certain pressure, where its fragility means that it is prone to break under precisely that sort of pressure. Should we regard the fragility as causally relevant to the breaking of a given glass, given that the role of the fragility may teach us little about the causation of the event? I think we should, though this may clash with common usage. The claim that a disposition programs for a certain effect, as fragility programs for the breaking of the glass, gives us at least the information that the breaking was due to the nature of the glass, not to any special influence. Why should it have to give us further information in order for the property cited to count as causally relevant?[7]

So much for the variety of causes under the program architecture. What now of the variety of causal explanations? Any discussion in which programming properties are identified will count as a variety of causal explanation in the sense in which such explanation is taken to provide information about causal history (Lewis 1986: 217). The identification of more general programming properties will provide comparative information on how the actual world might have been, consistently with the effect occurring; it just had to be a world where a bolt of lightning struck my house. The identification of more specific programming properties will provide more specific information on the exact nature of the actual

---

[7] This is quite consistent with denying that the disposition is a cause of the breaking. Causes, as Hume taught us, have to be distinct from their effects, and if a disposition is taken to be the higher-order property of having a property that gives rise to a given sort of effect, then it will not be suitably distinct in a given case from the associated effect; it will be manifested by that effect rather than causally giving rise to it.

world where the effect materialized; it will tell us that it was not just a world in which a bolt of lightning struck, but one in which the electrical discharge was of such and such a magnitude. Both forms of information may be useful, though for different purposes, and both are forms of information about a particular causal process of production.

The fact that these explanations provide different bodies of information on a given causal process, each body useful for a different purpose, means that there is no single right way of explaining an event. The program architecture allows for explanation at different levels, and each explanation will have its own merits, providing information that answers distinct questions.

The methodological lesson is that we should eschew explanatory reductionism, which would favor going to finer and finer grains of information in seeking the explanation of any event. We should embrace what I call "explanatory ecumenism" or pluralism. This is an important lesson in many areas, particularly in social science. There is no reason to have to choose between favoring individual-level accounts, for example, and explanations of a more structural, higher-level kind: explanations such as that which invokes urbanization to explain secularization, or a rise in unemployment to explain an increase in crime (Pettit 1993*a*: ch. 5). We should eschew methodological individualism, even if we embrace the ontological individualism that is discussed in Section 6 below.

But there is more to explanatory ecumenism than even this principle implies, for causal explanations do not exhaust the sort of explanation in which we are often interested, even allowing for the variety of explanations that count as causal on this account (Pettit 2002*b*: essays 2.3 and 2.4). The reason is that explanation is required to invoke controllers, and non-causal controls are often just as important as causal controls. Whenever a causal process leads to a certain sort of effect, we may say that it controls for that effect; in particular, that it controls actively for the effect, via the causal connections that are operative: it controls for the effect in the sense of making it more probable than it would have been in the absence of the process. But effects are often controlled for by factors that do not or need not be causally active in this way. They may be the products of virtual as distinct from active controllers.

A controller for a type of effect E—call it C—will be virtual under the following conditions. The effect E is normally occasioned not by C, but by some other factor, N (for normal). But in any case where N fails to produce E, then C steps into the breach and takes over the productive role. When C steps in like this, it actively controls for the appearance of E. But insofar as it is there as a standby cause, ready to intervene on a need-to-act basis, it controls for the appearance of C even when it is not actively in charge. It is a virtual controller of the effect in question. It rides herd on the normal mechanism of production, ready to compensate for failures in the process or to readjust the process so that it no longer fails.

Virtual control is nicely illustrated under what I think is the best account of why rational self-interest can be invoked to explain ordinary, non-calculative patterns of action, as in a well-known variety of social science. The claim is not that people are covertly or unconsciously consulting their self-interest in making the choices that the theory is supposed to explain. The better interpretation is that they are acting under perfectly ordinary forces of habit and custom, but that rational self-interest is in virtual control, so far as it remains the case, first, that if those forces serve a person ill, this is likely to become evident—the red lights will go on—and, second, that should the red lights go on, then self-interest will become an active force, rationally triggering suitable amendments. The virtual presence of rational self-interest may not be able to explain the generation of the behavior, or even its continuation, but it can explain the fact that the behavioral pattern in question is resilient, remaining in place like a stable equilibrium.

In our study of *The Economy of Esteem*, Geoffrey Brennan and I use the model of virtual control to give a realistic picture, as I think of it, of how the desire for esteem may shape much of human life, even while few of us ever give much explicit thought to considerations of esteem (Brennan and Pettit 2004). This topic is taken up in the final section.

Not only may rational interests virtually control a subject's behavior. So may regular beliefs and desires. In the next section I will be presenting a story as to how beliefs and desires can be causally relevant, programming for various actions and other effects. But while they can certainly have such a causal impact, it is worth noting that they may control behavior without always deploying such active control (Pettit 2001*b*: ch. 2). Consider a case where I take a certain route home out of sheer habit, or where I conform habitually to a certain rule or convention. It may well be that such behavior is often produced by blind habit, but that beliefs and desires remain in control so far as they are likely to be activated and to assume active control, should habit fail to produce the desired end: getting home or achieving a goal associated with the rule or convention. I won't return to this thought later, but it is worth keeping in mind in the discussion that follows.

The recognition that virtual controllers can be invoked in explanation of the resilience or stability of certain patterns of behavior makes it possible, to give a plausible gloss not just to rational-choice explanation and explanation of a more regular intentional sort. It can also help to show why functionalist explanation in social science need not be as ungrounded as many have come to think (Pettit 2002*b*: essay 2.4).

Such explanation tries to make certain patterns or institutions intelligible by showing that they have effects, in particular unnoticed effects, that are important for the interests of human beings. It might explain the popularity of golf clubs, for example, by the way in which they serve the interests of professional people in getting to establish contacts with others of their kind, and only with others of their kind. The standard critique of this pattern of explanation is that it would work only if the patterns or institutions had actually been historically selected for their utility in achieving relevant effects, and that in most cases there is no evidence of such selection. But that critique overlooks the fact that the explanation will serve to explain the resilience of golf clubs, just so far as there is virtual selection in place: just so far as it is the case that did golf clubs come under pressure, say through the imposition of heavy land taxes, then the interests of professionals would come into play and keep the clubs in existence.

The potential for useful functional explanation has been ignored in recent social science due to a failure to appreciate the role of virtual selection. Take the counterproductively severe level of criminal sentencing that prevails, arguably, in most contemporary societies. This may best be explained by the function it plays in reducing public outrage. For imagine what is likely to happen if sentencing comes to be more lenient in some category (Pettit 2002*a*). Even if the type of crime in question does not increase, even indeed if it becomes less common, still there is bound to be some offence that will occur, sooner or later, which would not have occurred had the sentencing remained at the earlier level. And if that happens, then the media will publicize it, the public will be mobilized in outrage and protest, and the politicians will respond, as electoral politics requires them to respond, by restoring the penalty to the old level, or a level still more severe. What keeps the sentences severe, then, is the function that severity serves in keeping the lid on public outrage. This will be so even if the selectional mechanism described has never actually been called into action; even if it remains wholly virtual in character.

I should not suggest, however, that this mechanism will operate robustly in all societies. It will work only under certain conditions; for example, when there are media with an incentive to sensationalize the crucial offence and when sentencing policy decisions are made by politicians who can be called upon to respond in the headline or soundbite. Nicola Lacey points out in her chapter that there have been circumstances in the past where the mechanism I describe has not worked to increase the severity of sentencing in the way I allege. Her evidence suggests either that the model is misconceived or, more plausibly, as I think, that its preconditions are not invariably satisfied. It would be of great interest to explore the historical variations under which the mechanism has not blocked reform of criminal justice sentencing, for this might have policymaking significance; it might suggest ways in which things could be improved. I myself would like to think that were sentencing policy put at arm's length from elected representatives, as interest-rate policy is put at arm's length, then that would make for an improvement (Pettit 2002*a*).

2. INTENTIONALITY, REASONING, AND FREE WILL

Minimal Intentionality

Like many naturalistic philosophers, I am inclined to think of a minded agent or intentional system in a rather deflationary way: specifically, in such a way that it requires the satisfaction of just two conditions. First, agency requires a system to be moved by scenarios that we may describe as its goals; the absence of such desired scenarios will routinely trigger behavior that is designed to put them in place, the presence of those scenarios behavior that is designed to keep them in place. And second, agency requires the system's behavior in pursuit of those goals to be controlled at the same time by beliefs—evidentially sensitive representations—as to whether its goals are realized or not, as to whether it can do anything to realize them or preserve them, and as to what exactly that is. The agent will act for the realization of certain goals, according to evidentially tuned representations as to how things stand at any moment. It will be a system of intentional states like desire and belief, as it is more often put, where desires select goals, and beliefs constitute evidentially sensitive representations.

On these minimal specifications, agency will not be the preserve of human beings; even a relatively simple animal or a piece of artificial intelligence may count as an agent. Each such entity can be a center of goal formation, a center of belief formation—evidentially sensitive belief formation—and a behavioral system whose actions serve those goals according to those beliefs. It need not always meet those conditions, or meet them perfectly, but to be an agent, it will have to satisfy them robustly within intuitively feasible limits and under intuitively favorable conditions.

Imagine a small robotic device, for example, that moves around an area the size of a table top. Suppose that scattered across this area are several cylindrical objects, some upright, some on their sides. And now imagine that it scans the area with bug-like eyes, then moves about and, using its prosthetic limbs, puts the cylinders that lie on their side into an upright position. Imagine in particular that it does this robustly, at least when the cylinders are not too near the edge of the table—perhaps it knocks them off in that case—and when the illumination is good. Even a device as simple as this will count as a mininimal intentional system; the goal that it pursues is to set the cylinders upright, and the beliefs that guide it in pursuit of the goal are the beliefs it forms about those cylinders.

The robot's attitudes are limited in domain insofar as it has only one motivating goal: namely, to keep the cylinders in upright position; and its representations involve only a few features: the locations of cylinders and their vertical or horizontal orientations. And its attitudes are also limited in spatial, temporal, and modal distance insofar as it only ever becomes disposed to act on the local, current context; its representational-motivational processing bears entirely on the here and now; it is a wholly reactive agent.

The minimal conception of agency and mind can be extended to include minds that are not so limited in domain or reach, as it can be extended to cover minds that are conscious and minds that reason. Some commentators prefer to reserve terms like 'mind', and related words like 'belief' and 'desire', for systems that are richer in such respects. Tim Scanlon suggests in his chapter, for example, that this may be the right way to go. I don't think that much hangs on the issue.

Let the terms be used as I prefer, and we can speak in non-minimal cases of the enriched mind. Let them be reserved for more significant exemplars of mind, and we can speak in minimal cases of the embryonic mind or the inchoate mind.

The Causal Relevance of Intentional States

One of the firmest intuitions that we have about ourselves, and about anything that we would want to dignify with the name of 'agent', is that belief and desire, and related intentional states like perception and memory, imagination and feeling, can be causally productive. It is because of what we believe and desire that we do the things we do. And, more generally, it is because of what we perceive or remember or imagine, judge or endorse, seek or value, that we adopt any of a variety of voluntary and involuntary responses. Intentional states of these kinds, although they are characterized by their intentional content—by what is perceived or endorsed or valued, for example—are causally powerful. They can make a difference in our experiences, actions, and lives.

How are intentional states supposed to do this? The view of those states that fits best with my background physicalism, and with the deflationary account of agency just given, is a version of 'functionalism', as it is called in the philosophy of mind; this has nothing to do with 'functionalism' as an explanatory strategy in social science. Whenever there is a belief or a desire of a certain variety, it will always involve a physical state of some kind: say, a neural configuration. And that physical state will count as the intentional state just so far as it plays a suitable function or role. It will have to play or come close to playing a suitable role, first, in causally interacting with other states; second, in causally interacting with the external world; and third, in eventually leading by a causal route to action. As this is true of a particular state that constitutes the belief that p, so something similar will be true at the same time as the other states with which that state interacts in earning its name, and true of the yet further states with which they interact in earning their names, and so on. Such states will earn their psychological names on a holistic or interconnected basis. The basis that establishes one state as the belief that p will serve at the same time to establish another as the desire that q. And so on.

Anything will count as a belief or a desire, then, and count more specifically as a belief or a desire with a certain content, just so far as it is a physical state that plays a suitable causal role, or comes close to playing such a role.[8] The physical state will realize or implement the appropriate belief or desire role. And the state

---

[8] The role envisaged is broad, in the sense of involving environmental objects, not just peripheral stimuli; hence it involves causal sensitivity to the environment of a kind that is often thought to be necessary to make content relatively determinate. For reasons that come up later in the discussion of rule-following and response-dependence, I think that contents will be quite determinate with reasoning minds. But I don't see any reason why this has to be so with simple, unreasoning intentional creatures; see Pettit 1993a: ch. 1.

that realizes that role in one agent, or in one agent at one time, need not be exactly the same state that realizes it in another agent, or in that agent at another time. The belief may in that sense be multiply realizable. For each type of belief, such as the belief that p, there may be many physical ways in which it is realized. And for each system of belief and desire and other such psychological states—for the system that each of us instantiates at any moment—there may be many physical or neural systems capable of realizing or implementing it. The belief-that-p type of state, at least in our species, may be realized by, and may correspond to, a disjunctive type of physical state: N1-or-N2-or-N3. The desire-that-q type of state may correspond to another such disjunctive state. And so on.

This functionalism about "the minimal mind", as I called it, fits nicely with the program model. We can readily think of intentional or functional properties co-programming for the production of action, for example, in tandem with physical properties: neural properties at one level, more basic physical properties at another. And we can endorse this pattern without suggesting that the intentional or functional properties are not really causally relevant; not causally relevant in the manner of the lower-level properties.

We can do this, indeed, no matter how we answer a related question that the functionalist picture leaves open. That is the question as to which of two possible candidates, which of two different functional properties, should be identified with the belief-that-p property. One candidate is the higher-order property of an agent that consists in his or her instantiating a neural or physical property, maybe this, maybe that, which plays the appropriate belief-that-p role; call this the "role property". The other is just the physical property, or perhaps the disjunction of physical properties, that plays the role. The model presented is consistent with either construal, though, for presentational reasons, I opt in *The Common Mind* for the role-property construal.

Peter Menzies offers an interpretation of my views that fails to register the extent to which I leave open these issues. Contrary to what he suggests, I do not think that the realizer-property construal of functionalism, or indeed of the program model, has to be rejected in favor of the role-property construal.[9] And I have never maintained that it is only the basic physical properties that do the real causal work and that more general, functional properties are a second-class citizen in the domain of production; usually I have explicitly left that matter open.

---

[9] Frank Jackson opts for the realizer-property construal in some of his independent work, as indeed I do myself, but this does not involve a rejection of the program model as such. Peter Menzies does not recognize this, I think, because he identifies that construal with the claim—criticized, as he says, in *The Common Mind*—that all there is to explanation of an event by reference to an intentional state, say the belief that p, is the claim that the referent of 'the belief that p', purportedly a physical state, is the cause of that event. Even on the realizer-property construal of the program model, invoking the physical state that is the belief that p is explanatory only in virtue of the fact that that state is the belief that p: it plays the appropriate role. Whether believing that p is a role property or a realizer property, the instance of that property has causal relevance in virtue of being the belief that p; it is its instantiating that property that programs for the event explained.

Menzies thinks that even if I do not restrict the realm of real causes in this way, still I am committed to an excessively demanding story about the presuppositions of intentional explanation at neural and other levels. He offers an interesting alternative vision of the explanations at such different levels, according to which we should not expect any robust relationship; this is because the explanations will work with models or sets of assumptions that do not match up straightforwardly. His approach swaps the ontological focus that I prefer—the focus on how in reality different levels of causally relevant factors must relate—for a more epistemological or methodological focus on the assumptions built into any causal explanation. I am not sympathetic to this move, but this is not the place to explore that general issue, or the more particular challenge he raises.

The Constraints and Desiderata of Rationality

The minimal mind described will be rational if it performs more or less satisfactorily in its own terms, embracing goals that can be fulfilled, forming representations that are faithful to its surroundings, and acting for the realization of those goals according to those representations. The core notion of the rational agent is that of an agent that functions more or less properly in this sense. Let a system fail to function satisfactorily above a certain threshold, at least within feasible limits and under favorable conditions, and its very title to the name of agent will be put in question.

There are a number of constraints of rationality that are immediately salient. An intentional system will operate satisfactorily in its own terms, and prove itself rational, only so far as the goals and representations on which it fixes satisfy certain constraints of compossibility or consistency. Let the agent try to act on an inconsistent set of representations, and it will seize up; it will just not function to order. Or let it try to enact an inconsistent set of goals—goals it is fixed on realizing, not just tempted by—and it will also stall. Again, an intentional system will operate satisfactorily only so far as the representations that it forms are more or less consistent with the ways things are, being updated by perceptual evidence as to how they are. Let it not be attuned in this basic manner to how things are, and are presented as being, and its representations will lead it to act in ways that systematically fail to serve its goals.

Not only are constraints built into the notion of an intentional system. So are certain desiderata. Suppose that an agent has certain representations that are consistent only with things being thus or so—that require things to be thus and so—on some issue where it has no current representation. Or suppose that the agent is fixed on certain goals whose realization is consistent only with things being thus-and-so, where it is not a currently explicit goal that they be thus and so. In each such case, a desideratum on the system is that it be able to see what its current representations or goals entail in this way, since this might have an impact on what it does; it might extend the current representations or goals, inducing no particular change in the agent; but equally, it might lead to an adjustment in those states. Let the system satisfy those desiderata of closure, and it will be better fitted to perform as an agent.

Apart from constraints of consistency and desiderata of closure, a further desideratum on any intentional system is that it be capable of forming beliefs in a way that is attuned to mounting, inductive evidence. This is rather harder to specify, since we have no good abstract account of what is involved in being inductively rational in this way, as distinct from being deductively rational in the satisfaction of consistency and closure. But intuitively, it should be counted with the other constraints and desiderata among the specifications that the intentional system would do well to satisfy. It would enable the system to perform more reliably in the role of an agent.

Reasoning

But although the performance of a minimal mind will have to be pretty impressive in this way, there is one respect in which it may fall far short of what our species is routinely capable of achieving. Not only do we human beings generally satisfy the design specifications for mind, as Daniel Dennett (1979, 1987) calls them. We also form higher-order representations as to what some such specifications are, thereby making it possible to recognize ourselves as rational and to reinforce our rationality.

Consider the way in which a minimally minded agent might conform to the rule of *modus ponens*. The system holds the belief that if p, then q, perhaps in a more or less habitual manner; it comes to form the new belief that p, say on the basis of incoming evidence; and then, more or less automatically, it goes on to form the belief that q (Cummins 1983). When this happens, there is no question of the agent forming the belief 'so, q' or 'therefore, q', for it need not have any representation—any higher-order representation—to the effect that the premises entail that q. The way most of us differ from such a minimally minded creature, however, is that we can form representations of this kind. We may not be able to spell out the rule of *modus ponens*, but we will be able, however implicitly, to register that propositions of the form 'if p, then q' and 'p' entail the truth of the conclusion 'q'. We will form a belief in that entailment, a sensitivity to the connection involved. Such a belief is a belief about the propositions involved, not a belief in those propositions. It is a higher-order or meta-propositional belief: a belief in the meta-proposition " 'p' and 'if p, then q' entail 'q' ".[10]

---

[10] This involves representation of more basically represented contents, or of constraints on such contents, not of the more basic representational states. 'Meta-representation' is usually taken to involve precisely this kind of state-representation, as in Sperber 2000; hence my use here of 'meta-propositional'.

When some minimally minded agents form the belief that q, we may say that they are rationally required to do so—required, so far as their beliefs that p and that if p, then q are fixed (Broome 2004)—and that they form the belief under the pressure of their sub-personal rationality: their susceptibility to such requirements. What difference is made by the fact that we human beings are also able to form and fix the belief in the relevant meta-proposition?

One difference is that if we do form such a meta-propositional belief, then we will be rationally required on two counts, not just on one, to form the belief that q: first, because of holding fixed the beliefs that p and that if p, then q; and second, because of also holding fixed the belief that 'p' and 'if p, then q', taken as given, entail 'q'. By forming the meta-propositional belief, we put an extra check in place on our belief-forming processes; we engage our rationality on an extra, meta-propositional front. The presence of the extra check is signaled by the fact that we are put in a position not just to form a belief expressed by 'q', but to form a belief expressed by 'so q' or 'therefore q'.

The fact that we human beings can form the meta-propositional belief, and other beliefs of that kind, also makes for a second difference. It means that we are able to ask questions about propositions like 'p', 'if p, then q', and 'q'—questions to do with their truth, consistency, and other relations—and to set out intentionally to let beliefs form within us in answer to such questions. The simple animal can set out to form beliefs about the objects that figure in the domain of its attitudes, asking itself whether someone is its owner, whether a noise is of dinner being served, and so on. In the same way, we human beings can set out to form beliefs about the propositions that figure in our expanded domain of attitude formation, asking ourselves whether some proposition is true or false, whether it fits with another proposition, or entails another proposition, or whatever.

These two differences mean, in combination, that we human beings can reason. We can adopt intentional means—that of asking ourselves suitable questions—with a view to imposing extra checks on the way in which our attitudes form and unfold. The activity of asking such questions, intentionally forming meta-propositional beliefs that will impose extra checks, constitutes what I think of as reasoning. We may pursue that activity in the context of forming beliefs or forming intentions or pursuing conjectures, and, depending on the context, it will help us to make sure of doing so rationally.

Suppose I wonder whether it really is the case that q, as I find myself inclined to think. One way of putting an extra check in place will be to ask appropriate questions about its connections with other propositions like 'if p, then q' and 'p' and about the truth of those propositions. Thus I may enunciate the entailing propositions as presumptive facts, or explicitly ascribe truth to them—I may just say the sentences to myself—and then implicitly register the entailment in the spoken or unspoken words 'so q'. The strict meaning of that remark is that it is the case that q, because it is the case that p and that if p, then q. But if I am checking my beliefs, then the message I will use it to communicate to myself, and to any audience, is that I ought—I ought rationally—to believe that q.

Suppose, again, that being focused on action, I wonder whether making 's' true in the context of 'r' really is a reliable means of making 't' true. One way of putting an extra check in place will be to ask questions appropriate to intention formation as distinct from belief formation. I may review intentionally the grounds for assuming the reliability of that means, going through a parallel form of thinking about the truth of 'r', the connections between 'r', 's', and 't', and registering the result in words such as 'so if s, t'. Again the literal meaning of this conclusion is that it is the case that if s, then t, because it is that case that r and that if s and r, then t. But if I am wondering about whether to try to make 'r' true in order to make 't' true, then the message will be that I ought to try to make 'r' true.[11]

Reasoning may not go very deep, since it presupposes the sub-personal rationality that will make the checks effective; at some point such rationality has to be presupposed, on pain of infinite regress (Carroll 1895). Neither does reasoning often materialize in full active dress: it is present in most of our reflections only in a virtual, background position; it typically makes its appearance when a red flag goes up, indicating that special care is needed. And finally, when reasoning does materialize, it may play a less than essential role in our attitude formation, reinforcing the direction in which our spontaneously unfolding attitudes were going, rather than inhibiting or correcting it; inhibition and correction are certainly possible, but they are not the order of the day.

All of this conceded, however, it is difficult to overemphasize the importance of reasoning. In the absence of a capacity for forming meta-propositional beliefs, and intentionally imposing checks on my mental life, I would be locked into an inscrutable, if more or less rational, process. My beliefs and other attitudes would evolve blindly: that is, without any capacity to recognize that they are the right attitudes to form, in the light of rational constraints and desiderata. And if blindly, brutely: that is, without any capacity to regulate my own performance so as to enhance the prospect of satisfying those specifications.

Bayesian decision theory gives us a wonderfully systematic, if idealized account of what we should expect from a blind but rationally performing agent, for it assumes no reasoning whatsoever (Pettit 2002*b*: essay 2.2). The Bayesian agent updates its beliefs by conditionalization, starting from some randomly ascribed prior probabilities: if it previously assigned a probability of degree x to 'p, given q', and it learns that q, then it assigns probability of degree x to 'p'. And, again, the Bayesian agent forms its preferences and decisions subject to the constraint of

---

[11] John Perry (1979) observes that in order to do X, an agent must have not just a desire that X be done, but a desire to do X, where this can be expressed in the form 'I desire to X' or 'I desire that I X', but not in the form 'I desire that Philip Pettit do X': if there is reference to the agent, then the indexical 'I' is essential. A similar lesson applies in reasoning (Burge 1998). Thus the 'I' is essential in the message given here and in the previous case.

maximizing expected utility; if the expected utility of 'p or q' is y, then 'p' and 'q' must have utilities such that the sum of the utility of 'p' times the probability that p and the utility of 'q' times the probability that q must be y. But for all that the theory requires, the Bayesian subject may do this entirely blindly. The agent need have no beliefs or degrees of belief about conditionalization, no beliefs about the maximization of utility, no beliefs even about the utilities it is supposed to assign to different scenarios and options. It may be perfectly, inhumanly rational, yet lack anything on a par with our capacity to reason.

Reasoning takes human subjects into a new space, enabling them deliberately to put checks on their own performance as intentional systems. By reasoning, human beings can regulate how their attitudes form and lead to action. In the cases mentioned so far, this self-regulation occurs fairly automatically, with the recognition that certain premises entail a certain conclusion serving more or less immediately to elicit or reinforce a belief in that conclusion. But self-regulation may sometimes involve a policy of much more active intervention in one's mental life (McGeer 1996; McGeer and Pettit 2002). Suppose that I am a gambler and am led by reasoning to realize that a string of heads in a series of fair tosses does not make tails any more likely on the next toss. It may require a high degree of self-policing for me to remain faithful to this insight in the predictions I make, and perhaps rely on, at the casino. The control exercised by reasoning in such cases will have to be imposed with the force of a lash. And as it is in certain forms of reasoning about what to think, so it will often be with reasoning about what to do. In many such cases it is likely that reasoning will have its reinforcing or corrective effect only insofar as it is supported by devices, as we think of them, of self-control.

The considerations that agents take into account when they reason are naturally described as reasons; in the *modus ponens* example, the relevant reasons will be that p and that if p, then q. The minimally minded agent takes account of reasons, without recognizing them as reasons, when it is prompted by its beliefs in the relevant propositions to form the belief that q. We human beings take account of reasons, treating them as reasons, when we are moved not just by those beliefs, but also by the meta-propositional belief that 'p' and 'if p, then q' entail 'q'; that we treat them as reasons shows up in the use of the 'so q' or the 'therefore q'. But we human beings, it should now be clear, can also go one better, introducing the word or the concept of a reason, and forming not just reason-providing but also reason-ascribing beliefs: beliefs to the effect, for example, that we have reason, even good reason, to believe that q, and so that we ought to believe that q. What we ordinarily call reasoning may or may not involve reason-ascribing beliefs, but it must involve reason-providing beliefs of the meta-propositional kind.

Given the capacity to ascribe reasons, we can characterize the fact that p and that if p, then q, as a substantive reason for believing that q. But we can also do something new: we can describe the fact of believing, fixedly, that p and that if p, then q, as a structural reason for believing that q; we can think that we have structural reason, as we can think that we have substantive reason, to believe that *q*. The terminology of 'substantive' and 'structural' is used by Tim Scanlon in his searching chapter on the normative character of structural reasons. Substantive reasons are reason-providing facts or presumptive facts that will weigh with any rational agent; structural reasons are facts about the attitudes of the agent that will require certain other attitudes to obtain — or a certain attitudinal pattern to obtain — if the agent is to be rational.

Scanlon rightly notices that by my lights rationality is derived from what well-ordered agency requires and that certain considerations will count as reasons in virtue of their relevance for the non-defective performance of an agent. But in case his discussion suggests otherwise, I should elaborate on two important aspects of the view I like.

The first is that I understand rationality in a broad, rather than a narrow, sense. If rationality is taken narrowly, then it will be a failure of rationality not to conform one's beliefs to the evidence one has actually registered, but not a failure of rationality not to conform one's beliefs to the evidence that is available to be registered, should one pay due attention. And if rationality is taken narrowly, then it will be a failure of rationality not to form an intention to do something that is supported by one's beliefs and desires, but not a failure of rationality to fail to enact that intention. I take rationality on each front in a broad, rather than a narrow, sense.

A second important aspect of the view I like is this. While reasons will count as reasons for an agent like one of us in virtue of their connection with rationality in the broad sense, this does not mean that their normative force as reasons consists, as we agents see it, in that connection. Suppose I see a fact — that *p* and that if *p*, then *q* — as a substantive reason for believing that *q*, letting it move me to think, 'so *q*' or 'therefore *q*'. The normative force registered in the 'so' or the 'therefore' — the normative force articulated when I self-ascribe such a conclusive, substantive reason to believe that *q* — presupposes that I am rational; it would not register with me, were I not rational. But it is not rightly analyzed along the lines of a hypothetical imperative like this: "if I am to be rational I should believe that *q*; I want to be rational; therefore I should believe that *q*." If I am rational, I will feel the force of the sort of consideration given, seeing it as a reason. It does not follow, however, that I must see the force of the reason as deriving from the way in which it connects with my rationality. I would not find a joke funny if I did not have a sense of humor; but it does not follow that to see the joke as funny is to see it as connected with my sense of humor.

What goes for substantive reasons goes equally for reasons of a structural kind: reasons, essentially self-ascribed, that mention certain attitudes that I already instantiate. I may self-ascribe a reason to believe that *q* on the grounds that I fixedly believe that *p* and that if *p*, then *q*, so that not believing that *q* would be irrational. But this does not mean that I see the force of the reason as deriving from the instrumental connection between believing that *q* and proving to be rational. It may derive simply from the fact that any substantive reasons I have for believing that p and that if p, then q, are also substantive reasons for believing that q; this, with the force of the substantive reasons explained on the earlier, rationality-connected lines.

Free Will and Free Thought

Whenever agents are subject to structural or substantive reasons, there is a basis for saying, as we noticed, that they ought to do this or they ought to do that. They are suitable addressees for prescriptions, whether the prescriptions are made by others or by the agents themselves. If it did not make sense, in any domain, to address a prescription to an agent, then it would not clearly make sense to say that the agent was a reasoning subject.

But 'ought' in the sense associated with addressing a prescription implies 'can', as one of the oldest philosophical clichés declares. So the notion of a reasoning subject goes with the idea of a subject with a distinctive capacity. Wherever it is appropriate to say that the agent ought to display certain responses, in virtue of a sensitivity to structural or substantive reasons, it will have to be the case that the agent can display those responses. What the agent is enjoined to do, as a reasoning subject, the agent must clearly be capable of doing.[12]

This observation suggests a line on free will and, as we will see, on free thought. We naturally think of free will as the capacity to act in any of a number of ways: the capacity to act as we decide or intend or, precisely, will. This way of thinking engenders a difficulty, however, for it's not clear what is so good about acting out of our will if what we will is not itself subject to our will, as Hobbes argued. Yet, if it is subject to our will, then there is a question as to whether that further will is subject to our will, so that a regress looms. The observation made about the connection between reasoning and capacity, however, suggests a different tack and a way out of this difficulty.

Why not take the capacity that we associate with free will to be nothing more or less than the capacity that is implied by a sensitivity to the discipline of reason: the capacity to register and respond to the perceived demands of reason, structural and substantive? The discipline of reason is the discipline of what is right or *orthos* according to the reasons available to the agent; what 'right' means, in this usage, is that which has the support of relevant reasons. So why not hold that free will should be identified with what Michael Smith and I have called 'orthonomy' (Jackson, Pettit, and Smith 2004: essays 13, 17); that is, with the capacity to be guided by the *orthos* or 'right', according to available reasons.

---

[12] This point marks out the 'ought' judgments in question, and the reasons they engage, as injunctive rather than evaluative in character. The evaluative 'ought' or 'reason' indicates not what an agent is enjoined to do, but what it would be good if the agent did: what, if the agent were a better and different agent, he or she would do. On this issue see Pettit and Smith 2006.

'Autonomy', which is often used as a synonym for free will, means the rule of the self as distinct from the rule of the non-self. 'Orthonomy' means the rule of the right rather than the rule of what is not right. The antonym of both words is heteronomy. As the antonym of 'autonomy', 'heteronomy' means the rule of the non-self. As the antonym of 'orthonomy', it means the rule of the non-right; it contrasts with 'orthonomy' as 'heterodoxy' contrasts with 'orthodoxy'. The orthonomy approach to free will has many elements in common with a range of recent authors (Wolf 1990; Wallace 1996; Fischer and Ravizza 1998; Watson 2003, 2005) and derives its inspiration from a paper by Peter Strawson (2003), originally presented in the 1960s, on 'Freedom and Resentment'. Strawson argued that free will is the capacity we suppose in those we treat as fit targets of reactive attitudes like gratitude and resentment. We argue more generally that it is the capacity we suppose in those we take to be subject to, and sensitive to, reasons, whether or not their performance is in the domain of reactive attitudes.

One consequence of the orthonomy approach, which Michael Smith and I highlighted, is that we have to take people to be able to enjoy something like free will in the formation of their beliefs as well as in the formation of their desires and in the performance of their actions. If someone has the capacity to track relevant reasons in the things they come to hold as well as in the things they come to seek, then they must be regarded to that extent as enjoying a certain freedom: a freedom of thought, as we might describe it, rather than a freedom of volition.

This should not be surprising or scandalous. There is certainly a contrast between the belief-forming habits of the reasoning creature and the belief-forming habits of the unreasoning agent. And there is nothing absurd about the idea that such a person should be said to hold his or her beliefs freely, the unreasoning counterpart not. We may be less conscious of the freedom of our thoughts, given that we cannot have the experience, all too common in the practical sphere, of our thoughts coming apart from our reasons. While we are all aware of desiring one thing while holding that the reasons support another, we do not have the same access to thinking one thing while the reasons support another. How we think will affect what we take the reasons to be; if we think that something is the case, even think this against the reasons, then that is how it will seem reasonable to us to think.

Extending the notion of orthonomy from action to belief and desire has many advantages. One is that it shows how rich the ideal of exercising orthonomy is. It will encode not just the ideal of answering to all the structural reasons associated with satisfying the demands of rationality within oneself. It will also encode the ideal of answering to the substantive reasons for beliefs and desires that are available in what one recognizes as evidence, including the evidence of what is prudentially or ethically desirable or undesirable.

With any capacity, orthonomy included, there will be three conditions to distinguish: lacking the capacity; having the capacity but not exercising it;

and having the capacity and exercising it. Those who lack the capacity will include non-human agents as well as humans who suffer from serious mental malfunction. Those who have the capacity but do not exercise it, or not on this or that occasion, will be human beings who underperform, perhaps from some variety of unreason, practical or theoretical. And those who have the capacity and exercise it will be human beings who act orthonomously, whether by spontaneous virtue or by the effect of discipline and self-control.

It is crucial to this picture that you may have the capacity to be orthonomous, say in respect of a given set of practical options, yet manifest or fail to manifest it. The fact that you act in the presence of the capacity means that you are free, and the fact that you exercise the capacity means, in addition, that you are virtuous or self-controlled: you are performing up to par. You may fail to be virtuous as a result of negligently failing to recognize the demands of certain structural or substantive reasons, or as a result of recognizing but not responding to the demands. When you fail, we usually postulate the presence of a blind spot or an *idée fixe*, an obsession, a compulsion, or weakness of will—under whatever name, some lack of virtue or self-control.

Thinking of free will and free thought in the image of orthonomy makes it relatively unsurprising that it should be present in natural systems like you and me, who are subject to control by physical law, deterministic or otherwise. That an action is free does not mean that it is the product of something other than natural causes: say, the product of a non-natural *volonté* such as Descartes postulated, or a sort of agent causation that is not mediated by particular sequences of events. It will mean only that it is an action performed in the presence of a certain sort of capacity in the agent as a whole. That capacity is susceptible, we may assume, to a naturalistic, ultimately neural analysis. So there need be no difficulty in thinking that free will and free thought can occur in mundane creatures, not just in the other-worldly beings imagined in religious and related traditions.

However attractive in this way, however, the account will still have to explain some problematic connotations of the idea that people are free in the way they think and decide. If you are said to be free in doing or thinking something, then in common usage that suggests, first, that it is such that you could have done otherwise; second, it is something for which you can be held responsible; and, third, it is a commitment with which you are identified: it bears your signature (Pettit 2001*b*). If psychological freedom is orthonomy, then there ought to be a basis for explaining why those connotations hold. I will try to explain the basis for the third connotation when I turn later to co-reasoning and conversability. But here I should say something briefly about the first two.

Is it the case that the free agent or free thinker could have done otherwise, on the account given? Yes, though in perhaps a deflationary sense. If we hold everything fixed right up to the moment of decision, then there may have been no possibility that things might have turned out otherwise. But that is quite consistent with its being the case in another sense that the agent could have done otherwise. Suppose the agent did well. Then he or she, if orthonomous, manifested their capacity in that choice—their capacity to do the right sort of thing—and could have done otherwise in the sense that had the reasons required something else, then that is what they would have done; or would have done, unless blocked. Suppose the agent did badly. Then he or she, if othonomous, possessed the capacity to have done the right sort of thing instead—to have gone with the reasons—and could have done otherwise in the corresponding sense; the agent's action was out of type, and did not reflect what he or she was capable of.

What the agent does well, then, is done in manifestation of a capacity to track the reasons, not just as a fluke. What the agent does badly is done out of character, not reflecting their continuing capacity to track the reasons. Those are the features that are marked, or that ought to be marked, in talk of what free subjects could have done, as distinct from what they actually did.

That an agent could have done something else in this sense—the sense of having the capacity required for doing it—does not mean in a given case that there was a situation-specific possibility of doing it: the sort of possibility envisaged by those who believe in non-naturalistic or contra-causal free will. The agent might have been blocked from doing it, so far as there was a factor there—a virtual controller, in the term introduced earlier—ready to interfere in the event of their trying. We can even concede that the agent might have been blocked from trying to do it by such a virtual controller, if the idea of stopping a person from even trying to do something is coherent. The sense in which orthonomy means that a free agent could always have done otherwise than he or she did does not require that the other action must have been a real alternative possibility.[13]

Once psychological freedom is cast in this way, of course, then there can no longer be a bright line between the cases where agents are free and the cases where they are not. First, capacities come in degrees, depending on the agent's level of mastery and the level of difficulty presented by the environment. And second, there may be no salient break between cases where we say the capacity is present and cases where we say it isn't. Neither implication need be troublesome, however; each fits with common practice. If our traditional ways of thinking about free will and free thought suggest that there ought to be sharp lines where we only find fuzzy areas, that may be due to a fault in those ways of thinking.

---

[13] Frankfurt (1969) argues that being responsible for something does not presuppose the capacity to have done otherwise, since the agent might have been blocked from doing otherwise, whether in the ordinary or the radical sense. I agree, as the qualification about the absence of blocking indicates. Thus I do not embrace the principle of alternative possibilities that his argument is meant to undermine. There is a large literature on these issues. For a line that is congenial to that adopted here, see Smith 2003. I was helped by conversation with John Maier on this point.

The second connotation on which I promised to say something links freedom with responsibility. Does the fact that you did something orthonomously mean that you can be held responsible for it? You may act orthonomously and not be fully responsible for doing something, as when you are coerced by another: in dealing with a robber, you orthonomously give up the money you are carrying rather than forfeit your life. Even if the money belongs to another, then, you will not be fit to be held fully responsible in such a case; you will have an acceptable excuse. I shall return to this point later, arguing that for freedom in the encompassing sense in which it is equivalent to fitness to be held responsible, it is essential to enjoy a certain relational status vis-à-vis others — one inconsistent with hostile threats — as well as having the ratiocinative capacity associated with orthonomy (Pettit 2001*b*). But the question now is whether, even in the absence of a problem with coercion, orthonomy is enough to guarantee fitness to be held responsible.

It may not seem to be enough, for this alleged reason: that someone can be held responsible for something only if they are regressively or recursively responsible (Hurley 2002; Pettit 2005*b*). According to this thesis, you can be held responsible for something only insofar as it can be causally traced to you. The matter for which you are held responsible must be due to you immediately, or, if it is the effect of other factors, then those factors must be due to you; at the end of the causal regress, you must stand out as the originary source. But many of the things you come to do or hold, no matter how orthonomous you are, will be the product of habits or states of mind that are due to your biology or background. So how can you be held responsible for them?

I deny that you can be held responsible only for what is causally traceable to you, as the thesis has it. The more plausible claim, rather, is that you can be held responsible only for what is within your control, where control may be active and causal or virtual and non-causal. Once that point is clear, the problem of recursion no longer looks insurmountable.

Insofar as you are orthonomous, you will have a capacity to track reason in every aspect of your nature that is responsive to reason. This need not mean that you actively control every relevant habit or state of mind, regenerating it under the pressure of reason; it couldn't realistically mean anything of the kind. Rather it will mean that you virtually control such states and habits, being the sort of creature who will be triggered to reconsider and perhaps revise any that give rise to problems. Such virtual control, guaranteed as it is by orthonomy, will be sufficient to ensure that you can satisfy the need for recursive responsibility. And it does not raise any of the problems that come up under the assumption that responsibility requires a recursion in active, causal control.

There will be more to say on psychological freedom when we come to discuss co-reasoning and conversability later. But before coming to such topics, it will be useful now to digress on some issues of metaphysics and epistemology that arise in light of our discussion of reasons and reasoning.

3. RULES, RESPONSE-DEPENDENCE, AND VALUES

Reasoning and Rule-following

Whatever form is ascribed to reasons, and whether they be structural reasons or substantive reasons, treating them as constraints on your performance will amount to following them in the sense in which you might be said to follow rules. You will have to understand or identify them, being able to recognize what they require over an indefinite range of cases. You will have to be able to regulate your performance with a view to satisfying those requirements. You will have to remain open to the possibility of misidentifying the requirements or of failing for other reasons to satisfy them; you will have to remain exposed to error. And all of this will have to be something that you are in a position to recognize.

The rules that you follow in this sense will include the rule for *modus ponens* reasoning, as well as other rules of logic. But they will also include rules like that whereby it is right to believe that p if and only if it is true that p; it is right to ascribe the property 'F-'to an object x if and only if x is F; and so on. Among those rules, some will have to be basic from your point of view: they will have to be rules that are not defined by other rules and not followed on the basis of following other rules. And this takes us to a deep, intriguing question, first given prominence in Wittgenstein's work (Wittgenstein 1958; Kripke 1982; Miller and Wright 2002).

How is basic rule-following possible? How is it possible for a simple creature like you or me, starting from a point that is free of normative connotations, to target a rule in the required sense? How is it possible for us, as purely naturalistic systems, to break into the space of rules and reasons in the first place? This is a basic challenge for anyone who thinks that reasoning is important to mental life. I describe the story that I favor as an ethocentric account, because it gives an important role to habit and practice, which both answer to the Greek notion of *ethos* (Pettit 1993*a*, 2002*b*, 2005*d*).

The ethocentric story is built out of a number of claims, and in documenting them, I will assume that we are concerned with how people might grasp the notion of a certain property or predicable, say 'F-', and learn to treat it as a guide to what they should think and what they should say—as a rule for identifying when they should and when they should not hold that something is F. Let the property be that of geometrical or quasi-geometrical regularity. This is a property that we can imagine people grasping, and using to guide their predications, without being able to define or analyze it in other terms. It is a candidate, as we might say, for a basic rule of thought.

Presented with examples of regular and irregular figures, the first postulate in the ethocentric story is that people will develop manifestly convergent dispositions or habits of extrapolation, and will be able to use a set of exemplars to illustrate the property of regularity for themselves and each other. Each will think that it is *that* property, the one exemplified by triangles and circles and squares, and will assume that they can go on reliably, putting confidence in the disposition triggered within them.

The second postulate in my story is that people will take the property presumptively identified in exemplars to be an objective, intersubjectively accessible entity. This will appear in the fact that they develop a practice of treating any interpersonal or indeed intertemporal divergence of ascription as a sign of a limitation or obstruction to the access that one or the other side has to the property. Let them go different ways in the application of the term 'regular' to a given figure, and they will tend to baulk. They will not continue happily on different tracks, but will be disposed to take steps that have the effect of indicting one or the other as being subject to a limitation or an obstacle. They may not agree on who is in error, but they will each assume that someone is and, if they do not correct themselves, that it is someone else.

Finally, the third postulate in the ethocentric story is that there is a fact of the matter, given the practice in which they are involved, as to who ought to be indicted in any case as mistaken. The right factors for them to identify as grounds for indictment—the right factors, by the lights of their own practice—are those that can best explain failures of access, consistently with the presumption embedded in the practice that the property is accessible in principle to all: viz. that no one can be discounted *ex ante* as an interpreter of the rule. The idea of best explanation here is that which leads us to say that it is better to indict one person with being color-blind, taking most others to see things correctly, than to privilege that one person's position and deem the run of human beings to be subject to some limitation or obstruction.[14]

On this story, the enterprise of giving a common, objective referent to a term or concept like that of regularity will be fraught with vulnerability. For it may turn out that people's dispositions do not after all converge; or that by some accepted criterion there is nothing objective there that generates them; or that there is no good explanatory reason why some factors should be thought the right ones to indict. Should any of these possibilities materialize, then the project of orientating by a common referent or beacon—the project of triangulating on an objective reference point—will flounder (Price 1988). People will be involved in a degenerating referential program. They may coordinate in their usage, but the coordination will not be objectively constrained in the manner promised in the practice; it will amount at best to mutual conventional adjustment, not to triangulation on a common point of reference.

---

[14] Those factors may leave it underdetermined whether the property should be taken to be realized in one or another sort of case, and if they do, of course, then at that point whatever convention users adopt will be the correct one.

Still, this is just to look on the dark side. The brighter aspect of the story is the suggestion that, despite being naturalistic systems in continuity with simple animals, we can bootstrap our way into rule-following, and ultimately into reasoning, by authorizing our convergent extrapolative dispositions, recruiting them to the epistemic purpose of identifying a presumptively common rule, and then vindicating that presumption by running a non-degenerating referential program under which any interpersonal or intertemporal discrepancies in people's responses prove to be appropriately explicable.

The story told may be thought to over-intellectualize people's referential capacities. But, as I construe the account, it does not do this. The story as to how people grasp and accept the guidance of a rule of thought—say, the property or predicable of regularity—is analogous to an account that might be given of how people grasp something as simple as the route across a complex city or park and set out to follow it. I can grasp a route and not be able to describe or map it. I may grasp it so far as I confidently and justifiably trust myself to be able to start out in the right direction and then, at every later turning point, be able to tell at that point how I should go on. I may even grasp a route in tandem with certain others so far as we each confidently and justifiably trust our group to be able to do these things under the pressure of mutual interrogation and interaction. For all that my story about rule-following implies, people's grasp of the basic rules of thought, the common referents by which they aspire to orientate semantically, may be of the same highly practical, untheorized kind.[15]

The ethocentric account of rule-following does not strictly entail that as rule-followers you and I have to form community; I might in principle try to establish a community with myself over time. But the account does entail that if you and I are able to know that we follow the same rules, as we generally assume we can, then we must enter into a community in which we each authorize the other, allowing that either of us may be subject to limitations or obstructions in access to those rules (Pettit 1993*a*: ch. 4). With the rules we follow in ordinary doings, we assume as a matter of routine that they are equally accessible, at least in principle, to all. And we effectively vindicate that assumption by the high degree of communicative success that we achieve. We may diverge on various matters of judgment, of course; for example, you may think that there are entities with certain sets of properties, I may think that there are not. But we much more rarely diverge on the meaning of the terms or concepts employed in those

---

[15] This aspect of ordinary understanding and assumption explains why philosophy has a substantive role to play in articulating and interrogating the working premises of ordinary thought (Pettit 1998, 2004*d*). What we may understand only in a practical, untheorized way in everyday thought, philosophy can enable us to understand in a more analytical, examinable mode. The paradox of analysis was supposed to be that if an analysis of our ideas told us something new, then it couldn't properly be an analysis. This paradox disappears once we realize that the practical mode of understanding associated with everyday thought is quite different from the theoretical mode associated with philosophical analysis.

judgments. We routinely achieve conceptual consensus, or something close to consensus, even as judgmental consensus escapes us.

One important upshot of this account is a lesson about interpersonal accessibility (Pettit 1993*a*: ch. 4; 2002*b*: essay 1.4). The story means that with words that serve as markers of basic rules for people, the referents of those words—the predicables corresponding, for example, to certain predicates—will be fixed for each only on the assumption that they are fixed for all. The worry that such a word means one thing for one person, another for another person, where the parties are successful participants in the same successful practice, is nothing less than the worry that the word does not have a suitably fixed referent at all. The condition on which each can think that the word is targeted on an objective semantic value is that it is targeted in the mouths and minds of everyone in the community on the same target. This result connects quite smoothly with the topic of co-reasoning to which we shall be turning later.

Rule-following and Response-dependence

According to the story told about how we follow basic rules of thought, gaining access to an unanalyzed predicable like regularity, thinking or reasoning presupposes a contingency of our nature: viz. that we are the sorts of creatures who will find ourselves disposed to extrapolate in a certain direction under exposure to examples. Presented with examples of triangles, circles, and squares, especially when these are set in contrast to figures of a squiggly nature, we will naturally be disposed to put rectangles and diamonds and trapezoids in the same class. And if a word is introduced in reference to the presumptive commonality amongst triangles, circles, and squares—I say nothing on how we master this naming game—then we will be naturally disposed to use that word of these further figures too, but not of anything that we find squiggly.

The rule-following problem is often motivated by the fact that everything is like everything in some respect, and that from any finite set of samples there will be nothing inherently wrong about extending the set in any of an indefinite range of directions. A mind that was truly open, perhaps the divine or an angelic mind, would find nothing in such a finite set to direct it to one pattern of extrapolation—the one predicable we call 'regularity'—rather than to another. The reason we go in one direction is due, precisely, to the fact that our minds are not open but are predisposed in that direction. This is a happy fault—a fortunate form of intellectual closure. It enables us to be able to target the property of regularity, letting the examples presented serve to exemplify it: that is, serve as samples in the way a tailor's swatch provides samples of different patterns of fabric (Goodman 1969).[16]

---

[16] It might be, of course, that what is identified as a single predicable by the convergent inclinations that people display under what prove to be favorable circumstances is not, from a

It should not be surprising that we tend to extrapolate in one direction rather than another, given a finite set of examples. I assume, as in the picture of the minimal mind, that even simple animals form beliefs or representations, ascribing this or that property to this or that particular. This assumption means that such animals must be predisposed to find certain properties or classifications salient and others not. Mother Nature will have provided them with this predisposition, letting them become attuned to categories that partition the world along lines that facilitate their survival and success. And what Mother Nature has done for other animals, she will also have done for us, thereby taking us to the point where words can be introduced and given common referents.

If I can gain access to certain properties and to other semantic values only in virtue of something that I bring to the world, thanks to my evolutionarily shaped nature, then that means that my access is dependent on the responses to which that nature predisposes me. I may be able to master the term 'regular', forming the appropriate concept, but my mastery will be dependent on having the response that makes a certain similarity salient, other similarities not. And what is true of such a presumptively basic term—the sort of term that is not learned just on the basis of definition—will be true of any term or concept that figures in the same basic way within my psychology.

This observation supports the claim that response-dependence is a global phenomenon, holding of the terms and concepts that are basic for any user (Jackson and Pettit 2002; Pettit 2002*b*: part 1; 2006*g*).[17] But this is not as controversial a doctrine as some have taken it to be (Devitt 2004). The crucial point to grasp is that there is a large difference between saying that the non-parasitic mastery of a predicate is response-dependent and saying that the predicate itself is definitionally response-dependent or, even more extremely, that the property it ascribes is ontologically response-dependent.

A predicate would be definitionally response-dependent if understanding it required having an independent understanding of the response in question. An example might be the predicate 'is nauseating'; to understand what this says, you have to understand the nature of the nausea response. And, to go to the other case, a property would be ontologically response-dependent if it was such that it could not exist without the response. An example might be a property like 'is

---

further point of view, a single property but rather an equivalence class of different properties. This means that we have a choice. We can try to live with that result, arguing that if the properties in that class are such that they will never come apart in a way that can register with us, then we need not worry about their multiplicity. Or we can introduce at this point the idea, due to David Lewis (1983), that among the properties available for the equivalence class one will be truly eligible for being designated by our term and concept, and it will inevitably be the referent (Pettit 1993*a*: postscript). I would prefer to live with the first approach; the second, 'magnetic' theory of reference has an other-worldly feel.

[17] I do not necessarily suppose that the same terms will be basic for all. Someone who came to master a geometrical definition of 'regularity', so that the term ceased to be basic, would still use it with the same meaning and reference as someone who had only a basic grasp of it.

envied' or 'is a cause of envy', as distinct from 'is enviable'; unlike enviability, being envied or being a cause of envy requires the existence of the envy response.

No predicate is required to be definitionally response-dependent, no property to be ontologically response-dependent, on my story. Take the predicate 'is regular' once again. The property this ascribes is not ontologically dependent on any response in us; if it obtains in the world, then it would obtain in the world independently of our presence there. Neither is the predicate involved definitionally response-dependent. In order to understand it, seeing how to extrapolate appropriately, I must respond to examples with a sense of what is salient about them and of where they point in partitioning other items into those that are of a kind and those that aren't. But I may have this response, and may be able to understand the predicate without having any independent understanding of the response that consists in finding a pattern salient; it may take philosophy to make me aware of the nature and role of the salience response.

That our mastery of basic terms or concepts is response-dependent, then, is consistent with realism about the discourses in which they figure. Take any set of response-dependently mastered notions, and consider the sort of talk and thought, however individuated, in which they figure; this may be talk about causality, or the mind, or matters of value, or possibility and necessity, or any of a range of topics. Realism about any such discourse will involve three distinct claims: first, against expressivism, that its characteristic claims are truth-conditional, not mere expressions, even expressions in a language of 'minimal truth', of non-cognitive states; second, against error theory, that those claims are not systematically undermined by the non-existence of some element involved in the truth conditions: say, some property the claims typically ascribe; and third, against an anthropocentric or idealist revisionism, that the truth conditions are as demanding as they seem intuitively.[18] Realism in that sense is in no way compromised by the recognition that semantic mastery is often response-dependent.

Still, the recognition of response-dependence does have some surprising implications. Let favorable conditions be defined as conditions in which those factors that are indicted as limitations or obstructions under a relevant practice are absent. For any response-dependently mastered term or concept, F, then, it will be a priori knowable that something is available to be named as F if and only if it is such as to give rise to the appropriate response under favorable conditions. It will be necessary and sufficient for the denominability of something as F that it be the sort of thing that occasions the relevant response in favorable conditions.[19]

---

[18] This is a slight variation on the account of realism in Pettit 2002*b*: part 1. I am indebted to a discussion of the topic with the graduate students at the Research School of Social Science, Australian National University, January 2006.

[19] I moved to this cautious formulation, employing the notion of denominability, once it became clear to me that the fact that something is denominable as 'F' only if a certain condition holds does not entail that it is F only if the condition holds. See Pettit 2002*b*: essay 3.3.

And this will be a priori knowable, being knowable on the basis of considerations to do with how a basic term like 'F' is mastered and gains its meaning.

I chose to employ the word 'response-dependent' in characterizing terms and concepts that are response-dependently mastered, because Mark Johnston (1989, 1993) had introduced it to characterize terms and concepts that are governed by just this sort of a priori biconditional. This may not have been a happy choice of terminology. For the terms and concepts that Johnston had in mind support a priori biconditionals because of being definitionally response-dependent, not because of being response-dependently mastered.[20] They are terms and concepts designed to pick out features that we conceptualize as dispositions in things to elicit certain responses, so that understanding them requires understanding the nature of the responses elicited; for our purposes, they might better be characterized, in Johnston's own phrase, as response-dispositional rather than response-dependent.

The terms or concepts for secondary properties like color and taste and texture are usually linked with a priori biconditionals on the grounds that they are definitionally response-dependent. One interesting lesson of the approach taken here is that even such terms may engage such biconditionals, not for that reason, but only in virtue of being response-dependently mastered. I think that color terms and concepts are certainly like this.

It is not because of recognizing that something elicits a red sensation and that conditions are normal that I understand 'red' and know the object is red. I understand 'red' response-dependently insofar as I have sensations that make red things saliently similar, in situations that do not give rise to intertemporal or interpersonal divergence; and I know that an object is red insofar as it displays that similarity in the absence of factors I have reason to regard as obstructions or limitations. But despite the connection to sensation, I need not become aware of sensations or develop an independent understanding of them in order to have this capacity (Pettit 2004c).

What marks off secondary properties, as they are called, on this account? On the world's side, the fact that they play a relatively narrow explanatory role; color explains a lot less than volume (Wright 1992). On the subject's side, the fact that the corresponding concepts are response-dependently mastered in a distinctive fashion. Some primary properties—e.g. volume and motion—may be conceptualized on a response-dependent basis, of course, but the responses presupposed will always involve multiple modalities of sense; thus we register volume and motion by both sight and touch. Secondary properties, such as color or taste or texture or sound, are conceptualized on the basis of their effect on one sense only. What makes them secondary is not the nature

---

[20] The terms and concepts with which I have been concerned should also be distinguished from the extension-determining notions that Crispin Wright brought to the discussion. See Wright 1992: 108–39.

of the properties as such but rather the character of our access to those properties.[21]

Substantive Reasons and Values

The discussion of rule-following and response-dependence gives us a perspective on the notion of rightness, in the sense in which this refers us to that which has the most support from substantive reasons. 'Right' in the sense in which it refers to that which has the most support from structural reasons is a covertly indexical term that is relativized to the individual whose structure of attitudes is presupposed. If I hold unquestioningly by the belief that p and that if p, q, then it is right relative to the structure of my attitudes—right-for-me—that I believe that q. 'Right' in the sense in which it refers to that which has the most support from substantive reasons will not be indexical in this way: it will mean 'right, period', not 'right-for-me' or 'right-for-you'. That which is right, period, will be that which is supported by considerations that are relevant to each of us in the same way.

There are clearly substantive reasons for believing things, as in the reason for believing that p that is given by the fact that p or the truth of 'p'. That fact makes it right to believe that p, not just for me, but for you and for anyone else; believing that p is right, period. Moving from beliefs to desires and actions, however, the big question is whether there are substantive reasons for someone to seek a certain result or to perform a given action; reasons that make it right, period—substantively, not just structurally, right—for the agent to take that line. Can we extend the notion of substantive rightness from belief-like attitudes that aim to fit the world to desire-like attitudes, and to related actions, that aim to make the world fit them? Can we find rightness-makers, in this sense of rightness, such that by common lights it is right for someone to seek or do something just in case the rightness-makers, the substantive reasons, make it right to do so?

Given that we routinely achieve conceptual consensus, identifying common predicables on the basis of communal triangulation, there is no principled difficulty that blocks the appearance of common rightness-makers. We can achieve consensus in the construal of relevant concepts from a basis of shared response.

---

[21] Is redness the physical property in things—or a disjunction of such properties—that makes them look red in suitable circumstances? Or is it the higher-level property of there being a physical property, maybe this, maybe that, that has this effect? The mode in which access is secured on the story of response-dependent mastery probably suggests that the stronger candidate is the lower-level, physical property, but I do not explore that issue here. I also ignore the role of the further distinction between the rigidly and flexibly designated property: the property that is picked out as the actual property that plays a certain role, e.g., or the property that happens to play a certain role. And I ignore the possibility of picking out properties in a response-dependent fashion, without any assumption that they have to be realized in our experience; I discuss such abstract concepts in Pettit 2002*b*: essay 3.3 and in Jackson and Pettit 2002.

Suppose, plausibly, that the following conditions obtain. First, people find various properties of potential actions and states of affairs attractive or aversive and, perhaps for that very reason, saliently identifiable; what makes a property attractive or aversive is that it will introduce a difference in attraction between any two otherwise indifferent scenarios (Pettit 2002*b*: essay 2.2).[22] Second, people authorize one another in naming and conceptualizing such a property, and naming it as a property that makes for a positive degree of attraction or aversion, though not perhaps the same degree on all sides. And, third, this strategy is vindicated insofar as people achieve a conceptual consensus: they successfully implement the assumption that any discrepancy in recognizing the presence of the property, together with a suitable desiderative valence, is due to the operation of factors that can be treated as limitations or obstructions.

The properties identified in this sort of exercise would naturally be capable of playing the role of common rightness-makers or wrongness-makers amongst the parties involved. Each would be able to argue for the substantive rightness or wrongness of a choice or policy, justifying it to others, by showing how it served to promote such commonly valued properties. The properties would conform to the profile of what are often called "thick values", answering to words like 'fair', 'kind', 'honest', 'sincere', and the like. They would contrast with the thin values of rightness and wrongness—rightness and wrongness, period—whose ascription they serve to justify. And they would equally contrast with the thin values of goodness or badness, where goodness might be taken to require a modicum of thick value, badness a modicum of thick disvalue.

Thick values, understood in this way, may prove puzzling on a number of counts. First, they are properties that are meant to obtain in a naturalistic world; they obtain or fail to obtain as a matter of fact. Second, they are properties that are supposed to be capable of making it right to desire or do something; contrary to a well-known Humean prescription, they allow a transition from 'is' to 'ought'. And third, they are properties such that the recognition that they are present is connected with motivation in more than a merely inductive fashion: contrary to another Humean supposition, belief in their presence is not really distinct from a corresponding state of attraction or aversion (Smith 1994).

These features cease to be troubling under a view of values that Frank Jackson and I labeled 'moral functionalism' (Jackson 1992; Jackson and Pettit 1995; Pettit 2001*a*). According to this view, thick values are natural properties that are identified by the role they play in engaging with our desires and our practices of reasoning about rightness. The concepts in which such properties become available to us are response-dependently mastered, though in a distinctively complex way.

---

[22] I argue that it is important to recognize the role of such properties, and the way decision theory abstracts from them, in Pettit 2002*b*: essay 2.2. For an exchange with Jamie Dreier on the topic see Pettit 2005*d*.

Take a term like 'fair'. I learn the meaning of 'fair', so this story goes, by seeing
the connections of the property with certain descriptive paradigms; by finding
those paradigms attractive in situations where there is no reason to think that I
am subject to relevant impediments or limitations; and by learning that fairness
is superveniently fixed by descriptive character: there is no difference in fairness
without a descriptive difference. But in learning the term I will also have to
see its connections with properties picked out by other terms: with substantive
rightness, as in learning that fairness is a reason why something may be right;
with politeness, as in learning that fairness is a more important rightness-maker
than politeness; with impartiality, as in learning that impartial people reliably
desire fair outcomes; with justification, as in learning that the fairness of an
option chosen may enable me to justify myself to others in making that choice;
and so on. And if I learn the meaning of 'fair' by seeing the connections between
fairness and the properties picked out by other moral terms, then I will at the
same time learn the meanings of those other terms by seeing the connections of
the properties they pick out with one another.

This picture is functionalist insofar as moral properties are associated with
roles they play in moral reasoning, and play in a holistic, interconnected way.
But moral concepts, on this picture, are still mastered on the basis of more
or less spontaneous responses and associated practices. How do people come
to believe that there are paradigms of fairness, as with a principle like 'Heads
you win; tails you lose' or 'I cut, you choose'? Not necessarily by explicitly
registering that such examples are paradigms, but simply by treating them as
more or less non-negotiable instances of the property. How do they come to
see fairness as an attracting property? Not by being taught the connection, but
by finding the property attractive in the presumptive absence of obstructions or
limitations. How do they come to hold that fairness is descriptively supervenient?
Not necessarily by giving their assent to a principle of supervenience, but simply
by being disposed to reason from the claim that two or more options differ in
fairness to the conclusion that there is some descriptive difference between them.
How do they come to hold that fairness is a *pro tanto* reason for thinking that an
option is the right one to choose? Not necessarily by spelling out that principle
of inference, but simply by being disposed to treat fairness, other things being
equal, as a reason for ascribing rightness.

This view of thick values—and indeed, of thin values too—makes it possible
to explain their problematic features. While the values are properties of the natural
world, they are properties—or equivalence classes of properties—that are individuated by a role they play. While they are properties that make for the rightness
or wrongness of options, they do so only because that is part of the role they are
given when people treat them as rightness-makers. And while they are properties
that are inherently motivating—if motivating in different degrees for different
people—that is because they are picked out to play their distinctive role only
insofar as they reliably arouse a non-negligible degree of attraction or aversion.

This last feature makes the concepts response-dependent in a distinctive manner. Not only will basic evaluative concepts be capable of being mastered only by creatures sensitive to the similarity between paradigms of their application and disposed to make suitable connections with other evaluative concepts. They will be capable of being mastered only by creatures in whom suitable desires are occasioned by such paradigms, and by extensions from those paradigms. Anyone who registers the presence of such a property, then, and does so non-parasitically on the responses of others, will experience the affect associated. There will be an intimate, more than inductive linkage between believing in the presence of the property and experiencing a certain degree of attraction or aversion.

Moral functionalism is an appealing doctrine. It represents ethical utterances as truth-conditional assertions, contrary to expressivism; it ascribes a credible truth-conditional content to them, contrary to error theory; and it does not revise our understanding of that content in a debunking, counter-intuitive way, contrary to a doctrine like subjectivism: this would take such assertions to self-ascribe attitudes of approval.[23] It amounts, in short, to a realism about moral discourse.

This realism does not entail, however, that there are determinate answers available to all questions about whether a given course of action is right or wrong. The thick values that people recognize in common are likely to have different weightings, under the assumptions made. As I said, people may each recognize a property as attractive or aversive, but do so with different degrees of attraction or aversion. For all that the story tells us, then, there is no saying how much convergence people will be capable of achieving in judgments of right and wrong. This will be true of judgments bearing on particular actions and policies and of judgments bearing on the institutions established in the course of social and political life.

How should people go about deciding questions of right and wrong, starting from the framework provided by shared concepts of thick and thin value? Moral functionalism provides support for the intuitively sensible method of ethical argument that John Rawls (1971) calls 'reflective equilibrium'. If our ethical terms and concepts are interlinked, then in thinking out our views as to where they apply—in applying and extending the theory that they encode—we will have to go back and forth between consideration of the particular applications we are inclined to support and consideration of the conceptual linkages we feel obliged to sustain; we will have to equilibrate our judgments in the two areas, shuttling reflectively between them. As a view of how our moral terms gain reference, and substantive reasons get established amongst us, moral functionalism supports this methodology but otherwise leaves open the direction that ethical or moral theory should take.

---

[23] For an argument that expressivism is in danger of collapse into such subjectivism, not representing a really stable point of view, see Jackson and Pettit 1998, 2003.

4. PHENOMENAL CONSCIOUSNESS

The Problem

There is little problem in explaining how I can know what I believe or want
or intend, under the assumptions I have defended about reasoning and self-
regulation. As a reasoning subject, I am committed to believing that which I
ought in reason to believe, to deciding that which I ought in reason to decide,
and so on; and as a self-regulating subject I am capable of ensuring that I live up
to the beliefs or decisions that I prescribe for myself. Suppose I am asked whether
I believe that *p*. I can answer by asking myself whether *p*; by announcing that
I believe that *p* if and only if reason suggests that *p*; and by then backing that
announcement with the authority of a self-regulating subject: someone who can
keep himself or herself tuned to what reason appears to support (McGeer 1996;
Moran 2001; McGeer and Pettit 2002).

But self-knowledge in this sense is distinct from what is now generally described
as "consciousness". A mental state or event will be conscious, in current usage,
just so far as there is something it is like to be in that state or to undergo that
event (Nagel 1986); just so far as it has what is often described as a phenomenal
presence for the subject. And the fact that I know what I believe or desire or
intend does not make such a state conscious in the phenomenal sense. Only
'experiences', to use the word that comes naturally to mind, are conscious in this
special sense. And it is the consciousness of experience that concerns us now.

Consciousness in this sense raises an obvious problem for physicalists. I
sketched an account of how a physical state can be intentional, constituting a
belief or a desire with a certain content, just so far as it plays a certain functional
role in interaction with other physical states. The problem is to give a similar
account of how a physical state can be conscious, identifying some physically
unexceptionable aspect that might ensure that there is something it is going to
be like for a subject to be in that state.

There are two distinct problems, in my view, that physicalists have to face.
The first is to give an analysis of what is involved in there being something it
is like to be in a certain mental state; this analysis of phenomenal consciousness
may be stipulative in character or purportedly faithful to ordinary understanding.
And the second is to show how the presence of consciousness, so analyzed, can
be realized by certain neural states in a person.

This is not an uncontroversial statement of the challenge. Some thinkers hold
that there is no possibility of analyzing phenomenal consciousness, and even that
there are no reliable marks or characteristics of consciousness; we know what
consciousness involves, so the line goes, just by seeing what it is in our own case.
If we take this view, and still want to be physicalists, then the best we can do
is to find physical phenomena that we can pair off with conscious appearances,

postulating basic, not further explicable identities between them. The fact that we cannot say anything informative in analysis or characterization of consciousness means that we cannot explain any identification we postulate between neural state N and conscious state C by showing that the physical nature of N makes sense of why it is the conscious state C. We cannot say: the components or characteristics of C, qua conscious, are x, y, and z; the physical nature of N ensures the presence of x, y, and z; and so it makes good sense to identify C with N. All we will be able to do is to posit that C is N, admitting that there is nothing about N that makes it a saliently suitable candidate for identification with C (for an overview, see Pettit forthcoming, *a*).

I do not know how to persuade people who think that there is no putative analysis of consciousness available that they are wrong. But I think they *are* wrong, for reasons that should appear in the course of the following discussion. Thus I reject the idea that the best we can do as physicalists is to posit blank, unilluminating identities between neural states and states in the conscious or phenomenal or experiential realm. I hope that we can do a lot better than that.

Consistently with that aspiration, I envisage a two-stage procedure of argument whereby we can try to make physicalistic sense of consciousness. In the first stage, I put forward a hypothesis as to what consciousness involves. On the analysis suggested, consciousness materializes when a subject achieves a meta-perceptual representation that parallels the meta-propositional representation that reasoning requires. In the second stage, I go on to test that hypothesis by looking at how far it can make sense of what are taken to be the data on consciousness. Here I start from the challenges that are formulated in the literature against any reductive account of conscious phenomena. These phenomena include the look available to us in a conscious visual state; the sound, feel, smell, or taste available in one of the other perceptual modes; or the pain or pleasure, the tone or tingling or pressure, that is characteristically registered in bodily sensation.

Representing the Represented-ways Things Are

Representation, as suggested earlier, is a matter of functional adjustment. Let us put aside the problem that representations come together in a system and that it may be difficult to identify what one representation does on its own (Stalnaker 1984). A subject will represent a way things are, we may then say, insofar as it is in a state that meets two distinct sorts of conditions. First, there is a generally robust connection—one that obtains in favorable conditions, however they are cast—between the form the state takes and the way the environment is configured; and second, the form taken by the state tends to lead the subject to behave in a manner that is appropriate, given its goals, to such an environment. The state will represent a property as instantiated insofar as, first, it generally materializes in the presence of that property, or of evidence of that property, and disappears in its absence; and second, it plays the role of prompting the subject to behave as the instantiation of that property makes it appropriate to behave, given the subject's goals and other states.

Representation of a property as instantiated may occur in a subject without any representation of the property as represented. The subject may respond appropriately to inputs, and may act appropriately under the effects of those inputs, even if all of this transpires in the dark of the brain. The simple predator may adjust to the rustling sound of potential prey, representing the presence of prey behind a bush or a clump of grass; it may then act out of a desire for food, as that representation makes it appropriate to act: it may put itself in a position to pounce; and this may transpire without any higher-level representation of the prey as a represented target—as a target that is represented as instantiated but that may prove not to be instantiated.

Such a simple, representational subject will be lost in the world it registers. Its representations will take it into the world, without any indication of being representations; they will offer a transparent, undetectable glass in which the world is apparently present. The subject will be attuned to how the world is, as it shows up in those representations, and will adjust to the way it is in light of its goals. But it will do so in complete neglect of what makes the world available—its own representational states. Its transactions with the world will sometimes be unsuccessful, because its representations misrepresent how things are. But they will misrepresent without the misrepresentation becoming salient—without the glass fogging up and becoming visible. The predator will not register the difference between pouncing on something mistaken for prey and pouncing on prey that slips out of its grasp and sight.

There will be nothing, intuitively, that the world is like for such a creature. The way things are will register with the creature, leading it to adjust and react appropriately, but the creature will not register the way things are as a way they are: it will not see it as one among a number of contrasting ways they might be. Putting it otherwise, the way things are will be represented *in* the creature, priming it to take suitable initiatives in its environment. But it will not be represented *for* the creature; it will not in itself be a potential object of attention (Cummins 1983). If the way things are is not represented as such—if there is no representation of the represented-way things are—then the way they are cannot have any phenomenal presence for the subject. Not being an object of attention, there cannot be something it is like for it to materialize. The phenomenal-way things are—the something-it-is-like-ness they display—has to be a represented-way things are.

The Perceptually-represented-ways Things Are

But not any represented-way things are will count as a phenomenal-way things are. Suppose I believe the proposition that it is raining beyond my curtained window. Aware of holding this belief—perhaps a belief prompted by the unreliable evidence of a pitter-patter sound—I may not only represent rain as a property instantiated outside, I may represent it as a represented-property. I may come to form a belief about how things are according to my representation. In doing this, however, I can hardly be said to enjoy any form of phenomenal consciousness. The example shows that representational recursion—representing properties as represented or indeed as represented-as-represented, and so on—is not enough to guarantee the presence of consciousness. Something else is necessary.

What is needed, I suggest, is that the represented-way things are at the base of the recursion be perceptual, not just propositional. It has to involve perceptual representation, whether of the world or of the subject's own body, not just belief that the world or body is thus and so. The representation of certain properties as represented, whether as propositionally or perceptually represented, will always itself be propositional. It will involve the belief that the way things present themselves is a represented-way they are, and it will facilitate the formation of further beliefs about how exactly they are represented: that is, about the content of the representation. For phenomenal consciousness, the represented-way that things are believed to be has to be a perceptually-represented-way they are; it cannot just be a way they are believed but not perceived to be.

Propositional representation represents a particular property or set of properties as instantiated or not instantiated, whether in the manner of a particular, an existential, or a universal claim. It is a more or less atomistic form of representation that picks out certain properties and focuses on them in isolation from others. Perceptual representation, by contrast, is holistic in character. If it represents the presence of a particular color, it will also represent the presence of a particular shape; if it represents something as at a certain distance from the subject, it will also represent it as in a certain direction; if it represents it as lying to the left of another object, it will represent it as lying to the left of anything on the other side of that object; and so on. Perceptual representation can be mined for ever more fine-grained information about the qualities present in the perceived field, with attention given now to this quality, now to that. Where propositional representation is digital, in the manner of an electronic watch that tells just hours and minutes, perceptual representation is analogue in form; it resembles the watch-face that at any moment gives us indefinitely fine-grained information on just how much of a minute has passed (Dretske 1999).

The holistic character of perceptual representation gives it a certain autonomy in relation to propositional representation. Subjects like you and me may check our propositional representations against our perceptual ones, going back and forth between the rich stream of perception and the more austere process of belief formation. But because the two representational modes are so different, they are relatively autonomous. Thus, even when I form beliefs that go counter to my perceptions—even when I judge that the stick I see in the water is not bent—still the perceptions remain in place, refusing just to go away. The perceptual stream, as it is sometimes put, is encapsulated or insulated against the presumptively corrective information that is registered at the propositional level (Fodor 1983). Propositional representation may be hair-triggered to the lightest pressure of evidence and argument—though even that is doubtful—but perceptual representation is sticky and hard to budge.[24]

Given the holistic, encapsulated nature of perception, there is a big difference between the case in which a subject represents certain properties as propositionally represented and the case in which the subject represents them as perceptually represented. The propositionally-represented-way something is will consist in its being represented as instantiating this or that atomistic property. The perceptually-represented-way something is will consist in its being represented as instantiating an open, holistic network of properties. The former is going to be something abstract, then: something whose features are exhausted in the description that tells us what object is represented, and what property or properties it is represented as instantiating. The latter is going to be decidedly concrete. It will have aspects that far outrun any description we may offer of its object or content. These aspects will be as endless as the properties that the object is represented as instantiating in the dense, analogue materials made available, for example, in sight or hearing, taste or smell or touch.

The difference made by the holism of perceptual content is amplified by the difference that its stickiness makes. Whereas the propositionally-represented-way an object is will just be the way it is according to the final beliefs of the agent, the perceptually-represented-way it is may come apart from the agent's beliefs. It will be a feature of the world-in-relation-to-the-subject that remains stable and inspectable, even as the subject denies it credibility, or only registers one or another proposition that it supports. As the agent's beliefs crystallize and change, the propositionally-represented-ways of things will alter in immediate response. Not so with the perceptually-represented-ways of things. These will remain in place, offering grounds for forming more beliefs that can be articulated at any moment. And, being relatively encapsulated against propositional information, they will often remain in place even when they run counter to the agent's final beliefs. They will retain a detail that outruns the articulation of the subject's beliefs, and they may do so, even in defiance of those beliefs.[25]

My hypothesis at this first stage of argument is that consciousness in the phenomenal sense envisaged in the literature appears just when subjects register the perceptually-represented-ways things are. To see consciously is to see and

---

[24] While perceptual and propositional representation may come apart like this, however, it is important to note that normally they will not do so. Thus, what an agent believes in this or that scenario—what the agent authorizes and is prepared to act on—may just be the perceived way it is, with attention focused on this or that element. It may not be broken down into any more atomistic, propositional elements. The difference between propositional and perceptual representation is a difference on the side of content. Either sort of content may be believed, or belief may be held in suspense, as in the deauthorized but robust perception of the stick as bent.

[25] I should say that I do not take this position to imply a line on how far the content of perception is conceptual. See McDowell 1996.

then, in addition, to be positioned to form indefinitely many beliefs about how things are according to that visual representation. To hear consciously is to hear and then, at the same time, to be positioned to form indefinitely many beliefs about how things are according to that aural representation. To consciously feel a tingle in one's foot is to feel the tingle—and so to be primed to scratch or stretch—and at the same time to be positioned to form an indefinite range of beliefs about how things are according to that representation: about the position or sharpness or constancy or painfulness of the tingle.

In every case of conscious perception, the way things are according to the perceptual representation will itself be available as something about which to form beliefs; it will be propositionally represented for the subject. How will you know the ways things are according to your perceptual representation? Arguably, in the way you know how things are according to your propositional representations. You will look to the world, rather than looking inside, and ask how they are—how they perceptually are. In reporting on how they are, then, you will identify the character of your representations: in this case, your perceptual representations (Bar-On 2004; McGeer 2005).

Any perception will be rich with properties that are there to be registered in this way by the subject. The properties of the visual experience will be that it is as of something red, as of something at such and such a distance, as of something gradually receding, and so on. The unconscious perceiver may register the redness, the distance, and the recession, and adjust appropriately. But only the conscious perceiver will register those properties-as-represented. And it is those properties-as-represented that provide the stuff of phenomenal consciousness.

To adopt this hypothesis is to be an intentionalist or representationalist about consciousness (Harman 1990; Byrne 2001; Jackson 2003; Pettit 2005a).[26] It is to hold that the phenomenal character of a mental episode is logically fixed by its representational content: it is supervenient on how things are represented—represented as perceptually represented—as being. Let that content be fixed, and the phenomenal feel will be fixed at one and the same time. Such an intentionalist analysis of consciousness is attractive because, on the account sketched earlier, content is itself supervenient on functional role, and functional role is physically explicable. Thus we can be confident that if the analysis is correct, then consciousness can be realized in purely physical creatures and so, assuming physicalism is correct, in creatures like us. The content of a representation—or, strictly, of a system of representations—is fixed by the environmental cues to which it is sensitive and by the responses that it elicits or would elicit in different environments, as the subject seeks in those scenarios to

---

[26] The intentionalism supported here is quite distinctive, however. Not just any kind of representation, not even any kind of perceptual representation, will ensure that there is something it is like for the world to be represented thus and so. It is only recursive, perceptual representation that will deliver that result: the sort of perceptual representation in which the subject becomes positioned to represent the perceptually-represented-ways things are.

realize certain goals (Stalnaker 1984). And the existence of such environmental and responsive connections is physically unexceptionable.

Susan Hurley and Alva Noë raise the question in their chapter as to whether my account of consciousness is meant to be a priori, and suggest that in any case it is not a functionalist analysis, a priori or otherwise. I think of the proposed analysis as an a priori account of how consciousness ought to be understood, whether or not it is revisionary of ordinary understanding; it will be revisionary, if ordinary understanding is infected with the belief in qualia that I discuss below. The analysis is broadly functionalist in character, suggesting that consciousness is going to be fixed in place by the complex, multi-level processing required for the representation of the perceptually-represented-ways of things. I think that Hurley and Noë need not object to this, since they appear to have a narrower account of functionalism in mind when they say that my account is not functionalist.

But if the account given so far can be depicted as a priori in character, I should add that the psychological story sketched later, when I respond to a salient challenge, is not a priori in the same way. This story is in the same family as that which attracts Hurley and Noë themselves, and belongs in the realm of empirical speculation, continuous with the sort of theorizing that is typical of science. It outlines an account of the perceptually-represented-ways things are when perception, in particular color perception, is phenomenally conscious. The idea is to rough out a plausible but not a priori demonstrable account that can gird us against the common belief in qualia.

The Challenge to the Hypothesis

The story just developed can be reformulated with the notion of a perceptual seeming or appearance. That there is a perceptual seeming or appearance presented by things just means that the subject registers the perceptually-represented-way those things are. There is a way that things are perceptually and holistically represented such that, being itself available to propositional representation, it can be interrogated for its more atomistic features. According to the story just developed, it is the presence of such perceptual seeming or appearance that constitutes consciousness. Reformulating the account in these terms makes it possible to formulate neatly the challenge to which it is most saliently subject.

That there is a seeming or appearance means, in functional terms, that the agent is primed to adjust and react in a suitable manner. I will believe that things are thus and so, according to functionalism, in virtue of my being in a state that is attuned to a certain scenario and that tunes me to respond in a way that is appropriate, given my goals, under that sort of scenario. Applying this account here, we may say that things will perceptually seem to me to be a certain way in virtue of my being in a perceptual state that meets suitable attuning and tuning requirements. If it seems to me that there is a mug of coffee at such and such a distance and in such and such a direction from my right hand, then that will be because I am in a type of state that meets two conditions. It is holistically attuned to, among other things, the perceptually registered position and distance of the mug relative to my right hand: the perceptually-represented-way it is in those respects. And it enables me to ask the question as to whether this is the actual position and distance of the mug from my hand and, in response, to come to believe that it is, or indeed that it isn't.

The challenge that any such account will face is that there is apparently more to phenomenal perception than the presence of such functionally characterized seemings or appearances. A powerful modal intuition works against an equation between how things seem to be in visual perception, for example, and the concrete look that they have for a given individual (Chalmers 1996). We can imagine things continuing to seem a certain way in visual perception, so the idea goes, while the look that they have changes; and, conversely, we can imagine things looking the same way while the way they seem to be varies. Looks and seemings, so the idea goes, are doubly dissociable.

The most famous illustration of this alleged possibility is provided by the spectrum inversion that many people find plausible. Under such an inversion, say as between two individuals, what looks green to you might look red to me, although our perceptions would play the same functional role, and the way things seem to be would be indiscernible; we would each class the same things with the same things, and adjust our behavior to the same discriminations. If such inversion is possible, whether across different persons or within the same person at different times, then how things seem can be the same while looks vary, and how things look can be the same while seemings vary.

This modal intuition is apparently given support by a corresponding epistemic intuition, although whether it is or is not supportive is actually quite dubious (McGeer 2003). The epistemic intuition is developed most famously in Frank Jackson's (1982, 1986) thought experiment, where Mary is a scientist who knows all the physical facts—all the facts there are, according to physicalism—but who has spent her life in a black and white room, scanning things on black and white monitors. Would Mary discover a new fact on leaving the monochromatic room and learning, not just how things seem to people when they see red or green or blue—she knows that already—but how precisely red or green or blue looks? The epistemic intuition, allegedly, is that she would indeed learn something new, and that how colored things look, therefore, cannot be reduced to how they seem: that is, to what perceptual information they are represented as giving.

The intuitions that argue against equating looks with visual seemings, sounds with aural, smells with nasal, have as a common element the supposition that looks and sounds and smells are individuated on the basis of an intrinsic property, not in the functional way in which seemings are individuated. Let the functional role of two seemings be the same, and they will be the same seeming. Not so, according to these intuitions, with looks and sounds and smells and feels. Each of those phenomena has its own intrinsic, functionally dissociable character. The phenomena count as qualia, in the technical philosophical jargon, not just as seemings; they are perceptual seemings construed so that their essence is to have a certain intrinsic character, not any particular functional role. We may view a statue as a lump of clay and individuate it on one basis, or as a statue and individuate it on another. And similarly, so this line would go, we may view a seeming as a quale and individuate it by intrinsic character, or as a seeming and individuate it by functional role.

The question raised here is the crux of the issue, as I see it, between physicalism and non-physicalism about consciousness. If qualia are allowed, then it is always going to be logically possible to have a world that is identical to the actual world in physical respects but that lacks qualia or that displays different qualia. The physical cannot fix qualia by the functional organization it incorporates, since qualia are not functionally characterized. So, for all that the physical nature of the world appears to require, there may or may not be qualia present, or there may or may not be this or that pattern of qualia. Physicalism falls if qualia stand.

Responding to the Challenge, 1

My own belief is that qualia are illusory and that all that phenomenal conscious-ness requires is perceptual seemings or appearances. I do two things to try to bolster this view. First, I argue that seemings are much better candidates for the role of conscious phenomena than is generally recognized—this takes me into an area of empirically grounded speculation—and that the failure to see this may explain the intuition that only qualia can fill that role. And second, I hold that we should not be surprised if this denial of qualia continues to seem unsatisfying; there is a debunking explanation available for why the belief in qualia may continue to appeal.

Seemings look like poor candidates for the role of conscious phenomena when the representational role that they have to play is characterized in too restricted a manner. What is it for something to seem red? This is often taken to mean: it seems to be of such a character that the subject can discriminate it from things of other colors and class it with things of the same color. But then the intuition that something might seem that way and look green rather than red gets to be very powerful. It appears that how the color looks cannot possibly be exhausted by how its bearers seem—by how they are represented as being perceptually represented—when they seem red.

My first move in arguing for the equation between look and seeming in this case is to emphasize the richness of the role that a seeming or appearance of red has to play. When something seems red to you, and that seeming is veridical, then the perceptually-represented-way it is has to do a number of things, and do them manifestly: that is, do them in a manner that is accessible to you in recursive representation. First, it has to enable you to sort the object with other red things and mark it off from non-red things, across changes in your perspective, changes of background color, and changes of lighting. Second, it has to enable you to track the object under similar contingencies: as you move or it moves, as the background colors change independently or as a result of such movements, and as the lighting waxes or wanes. And third, it has to do these things in a way that activates suitable expectancies. Let something seem red to you, a practiced color-perceiver, and it will naturally engender expectancies to the effect that it will continue to seem red—it will continue to provide whatever is required for the continued capacity to sort, contrast, and track—even as things change in this or that respect. If such expectancies prove to be misplaced, then the red look of the object will count as misleading or illusory.

Think of the optical state you are bound to be in when you see something as red. This will involve a state of retinal excitation, of excitation in the optical nerve and associated brain areas, and of engagement with those parts of the brain involved in generating the required expectancies. When something seems red, the information that is processed in this dispersed optical-cum-neural state becomes available for propositional interrogation, as information provided by the object itself. The state does not involve a bodily disturbance of the kind that can be registered in the fashion of a tingle or strain in the foot. But it can be registered in the representational properties it has: in its depicting the object as a bright red, different from those other reds; or as something quite like this or that orange item; or as an object starkly contrasted with that brown background; and so on. And that is all that is involved in there being a red look that the object has. The seen object has the presence to my visual system that enables me to classify it, discriminate it, track it suitably over the relevant contingencies, and form expectations as to the presence it would assume under various changes; and it is present in such a way that it is propositionally interrogable.[27]

Could the object have this interrogable presence—could it seem the way it does—yet have a different look? My suggestion is that as we see just how much has to be done by the visually-represented-way the object is, and done in a manner manifest to me, it becomes harder and harder to think that it might do all of this, yet assume a different look. What it is for something to look the way a red object looks is for it manifestly or interrogably to have the visually-represented-profile

---

[27] One slight misgiving I have about the way things are phrased by Hurley and Noë is that they speak not about the presence that things would have under certain variations, but about the changes in patterns of sensation that such variations would produce; that seems to leave the notion of sensation, itself associated with phenomenal consciousness, undischarged. My misgiving is shared with Clark (2006). A related difference worth mentioning is that they focus on the changes that can be brought about motorically; hence the reference to sensorimotor contingencies, rather than sensori-situational contingencies. They may be right, of course, that the motorically manipulable changes are of particular importance in enabling a subject to see red or any other color.

of something that primes me to be able to sort, contrast, and track in a suitable way, and do so with appropriate expectancies. Seeing red is an optically tuned, ability-tuning state, maintained in the presence of certain expectancies. And being in this state will become a conscious episode when its representational deliverance—the visually-represented-way things are—becomes available for propositional interrogation and representation.

One way of making this claim intuitive is to put it in parallel with a claim about how an object will look when it looks like it is moving (Pettit 2004*e*). Just as color-blindness means that things do not look colored, so there is a condition, kinetopsia, which means that things do not look like they move; when they move, the impression is of a kind with seeing things jerk from one position to another under stroboscopic lighting. Think now of how things will be for someone who ceases to be kinetopsic. Clearly there will be a big shift as the person becomes capable of being perceptually tuned to movement and as the state thereby elicited tunes the person to duck spontaneously when something approaches, or to reach out and grab it at a suitable point in egocentric space, or to intercept it at some later point in its trajectory. When this visually-represented-way the object is becomes available for propositional interrogation, then the object, plausibly, will assume a certain look.

Can we imagine that look changing, while the ducking and grabbing abilities it tunes remain the same? Not easily, I think. And the imaginative difficulty here should suggest that we ought to feel a similar difficulty in the color case. As it is hard to think of slow-moving things having the look of fast-moving things, while still tuning the same abilities in us, so it should be hard to think of red things having the look of green things, while still tuning similar abilities. Can we imagine that someone kinetopsic who knows all the theoretically available facts about the movement of an object lacks knowledge of some fact that the non-kinetopsic can register? Surely not: the difference between the kinetopsic theorist who knows all about the motion of an object and the non-kinetopsic counterpart is a difference in how the same facts are known, not a difference in the known facts themselves. And as this seems obvious in the motion case, so it ought to suggest a similar lesson in the case of color.

The novelty of this approach to looks, and by extension to other conscious phenomena, is that it reverses the assumption made in common sense that how something looks when it looks red or looks moving explains the adjustments and expectancies of a subject in tracking the object, reaching out to grab it, and so on. On the story told here, it is because of the abilities tuned by the perceived object, and because of the expectancies that go with these abilities, that the object has the look it has, and not the other way around. Those abilities are tuned at a sub-personal level and the object consequently assumes a perceptual profile of a certain kind: a profile that goes with a certain look, when it becomes propositionally represented and interrogable.

The story told here has much in common, as they emphasize in their chapter, with the approach taken by Susan Hurley and Alva Noë. They give a very helpful characterization of the ideas we share, going on to raise a nicely turned problem that we face in common. The problem is how to characterize the synaesthetic perception of color: say, the perception of redness surrounding certain words or sounds. There is a look of redness here, for sure, but it does not appear on the basis of the sorts of capacities associated with regular looks. So what to say about what is going on?

On the approach I like, as I argued elsewhere (Pettit 2003*c*), the red look that something has may fail, not just because the object that robustly looks red—say, because of the red glasses you are wearing—proves not to be red, but also because the expectancies that are raised, and raised manifestly, by the red look prove not to be accurate. The red look is not just misleading, it is not even robust; and it is appropriate in such a case to speak of an illusion of redness, not just of a misperception of something as red. The obvious response to synaesthesia, as Hurley and Noë argue, is to say that the synaesthete undergoes illusions of redness and of other colors on being presented with the words or sounds that appear clothed in color.

But is this right? Not on the face of it, they say, since the illusion does not go away and is quite robust in its own right. It seems more appropriate to hold that what the synaesthete experiences is not an illusion of surface redness but a different sort of redness. I have nothing illuminating to say on this issue. We know already that it is not just the surfaces of things that look red or blue or whatever—I have only been concerned with surfaces here—but also lights and liquids and gases and so on. Perhaps there is some unified story under which the synaesthete can be reckoned to see another sort of red, rather than have an illusion of surface color. I doubt it, and am still drawn to the illusion story sketched and rejected by Hurley and Noë. But there are difficulties, no matter how we turn.

This discussion has focused in particular on vision. But we may assume that touch and hearing, taste and smell, work in a parallel way. Each mode of representation will have a phenomenal counterpart of a look, so far as the perceptually-represented-way in which it casts a scenario becomes represented in the agent: becomes a way, fixed in the relevant modality, that the scenario seems to the agent to be.

Three of these sensory modalities—touch, taste, and smell—have one further distinctive feature. They often have a distinct hedonic register, occasioning quite a local pleasure or pain. This does not make for a special problem. Every representation serves to guide behavior appropriately: typically, it will dispose the agent to adjust in an appropriate way, conditional on the agent's goals. But there is no reason why representations might not have such a response-shaping function built into them, independently of goals: no reason, as we might put it, why Mother Nature should not have selected them to play this role quite independently of contingent goals.[28] And arguably, that is what happens when not only is there representation of a perceptually-perceived-way things are, whether in touch or taste or smell, but the way things are represented as being is designed to attract and give pleasure or repel and give pain. The representation may have a hedonic valence—an inherently attractive or aversive aspect—built into it.

What, finally, of bodily sensation? In bodily sensation you will not perceptually represent a way the world is, but rather a way your body is. You will register the throbbing in your arm, the pounding in your head, the knotting in your stomach, the cold in your foot, the tingle in your neck. Such bodily perception will normally have a hedonic valence like touch and taste and smell. But it will be distinct in other ways. With external perception there are sensory materials recruited to a representational purpose, and in becoming capable of interrogating what is represented, those materials will be assembled as ways in which things are presented. The perceptually-represented-ways that things are will be constructed out of such materials: the way something looks will be presented in shape and color; the way something sounds will be presented in timbre and tone; and so on. There is no analogue to this in bodily sensation, as it is not mediated by any sensory modality.

The agent in bodily sensation will mainline the throbbing or pounding or knotting, the cold or the tingle, as if without a distinction between knower and known. There will always be such a distinction, as is evident from the fact that you can have a sensation as of something happening in a phantom limb. But the distinction will not be so marked, because there is no room for error in the ascription of a throbbing or a pounding or a knotting. Error is possible through misidentification of the bearer of that property—the part of the body where it materializes—but no error can come about through misattribution.[29]

Is this a problem? Not necessarily. The fact that what one represents in sensation is a throbbing or a pounding or a knotting is fixed by the hedonic valence of the representation, we might say. To register a pain in one's arm is to register a part of one's arm painfully: that is, in a way that tends to make you wince and nurse it. To register a pleasant tingle in one's foot is to register a part of one's foot pleasurably: that is, in a way that tends to keep you in position, for example maintaining exposure to any presumptive cause. And to register different kinds of pains, or different kinds of pleasures, will be to register the relevant body part as inviting different responses, whether in easing the pain or prolonging the pleasure. The pain will be an itch insofar as it is eased by

[28] Some beliefs serve as habits of inference without surfacing as matters endorsed in premises; indeed, for reasons of regress, some beliefs have to serve in that way. Such beliefs will also have a goal-independent role to play in prompting assent to suitable conclusions. On the contrast between desires and habits of inference see Pettit 1993*a*: ch. 1.

[29] The case is the reverse of what happens with ascribing attitudes to oneself, where there is no room for error through misidentification, but there is room for error through misattribution. See Evans 1982.

scratching, an ache insofar as it is eased by gentle rubbing, a strain insofar as it is eased by stretching, and so on.

This feature of bodily sensation has an important implication, bearing on animal consciousness. It is quite conceivable, as I argued, that external perception should not involve any recursive representation and should be non-conscious. But this is not conceivable in the same way with bodily sensation. Being essentially hedonic, the properties registered in bodily sensation could not exist without being represented; there is no such thing as an unregistered pain or pleasure, no such thing as a pain that does not seem painful or a pleasure that does not seem pleasant. The way things are in your body when you register pain or pleasure, then, has to be a represented way they are: a way they seem. So, when you become aware of a pain as something to ease, or a pleasure as something to indulge, you are aware of a perceptually-represented-way your body is; you are confronted with a way it seems. It is with a view to changing the way it seems that you act as you do in search of relief from the pain or reinforcement for the pleasure.

On the account given here, then, there is no bodily sensation without phenomenal consciousness. This is an attractive result, as it makes it possible to think, in line with intuition, that even simple animals whose worldly perceptions are not phenomenally conscious may have conscious perception of pain and pleasure in their own bodies.

This claim about simple animals can be supported by a further observation. One of the features of consciousness, marked since at least the time of Descartes, is that with a conscious phenomenon there is always a feature that one knows unmistakably. This is present with the pleasure or the pain, for one cannot be wrong about feeling pleasure or pain. And it is also present with perceptual seemings that bear on the external world. When the perceptually-represented-way things are is represented propositionally as having these or those features, when it seems to have those features, then there is no room for the thought that the seeming might be mistaken. There is a distinction between how the world really is and how it seems to be, since we have ways of proving that certain seemings are false. But there is no distinction between how the world seems to be and how it seems to seem, since in ordinary experience there is no way of marking such a difference.[30] The unmistakability of bodily sensation is also found in the other cases where I posit phenomenal consciousness.[31]

[30] This claim is limited to ordinary practice. On some interpretations, recent experiments have demonstrated the possibility of a certain mismatch between the perceptually-represented, ability-tuning way something is and the subject's propositional representation of that perceptual content. Subjects who judge that objects like identical Titchener rings—rings set within other rings that do differ in size—are judged to have different diameters, even as the ways their hands adjust to grasp those rings are the same. See Milner and Goodale 1995.

[31] Unmistakability should be distinguished from unmissability. Contrary to what is sometimes taken as Cartesian wisdom, I may miss or overlook certain features of a conscious experience, even if I am not capable of being mistaken about them when I do register them. Suppose that two pains, A and B, are indistinguishable in conscious experience, but that A proves to be distinguishable, B not,

Responding to the Challenge, 2

On this story, the way in which things are functionally organized in the physical material out of which we are all composed ensures that there will be phenomenal consciousness. The look or the smell or the feel of things will be generated by the presence of a functionally characterizable seeming, as a matter of analysis. So far as the physical way in which the brain is organized ensures that the appropriate functioning is present, therefore, it will ensure also the presence of the look or the smell or the feel. But those claims may just not sound plausible. For, to recall the spirit of the modal and epistemic intuitions canvassed earlier, recalcitrant intuitions will remain in place.

Surely we can still imagine the presence of suitable functioning, and even the presence of the corresponding seeming, and yet allow that the relevant look or smell or feel might not materialize? There is no necessity of conception, it appears, that will take us from the recognition of such an unproblematic configuration to the look of the sunset, the smell of the coffee brewing, the feel of the familiar, dreaded headache. Notwithstanding our best efforts to explain why the theoretically describable, functional pattern guarantees the presence of the phenomenal gestalt, there still remains an intuitive gap. We find ourselves gripped by the intuition that despite all that has been said, the configuration might remain the same and the gestalt shift. If physicalism about phenomenal consciousness is sound, as I think it is, can we explain why this intuition continues to have a hold on our minds?

According to my preferred sort of physicalism, the relation between the functional organization of the brain and the presence of phenomenal consciousness is like the relation between the distribution of pixels in a frame—a distribution that can be characterized in a series of coordinate pairs—and the presence of a particular shape or picture there. We may not be able to see why such and such a distribution of pixels, such and such a set of coordinate pairs, should make such and such a shape. But once we recognize how the pixels make the picture, we can see that with a suitable distribution fixed, there will be a corresponding shape fixed. We do not have any lingering intuition that the pixels might remain the same but the shape and picture begin to shift. The question we face, then, is why things aren't like that in the case of phenomenal consciousness.

Things do seem to be like that in the case of the representational capacity that we take to be fixed in place by functional, physical organization. There is little or no difficulty in the idea that if a creature's brain is arranged so

from a third pain, C. This implies that there is a feature of A, overlooked in the comparison with B, that is consciously registered only in the comparison with C. I was not mistaken in thinking that A and B were indistinguishable: they were indistinguishable in the properties consciously registered in comparing them. But I missed a feature of A such that had I not done so, then they would have been distinguishable. My thanks to Michael Smith for alerting me to this issue.

that certain states co-vary with sensory evidence as to how things change in certain ways, and if they guide the agent's goal-seeking actions in response to those changes, then they count as representational states. We may think that some further conditions need to be fulfilled for representation proper, but we will readily see that something along the lines of the functioning described is going to be sufficient for representation to occur. The question, once again, is why phenomenal consciousness is different; in particular, why it is different if physicalism is sound in this case too.

My suggested response is to think about a different analogy from that with the pixels and the shape (Pettit forthcoming, *a*). Consider a case where the coordinates determine a shape, as before, but also determine something else—call it a profile—at the same time. The profile is a distally discernible property of the shape. It is something that can be seen in the shape, but only when you stand at a certain distance from the frame or grid. The man-in-the-moon is a profile in this sense. And so is the figure that emerges in certain impressionist paintings, when you stand back at an appropriate distance. As the coordinates in a frame may fix the presence of a regular, proximally discernible shape, so, clearly, they may fix the presence of such a distally identifiable profile. The same argument will apply in the two cases.

But there is still an important difference between the two scenarios. In the shape case, it is possible to go back and forth between plotted coordinates and the shape, since they are observable from the same viewpoint, and to see how the pattern of determination or dependency goes. But in the profile case nothing similar may be possible, for you may not be able to go back and forth in the same way, tracking specific dependencies of profile on coordinates. Look close enough to detect the plotted coordinates, and you won't see the profile. Go far enough away to see the profile, and you won't be able to detect the coordinates plotted. We may even imagine that you cannot take notes or form reliable memories at either position on what is observed—the pixels or the profile—at the other.

In the shape case you will naturally develop a sense of how pixels fix shape, banishing any idea or intuition that the coordinates or dots might remain the same and the shape vary. But in the profile case your conviction that the pixels or dots determine the profile may not give rise to a similar intuition of invariability. Not being able to determine the specific dependency of the profile on the pixels, you will not have the same intuitive sense that if the pixels remain unchanged, the profile must remain unchanged. You are liable to have illusions about how the coordinates might be preserved and the profile still vary. You will have a sense of the profile—an ability to recognize and imagine it, for example—that floats free of your representation of the coordinates. So, although you believe in an abstract manner that there is a pattern in the coordinates that guarantees the presence of the profile, it may seem that you can imagine the coordinates remaining fixed while the profile varies. You won't have the concrete, working sense of the dependency of the profile on the coordinates that would banish such illusions of imaginability and conceivability.

I think that things are similar with the relation between phenomenal consciousness and physical, functional configuration. Indeed, I think that they are also similar with the relation between free will and physical configuration, and between rule-following and physical configuration, but I shall not pursue that point here (Pettit 2000c; forthcoming, a). Just as a shift of perspective is involved as I now see the pixels, and now see the profile, so a shift of perspective—a much more radical shift of perspective—would be involved in my now seeing the functional way in which my brain is organized and now seeing the way in which things appear to me as the bearer or user or owner of that brain. Thus it is not surprising, even if my sort of physicalism is sound, that the functionalist analysis should leave us with intuitions that remain in tension with it.

We all have the experience of looking at pop-out picture books but not having the picture pop out. With the pixels and the shape they construct—even the pixels given in coordinate pairs—experts might just be able to see the shape in the coordinates, and experience something close to pop-out. They might be able to see the shape in the array of numbers in the way most of us can see a diagonal in a set of coordinates such as (0,0), (1,1), (2,2), (3,3), and so on. But with the pixels and the profile, as I have described the case, pop-out is almost completely blocked. I think that the situation is similar with functional organization and phenomenal consciousness, and that this explains the tenacity of our anti-physicalist intuitions. We suffer from a deep derivational deficiency in this case, as in the case of the profile. And we are likely to remain subject to that deficiency, short of a transformation in the technology available for aligning brain analysis with subjective experience.

Hume is well known for arguing that the experience of having one sort of event more or less invariably precede another leads us, mistakenly, to posit a necessary connection—by his account, a causal linkage—between the first and the second types of occurrence. The derivational fallacy that he imputes to us is the inverse of the derivational deficiency alleged here. In his case, there is no necessary connection between the distinct events envisaged, and the problem is that there is an experience of being led by the occurrence of events in the first category to the expectation of the occurrence of events in the second. In our case, there is a necessary connection between physical and psychological phenomena—the sort of connection that exists between dots and shape—and the problem is that that there is no experience of being led by variations in the first domain to the expectation of variations in the second. It is this that puts the experience of pop-out beyond our reach.

Hume's problem is that our psychological habits induce us to posit among things connections that do not exist there, while the problem here is that there are connections among things that our psychological habits do not induce us to posit. There is an allegation on both sides that mind and world are misaligned at the level of epistemic impulse, but where he indicts epistemic impulse as a source of error—it indicates the presence of a non-existent relationship—I indict it as a source of ignorance: it fails to signal the presence of a relationship that on my account does indeed obtain.

5. CONVERSABILITY AND MORALITY

From Reasoning to Co-reasoning

The ability to reason, as suggested earlier, is an instance of the ability to follow rules: the ability to identify a constraint on your performance over an indefinite range of cases, guide your behavior with a view to satisfying that constraint, yet do so in the knowledge that there is room for getting the demands of the constraint wrong in any given case. Whether the reasons to which we try to adjust are structural or substantive in character, in Tim Scanlon's distinction, they present themselves to us as guidelines to which we can be held responsible, and guidelines by which we may hope to self-regulate where regulation is necessary, because our spontaneous habits don't keep us on track. The reasons that move us may be that those premises we accept entail that such and such is the case; that the presence of this or that property means that an option is desirable; that this or that object of perception is of a kind with certain others, and is therefore an instance of a relevant property; and so on.

In the discussion of rules, we also saw that the most straightforward explanation of how we identify basic rules for ourselves, seeing them as at once accessible and mistakable, is that we authorize one another equally with ourselves as interpreters of the rules. This mutual authorization means that we naturally assume that one or more of us must be mistaken if we go separate ways in applying the rule: one or more of us must be subject to a limitation or obstacle in interpreting it. And assuming that, we therefore see the rule as that objective or intersubjective constraint that will show up reliably if and only if those factors that deserve to be seen as limiting or obstructing are absent.

This in turn means, as I noted, that with rules established by such a process of triangulation, there is no problem about identifying the rules that others in our community of usage are following. The condition on which a rule gets identified as a determinate but missable target is that it is our rule: it is a rule identified on the basis of a practice in which we are all participants. The factors that affect access to the rule—the limitations and obstacles postulated—are defined, precisely, as factors that best explain divergences between us, assuming that none of us can be discounted *ex ante* as an interpreter. If you or I manage generally to follow such a rule, therefore, then we are well positioned to know the rule that we each aspire to follow.

Putting these points together, we can say that the basis on which most of us learn to reason is a basis on which we will be able also to co-reason. If I am able to identify reasons relevant to a process of theoretical or practical thought, and am able to keep a check on myself in an exercise of explicit reasoning, then I will be able to call you in to play a similar role. I can be confident that you too will have the capacity to identify the reasons to which I wish to sensitize my thinking, and that you may be able to serve me well in calling my attention to relevant considerations.

When I reason with myself, I am attentive to certain structural or substantive considerations, and monitor where my thoughts are leading me, with a view to satisfying the constraints that those considerations impose. I adopt the position of an *amicus curiae*, a friend of the court, in keeping an eye on where my rational processing is taking me as my beliefs and desires evolve and as they condense into intention and action. I am like a counselor to myself, letting my thought processes evolve spontaneously and intervening only when a slip causes the red lights to go on, or when I independently decide to do some checking.

If reasoning with myself has the aspect of self-counseling, then reasoning with you or another is an exercise in which we each play counselor to the other, helping one another to see where reasoning should lead us. It is an exercise in which we each play *amicus curiae*, friend in the forum of the other's thought. We put ourselves at each other's disposal, offering but not imposing the help that we think we can provide; and we are ready to help, whenever we are called upon to comment. We are mutual counselors, committed to a practice of epistemic collaboration (Pettit and Smith 2004).

Co-reasoning in Conversation

How common is such co-reasoning in ordinary conversation and exchange? There are three styles of conversation that are worth distinguishing. At one extreme is the peremptory approach in which you assume unquestioned authority, threaten or intimidate other people, or even exercise force at the same time that you address them. At the other extreme is the approach in which you explicitly present yourself as a counselor or co-reasoner. And in between is the more relaxed approach where you behave in a manner that is neither of a counseling nor a peremptory character. You joke or tease or cajole your interlocutors; you entertain or regale them with stories; you gossip or complain or bring them up to date on local doings; you comfort or charm them; and so on.

While much conversation is surely of this relaxed kind, it goes on the counseling side of the ledger rather than on the peremptory. The current of such convivial exchange will quickly break up if it comes to be assumed that the background is one of unquestioned authority, coercive threat, intimidation, or violence. The conversation can continue in its even flow, only insofar as such interventions are off the table. The absolute monarch may be surrounded by courtiers and jesters, but cannot expect to have companions with whom to share in unforced conviviality.

Peremptory exchange is the exception, then, in the practice of conversation, contrasting with the other two varieties, counseling and convivial, reason-mediated and reason-friendly. Very little conversation in ordinary life is of this kind. The peremptory instruction of the manager, the challenge of the police officer, or the mugger's demand for cash may belong clearly in this category. But they are scarcely representative of the run of human exchange. And in some settings they may occur with reasoned licence. As we set out on the grueling mountain climb, we may agree on a reasoned basis that the leader of the group will be given unchallengeable authority to command. And what is true of that context may hold equally, if less explicitly, of many situations in which we let one or another person dictate what the rest of us do.

If this is right, then in most human conversation we present ourselves to one another as counseling or convivial, reason-mediated or reason-friendly, in character. But it must be said immediately, of course, that we are not always as we present ourselves. We may pretend to be counselors but do so insincerely.

One mode of insincerity arises where we reserve the power to resort to force or coercion, should the counseling that we practice not lead someone to behave as we want them to behave. Here we aspire to virtual control of our interlocutor, being happy to reason, but only so long as it gets us what we seek. Another mode of insincerity involves a search for what, broadly, we might describe as deceptive control. We may suggest candor and withhold information or seek to deceive another. We may suggest commitment to a future course of action, but have no intention of complying. We may speak with a view to distracting and misdirecting our audience rather than genuinely engaging them in collaboration. Or we may address others, perhaps from the rostrum or the pulpit, and aim only at mesmerizing them with rhetoric and bending them to our point of view.

Although reason-mediated and reason-friendly conversation may be insincere in character, however, it should be distinguished sharply from peremptory communication. The very fact that speakers pretend to work within the bounds of co-reasoning means that they inevitably expose themselves to adjudication in terms of the standards with which we expect co-reasoners to comply. Hypocrisy is the tribute that vice pays to virtue, and indulging in the hypocrisy of insincere exchange means acknowledging as relevant yardsticks of performance—yardsticks that have a presumptive hold on us—the standards of veracity and candor that genuine co-reasoning requires.

Reason-mediated conversation, it should be noted, need not have the austere, scholastic form of seminar exchange. The arguments that you offer in an attempt to persuade me of something may be elliptical or, in the old term, enthymematic; they may be wholly implicit, as when you draw my attention to something and let me fill in the missing lesson; or they may take the form of a story or a parable, in which you invite me to see things another way. And apart from that, the arguments you present may be offered in the spirit of ironic or sarcastic or mocking comment, not just in literal speech. You may need resort to such tactics in order to knock me out of my complacency or let me see how stupid, even risible, my point of view is. There is nothing inherently inimical to reason in the resort to such moves.

Nor is there anything necessarily inimical to reason in employing metaphor and image, and all the colors of persuasive overture, in trying to win me to your point of view. It may be impossible for me to be able to live with the conclusion to which you sincerely believe reason directs me without that conclusion being made to seem habitable to someone of my particular background. It may be necessary for you to move me at the level of sentiment as well as understanding in order to see the truth.

The rise of modern science prompted a panicked retreat from rhetoric on the part of seventeenth-century figures like René Descartes and Thomas Hobbes (Skinner 1996). The retreat may have been rational, given the widespread abuse of classical techniques of rhetoric. And it may have been useful in giving prominence to the austere discipline of experiment and deduction that the new science rightly championed. But there is no escaping the need for rhetoric in human exchange, even exchange of the highest, reason-mediated kind. The emphasis on the importance of reason, then, should not be taken to imply any hostility to rhetorical technique. We all recognize that if we are to advertise our meetings or our wares appropriately, then we should not hesitate to use whatever we know of graphic design. We should be as willing to design and decorate our discursive messages as we are willing to design and decorate our visual ones.

Conversability

We have seen what co-reasoning involves, and how prevalent it is in ordinary conversation. I turn now to the assumptions we make when we treat someone as worth co-reasoning with—as conversable. The assumptions amount to treating the person as orthonomous, and orthonomous in relation to a body of commitments engaged over time.

In treating me as a worthy interlocutor, the basic assumption you must make is that I am capable of reasoning about what to think and do: that I am capable of recognizing reasons and regulating myself according to those reasons. If you are to see me as worth counseling on issues of what to think, then you must believe that in the domain where you talk to me I am not hopelessly subject to blind spots or *idées fixes*, biases or fallacies or paranoia. And if you are to think me worth counseling on what I should do, or what we should do together, then again you must believe that in the relevant areas I am not excessively prey to obsession or compulsion, temptation or weakness of will. You will have to treat me as possessing, if not always exercising, orthonomy in the realm of will and thought.

When you hold me to the demands of reason in this way, however, you will have to make an assumption about my existing commitments. If you are to apply the expectation of consistency to me, for example, then you will have to ascribe a body of beliefs or judgments to me, and then explore how far it is a consistent set. Where, then, are you to find a base for ascribing such commitments?

You are likely to identify a suitable base, at least partly, in the record of avowals that I build up over time. You cannot converse with me seriously unless you assume that I will not at any point in your conversational dealings with me declare that it was a past counterpart who acknowledged a certain truth or commitment and not I—not I, considered as the same center of reasoning. If you have to think me worth talking to, then you must assume that I will own the past words that I uttered as having a special bearing on what I can now claim reason to think or do. I may explicitly disown some words at any point in our exchange, announcing a change of mind or heart; certainly I may do this when the words did not amount to a promise. But I must at least acknowledge that this is a necessary step. The default assumption will be that I can be held to any words I have not explicitly disowned.

At this point we can see why the notion of orthonomy goes so closely with the assumption that what is freely said or done bears the signature of the agent; this is a connotation of free will and free thought that I promised I would come back to. Anything that I knowingly and freely say or do is something, inevitably, that I must own as one and the same agent continuing over time. I am not allowed to think of it as a visitation from outside, something that happens within me rather than something I personally author. The cost of thinking about it in that way would be to undermine any aspiration to conversability and any prospect of relating to others, or indeed to myself over time, in the manner of creatures who can give their word and be held to it.

The conversable subject, understood in this way, counts in a familiar, functional sense as a person. In this sense, persons are intentional subjects who recognize what is expected of a reasoning subject that self-identifies over time and who acquiesce in being held to such expectations (Pettit 2001*b*). When you take me to be conversable, you personify me or treat me as personifiable. I am someone, you take it, who can recognize the demands of reason over time, and apply them to myself. I am someone who invites the ascription of thoughts to the effect, for example, that I observed things in the past to be thus and so and ought now to conclude such and such; or that I promised in the past to take this or that attitude and ought now to opt for such and such a course of action. Let me now think or act in an inconsistent manner, where there is no question of disowning that past, and you have my implicit permission to invoke the expectations that I licenced and to use them in criticism of my performance.

Orthonomy, conversability, and personifiability, as this makes clear, are close to being synonymous ideas. To be orthonomous, to have the capacity to go with reasons, is to be conversable, at least once it is clear that the orthonomy engages a growing history of commitment. And to be conversable in that sense just is to be personifiable. Children and others may not count as full persons in this sense, but that need not make for a serious objection. They can count as persons on the grounds of being agents who are conspecific with full persons, and may be capable of being inducted into the practice in which persons recognize one another.

The upshot of this approach to personhood is to identify a sense in which we should reverse the ordinary presumption that you can hold me responsible for acting contrary to such and such a promise, or for making declarations contrary to such and such an assertion, because I am the same person with the agent who made that promise or assertion. There is a sense, on this account, in which I am the same person with that agent because I can rightly be held responsible for the things that agent said or did, and not the other way around. To be a person is to be an agent who can be held responsible to the demands of reason, and to be the same person as a past agent is to be someone who can be held responsible to the demands of reason as they are engaged by the record of sayings and doings that is shared with that agent.

As mentioned earlier, it is always going to be possible for me at any moment to disown many of the things said or done—though not perhaps the things promised—by my past counterpart. I may be said to be the same self as my own person in the past only insofar as the shared record of commitments is not substantively disowned in any measure. I am no longer the same self as that person, I may say, indicating a past counterpart who held foreign beliefs and did things alien to my current inclinations. Selfhood is built up as a side-product of the growing record of commitments that continues to be endorsed by a person. Ruptures occur only when that record becomes thinned out as a result of what the present person has disowned.

Conspiring in Conversability

When you take me to be conversable, you may do so only in a qualified way. You may converse with me on a range of issues, theoretical or practical, yet think that there are some questions where it is of little benefit, at least of little benefit for you, to try to debate with me. You may converse with me on good days and yet recognize that I am not always so reachable: a certain sort of passion or anxiety or addiction can render me fairly obtuse to what you have to say. And even when you think I am conversable, you may recognize that it may take a lot to move me in reason's direction; I may be resistant, even blindly resistant, to the changes of mind you recommend.

Conversability is a capacity that may not be manifested or exercised all that often, then, or all that easily. It may prove scarce of supply and shy of display. But why in that case do we so readily ascribe conversability to one another, and expect to have it ascribed to us? Why do we treat many failures as failures to exercise conversability, not failures to possess it? And even when we come to believe that conversability is lacking on some questions, why do we insulate those failures and expect to find the person conversable on more general matters?

My answer is that we conspire in the assumption that, short of the extremes that drive people to asylums, we are all of us pretty well conversable. The conspiracy takes the form of being ready to overlook one another's failures to manifest conversability and to insist on believing that when we fail in this way, we typically act out of character. We fail to exercise orthonomy, but we do so under the influence of one or another contingency, not for lack of the capacity itself. This mutually shared commitment to the ascription of conversability is often upheld in the teeth of contrary evidence. And when it is suspended, as we saw, it is generally suspended only in relation to certain topics or times. That is why it has the aspect of a conspiracy.

But while the conspiracy may not always be epistemically reasonable or convincing, it makes good practical sense. Perhaps I fail to think or act in the manner that your counsel, by my own admission, ought to have elicited. Are you to think of me as someone beyond the pale of reasons, then, fit only for the influence you might hope to exercise by deception or coercion or force? Are you to think of my ill-doing, if I did ill, on a par with bad weather or bad luck? And are you to think of anything good that I may later do as just a bout of good fortune? Are you to think of me, in short, as a force of nature? This might be an epistemically reasonable conclusion, at least on the short run of evidence available to you, but it would not make good practical sense. It would prematurely close off the possibility of our achieving a co-reasoning relationship. And it would undermine the chance of your reasoning with me to advantage, bringing me to a higher pitch of performance.

Not only does the conspiracy to ascribe conversability make practical sense in this way, it may also be motivated by a constraint of symmetry. We each have to ascribe conversability to ourselves when we reason in the first person (Pettit and Smith 1996). When I reason with myself about what to think or do, adopting a deliberative stance, I have to think of the options before me as options I just can adopt: they are within my control so far as I can go with the reasons in determining which direction to take. Again, as I remind myself of where the evidence or the argument leads, I have to assume that I will myself be responsive or sensitive to the reasons presented in this exercise. But if I have to self-ascribe such control and sensitivity in conceiving of myself as a conversable agent, then I must think it reasonable for you to remain robustly committed to seeing me in the same way. You will not see me as I see myself, unless you remain confident that even as I fall short of satisfying reason's demands, I remain a creature of reason; I act in the presence of a capacity that I fail to display.[32]

---

[32] The commitment to seeing one another as conversable may be supported by the necessities of child development. It is now close to orthodoxy that in raising our children, we consistently over-interpret what they say and do, treating them as having achieved levels of understanding and responsibility that are well beyond them. In doing this, so the lesson goes, we help to elicit the very mentality that we ascribe. We 'scaffold' the children's development, giving them a conception of

The imperative to ascribe conversability, and to invite its ascription, explains why, as Kant emphasized, the capacity for free will and free thought is not just a theoretical postulate of folk psychology. It is an inescapable postulate, we might say, of personal and interpersonal reasoning. We can reason with ourselves, and with one another, only insofar as we are prepared see ourselves as free centers of thought and decision.

But conspiring in conversability is not conspiring in a flattering form of collusion. Suppose, despite earlier discussion with you, that I fail to remember the lesson of the gambler's fallacy, fail to keep away from the dreaded drink, or just fail to act on my declared intentions. When you respond by insisting that I had the capacity to have done otherwise, being a conversable creature, you are not inviting me to think more kindly of myself. You are calling me to a higher standard than I am exhibiting, and inviting me to condemn and transcend my current performance. Rather than despairing of me, or just becoming resigned to the way I am, you are challenging me to realize that I could have done better: that I can register what reason requires, and that with some effort and practice I can learn to respond to reason's demands.

Not only will it be uncomfortable for me to endorse this view of myself. It will be uncomfortable for me to face the attitude that you will bring to bear when you respond in this way. In not despairing of me, you will deny me the indulgence and acceptance that you might give your errant dog. You will think me responsible insofar as you believe that I satisfied three conditions: I had a choice between significant options; I was in a position to see the options I faced; and I had the capacity to choose on the basis of reason between those options. You will assume, in other words, that I have little or no excuse for doing ill.

But you will not think this from the viewpoint of an indulgent therapist, or a forgiving friend. You will think me responsible from the perspective of someone who is entitled by the presumptive terms of our relationship to expect better; that is, from the perspective of someone who is entitled to complain, whether on your own behalf or that of another. You will not just *think* me responsible; you will *hold* me responsible. You will judge me from the engaged, emotional viewpoint of an interested party. You will resent me if I have hurt you; you will be indignant with me if I have hurt another. You will blame me and invite me to blame myself: that is, to register my fault and my guilt. You will see me, to my discomfort, as blameworthy; and you will invite me, to my added discomfort, to see myself in light of the same concept. Your blame will not be a welcome visitation, however tied it may be to the flattering assumption that I remain a creature of reason.[33]

themselves to which they may aspire and a conception that they may one day achieve (Bruner 1983). Perhaps the commitment to seeing one another as conversable creatures of reason is an expression in adulthood of this very basic imperative.

[33] I benefited from discussion with Gideon Rosen on this topic; he takes a different view from that at which I gesture here. The view taken is largely shared with Victoria McGeer, and is the product of many discussions on the topic.

Deliberative Exchange and Mutual Respect

This discussion of conversability should make clear that in the process of exchange with others, there is a natural ideal of deliberative exchange that comes to be salient to all parties (Pettit and Smith 2004). This is the ideal of seeking only reason-mediated or reason-friendly influence on one another. You seek reason-mediated influence on me when you offer me counsel in a spirit of sincere epistemic collaboration, happy to let me take your advice or leave it. You seek reason-friendly influence when you interact with me in a convivial way, establishing or extending our relationship, but not with a view to compromising the rule of reason.

When people reason together, one person will often exercise control over something that the other does, in the basic sense of making that action more probable than it would have been in his or her absence. But the control exercised in this case is consistent with the controlled agent's orthonomous choice (Pettit 2007*a*). It does not reduce that agent's capacity to reason—for example, as brain-washing or hypnosis might do. It does not forcefully remove any option, or replace any option by attaching a coercive penalty to it: the option-plus-penalty would be a different option, I assume, from the original alternative on offer (Pettit 2002*b*: essay 2.2). And it does not deny the agent knowledge of what the options are, as in deception. It leaves the agent in a position to continue to be able to think, and think rightly, of each of the options in play: I can do that; it is up to me. Deliberative control is consistent with orthonomy, because it does not make such can-do assumptions untrue or unavowable.

Deliberative control contrasts in this respect with the alien or alienating sort of control that is exercised by means of overt force or coercion; or, covertly, by deception or the stand-by invigilation practiced by someone who retains the power to intervene in such ways; or, more radically still, by manipulative brain-washing or hypnosis. Such alien control will do one of three things: reduce the person's power of choice; remove or replace an option in the domain of choice; or give the agent to believe that the options are other than they are, whether by means of the bluff or the lie. Thus it will make a can-do assumption false, or make it unavowable by the agent. The assumption will be false, if an option is removed, or would be removed did the agent try to choose it, or if the option is replaced through the attachment of a penalty, for example, or the probability of a penalty or obstacle, or through being made conditional on the goodwill of a stand-by invigilator. The assumption will be unavowable if the agent is led to believe any of those things or is misled in other ways about the options.

The ideal of deliberative exchange is realized when people put aside resort to such violations, credibly eschewing that sort of alien control over others. It will not be sufficient for the realization of the ideal that people do not actually perpetrate violations against someone, for if they retain the capacity to violate—if they have the power and knowledge required—then they will retain virtual control over that person. They must be subjected to a regime under which violation will be prevented or punished, or they must subject themselves to such a discipline. The ideal involves a practice of interaction between people in which violations are put beyond the reach of individuals or in which they put them beyond their own reach. People reason with one another, or relate in reason-friendly ways, but no one is able to exercise control over anyone else.

The notion of alien control is comparative in character. Some people will control others just as long as the balance of power—the resources of alien control—tilts in their favor. They have the power to make things worse for others, by resorting to force or coercion or deception or manipulation, without making things worse for themselves. They have a comparative advantage in the currency of such evils. They can impose the harms at will—the imposition of harm is an available option—and, equally important, they can impose them with relative impunity; whatever initial cost is involved, they can expect the violation to produce an overall increase in personal welfare.

The ideal of deliberative exchange gives us an interpretation of the notion of respect. You and I will respect one another insofar as we embrace the possibility of mutual influence—we do not avoid one another—but credibly eschew resort to any form of influence that is not reason-mediated or reason-friendly. We do not bestow this eschewal by way of a gift, retaining the power of resorting at will to unreasoned influence; we deny ourselves access to that influence, or we foreswear it on pain of a suitable censure or penalty. Thus, we set up a practice in which we each can command the respect of others. You do not depend on the good will or whim of others for the respect you enjoy, for they cannot deny it to you without hurting themselves. And what is true of you is equally true of each. The respect is mutual, and, inevitably, it is mutual as a matter of common awareness.

Kant's idea that we should treat one another as ends and not merely as means has its roots in the sort of practice envisaged. Respect is not primarily a matter of adopting an attitude, though it certainly has attitudinal requirements. And it is not primarily a matter of behavior—a matter of enacting prescribed action-types—though again it has behavioral requirements. Respect has two components: negatively, it requires a framework in which people are denied control over one another; and positively, it requires a disposition to engage with one another in reason-mediated or reason-friendly ways.

Respect in this sense is a practice that we can pursue only with other reasoning creatures. We may love or revere nature, and love or revere other sentient creatures, but in the relevant sense we cannot respect them. Respect is available only with agents to whom we can address reasons and from whom we can expect a similar form of address in return. It can materialize only between persons, in our sense of person. In the world as we know it, animals seek many different forms of influence over one another, as they fight for territory, compete for food, combine as mates, and raise their young. But, for all the available evidence supports, they never seek the influence that embodies respect in the manner of those of us capable of deliberative exchange. Respect may be an essentially anthropocentric ideal.

The practice of respect is intuitively very attractive, insofar as it rules out the pursuit of forceful and coercive, virtual and deceptive and manipulative, forms of control. But does it rule out too much? Does it rule out what we naturally think of as offers rather than threats? If you offer me a reward for taking a certain option, then aren't you rigging my reasons just as effectively as by threatening me with a penalty if I take any other alternative? The ideal of respect, interpreted in terms of deliberative exchange, will not be very attractive if it is undermined by such offers, at least when they are of a regular, non-mesmerizing kind: when they are not like the offer of drugs to an addict, riches to a pauper.

The ideal is not undermined by offers, I believe, because a crucial feature marks offers off from threats. Suppose that I have options A, B, and C before me, and you threaten me with a penalty if I do B or C. In that case you have changed my options so that they are now A, B−, and C−, where the minus sign indicates that the option taken will be attended by a penalty. But suppose now that instead of threatening me with penalties you offer me a reward—a refusable reward—for the choice of A. In this case you leave me with the original options, A, B, and C, and add on another option, A+, where the plus sign indicates that the option will be accompanied by a reward. The difference is that the penalty is inescapable, but the reward is not: refusing the reward, I can still choose A, or, accepting it, I can choose A+.[34] My original can-do assumptions remain in place: they are true, and they are accessible.

When you offer me a reward, of course, you may change the probability of my choosing A; indeed, you may change that probability in just the same measure as you would have done, had you threatened instead to penalize my doing B or C. But the crucial difference is that in face of the reward, assuming that it does not have a mesmerizing character, I preserve the orthonomy that I had before. I retain the options that I had before—I can choose A or B or C—and I retain the ability to reason about them; the only change is that I now have a further option: I can choose A+ instead of A or B or C.

The possibility of orthonomous capacity and choice is presupposed in any agent's decision making. As I deliberate about whether to do A or B or C, I have to think of those options as alternatives between which I can just choose, depending on how I assess the reasons. Were I to cease to think that I had such effective choice—were I to think, say, that taking B or C is impossible—then

---

[34] On this analysis, a non-refusable reward would have the same effect as a penalty, but that is intuitively alright. Why would you make the offer of a reward unrefusable unless you thought that I might refuse it? And in that case there is some evidence that from my point of view it counts as a penalty.

I would no longer have any grounds for deliberating. And were I to begin to think of the different choices not as matters subject to the control of my choice, but as different scenarios, each with its own probability of materializing, then I would equally have given up on decision making: I would have moved from a deliberative to a predictive stance. The attraction of an offer is that while it may shift the probabilities of my choosing one thing rather than another, it does not contract my power of choice; my options will not have been changed, only expanded.

This line on offers is supported by our explication of deliberative exchange. As my deliberative partner, you may give me advice on the options before me and on the reasons for and against each of them. And in the spirit of epistemic collaboration, you may point out that one option available is that of getting a third party to reward me for taking an option that will appeal to that person. But if you can point this out in relation to a third party, you can surely do so in relation to yourself. You can communicate that from your point of view it would be good if I took A rather than B or C, and so that you are willing to give me a reward if I make that choice and I want the reward. You can retain the profile of an *amicus curiae*, a friend of the court, while making me this offer.

To be orthonomous, as we know, is to have the capacity to recognize the reasons that bear on what you think or do and to self-regulate by those reasons. If you are to enjoy free will and free thought as a person amongst persons then it is essential that your relations with others allow that capacity unrestricted exercise, guarding you against the alien control of others, active or virtual. The status of commanding respect — the status of discursive control, as I have called it elsewhere (Pettit 2001*b*) — would guard you against such alien control. It would complement orthonomy, nicely reinforcing that ratiocinative capacity with a corresponding relational capacity. If you lack the ratiocinative capacity, then you will not be fit to be held responsible for what you do. But equally, if you lack the relational capacity, say because of living under the thumb or threat of another, then in many cases you may not be fit to be held fully responsible for what you do. The lack of either capacity may lead to a shortfall of freedom in the encompassing sense in which freedom can be equated with fitness to be held fully responsible; this is the sense of freedom explicated in *A Theory of Freedom* (Pettit 2001*b*).

Richard Holton is not inclined to find any appeal in this encompassing sense of freedom, and this explains a number of other differences between us. One difference is that he wants to say, contrary to the line in *A Theory of Freedom*, that coerced acts can be free. The idea is that when you give the robber your money, rather than forfeiting your life, you make a choice, and so exercise free will: in our terms, orthonomy. But I don't need to back away from this. As already noted, I agree that you may be orthonomous in the way in which your will and thought form under a coercive threat. I say only that you do not have freedom in the full sense associated with fitness to be held responsible; more particularly, you do not have the relation to others that such freedom requires. This ought not to make for a deep divide with Holton, since he accepts that coercion reduces responsibility, providing an agent with an excuse or even a justification for acting as he or she does. Like me, indeed, he thinks that coercive threats are different in this way from refusable offers, though he provides a different, interesting argument in support of that view.

Another difference that arises between us also derives from the fact that I focus in the book he discusses on freedom in the encompassing sense in which it requires both a ratiocinative and a relational capacity. He thinks that the emphasis on relational capacity is meant to suggest that if you are out of society, like Robinson Crusoe, then you cannot be a free person. But all I want to argue, of course, is that assuming that you exist in society with others—assuming, as I say, that you are a person amongst persons—you cannot be free unless you command the respect of others, having the status that I describe in the book as discursive control.[35]

The Ethic of Respect

If all this is right, then our reasoning and co-reasoning nature makes it inescapable that we should countenance certain substantive values and disvalues. A property will be treated as a value, on the account given earlier, insofar as it plays a certain role in our reasoning and co-reasoning, serving to support the rightness of certain choices, for example, and to justify those choices to others. What we have seen now is that if we endorse the practice of deliberative exchange with others, then we will inevitably give certain features of our situation and behavior roles that make them count as values and disvalues.

We will publicly endorse the practice of deliberative exchange, whenever we renounce violence and coercion—overt forms of disrespect—and present ourselves as potential co-reasoners. Even when we are insincere, we still sign up to that practice as the frame for the relevant relationship, inviting others to hold us to the expectations that go with that frame. Given that we understand what is involved in the practice, endorsing it will mean being disposed to recognize any instance of violence or coercion, or any sort of insincerity in the performance of one party, as something blameworthy. And this being a matter available to common awareness, it will mean recognizing that by everyone's lights—by the lights of everyone not explicitly bent on violence or coercion—such performances will attract the same condemnation. They will be properties marked in common awareness as paradigms of wrongdoing.

---

[35] He thinks that the relational capacity requires you to be able to justify in a radical way the things that you think and do—or at least "the moral conclusions" you reach—to others. But I take it that co-reasoning with others may only take you to those common considerations, however shallow, where you each see things alike.

The perspective of a rational agent gives us each a standpoint from within which certain reasons will have a natural grip; you would not be functioning as a rational agent if you were not sensitive to those reasons. The argument here, in parallel, is that the perspective of co-reasoners in deliberative exchange gives us a common standpoint from within which certain considerations will equally have a grip on us; we would not be functioning as co-reasoners if we were not sensitive to them in a parallel way. The argument, more particularly, is that if we are to aspire to participate in the practice of deliberative exchange, then we must be disposed to treat violence and coercion, deception and manipulation, as simply unacceptable. Indifference towards such overtures would not cohere with deliberative co-reasoning any more than indifference towards fallacies would cohere with rational, first-person calculation.

This is to say, in a phrase, that there is an ethic of respect inscribed in the most basic of human practices, and that it is as inescapable as those practices themselves. Kant looked for unconditional imperatives that would apply without any conditions or provisos. The ethic of respect encodes hypothetical or conditional imperatives only, prescribing that if we are to practice deliberative exchange, then we should avoid this or that sort of overture—and, more generally, should conduct ourselves in this or that fashion. But the fact that these imperatives apply if we seek deliberative exchange, and not perhaps otherwise, does not significantly weaken them. For this is a small 'if', since deliberative exchange is the default option in conversation with others. The prescriptions of the ethic of respect are minimally conditioned, if not quite unconditional, imperatives.

Beyond the Ethic of Respect

Notwithstanding their conditional character, there is one way in which the imperatives of respect would appeal to Kant. Like his unconditional counterparts, they represent constraints on how people should act, rather than goals or targets for their actions to achieve. A constraint on your performance identifies a general pattern that you are expected to instantiate in your own behavior and relationships. A goal or target identifies a general pattern that you are called on to promote; you are to do everything possible to ensure that there is more of it rather than less of it in the world overall, even if the action required does not instantiate that pattern itself. Take non-violence, for example. This would be represented as a goal if you were allowed to practice violence in order to promote more non-violence overall. It would be represented as a constraint if you were not allowed to make wholesale use of that justification: if at least certain forms of violence were prohibited, no matter what the overall gain in non-violence.

Respect is a constraint, not a target, under the ethic described. For a breach would not be justified within the ethic just because, for some perverse reason, it represented the best way of getting others, or even getting yourself in the future, to abide by the ethic. The breach might be justifiable in other terms—say, because it is the best way of bringing about a variety of independent goals—but it would not be justified within the strict terms of the ethic itself. That ethic requires that people instantiate respect in their relationships with others, not that they behave towards others in a way that maximizes the expected instantiation of respect. It is a code to which those who engage in deliberative exchange are expected to subscribe. And the code does not contain any provision allowing you to offend against the code because that will lead to a reduction of offences overall.[36] To expect otherwise would be like expecting the code of chess-players to provide for when the rules of chess playing may be broken for the sake of promoting fidelity to those rules overall.

We have seen, first, that the ethic of respect is deeply embedded in the most fundamental and basic of human practices; and second, that it presents us with constraints on behavior, not goals for behavior to promote. Does this mean that the most basic viewpoint in ethics is provided by a set of general constraints, not a set of general goals? Does it mean that non-consequentialism, rather than consequentialism, gives us the best theory of what is right?

Consequentialism, as I understand the term, holds that the yardstick or criterion of rightness, be it the rightness of an act or policy or motive or rule, is whether that particular variable promotes the good; whether it maximizes expected value (Pettit and Smith 2000). It may not make much sense to try to apply that criterion in decision making; it may even be counterproductive to try to do so. But the idea is that in assessing any initiative, perhaps only in hindsight, the basic question is whether its appearance made for an expected improvement in the world—an expected increase in neutral value. Non-consequentialism rejects this claim, arguing that there are some patterns of action or policy or whatever that call to be instantiated, not because they promise an increase in overall good, but for other reasons: they may be hailed as sacred dictates—the moral law within—or as means to the personal good of stakeholders, or whatever.

I think that consequentialism better reflects the patterns of moral reasoning that should command our allegiance as we seek reflective equilibrium in our views. In these patterns, so I think, justification is ultimately achieved by appeal to some identity of concerns and so, as consequentialism suggests, by appeal to a neutral good—potentially, a good-by-all-lights—that the justified initiative promotes (Baron, Pettit, and Slote 1997). But this being so, what should I say about the non-consequentialist character of the ethic of respect that is deeply rooted in our nature and practices?

The story told about the practice of deliberative exchange, and the emergence of the ethic of respect, is quite consistent with acknowledging that participants will come to recognize thick values in common, and will be able to invoke them

---

[36] What if the reduction in offences will be of direct benefit, not to others, but to the person himself or herself? I ignore the complication here.

in evaluation of deliberative exchange itself. The simplest property available for the evaluation of the practice is going to be the property of respect satisfaction. The partners in a practice of deliberative exchange should be able to appreciate the difference between having respect satisfaction in their lives and not having it. And they may be expected to name it as a commonly invoked value, on the pattern described in Section 3. It will be for them a property identified by certain paradigms; supervenient on descriptive features of the relationships that generate it; attractive to all, or at least to all who count as unaffected by certain obtruding or limiting factors; and connected suitably with rightness and justification and virtue.

If partners in deliberative exchange can countenance a thick value of this kind, then it is going to be possible for them to argue that maintaining relationships of respect is important on consequentialist grounds, promising to produce more of this value of respect satisfaction. But it will be possible also for them to argue, on similar grounds, that room should be made for occasionally breaching the requirements of respect. Suppose, as in an example from Kant, that if I truthfully answer a would-be murderer's question about where you are—if in that sense I treat the person with respect—then I will cause your death, thereby denying you all possibility of respect satisfaction. On the account emerging here I will be well within my rights to tell the would-be murderer a lie. Telling a lie may breach the ethic of respect, but on the very grounds that generally argue for the importance of that ethic, it is the best thing to do overall.

Consequentialism is available as a viewpoint to which I can retreat and reconsider my options when, as in this case, the red lights go on: when it becomes clear that following the automatic pilot provided by the ethic of respect—and thereby generating the good of respect satisfaction—is actually going to do more general harm than good. As we used the idea of virtual control elsewhere, so we can make good use of it here too. Consequentialism does not require me to weigh the pros and cons of every action or policy or rule—that, indeed, would be counterproductive (Pettit and Brennan 1986)—but it may require me to retain a virtual, consequentialist control over my performance, being alert to the red lights that tell me when important neutral values are at stake, and when it may make sense to break with routine, even a routine that is for the best in the vast majority of circumstances.

I think that while the ethic of respect is of inestimable importance in human life, it is equally important that we not fetishize it as if it were the beginning and the end of morality; this is at least a temptation for non-consequentialist theories of morality that stress obligations and rights as if they were imposed from elsewhere.[37]

---

[37] The best, philosophically reflective forms of non-consequentialism do not indulge this temptation. Take T. M. Scanlon's (1998) contractualist approach to ethics, for example. While it prioritizes principles to which none of us, relating as respectful co-reasoners, could 'reasonably'

One reason for keeping the ethic of respect in its place is that it presupposes a dispensation under which property is distributed according to a certain pattern, and does not itself engage that pattern. Thus, despite the fact that you are poor, we others will not be required under the ethic of respect to do anything for you; we can allow you to remain poor. And equally, despite the fact that you are rich, we others will be required not to take anything from you; we cannot actively deprive you of any property, regardless of how this may help others.[38] The ethic is under-demanding on the one side and over-constraining on the other. It restricts responsibility to the changes we make in the lives of others, and does not extend to include the unchanged ways that we allow others to be. We will return to this point in Section 7.

6. COMMUNITY AND INCORPORATION

Social Ontology

There are three important debates in social ontology, one centered on individualism, a second on atomism, and a third on singularism (Pettit 2004*f*). All of them relate to possibilities involving the intentional psychology that we ascribe to ourselves when we take our actions to be the more or less rational products of more or less rationally held beliefs and desires. In each case there is an issue as to how our psychology connects with life in society.

The individualism debate concerns the question of whether our individual, intentional psychologies are compromised in any way by social regularities: whether we are predetermined or predestined, notwithstanding our apparent intentional powers, to behave so that the regularities are sustained. The atomism debate concerns the question of whether we depend non-causally on having certain social relations with one another in order to instantiate certain psychological capacities, in particular the capacity to reason and perform as persons. And the singularism debate bears on whether there are centers of intentional attitude and action over and beyond individual agents; whether individuals can socially combine to form groups with minds of their own.

These debates are independent of one another, because there is nothing to rule out any of the eight possible combinations (Pettit and Schweikard 2006). The

object as principles for regulating our behavior, the principles do not just legislate for the behavior required of us when we are respectful; they also dictate how we should behave under conditions in which we are dealing with malefactors like Kant's would-be murderer, where we are not generally proving to respect one another, where natural circumstances are devastating, and so on; see Pettit 2006*a* for a description and assessment.

[38] Robert Nozick (1974) argues against forced redistribution precisely on the grounds of interpreting an ethic of respect in this way.

propositions defended so far in this piece argue in favor of individualism and against atomism. And, as I shall try to show, they naturally support a position according to which there are group agents or persons that, in an important sense, have minds of their own.

For Individualism

Individualism holds that in matters psychological, as limned in earlier discussions, we human beings are as we seem to be. We are centers of thought and feeling and agency who can strive, with some degree of success, to live up to what we generally agree are the demands of reason and morality. We are not the pawns and playthings of collective forces but are possessed, however imperfectly, of a capacity for independence in thought and action.

This sort of individualism contrasts with two traditions (Pettit 1993*a*). One holds that the familiar, intentional regularities associated with ordinary self-understanding—with *Verstehen*, as it is sometimes put—are overridden by the hidden, collectivistic regularities of history or sociology that are there to be uncovered in the pursuit of scientific explanation, or *Erklären*. The other holds that those intentional regularities are not so much overridden as outflanked by such hidden collectivistic laws.

The idea in the first tradition is that what the intentional laws of psychology require can conflict with what is required by historical or structural laws, and that where conflict occurs, the latter laws win out; thus our familiar psychology is limited by the requirements of scientific, collectivistic law. The idea in the second tradition is that we have been shaped by a process of social selection so as to be creatures who will only ever display intentional profiles—and who will only ever engage intentional regularities—in a manner guaranteed to save the social laws; our familiar psychology is rigged to serve the requirements of collectivistic order.

The individualism involved in rejecting the overriding and the outflanking theses conflicts with the disposition present in the writings of some classical anthropologists and sociologists, most prominently Émile Durkheim. The factors that he took to compromise intentional psychology range from the morphological features of a society, like the density of its population, to the norms or rules institutionalized there, to the currents of opinion and the enthusiasms which take over from time to time (Durkheim 1938; Lukes 1973). He argued that social facts of these kinds constrain intentional agents from without. Individuals, he urged, are not independent centers of thought and feeling and agency, contrary to the claims of self-determination made by 'the zealous partisans of absolute individualism' (Durkheim 1938: 4).

Against what I take to be the intended claims of Durkheim and certain others, I hold that the core deliverances of our folk psychology have yet to be falsified or transcended. Nothing in what history and social science have revealed—and nothing, going on the sample so far, that they are likely to reveal—has any tendency to undermine our sense of ourselves as relatively independent agents. The results of social inquiry and social theorizing can generally be squared with our folk psychology, even if this psychology requires amendment at the margins. And to the extent that this is not so, those results look downright incredible. How could any of the more or less tentative findings that social science is likely to generate ever persuade us that there is something misconceived about adopting the stance in which we see one another as conversable agents?

Rejecting individualism is an extreme and implausible option, but it may appeal because of an exaggerated sense of what individualism forbids. I should stress, therefore, that individualism on my understanding of it is a capacious doctrine. It allows that the best way of explaining social events may not be by reference to individuals, for example; we saw earlier that explanatory ecumenism is a better option than explanatory reductionism. It allows that while some people have effected great things on the social stage, still, many of the things achieved might have come about by another hand, had the individuals involved not been around. And it allows that people's opportunities for action may sometimes be so circumscribed that what they do is entirely explicable without reference to intentional antecedents. Such scenarios would not compromise our picture of intentional agency, and their possibility does not argue for a rejection of individualism.

Against Atomism

We might think of the issue of individualism as vertical in character, since the question is whether or not historical and structural forces act upon individuals from on high. The issue about atomism, by contrast, is horizontal in nature. It is the issue of whether individuals constitutively or non-causally depend upon their relations with one another for the possession of any particularly important human capacity: whether, in particular, they depend upon one another in this way for being able to reason and and perform as persons (Pettit 1993*a*; 2002*b*: essay 1.4).

If atomism is unsound, then there is a sense in which society comes before individuality—it is a precondition of the individuality we manifest—but the priority involved is very different from that which anti-individualism proposes. The claim is that for reasons of a constitutive or non-causal kind, individuals are incapable of manifesting a full human psychology on their own; the achievement of that sort of psychology is something that they can bring off only in community with one another. And that thesis is quite consistent with holding that the psychology achieved by grace of relations with others is just the familiar sort of psychology in which individualists believe.

Whereas individualism is supported by the views sketched earlier on rationality and reasoning, atomism is inconsistent with the particular story about rule-following that those views incorporate; indeed, it is also in tension with the emphasis on conversability and deliberative exchange. According to the story about rule-following, it is only in virtue of having one another as authorized, potentially discrepant voices that we are able to target the commonly accessible rules to which we try to stay faithful as we reason and think, whether on our own or in public debate. And if this is so, then it is not going to be possible for us to reason and think—or at least to reason and think with rules that are accessible to all—except in community with one another. Such mental activities will presuppose social practices.

The status or power that someone enjoys in a society depends non-causally on others holding certain beliefs about them and holding beliefs about their each having such beliefs; in this sense it is an inherently social property. The claim here is that, in a parallel manner, the capacity that someone has to think accessible thoughts depends non-causally on those others having been interactively identified as voices that they cannot ignore. These voices can serve as correctives of the person's own inclinations, providing an essential reality test. Trying to reason and think out of a history of community with such voices would be like trying to clap with one hand.

There is a second line of argument made available by previous considerations that might also be invoked to support a rejection of atomism. Apart from reasoning, a feature that is equally characteristic of the mind of human beings is the ability to perform as a person, engaging the expectations and reliance of others and inviting censure in the event of non-compliance. Following Hobbes, we might describe this as the ability to personate, as distinct from the ability to ratiocinate. This is the ability to represent yourself authoritatively—to speak for yourself, to give your word—almost like a duly appointed political representative. Some of the considerations rehearsed in the discussion of co-reasoning and conversability suggest that, like ratiocination, personation is dependent in more than a causal way on community with others.

Suppose that you are the solitary individual imagined in atomistic scenarios: the adult human being, sprung into existence without any contact with others; and suppose, contrary to the first argument, that you can reason with yourself over time: you have no difficulty on the rule-following count. Even on that supposition, it will still be impossible for you to give your word to yourself, or to speak for yourself to yourself, in the fashion of a person. It will be impossible for you to gain the distance on yourself that comes with living in the presence of others to whom you may commit yourself in that way.

How could you distinguish between releasing yourself from expectations that you may have engendered and changing your mind about what to think or do? How could you have access to the notion of creating expectations, given that you would have no one who relies on you? How could you be anything other than a subject that drifts, however ratiocinatively, from moment to moment, and mind-set to mind-set? Like reasoning out of community, personating out of community may be as impossible as clapping with one hand.

Against Singularism

The third debate in social ontology bears on singularism—I adapt the word from Margaret Gilbert (1989)—as distinct from individualism or atomism. The issue is how far people can unite to form intentionally minded agents of a group kind: agents that constitute institutional persons with minds of their own. The singularist maintains that group agents are not real agents, and that any talk of such agents is a *façon de parler* for referring to agents of the familiar, individual kind. If we speak of what such groups intend or believe or do, for example, the idea is that we are just indirectly speaking of what their members or officers, or a majority amongst them, intend or believe or do. It would be a serious error of double-counting, so the line goes, to imagine that when we have taken account of all the individual agents in any context, that still leaves a question as to how many group agents there are.

Anti-singularists deny that group agency dissolves in this way into individual agency. The idea is not the metaphysically outrageous one that the number of group agents and the dispositions of group agents might vary without any variation in the number or nature of individual agents; that would amount to positing an independent realm of group agency of a kind that would have to conflict with individualism, in the sense defined above (List and Pettit 2006). The idea is merely that groups can satisfy the sorts of conditions sketched earlier for when a behavioral system can count as the bearer and enactor of intentional attitudes.

Suppose that people each form the shared intention that they should act together for the promotion of certain goals: these may be given goals, or goals that are yet to be identified in some downstream procedure. On a familiar analysis of shared intention, this will mean that they each intend that they together promote the goals; they each expect others to play their part in the exercise; they each intend, given that expectation, to play their own part too; and all of this is above board, as a matter of common awareness (Pettit and Schweikard 2006).

The joint action sponsored by such a shared intention might not involve the creation, intuitively, of any center of intentional attitudes apart from the singular agents involved. The individuals might each act in pursuit of the goals according to their own beliefs about what it is best to do on any given occasion; if they are successful, that might just be because their beliefs happen to fall in line with one another.

But now suppose, in addition, that the parties also share the intention that when any one of them or any collection of them acts in pursuit of those goals, they should do so according to the same body of judgments; these will include judgments on the options available in any situation, on the best means for pursuing a given goal, on the relative importance or urgency of goals, and perhaps on whether to drop an old goal or adopt a new one. They can act on this intention by setting up a procedure for identifying the propositions that should guide them as a group. The group will not have different degrees of belief in such propositions, in the manner of an individual, but it can be said to judge in their favor. Judgment is like belief in being a representation of how things allegedly are, but, while it may bear on a probabilistic proposition or content, it does not come in degrees; it is endorsed or rejected, period.

Under these suppositions, it becomes very plausible to hold that a novel center of intentional attitudes will be formed, over and beyond the cooperating individual agents.[39] This center will be the group that employs its members as representative agents, charging them to pursue its characteristic goals according to its characteristic judgments. The group will have a procedure or practice whereby its goals and judgments are formed and individuals are selected to enact those intentional attitudes. Individuals will give this new agent life, insofar as they put their individual attitudes offline and place themselves in the service of the group's attitudes, as these are formed under the prevailing dispensation.

But won't the group goals be just a function of the members' goals, the group judgments just a function of the members' judgments? And in that case, shouldn't we think of the group, not as a novel center of intentional attitudes, but rather as a corporate agency or apparatus whereby the members manage to pursue more-or-less-shared goals according to more-or-less-shared judgments?

No, we shouldn't. Individuals cannot expect to put their judgments together in a body of judgments suitable for the guidance of a group without allowing the group to assume a certain autonomy; the same is true of goals, but it will suffice to defend it for judgments. The obvious way of putting member judgments together is by majority voting. But the 'discursive dilemma' shows that majority voting among perfectly consistent voters is liable to generate an inconsistent set of judgments—a set that is unfitted, therefore, to guide the group (Pettit 2001*b*: ch. 5; 2003*b*).[40] And an associated impossibility theorem shows that the problem is quite general (List and Pettit 2002).

In order to illustrate the problem, consider a simple group of three agents, A, B, and C, and imagine that under the pressure of decision and action, they have to form judgments, now on whether p, now on whether q, now on whether r, and yet again on whether p & q & r. All but A might vote for p; all but B for q; all but C for r; and, consequently, none for p & q & r: each

---

[39] The claim here is that a certain set of collective intentions may be sufficient for forming a group agent, not that it is going to be essential. I do not address the possibility of group agents who form without such collective intentions.

[40] The dilemma is a generalization in a number of ways of the doctrinal paradox that Lewis Kornhauser and Larry Sager had identified as a problem for collegial courts. See Kornhauser 1992*a,b*; Kornhauser and Sager 1993.

Table 1.

	p?	*q*?	*r*?	*p* & *q* & *r*?
A	No	Yes	Yes	No
B	Yes	No	Yes	No
C	Yes	Yes	No	No
Majority	Yes	Yes	Yes	No

would reject it because of rejecting one of the conjuncts. Under a majoritarian arrangement, these votes would have the group holding that *p*, that *q*, that *r*, but that not-*p* & *q* & *r*. The position would be as represented in the matrix shown in Table 11.1. The dilemma illustrated by such a case is this. The group may opt for responsiveness to individual opinion, in which case it will have to sacrifice collective rationality. Or it may opt for collective rationality, in which case it will have to sacrifice responsiveness to individual opinion. It cannot have it both ways.

If a group is to behave as a collective agent over time, it cannot be relaxed about the appearance of inconsistencies in the body of judgments whereby its members are to be guided when they act in the name of the group. It will form judgments on a need-for-action basis, not just for the pleasure of doing so, and if its actions are to be properly shaped, then those judgments must give a determinate and consistent lead. But as the record of its judgments builds up over time, the threat of discursive dilemmas will increase; there will be a growing likelihood that its existing judgments will require it to take a different line from that which majority voting would support (List 2006). Thus the group will have to be ready to form judgments on certain issues that break with the views of a majority, even the totality, of its members. It may have made judgments in the pattern of the A-B-C group on whether *p*, whether *q*, and whether *r*, and then find that voting suggests the judgment that not-*p* & *q* & *r*. In that case, it will have to revise one of its earlier judgments, breaking with the majority on that question, or judge that *p* & *q* & *r*, breaking with the totality of members on that issue.

The discursive dilemma shows that a group that tries to form judgments as a majoritarian function of the judgments of its members is more or less bound to fail. But could a group form its judgments on different issues as a non-majoritarian but still systematic function of the judgments of its members on those issues? It turns out not.

Take any procedure that treats every individual voter equally, giving no one the status of a dictator (anonymity), that is designed to work for any consistent sets of input judgments (universal domain), and that enables a group to produce complete and consistent judgments over ranges of suitably connected issues. No procedure that satisfies conditions of roughly these kinds will identify a rule or function—majoritarian or non-majoritarian—whereby the corporate judgment on every issue can be derived from the votes and judgments of members on that issue. No such procedure can establish a systematic relationship between the judgments of individuals and the judgments of the corporate organization (List and Pettit 2002).[41]

The upshot is that if individuals combine to act in pursuit of group goals according to a single body of group judgments, then the group will have to form judgments that are discontinuous with the judgments of members. In that sense it will have to prove itself a relatively autonomous center of intentional attitudes. Corporate agents do this routinely, of course, and without going to the extreme of making one individual dictatorial. They ensure that their judgments are not a function of the judgments of individuals, and not hostage to inconsistency, by any of a number of methods or technologies. They may let past judgments dictate their judgment on any logically connected issue, for example. They may let a single individual, or a subcommittee, decide what the group's judgments are in problematic cases. Or they may follow a straw vote procedure, whereby they decide as a group what line to take when straw voting suggests that they will have to deal with an inconsistency. Although the possibilities are legion, they all have one feature in common. Guarding against inconsistency, they all ensure that the intentional judgments of the group will not reflect, on a one-to-one pattern, the corresponding judgments among the group members.

One way of underlining the autonomy thereby accorded to the corporate entity is to observe that the position of the group in relation to its members will be a little like that which might obtain between an individual person and those he or she consults as advisers, generally accepting any view that a majority supports. The advisee will not be able to go along slavishly with majority opinions, since, as we have seen, these can be inconsistent with one another. Presumably the only satisfactory line will be to go along with majority opinion subject to the constraint of not allowing internal inconsistency. That policy will not dictate a uniquely best set of judgments to adopt, but it will at least ensure that the advisee remains a believer proper, not just a voicebox of those consulted (Pettit 2006*h*). In precisely the same way, the only satisfactory line for a group that is generally disposed to go along with the views of its members on any issue—say, the views of the majority—will be to do so under the constraint of ensuring that this does

---

[41] Nor is that all. Take any procedure that makes the judgments of the corporate body depend on the judgments of more than one individual, thereby ruling out dictatorship but without enforcing the equal treatment of individuals (i.e. without enforcing anonymity). Let this procedure, as in the previous case, work for any consistent sets of input judgments (universal domain) and enable a group to produce complete and consistent judgments over ranges of connected issues. No procedure that satisfies conditions of these still weaker kinds will identify a rule or function—majoritarian or non-majoritarian—whereby the corporate judgment on every issue can be derived from the votes and judgments of members on that issue; no such procedure can establish a systematic relationship between individual and corporate views (Dietrich and List, forthcoming; this develops Pauly and Van Hees, forthcoming).

not lead to inconsistency. And just as that policy will mark out an advisee as a believer in his or her own right, so it will do the same for the group.

Corporate Rights and Responsibilities

If this is right, then there is every reason to countenance corporate agents as well as agents of an individual stamp. While they must be composed and operated by individuals, they will have an intentional autonomy that forces us to treat them as agents in their own right. And not just as agents, indeed: also as personifiable entities. For just as individual persons can be aware of the demands of rationality, aspire to live up to those demands over time, and prove conversable in their relations with themselves and others, so corporate agents can do all of those things too.

Medieval legal theory was probably the first intellectual tradition in which corporate persons were properly and widely recognized as such (Canning 1980). The corporate entity was illustrated for people in that time by guilds and towns, monastic orders and parishes, indeed by the church itself. They thought of such a body as a *universitas*, a unity in many. And they held that while the *universitas* or corporate entity formed its goals and judgments, and enacted those attitudes, by courtesy of its members, those members did not think as individuals or *singuli* when acting for the group. They performed, rather, as *universi* or representatives, putting their mouths and hands—putting their very minds—at the service of the collectivity: the corporate persona.

Two questions of ethical importance arise with corporate entities or organizations. The first question is whether they have rights, and the second is whether they have responsibilities.

To say that corporate entities have certain rights, in the relevant sense, is not just to say that under a given system of law and custom—as a matter of positive fact—they are entitled to make such and such claims. It is to say, rather, that the system of law or custom ought to be such that it would entitle them to make those claims. It is to make a normative claim, prescribing how the rules of the system ought to be structured.

The rules governing corporate entities must determine how they may form, for what purpose, in what territory; how far they may change their sphere of activity at their own will; what constraints they may place on their members; whether they may merge with one another, divide into different entities, or exercise control over other corporate entities; how far their financial liability is limited to corporate funds; to what extent they are protected by the provisions that guard natural persons; and so on through a vast range of issues. The rules that actually shape corporate life, in particular the life of commercial corporations, have changed enormously over the past couple of centuries. In the early nineteenth century, for example, commercial corporations in many countries could only be formed by an act of the legislature, were restricted to a certain sphere and area

of activity, could not have ownership in one another, and were not protected by
the limitation of liability.

How to settle the abstract question as to what rules ought to be put in place to
shape corporate entities and establish their rights? How to adjudicate the pattern
of rule making that has actually emerged and stabilized, not just for commercial
corporations, but also for churches and associations, schools and universities,
professional bodies and political parties? It is not possible to develop a detailed
answer here, but there are two general points that I want to stress.

The first is that the question can be answered only by reference to individual
persons, and to what serves individuals best, however such service is meas-
ured—whether, for example, in consequentialist or non-consequentialist terms.
How it is best to organize things in social life is determined by how it is best
to organize them from the point of view of natural persons. The only plausible
perspective on the issue amounts to a moral, as distinct from an ontological,
version of individualism (Kukathas and Pettit 1990; Pettit 1993*a*).

The second point I want to make is that within any plausible system of rights,
it will be possible for corporate entities, within the limits set by the rules, to
enjoy relations of respect with other corporate entities and with natural persons.
The idea of conversability will remain in place, and the ideal of deliberative
exchange or respect will continue to be relevant. It will be possible and desirable
for relationships among persons, natural and corporate, to be governed by an
eschewal of all but reason-mediated, reason-friendly forms of influence. This ideal
might give us a basis for determining the rights, and the limitations on rights,
appropriate for corporate entities. A precondition of mutual respect, as we shall
see in the next section, is that people should enjoy liberty as non-domination in
relation to others. The rights that people are given when acting as corporations
ought to facilitate that liberty, and the limitations to which they are subject in a
corporate role ought to protect the liberty of others.

So much for the rights of corporates and the claims that they should be
allowed to make. What now should we say of their responsibilities? To hold in
the relevant sense that a corporate entity has certain responsibilities is not just
to say that certain claims can be made against it under the existing system of
rules. It is to say, in parallel with the ascription of rights, that the system of
rules ought to be such that those claims can be made against it. As in the rights
case, there is no possibility of arguing for the detailed set of responsibilities that
ought to be assigned. But there is a general point that needs to be defended.
This is that it is appropriate to treat the success or failure of a corporate entity
in discharging its assigned responsibilities in the way that we might treat the
success or failure of a natural person. There is every reason why we should
be prepared to think and hold a corporate entity responsible for the initiatives
it takes. And this is so, despite the fact that it may also be right to hold
members responsible for the part they played in enacting such initiatives (Pettit
2007*b*).

To think an individual more or less fully responsible for an action, by criteria that we outlined earlier, is to assume three things: first, that the person was an agent proper and faced a significant choice, involving the possibility of doing something good or bad, right or wrong; second, that the person was a believer with evidence available supporting beliefs that that is how things were; and third, that the person had a capacity to reason about the pros and cons of the options and enjoyed control over which option to take. The person will have to satisfy requirements, as we might describe them, of agency-plus-choice, judgment-plus-evidence, and control-plus-reason.

On the account given, corporate groups can clearly satisfy the agent-plus-choice requirement. And equally clearly, they can meet the judgment-plus-evidence requirement, being able to form judgments in the manner of an autonomous subject about the options available in any choice, about the reasons that support those alternatives, and so on. But can groups satisfy the control-plus-reason requirement? They will be able to reason insofar as their members can reason. But will they be able, in their own right, to exercise control over what is done in their name?

It may seem not. Whenever a group acts, it must always act via the intentional action of its members or those whom its members employ. And in that case it appears that control over the actions taken is in the hands of those members, not in the hands of the group as such. The members who act may do so according to the group's instructions, of course. But the instructions will always have to be issued by other members—perhaps those in an official position—and so the control that the group exercises at that level will also be exercised only in virtue of the control of individuals.

Sound though they are, however, these observations should not lead us to deny control of what it does to the corporate entity itself. The reason is that although it is always individual agents who carry out the projects of a corporate organization, the organization may still program for their being carried out.

Consider the example where the water in a closed flask is brought to the boil, and, as a consequence, the flask breaks. As the water boils—as the mean motion of the constituent molecules reaches a suitable level—it becomes likely to the point of near-inevitability that some molecule will have a position and momentum sufficient to break a molecular bond in the surface of the flask; and this is in fact what happens, leading to the collapse of the flask. The mean molecular motion of the water programs in such a case for the breaking of the flask, and the particular molecule that does the damage implements that program. Both play a role in the causal explanation of the event, with each exercising a different sort of control.

This example suggests an analogous structure in the control of those activities that are taken by its members in the name of a corporate group. The corporate group or body acts through the practices it puts into place to ensure that there will be someone, maybe this individual, maybe that, who will discharge a task that is targeted for fulfillment. As the boiling water programs for the collapse of the flask, so the corporate group programs for the completion of the job. And as the molecule with the required momentum and position implements the program in the water case, so the individual or individuals who actually perform the task implement the corporate program. The individuals are the ones who carry out the job on this model: they are the immediate causal operatives. But the corporate body, the collectivity acting as a whole, puts routines in place that allocate that job to those individuals, and that ensure a certain monitoring and backup by others.

This program architecture means that we should distinguish between the responsibility of an organization as an organization—and so the responsibility of the members as members—for what is done on a given occasion and the responsibility of those individuals who play a part in enacting the project. The organization will control things to the extent of arranging matters so that some agents will be there to act in the relevant role, while individual agents will control things to the extent of ensuring that it is they who actually enact the role. The corporate organization has control over whether the job in question is going to be done, it doesn't matter by whom. The individuals have control over whether it is going to be they or others who do the job.

The *Herald of Free Enterprise* sank in the English Channel in 1987, killing nearly 200 people. An inquiry described the company as sloppy and its actions as inexcusable, but no one individual or set of individuals could be identified as culpable enactors. The accident occurred as a result of those agents following accepted, inadequate procedures. And there were no salient individuals who could be assigned enactor responsibility for having failed to examine or recommend a change in the procedures. On the analysis offered here, the company should still be held responsible as a whole. It programmed for that sort of failure, or failed to program against it, as a result of having an inadequate constitution. And since any organization will have the capacity to review and amend its constitutional procedures—since it will have control over whether the constitution remains unchanged or not—the company in a case like this can reasonably be held responsible for what was done as a result. There will be full responsibility accruing to the corporate entity, and so to the members as members, but there will not be a comparable measure of enactor responsibility.

The possibility of this sort of gap between corporate and enactor responsibility argues for the need to hold corporate organizations responsible as such (Pettit 2007*b*). Given that gap, it will be possible for individuals to combine in the achievement of an objectionable goal when none of them can be assigned proper enactor responsibility for the result. Let organizations be able to dodge responsibility of the kind that we ascribe to individual agents, and there will be a permanent possibility of a deficit in the ledgers of responsibility.

The fact that organizations can be held responsible in their own right means that there is no objection in principle to exposing them to the sanctions of the criminal law. I do not address the question of how organizations should be seen and sanctioned in the criminal law, but the issue is clearly deserving of attention. The fact that a corporate organization is the sort of entity that can be held responsible for its doings, and held responsible in the manner in which individuals are held responsible, clears the way for a more detailed consideration of the regime of sanctions, criminal and otherwise, to which such organizations should be subject.

Incorporation and Politics

Given the profile of coherent, responsible agency that incorporation can confer on a group, a natural question is how far the state, the government, and the various departments of government—the executive, the legislature, and the judiciary—ought to assume such a profile; and indeed how far, as a matter of fact, they do.

I have argued elsewhere that a number of political philosophies—in particular, the republicanism I go on to consider—argue in favor of requiring such agencies to incorporate and, as John Ferejohn puts it in his paper, display conversability (Pettit 2003*a*; List and Pettit 2005). Republicanism, for example, requires public agencies to be contestable, in the sense that they can be called to account, forced to justify what they do in certain terms, and exposed to judgment for how far the justification works. If the groups involved do not incorporate, committing themselves to embodying a coherent set of purposes and representations, then they will not make such contestation possible. They can be as undisciplined in the views they jointly uphold as an opinion poll sample or the collection of people who happen to live in the same zip code area. But republicanism is not alone in suggesting that it would be undesirable for public bodies to be like this. As Ferejohn himself says, conversability is required in order to treat people's interests appropriately; and this, no matter what the criterion of appropriateness.

I think as a matter of fact that public bodies generally aspire to such coherence and conversability. The collegial court aspires to defend the position of the court over time, even if, like any individual agent, it occasionally sets aside past judgments as no longer exercising a presumptive, precedential constraint on its decision making. And the executive agency operates in the same way, committing itself to being able to give a coherent account of its decisions over time, though allowing for big breaks—as with a change of government—when a batch of prior judgments is set aside.

What of the legislature? Here I think that there are big differences between Westminster and Washington. In the Westminster Parliament, the necessities of upholding an executive mean that a more or less permanent majority is formed for the period of a Parliament and, being capable of controlling the legislature, it commits to a more or less coherent, contestable package of policies. Thus the Parliament assumes the profile of an agent, albeit an agent, once again, that sets aside many prior commitments when there is a change of government.

In the Washington Congress, things are very different, since parties are not disciplined by a need to uphold an executive and are not in a position to impose legislative programs. Each issue voted on has to find its own majority, and the upshot is that there is a much greater possibility of incoherence over time. Is this a serious problem? Not in general. Party leaders will have incentives to guard against incoherence; it doesn't make for good law, and doesn't go down well with the electorate. And besides, the courts serve an important function in interpreting congressional judgments in a way that preserves consistency.

John Ferejohn has an excellent discussion of some different ways in which bodies like these, and other corporate entities, might ensure the coherence that is required for agency. He takes me to task for suggesting that only smaller, cohesive bodies can ensure this. If I have ever suggested that—he finds the idea in Pettit (2003*b*)—then I withdraw the suggestion; I agree with what he says.

Drawing on that same source, Ferejohn also takes me to suggest that groups can achieve coherence and conversability only by relying on what I have called the premise-driven procedure, or a close variant; this would have members vote on the premises in any problem—on '*p*', '*q*', and '*r*' in our schematic example—and let the conclusion be dictated by logic. Here I do protest, as I have always tried to keep open the various ways whereby, as I see things, coherence and conversability may be achieved in a group. I don't think that it is even clear which propositions that give rise to a discursive dilemma can be regarded as premises and which as conclusion; whether a proposition in such a set counts as a premise depends on the subjective matter of whether it has epistemic priority in the thinking of the person or persons considering the dilemma.

I agree strongly with Ferejohn that it is more natural to allow that all propositions on which a group seeks to make a commitment, or indeed has historically made a commitment, ought to be regarded as being in play during the deliberative process. One procedure that I have suggested as natural for a democratic body, for example, is the rule under which every issue is first decided on a straw vote basis; if it gives rise to inconsistency with prior judgments, the set of troublesome commitments is identified; and then the group determines which judgment in that subset ought to be set aside in the cause of attaining group consistency (Pettit 2006*e*).

7. LIBERTY AND REPUBLICANISM

Into Politics

This takes us to matters of politics.[42] The previous section provides us with an idea of the sort of corporate entity that the state and other political bodies can

[42] I benefited in revising this section and some connected discussions from searching comments received from Brookes Brown and Philipp Koralus.

constitute. And the section before that identifies the practice of respect that is central to questions as to how the polity should conduct and organize itself. In this section we will look at the ramifications of respect for the role or conduct of the state, and in the final section at its implications for how the polity should be organized.

We saw in our earlier discussion of respect that this is a benefit that people cannot confer on one another as a gift. If I exercise virtual control over you, having the power and knowledge required for intervening with relative impunity in your affairs, then you cannot command my respect; I may offer you the trappings of respect, but that is all that I will be able to provide. The first, negative requirement for your commanding my respect is that I lack such control, not enjoying a balance of punitive power in relation to you: that is, a balance of power in the imposition of force, or the making of threats, or in resources of deception and manipulation. Unless this is fulfilled, I can only pretend to meet the second positive requirement, which is that I should be disposed to relate to you in reason-mediated and reason-friendly ways. No matter what his wishes, the master, as Hegel emphasized, cannot hope to remain master, yet reason with his slaves, at least not on an open range of topics. He can only reason with them if he reasons as an equal among equals, and so he can only reason with them after emancipation, not before.

Given that respect is not something that people can confer on one another as a gift, we can see why from the point of view of respect, the polity may be necessary. In a world of unequal power, standing, and possessions, the better-endowed people will not be able to confer respect on others, no matter how good their intentions. Respect cannot be conferred, only commanded. But a central, coercive power can hope to establish a world in which people enjoy mutual respect, insofar as it can put in place a framework that removes or reduces the extent to which some people control others, and so makes it possible for respect to flourish. It can hope to do this, at any rate, provided it does not itself impose in a way that is inconsistent with respect. At the same time that it facilitates the enjoyment of mutual respect among citizens, it has to limit its own power sufficiently to have citizens command its respect in turn, and command it equally.

If there is a single problem that dominates political theory, it is that of imagining and designing a state that can facilitate respect among citizens without undermining its own capacity to respect them: that is, in effect, without giving itself control over the lives and affairs of any of them. Moved by this concern, libertarianism argues, for example, that the state ought to respect the choices of citizens equally, in the way they should respect each other's choices, except when they opt for disrespectful acts of force or coercion and the like. It ought to nurture and honor the liberty of non-offending citizens, minimizing its interference in their affairs. It ought to assume just the nightwatchman role protecting citizens against internal and indeed external dangers, and of punishing those who offend.

Other philosophies offer other accounts of what respect requires (Dworkin 1978), including the version of civic republicanism—we might call it 'civicism'—that I favor (Pettit 1997*b*). This starts from the fact, ignored in libertarianism, that differences in cultural connections, property holdings, and natural assets can undermine respect between citizens, if not quite so dramatically as acts of violence and coercion. They will give some people virtual control over others—virtual, alien control—and the existence of such asymmetries of power will mean that the weaker cannot command the respect of the stronger. And this will be so, even if the stronger happen to be entirely benevolent. So long as their power is not reduced or restricted, the prospects for an inclusive regime of mutual respect among citizens will be very poor indeed. In principle, people might reduce or restrict their own power, alienating the resources required; but in practice there is little chance of this happening outside of a political regime.

The core idea in the republican approach is that the state ought to try to reduce the extent to which some have alien control over others, protecting each against the force, coercion, deception, and manipulation of compatriots and outsiders, but also empowering them against the effects of damaging asymmetries. And it ought to do this, in particular, while binding itself in such a way that it does not control the very citizens whose lives it regulates in that manner. It ought to guard citizens against the danger of *dominium* or private power without exposing them to the danger of *imperium* or public power. This philosophy, as we shall now see, is like libertarianism in giving central place to the single value of liberty. But this is liberty in a sense in which it requires more than the absence of interference.

Liberty, Control, and Interference

The earlier discussion of free will and free thought identified a capacity, orthonomy, with which it is plausible to identify what we might call psychological freedom. Possessing this capacity to track the right is enough for free will and free thought, even if its exercise is otherwise blocked. But possessing this capacity is not enough for freedom in other, non-psychological senses, as appears in the fact that you can be orthonomous and not be fully fit to be held responsible for what you do. The exercise of your psychological freedom may be disturbed by physical incapacity, natural impediment, or of course the social constraint associated with being under the alien control of others.

The ideal of being guarded against alien control by others, including control by the state, is equivalent to a certain ideal of social freedom or, as we may also say, liberty. We saw earlier that the encompassing sense of freedom in which it means nothing more or less than fitness to be held responsible requires both the ratiocinative capacity associated with orthonomy and the relational capacity associated with being able to command the respect of others. Liberty in the sense in which it requires the absence of alien control by others can be identified with this sort of relational capacity or status. Requiring the polity to be concerned with reducing control is equivalent to imposing a concern with the promotion of liberty.[43]

What are the more salient ways in which you may fall under the alien control of others? In the recent tradition, it is almost always said that you will suffer such alien control to the extent that one of three things happens. Others intentionally—or at least negligently (D. Miller 1984)—take away an option or options, as in rigging your opportunities or exercising force; they put a block in place. Or others intentionally or negligently transform those options, as in imposing a penalty or threatening to impose a penalty; they put a burden in place. Or others, finally, make a credible pretense that they or others or perhaps nature itself have put such blocks or burdens in place; they impose subjective rather than objective blocks and burdens. These forms of intervention exemplify what is usually described as interference.

In standard accounts, especially among libertarians, liberty is identified with non-interference.[44] But the identification of liberty with non-interference is mistaken, if liberty requires the removal or reduction of alien control. There are two reasons why it fails, as we shall see. Since both of these reasons derive from the observation that control comes in many varieties, it may be useful to make some comments first on the varieties of alien control—I shall often say just 'control'—that someone may exercise over another.[45]

We have already made use in our discussions of the distinction between active and virtual control. In the first case the controller is causally implicated in the control; in the second the controller allows the causal process to evolve under independent factors, but stands ready to intervene where intervention is thought necessary. But there are two other distinctions worth putting on the page, both of which cut across the first divide.

One is the distinction between direct and indirect controls. You are able to control what I do directly, so far as you have a power of intervention or

---

[43] Social freedom, even understood as the absence of control, may seem to be too narrow a concern for the polity, on the grounds that it does not give sufficient attention to material but non-social ways in which the exercise of orthonomy may also be affected (Van Parijs 1995). But this is not so. Ensuring your social freedom in the sense intended here will require eliminating those material and related disadvantages that expose you to control by others. And that is not all. Suppose that you do not suffer social control, but material limitations mean that you have few effective options available. Those limitations may not trigger control by others, but they will mean that your liberty won't be worth very much. They may not compromise liberty in the manner of social control, but they will condition the range and ease with which liberty may be exercised (Pettit 1997*b*); they will reduce the worth of liberty (Rawls 1971). Thus the focus on social freedom leaves room—though I shall not explore it here—for a concern with reducing the extent to which liberty is conditioned, not just the extent to which it is compromised.

[44] Some thinkers restrict the notion of interference, arguing that liberty is compromised only when the choice of a certain option is rendered impossible, with a block being put before it. See Steiner 1994; Carter 1999. But others may wish to extend the notion further to include various forms of deception and manipulation. I opt here for the standard, in-between account.

[45] I am indebted in what follows to a wonderful series of discussions in a reading class on liberty with some graduate students at Princeton University.

instruction in relation to me. You are able to control me indirectly, insofar as you have deputies who can act in your interest in controlling me or you have put constraints in place that can have the effect of more or less ensuring that I act in your interest. Active control may be direct or indirect, and so, obviously, may virtual control. The distinctions cut across one another to create four possible types of control.

But there is also a third distinction that we need to put in place, between personal and proxy control. This is the distinction between the control you enjoy when you are the ultimate, personal source of control, active or virtual, direct or indirect, and the control that you enjoy when the ultimate source of control is another agent, individual or corporate, who has the status of a proxy or surrogate. Like deputy-based control, proxy control requires you to recruit another agent to your service. But a proxy will still be quite distinct from a deputy. Whereas deputy-based control is indirect, we may say that proxy-based is oblique. Deputies are responsive to the manifest wishes of a principal, whereas proxies are not. They act on their own wishes, but, whether by nature or design, they are such that by doing so they satisfy the wishes of the principal as well; thus they relieve the principal of the need for personal action, direct or indirect. The fact that someone acts in a way that happens to satisfy the wishes of another, even happens to do so reliably, does not make that agent into the other's proxy, of course. The person whose wishes are served must employ the agent for that purpose if he or she can be said to exercise control via their agency. That principal may have created or helped to create the proxy, as in establishing a corporate agency that can serve the interests of the principal or principals; or may have selected a person or group to play the proxy role; or may have situated himself or herself so as to exploit the efforts of the proxy; or may have taken steps to keep the proxy in existence and on track. To the extent to which your proxy has to share your interests, any control that the proxy exercises over me will serve as a proxy for your control over me. Whether that control be active or virtual, direct or indirect, it will relieve you of any need to try to exercise such control yourself; it will serve the same function. Your interests will dictate what happens at my hands, not because they are your interests but, rather, for a more complex reason: that they coincide with the proxy's interests, and that the proxy is more or less bound to serve your interests.

Back now to interference. The first reason why liberty is not identifiable with non-interference is that you as the interferee may exercise virtual or indirect or proxy control over whether the interference is to continue. That interference may materialize under your prior instructions, or subject to your continuing assent, or under threat of your retaliating for its being unacceptable, or in a context in which certain pressures force it to track the directions that you would give were you able to issue directions. In any such case you will retain control over what is done, not suffer alien control; you will be free insofar as you maintain a balance of punitive power in relation to the interferer. You may be able to block any interference in your affairs that does not conform to your wishes; in that case the interferer will not be able to act at will against you. Or if the interferer can act at will, you may be able to impose a burden on any act of interference, thereby holding out a prospect of escalating costs that will effectively inhibit the interferer; this will mean that the interferer will not be able to act with the relative impunity that control requires. Or you may be assured that these things will be done by a deputy or a proxy; you may exercise indirect or oblique control over the interferer.

There are many scenarios where this structure prevails. When your financial adviser makes choices for you in the investment of your assets, the interference practiced is under your virtual control, and does not take away your liberty. When your friends make a choice for you in a case where you are not available to be consulted—it may be a choice, after an accident, over what surgery to have (Sen 1983)—then the fact that they are bound to follow your wishes means that you are in indirect control. When the management of the corporation where you work demands a contribution to a medical insurance plan, the fact that you can rely on the control of your trade union—assuming this serves as a proxy—means that if the demand in accepted, it does not have the aspect of imposition.

This observation means that interference as such may not take away your liberty. It will take away your liberty only insofar as it is uncontrolled by you, being perpetrated at the will or by the judgment of another, and being perpetrated without exposure to any cost that you may impose. Uncontrolled interference will make things worse for you, without making them worse for the interferer. It will take away your liberty insofar as it is an arbitrary form of interference: it is guided by an *arbitrium*, a will or judgment, that is not your own, and that may cut across your own with relative impunity. Controlled interference will not have this effect. Should the interference not satisfy the interests you avow, you will be able to make things worse for the interferer without making them worse for yourself; and so the interference will unfold under your direction.

But there is a second reason too why liberty cannot be identified with non-interference. This is that even when others do not interfere with you, they may have a degree of virtual control over what you choose. Only virtual control is relevant in this case, as indirect or proxy control will itself count as a form of active interference: it may be imposed at arm's length, or by an independent hand, but it will still have to be actively imposed.

Suppose that some others are so powerful and so positioned, then, that should they not like what you choose, or should they not like your having a choice to make, they can interfere with relative impunity in what you do; they can impose blocks or burdens on you. In such a case, you may actively control what you choose, perhaps being unaware of the presence of those others in your life. But those others will have a degree of ultimate control over your choices insofar as you can do what you do—or at least do it with impunity—only when they allow or permit you to do it. You will live, consciously or unconsciously, under their management. Whatever you do in fulfillment of your orthonomous preferences, you will do by their grace and leave. They will be masters of your life, even if they are utterly indulgent or indifferent and rarely resort to active interference.

If you become aware that others have such virtual control over what you do in some domain, of course, you may well begin to provide them with incentives for not actively interfering. You may censor what you do, so as not to put them offside; and you may try to curry their favor or ingratiate yourself with them. In short, you may try to keep them sweet. But such efforts, unlike the ability to block or burden any interference on their part, will not reduce the control they enjoy. On the contrary. Just as the offers of another will not put you under that person's control, but only expand the options that are available to you, so your overtures will have the same effect here. The powerful will be able to enjoy your favors and still impose their will, or, as they could always do, they will be able to impose their will without enjoying any favors; they will have an extra option at their disposal. The probability of their interference may be reduced, but, paradoxically, they will have an enhanced degree of control in your life.

Jeremy Waldron asks in his chapter whether the fact that others have the potential to interfere arbitrarily in your life need matter if there is only a very low probability of that potential being exploited. Others will have the potential to interfere arbitrarily in your life to the extent that attempted interference is neither blocked nor burdened. But we can now see that others might have that potential and be very unlikely to interfere, because of all the incentives you can provide to keep them sweet. Such a case illustrates the possibility denied by Waldron: that the potential which others have of interfering in your life can matter greatly to you, even when the probability of their interfering is close to zero. You may have provided incentives to reduce the probability of interference by the powerful close to zero—like Rigoletto, you may be a very charming court jester—but by that very token you will have emphasized and enhanced the control of the powerful over you.

The upshot of these considerations is that interference is neither sufficient nor necessary for a loss of liberty. It is not sufficient, because the interference of another may be subject to your virtual or indirect or proxy control; only uncontrolled or arbitrary interference will reduce your freedom. And it is not necessary, because you may be controlled by others without any active interference, direct or indirect, personal or proxy, occurring; they may have the virtual control that gives them a degree of mastery in some aspect of your life and affairs. Jeremy Waldron accuses me of eclecticism in designing a conception of freedom in which two distinct elements are emphasized: the arbitrariness point and the capacity point. I hope that this discussion of the connection between freedom and control will help to show why the two elements are intimately connected.

One final observation. In introducing the notion of control among people, I said earlier that I will control you only insofar as the balance of punitive power tilts in my favor. I can impose a block or a burden on you, and expect to be better off for doing so. I can make things worse for you without making them worse for me. This is an important key to understanding the notion of freedom in the sense in which it requires the absence of alien control by others, not just the absence of interference. For it means that just by having the capacity to burden my interference, not just to block it, you may avoid my control. And it means that when a third party can impose appropriate costs on my exercise of interference—or even when nature itself does so—then equally you may escape my control; and this, consistently with not being controlled by that third party either.

This observation is important, because it points us towards an ideal in which people may enjoy the absence of alien control by others—or, more plausibly, enjoy it in a high degree—even when the apparatus of protection and empowerment that secures this is relatively lightweight; even when compliance with the law emerges, as it does in most sectors of society, on a relatively willing basis (Tyler 1990). We do not have to see one another bound in straitjackets, nor do we need to have towering walls surround us, before we can credibly claim—and claim in encouraging awareness that our compatriots make complementary claims—to enjoy something close to the absence of control required for liberty. In the most harmonious society, of course, there will always be some who are prepared, even at enormous risk or cost to themselves, to try to impose on others; whatever of the poor, we will probably always have the psychopaths and the zealots with us. But this melancholy fact makes for a special problem, and one from which I abstract here.

The Republican View of Liberty

Liberty does not require the absence of interference in your affairs, then, but the absence of uncontrolled or arbitrary interference. And it does not require just the absence of such arbitrary interference, but also the absence of access on the part of others to arbitrary interference in your affairs. To the extent that another has access to arbitrary interference in your affairs, the other will be a master, or *dominus*, in your life. Thus, invoking ideas already current in classical Rome, we can say that freedom in the sense in which it involves the absence of control by others is freedom in the sense of non-domination. It requires living without subjection to a master: living without *dominatio*, or domination; living the life of a *liber*, or freeman, not the life of a *servus*, or slave (Pettit 1997*b*; Skinner 1998; Honohan 2002; Viroli 2002; Maynor 2003; Skinner 2007).

The tradition of associating freedom with non-domination was important not just in classical Rome, but also in the revival of Roman republican ideas in Renaissance Italy, in the England of the Civil War and Glorious Revolution, in America at the time of the War of Independence, and in the course of the French Revolution. It served in those places and periods as a base for expressing a dual demand on government: first, that government should protect each citizen from the dominating power of private parties, local and foreign; and second, that government should be constituted so as to offer a non-dominating form of public protection against private domination. In emphasizing those two more or less common demands, of course, I am selecting from a variety of ideas that were only partially shared across the different incarnations of republican thought, as Jeremy Waldron mentions. But I see no harm in doing so, provided that I do not misrepresent the exercise.

The first of the republican demands is a demand for guards against private power, or *dominium*, as I put it earlier; the second a demand for guards against public power, or *imperium*. For a number of reasons the emphasis in the tradition was mainly on the second demand. This is because the citizenry envisaged in politics, right down to the end of the eighteenth century, was invariably restricted to propertied, mainstream males, and the principal danger that they faced was from public power, not private. So long as the state gave citizens a reasonable standing before the law and protected them against outside danger, their personal resources would do the rest in ensuring them against private power. Not so with public power. There was little to ensure them against a government that was driven by the will of an absolute monarch, or a colonial state, or a self-serving faction, or anything of that kind. Government had to be strong enough to protect the borders, to establish a rule of law, and to guard against being taken over by a foreign power. But how was government to be stopped from dominating its citizens? The question was: *Quis custodiet ipsos custodies?* Who will guard against the guardians themselves?

Apart from the notion of liberty as non-domination, the second great legacy of republicanism was the suggestion that a certain sort of political constitution or dispensation, often taken to be exemplified by classical Rome, offered the one and only recipe for restricting government's power of domination without rendering government ineffective. This idea took many forms, as it was interpreted and applied in various contexts, but the recurrent elements are familiar. Since the constitution envisaged was most remarkable for the fact that it embodied elements of monarchy, aristocracy, and democracy—and since this mixing was taken to give it stability—it was often described as a dispensation for mixed government, a mixed constitution.

This dispensation required that the different sectors of society should be represented in a balanced government; that government should be run with an eye to the common good—the presumptively salient common good—of those in different sectors; and that various restrictions should be built into the way in which government is conducted to guard against a lack of balance and a failure to empower that common good. The protections envisaged became staples of political theory from the time of Renaissance republicanism down to our own day. They included the rule of law, the dispersion of power, election to office, limitation of tenure, and invigilation by an active citizenry who, ideally, would rotate in and out of office.

The republican idea was that the protection of the law and the state would help to ensure that no one was controlled by private parties, not even virtually; and that the constitutional framing of government would help to ensure that it was ultimately controlled by the citizens, even as it interfered in their lives with taxation and law and punishment. Thus the promise was that while the state and the law interfered with the citizenry in order to protect them from one another and from foreign dangers, this form of interference materialized under the control of citizens and would not be arbitrary and dominating in character.

It is one thing to say that government will not be a power of arbitrary interference in someone's life to the extent that that person has a degree of private control over how government interferes. It is quite another thing to say that it will not have such a power in the person's life to the extent that citizens generally have control over the interference. The assumption in the republican tradition, however, was that each citizen would control government, insofar as the citizenry as a whole reflected his or her interests—those held in common with others—and was able, as a proxy controller, to impose a direction and keep a check on the interference perpetrated. Under such conditions, it was postulated, the interference of government in people's lives would not be arbitrary, at least not in any substantive measure. We will return to this theme in the next section.

The upshot of this republican way of thinking about government is an image of free persons as citizens incorporated in a matrix of law and government that would empower each, giving them independence and standing in relation to one another and in relation to the power of law and government itself. This status would generally be a matter of common knowledge, and so the free person became cast as someone capable of walking tall, looking others in the eye, and not having to resort to the tawdry tactics of the subservient in trying to provide the powerful with incentives for not interfering. The free person would not have to fawn or toady or kowtow, not have to doff the cap, tug the forelock, or bend the knee, not have to seek anyone's leave or favor in the pursuit of ordinary business. To this day it remains an appealing image.

The republican ideal of liberty, as all of this makes clear, took the main bearer of liberty to be the person. You could be free only in a situation where you had or approximated a certain standing (Pettit 2006*c*; Skinner 2007). How did this standing relate to the freedom of your choices? A choice would not be free just because no one was disposed or even able to interfere; it would have to be the case that no one had this disposition or capacity because of your standing—in the case of the ordinary citizen, your standing in the law and culture. Nor would a choice be unfree just because the government used the law to interfere and rule out some option; this interference would not represent an offense against freedom if, in effect, it was licensed or mandated by the presumptively reliable proxy represented by the citizenry as a whole. Like the natural obstruction, such a restriction of choice would reduce the range within which you could exercise and enjoy your freedom as non-domination—and would be a bad to that extent—but it would not be equivalent to the dominating restriction of choice. It would condition but not compromise your liberty (Pettit 1997*b*: ch. 1); it would reduce the value or worth of your liberty, not the liberty itself (Rawls 1971).

Jeremy Waldron raises some interesting questions in this connection. One is whether freedom of choice or freedom of the person is prior. As just explained, the republican approach suggests that choices are free in virtue of the freedom of the person choosing, not the other way around; thus the freedom of the person is certainly prior to freedom of choice. But what of the relationship between the freedom of a person and the freedom of a society, to turn to another question of Waldron's? I think that the notion of a free person is intelligible independently of the notion of a free society, not the other way around, so in that sense priority goes to freedom as it applies to persons. But there is also something to be said on the other side. What makes persons free in the world we know is the protection and empowerment that the institutions of the free society give them. And those institutions give persons the defense required for freedom in the way that antibodies give an animal immunity to a disease. They constitute or establish people in their freedom; they don't bring freedom about just as a contingent, causal consequence (Pettit 1997*b*: ch. 3).

The Retreat from Republicanism

The republican way of thinking about liberty was challenged directly by Thomas Hobbes in the seventeenth century and, with lasting effect, by Jeremy Bentham and other utilitarians in the late eighteenth; they shaped the body of opinion associated with what came to be known as classical liberalism and, later, libertarianism.[46] Bentham and a growing group of followers and fellow-travelers argued for two views that directly challenged the tenets of classical republican doctrine. They held, first, that a choice is free if not interfered with, even when others have a virtual form of control over the chooser; and second, that it is unfree if interfered with, even when the interferer acts, like the ideal republic, under the ultimate control, virtual or indirect or proxy, of the interferee.

The shift from liberty as non-domination to liberty as non-interference had an enormous impact. It meant that even when citizenship began to be extended to include workers and women, as utilitarian reformers argued it should be, it remained possible to equate citizenship with liberty, without any revolution in the status quo. Neither workers nor women could be represented as free under

---

[46] Jeremy Waldron takes me to task for maintaining that Hobbes and Bentham espoused this approach out of ulterior motives. If I ever suggested that those motives operated as conscious designs, or were the only pressures operating in their thought, I am well rebuked. I absolutely agree that both figures had massive intellectual projects on hand, and that their thought was shaped in great part by where the logic of their projects took them, not just by local, historical influences. For the record, my reading of Hobbes has recently shifted. See Pettit 2005*c*.

the conception of liberty as non-domination, since they were manifestly under the control of masters and husbands according to the law and culture of the nineteenth-century world. The extension to them of liberty as non-domination would have required a revolution. But they could easily be represented as free under the novel conception of freedom as non-interference. They would be free, regardless of their lack of standing and power, so long as their masters and husbands chose not to interfere with them.

Not only did the shift in ways of thinking about liberty have this domestic impact. The change also made it possible to argue that a colonial power did not make the subjects of that power unfree. According to the new way of thinking, the citizens of any state, being subject to the coercion of the law, were deprived to that extent of their freedom. But then, so the argument went, the subjects of a colonial power were made unfree only in the same measure. There was no real contrast, not at least in the ledgers of liberty, between the position of the domestic citizen and the colonial subject. This argument was powerfully mounted by John Lind, a friend of the young Bentham, in a defense of the rule of the British Parliament over the American colonies (Lind 1776).

The effect of the new development in thinking about liberty was to break the connection between liberty and power: in particular, the power of the free person against other individuals, against the collective, and indeed against the sorts of corporate organizations discussed in the previous section. In the new perspective, the issue of concern with liberty was not how to give power to persons, enabling them to resist one another's alien control and command mutual respect. The issue was how to maximize the prospect of free choice. If the best prospect of free choice required radical disempowerment, as in the rule of a benevolent despot, then this was what the cause of liberty supported; the point was already made in 1785 by one of Bentham's most influential colleagues, William Paley (1825). No greater reversal of the republican perspective could be imagined.

Republicanism and Public Policy

We have seen that social freedom or liberty should be understood as the sort of liberty required for escaping the control of others and being able to command their respect. But in the natural course of things, that liberty is often lacking, with some individuals having so much more talent or property or standing—in a word, power—that they can exercise a degree of alien control over others. This effect may come about so far as the extra power gives them control over the affected individuals themselves or control over the way collective government is run.

Republican theory holds, in consequentialist vein, that social and political institutions ought to be organized so that the enjoyment of liberty is maximized and the practice of mutual respect enhanced.[47] The idea, as we have seen, is that this can and should be done by the efforts of the state in empowering and protecting individuals against one another, curbing *dominium*, or private power; and more particularly, that it can and should be done by a state that does not thereby assume an uncontrolled or arbitrary position in people's lives: it curbs *imperium*, or public power. The state will identify a range of choices wherein each individual should be protected from, or empowered against, the control of others: these areas of choice will count as the liberties entrenched in the system. And, all going well, the state will implement this program in a manner that does not expose people to an arbitrary degree of control on its own part.[48]

We turn in the next section to the issue of how the state can guard against itself perpetrating an arbitrary form of control. But it may be useful, before leaving this, to explore the sorts of measures that the republic might take on the first front, looking at the kind of public policy that it is likely to support. Since policy depends so heavily on empirical as well as normative assumptions, however, it is not possible to say much. I will restrict myself to some illustrative observations on the impact that the republican ideal would have in three areas of policymaking: social security or welfare, criminal justice, and foreign relations.

The main issue in welfare policy is how far the state should go in drawing on the funds provided by taxation to ensure people in general, and in particular the poor, against those forms of dependency that derive from inadequate resources, lack of education or information, medical need, and reduced access to justice. Without considering the sort of intervention that the state might make in these areas, we can see that non-interference theorists will think, first, that any intervention involves coercive taxation, itself an instance of the very loss of liberty that should be prevented; and second, that the interventions made may not be required by liberty as non-interference, so far as dependency fails to trigger actual interference by others. They will be able to make only a very uncertain connection between the promotion of freedom as non-interference in itself and the establishment of a welfare system. A line that might attract many will be to say that rather than having the state tax the rich to help the poor, we should rely on the philanthropy of the rich to have this effect—we might even provide tax breaks to facilitate it—and ensure people only against the most extreme cases of emergency.

The view that a republican perspective would support is very different (Pettit 2006*d*). On this approach, the taxation needed to build a social security system

---

[47] Should the target for maximization be equal liberty or just liberty? I think that this may not matter, since the best way of increasing liberty at any point will be by further equalizing it, as argued in Pettit 1997*b*: ch. 3; see too Lovett 2001. But I am happy, if this proves necessary, to make the goal equal liberty, rather than liberty as such.

[48] The issues of choice wherein the state will protect and empower people constitute the standard liberties. Notice that on the republican approach these liberties will have a unity, deriving from the fact that their protection, intuitively, is going to be required for the standing of the agent as a free person amongst persons. It will not be an ad hoc list.

may not count as domination, and so not as the primary sort of offence against liberty; it may represent a suitably controlled, so non-arbitrary, form of government interference. More on how this might be the case in the next section. And on this approach, the provision of welfare may count as essential for protecting people against dependency, and the consequent loss of republican liberty; it may be necessary, even when the dependency does not trigger active interference. Welfare provision will be a more acceptable policy option, then, on the republican approach; and the condition of dependency against which it is designed to protect will be a less tolerable social ill; indeed, it will not be a social ill that even philanthropy can rectify, since philanthropy reinforces dependency. There will be a lighter burden of justification in arguing for welfare provision, and there will be a heavier benefit available to outweigh that burden.[49]

One aspect of social organization that is crucial to welfare policy is the property system—the allocation of titles and rights of ownership—that the law supports. I think of the state as intervening in a form of social life in which there will always already have been property conventions in place and an associated pattern of mutual interaction and individual reliance. This means that there will be a default presumption in favor of the claims sustained under those conventions. Nonetheless, the cause of freedom as non-domination may still require reorganization or redistribution on the property front; this will be required when poverty-related dependency triggers domination.[50] I am at one with Jeremy Waldron when he insists that the concept of freedom should give us a resource for thinking about the shape that the property system should assume. But I agree with him from a distinctive viewpoint. The ideal of liberty provides us with a standard by which to assess the property system and determine amendments that ought to be made to it, but the enforcement of the amended system need not impinge on the liberty—the freedom as non-domination—of those who live under it. The enforcement of the system will restrict people's choices, conditioning them in the same way as natural obstacles, but it will not compromise this liberty in the way that uncontrolled or arbitrary interference would.

Republican thought has an equally salient lesson for criminal justice, though again it is not possible to elaborate it in the absence of empirical guidance as to the effects of different policy initiatives (Braithwaite and Pettit 1990; Pettit 1997*a*, 2002*a*). The lesson is that the criminal justice system should be designed, first, to criminalize only those activities that are directly inimical to liberty

---

[49] These observations would also argue that paternalistic interventions designed to guard people against the certain dangers—say, requirements that they insure themselves medically or in other respects—may be easier to justify in the name of freedom as non-domination than in the name of freedom as non-interference.

[50] It may also be held to be required when poverty restricts or conditions the range or ease over which freedom as non-domination can be enjoyed. As mentioned in n. 43, I am abstracting here from the case for relieving such conditioning of liberty as distinct from relieving the domination that compromises liberty.

as non-domination: these will be acts intentionally or negligently designed to impose control on someone; and, second, to impose sanctions that will serve to undo and guard against the harms done to such liberty, and only those harms.[51]

What are the harms done to liberty as non-domination by the uncontroversially criminal act; say, an act of theft? They fall into three categories. First, a person's exercise of liberty as non-domination will be restricted or conditioned by the loss of resources—the worth of that liberty will be reduced—just as it might be restricted by a natural accident involving the loss of the object stolen. Second, the victim's liberty as non-domination—the person's protected status—will be denied or compromised by the assumption of a dominating power, and the assertion of alien control, on the part of the thief; this would not be a distinct harm under the notion of liberty as non-interference. And third, the general prospect of suffering such ills will increase with the occurrence of the crime; the quality of protection available to people generally will have been put in question, with a consequent loss of confidence.

The criminal justice system should impose a sanction that is commensurate with the relative culpability of an offender in committing such an act. And the sanction imposed should serve, to the greatest extent possible, to redress the problems occasioned by the crime. First, the sanction should help to provide restitution or compensation for the victim, something that may be feasible with theft but not in many other cases—above all, not in the case of murder. Second, it should serve to vindicate the protected, undominated status of the victim or the victim's ilk. And third, the sanction should be of a kind that helps to reaffirm the level of protection that the crime put in question, providing a deterrent for offenders generally and restraining or deterring the offender in the case at hand.

These ends are going to be hard to achieve, and they will be particularly hard to achieve under standard assumptions about the role that the state should play in the area of criminal justice. When the system is run as a hierarchically organized exercise, with the full power of the state at issue in every instance, there are multiple dangers: that the state or community will get cast as the main complainant, rather than the victim; that the only controls envisaged in deterrence of crime will be heavy-handed penalties; and that the state will connive in what Montesquieu (1989: 203) described as a 'tyranny of the avengers', giving punitive expression to the horror and outrage that crime naturally elicits.

One of the main voices of protest against these dangers has been John Braithwaite, and in his chapter he reminds us of the case for instituting the sorts of conferences supported by the restorative justice movement; in certain areas these can be made available as an alternative to the ordinary courts (Braithwaite 2002).

---

[51] Whether to criminalize and sanction a liberty-inimical activity will be determined by how far criminal sanctions can be productively imposed. Activities that escape sanction under this provision will still be subject to blame and condemnation, of course, and the civic culture of an ideal republic might be expected to inhibit and reduce their incidence.

The defendant in such a conference, admitting culpability, is joined by nominated friends or family to discuss with the victim and the victim's chosen companions the best way in which amends can be made. This sort of process makes it feasible to achieve the three outcomes discussed. It facilitates the provision of whatever compensation is available, it makes room for a powerful form of victim vindication—the credible apology of the offender—and it activates controls of an informal, networked sort that often promise to be more effective than direct, state controls. The republican approach to criminal justice makes room, quite comfortably, for this sort of institution.

The striking advantage of republican theory in this area is that it provides a plausible, consequentialist goal for the criminal justice system to promote—the enjoyment of liberty as non-domination—yet does so without running the risk, often associated with consequentialism, of confusing the criminal justice system with a system for the regulation, even manipulation, of potential offenders. On the approach taken here, punishment is appropriate only when it serves, perhaps among other ends, to express condemnation and blame, and, consequently, punishment should be directed to undoing the harm done to the victim. Yet, according to the line taken, punishment should also be shaped to a beneficial, social purpose: that of promoting the enjoyment of liberty as non-domination. It is not a mechanical exercise of punishment for punishment's sake, or punishment for the sake of providing payback, or anything of such a mindlessly retributivist kind.

Nicola Lacey is generally sympathetic in her chapter to the line I take here, but she draws attention to one important danger. She is supportive of the way I understand responsibility, congenially emphasizing the extent to which it makes room for character and attributability to character, as well as bare accountability. But she points out that celebrating the fact that criminal justice applies only to the blameworthy—insisting that it must in that sense be fair—can cover up the rather less palatable fact that often the system serves in a divided society to legitimate a form of regulation that demonizes those on the receiving end. That problem has to be addressed in any comprehensive consideration of how to institutionalize criminal justice.

I welcome this caution. It forces us to recognize that the criminal justice system involves many different, interacting components, ranging from the system of criminalization to the surveillance regime, to the routines of arrest and prosecution, to the court hearing and sentencing procedures, to the institutions for the imposition of sanctions (Braithwaite and Pettit 1990). No policy in the area can afford to concentrate on one component in this complex system to the neglect of others. If I have concentrated here on issues of sentencing and the treatment of convicted offenders, that is only for want of space.

The third area of policy that is worth commenting on briefly is that of international relations. The ideal of liberty as non-domination has a distinctive resonance in this domain, as in a number of others. The reason is that it gives us reason to worry not just about the active interference of one state in the affairs of another—military, diplomatic, commercial, or whatever—but also about the imbalances of power that may affect a society.

If the society that certain individuals belong to is dominated by another agency, in the sense of being exposed to the arbitrary interference of that power in its affairs, then, other things being equal, those individuals themselves are subject to such a controlling power. Their fortunes will tend to ebb and flow with the fortunes of their own society, and if the society's fortunes are hostage to an alien power, then so are their own. The domination of a society or a people may come about when another state has a greater degree of interfering power; but it may also materialize when multinational corporations or churches or other movements have that sort of power in relation to the society. After all, such organizations, like states, are going to have the profile of agents according to the account given earlier. And their power of interference in the affairs of a society and its people may be quite considerable.

If the domination of societies by foreign states and multinational organizations is cause for complaint, according to the republican ideal of liberty, then what correctives are available? The only remedy on offer for weaker societies is going to be one of multilateral action. This may take the form of affiliating and making common cause with similarly situated societies, say in a trade bloc. But equally, it may take the form of signing up to international treaties and organizations, and to the rule of international law and convention. The first, partial association with others might be described as plurilateral; the second, encompassing kind as totilateral.

Establishing international associations, plurilateral or totilateral, does not necessarily mean introducing a world state or even regional state-like entities, such as the European Union. While any system of mutually supportive states will require continual monitoring and maintenance in order to counter centrifugal, free-riding pressures, there is no reason in principle why it should not be able to survive. It should be kept in place by the continuing interest of the affiliated parties; it should strengthen with the appearance of interlocking networks, connecting the authorities and officials of the different societies (Slaughter 2004); and, given enough debate about matters of common concern, it should generate a recognition of some minimal values that are recognized on all sides, regardless of other differences, as relevant to the resolution of shared issues (Rawls 1999).

In his chapter John Braithwaite emphasizes the extent to which networks of international control have actually materialized, giving us power, not just as citizens of our countries, but as denizens with claims in many lands. These networks, he thinks, hold out the prospect that individuals at the nodes of governance that these networks make possible can exercise forms of protective control, to the benefit of ordinary people. The idea is that the United Nations committee, or the standard-setting body, or the non-governmental organization, can serve in the protection of ordinary individuals against domination, including the domination of their own state. I warmly agree, subject to the proviso that he himself emphasizes (Pettit 2006*b*). This is that those bodies are themselves subject to control in the interests of ordinary people, being forced to give an account of themselves on agreed terms and being accessible to effective contestation. This theme will recur in discussion of democracy.

8. DEMOCRACY AND REGULATION

From Republican Control to Democracy

Republican thinking argues that the state is necessary to protect people's liberty as non-domination on a variety of fronts. But equally, as we have seen, it argues that the state itself must conduct its business in such a way that it is not a dominating presence among them. It must not undermine the regime of respect to the extent of becoming an uncontrolled source of interference in their lives and affairs. The state must be a public affair, a *res publica*—a commonwealth, a free state—and must answer to the wills of members of the public, not be imposed on them as an alien form of control.

The state inevitably interferes in the lives of citizens, whether in taxing them, legislating for them, or penalizing them for a breach of the law; and this interference, we may suppose, is required for purposes of promoting their freedom as non-domination. But the idea is that the interference practiced should be itself under the control of citizens, and to that extent not represent a form of domination. It should contrast sharply with the interference of the civicly uncontrolled state like the absolute monarchy or the colonial regime. It should contrast even with the rule of the benevolent despot; while the despot may have interests in common with citizens, there is no constraint requiring that this be so.

According to republicanism, non-arbitrary interference in a person's life is equivalent to the sort of interference that that person controls. But the interference practiced by the state in someone's life cannot be subject to the control of that particular person, of course, short of his or her enjoying a veto power over government. So how can republican theory avoid giving everyone a veto—impossibly—over what government may do?

The answer that is assumed implicitly in the republican tradition has three elements:

- The corporate people can control government, whether through exercising or constraining state power.

- Specifically, the people can control government for the perceived common good: that is, in the public interest.

- Consequently, the people can control government as a proxy that acts for the perceived interests of individual members.

The republican image of the free state, the undominating commonwealth, exemplifies a certain conception of democracy, though the word 'democracy' was not traditionally used in this context (Manin 1997). The *demos*, or people, considered as a corporate or quasi-corporate entity, is to have *kratos*, or power, over government, with things being organized so that the controlling *demos* acts for a goal—the perceived, common interest—that goes proxy for the personal interests of individual citizens. Democracy is understood in a corporate way. And it is justified on the grounds of promising to do well by interests with which each citizen can identify.

In what follows I sketch the broad outline of the democratic theory that the approach supports by looking in some greater detail at each of the three elements distinguished. I emphasize that this is a sketch, based on existing publications (Pettit 1999; 2000*a,b*; 2001*b*; 2003*a*; 2004*b*; 2006*b*). I hope to develop it further in later work.

The People can Control Government

The first element in the approach involves recognition of the people as a sort of corporate entity in which individuals unite for the pursuit of certain ends. We know that incorporation normally requires members of a corporate body to intend, however implicitly or reluctantly, that they together act for a certain body of goals according to a certain body of judgments; goals and judgments may be identified by reference to a list or, more plausibly, by a procedure for generating them. Each of the members is willing to do his or her bit, however small, in ensuring this result; each does this, at least in part, because of expecting that others will do their bit in turn; and all of this is above board, as a matter of common awareness.

Clearly, it is possible for the members of a polity to incorporate in this sense. Two extreme ways in which they may do so are represented by what Hobbes sees at one end of a spectrum as the democratic mode of incorporation and at the other as the dictatorial mode of incorporation associated with monarchy. Democratic incorporation requires each member of the group, assuming that others do likewise, to authorize majority opinion in assembly voting; Hobbes is insensitive to the problem of the discursive dilemma. Dictatorial incorporation requires each member, assuming that others do likewise, to authorize a single individual to speak on behalf of the group as a whole. In the one dispensation the assembly's majority voice is to identify the goals and judgments of the people incorporate; in the other the dictator's say-so is to serve in this role.

Majoritarianism and dictatorship, so understood, represent two different technologies of group formation. We know that the majoritarian technology is flawed, since it will generate inconsistencies in the face of discursive dilemmas. Putting this flaw right won't be easy, given the size of the assembly envisaged here (Pettit 2003*a*, 2006*e*). But let us assume that it can be rectified, with the assembly being disposed, as under the straw vote procedure, to monitor and resolve any issues of inconsistency that arise from its majority judgments. Under each of these technologies, then, quasi-majoritarian as well as dictatorial, the people can act as a collectivity: a corporate agent.

This is all that is needed to support the first element in the republican picture. But we should notice that there are many technologies whereby the people in a polity can form a group agent that lies between these two extremes. In a quasi-majoritarian assembly, members of the people keep the formation of goals and judgments in-house. In dictatorial authorization, they outsource this exercise completely, giving it over into the hands of the monarch. But clearly, there are many possibilities that lie in between.

When they require something to be done in the name of the group, the assembly or dictator may have to play an active role themselves or identify suitable agents to act for them. What distinguishes each mode of collective formation, then, is that there is a divide in time and logic between the formation of will and the enactment of that will, whether by the members or by hired enactors. But that observation suggests a wholly different kind of group formation. In this mode, the enactors would be appointed prior to the formation of a particular will, not after it. And they would be able to act on behalf of the group, but only subject to the indirect or virtual or proxy control of members. Indirect control might take the form of prior instruction, virtual control that of monitoring with a capacity for intervention, proxy control that of organizing things so that they are subject to a controller with similar interests.

This novel mode of group formation has two aspects to it. On the one hand, the members of the group authorize enactors to act for them; they thereby make themselves the ultimate authors of what the enactors do. On the other hand, the members impose limits and checks on what is done by the enactors in their name, much as an editor, rather than an author, might do. The structure is one of authorization combined with editorship. The editorial controls, like the controls that any editor might put in place, will include prior guidelines or instructions on what should be done; monitoring and occasional intervention in amendment or reversal or what is done; and the introduction of regulatory devices—rewards or penalties—for making sure that it is in the interest of enactors, or certainly not against it, to act as the group requires.

Where the assembly and dictatorial modes of group formation are top-down, with the assembled or dictatorially represented people giving instructions to enactors, the authorial–editorial model is interactive. It requires a continual to-and-fro between the people and those who act in their group name. Not only will members be active in appointing enactors, then, they will also be active in invigilating the enactors in government for the extent to which they are in breach of guidelines, or in conflict in some other way with the presumptive goals or judgments of the people. They will be active, not just in electing to government, but in contesting what is done by government. Some individuals may be appointed as authorized invigilators, in which case their contestation will automatically carry weight. When private individuals contest what the enactors do, their challenges will presumably be given weight only if they are upheld in some designated forum.

This picture of how the people can control government may seem to occasion problems insofar as the people, as such, never or hardly ever acts; it is always individuals, or small groups of individuals, who act in its name. But this, as we know, is not a reason for thinking that it is purely an interpretive conceit to ascribe control to the people. Our discussion of incorporation should have made clear that while it is always one or more individuals who do the things the people does, it is the people together who ensure that there will almost always be some individuals in place to do those things. The people can program for what its members produce.

The People can Control in the Public Interest

Let something be in the perceived, common interest—for short, in the public interest—if people are robustly disposed to avow it as a common interest, where robustness means that they are disposed to avow it as a common interest across most times, scenes, and moods. The question to which we now turn is whether there is a mode of incorporation under which we might reasonably suppose that the people will control government in the public interest, so understood.

If the people incorporate under a dictatorial constitution, then there is little or no prospect that they will be able to control government so that it is in the perceived, common interest. There is nothing to stop the dictator working for his or her own interest, and only the most implausible of Hobbesian arguments would suggest that there is likely to be a coincidence of that private interest with the interest of the public.

The prospect of the required sort of control may look a lot better if people incorporate under the assembly model: say, with a modification of majoritarian voting that builds in safeguards against discursive dilemmas. But still the prospect does not look very good on that scenario either. For, as the long tradition has it, there is always going to be a threat of majoritarian tyranny in such an assembly. Let there be a stable minority whose interests diverge from those of most members, and there will be a real danger of government being conducted in a way that does not respect their interests. And if government does not respect the interests of such a minority, it cannot be in the perceived, common interest; its policies will not be ones that members of the minority are robustly disposed to avow as common.

Democracy by assembly is close to the ideal envisaged in Rousseau's (1973) *Social Contract*, but he sought to get around the problem of majoritarian tyranny by requiring people always to vote with a view to matters of shared and not divisive concern, legislating in a rule-of-law manner. This protection will not be very secure, however, unless more is done than Rousseau contemplates to impose such a constraint. And there is a serious problem that the successful imposition of the requirement would bring in its train. The assembly would not be able to lower its gaze and pay attention to what is done in particular application of its general decrees by the ministers it appoints; and such enactors, therefore, would be able to interpret and implement the laws in their personal or factional interest (Urbinati 2006).

The authorial–editorial model, happily, offers a much more promising method for enabling the people not just to control government, but to control it in the public interest. I sketch a defense of this claim, looking first at how we should understand the public interest and then at what the prospects are, under an authorial–editorial design, for ensuring that the people will control government in the public interest.

The perceived, common interests of people incorporating in a group should not be identified with the common, perceived interests shared amongst members of the population: the interests, in other words, that are at the intersection of different people's sets of recognized, personal interests. There may be only a small overlap between such pre-given, personal interests (Waldron 1999). And whatever overlap exists may wobble wildly across time, as people's interests and perceptions shift (Goodin 1996).

But if the public interest of a people or group is not determined by the overlap of their personal perceived interests, what is its relation to such interests? The connection I propose is that the perceived, common interests of a group are those policies or measures that satisfy the following, higher-order condition: it is in the perceived personal interest of each that the group as a whole promote those measures or policies on a collective and, if necessary, coercive basis. Although some policy may not be in someone's personal interest, in view of the greater appeal of certain alternatives, it can still be in that person's higher-order interest: it can be in their interest that there be a collective, coercive agency—in effect, a government—that enforces that policy (Barry 1965; Pettit 2004a). Policies that do not fall at the intersection of people's personal interests, this being a small and unstable set, may satisfy the higher-order condition, and such policies will count in my usage as being in the public interest.

It is entirely plausible to suppose that there are some policies that fit the higher-order condition and count as in the public interest. The condition will obviously be satisfied by conventions that need to be collectively and coercively imposed, like driving on the right or left of the road; here no one minds on which side people drive, provided they drive on the same side. But it will also hold with norms over which people have rival preferences, as with rules that determine the titles and rights of ownership. It will presumably be in everybody's interest to have some system of ownership in place, even though any one system chosen will suit some more than others. Or at least that is likely to be the case insofar as the system is egalitarian in the intuitive sense of treating individuals as equals, displaying equal concern and respect for all (Dworkin 1978).

But is it going to be too easy, perhaps, for policies to fit the higher-order condition and count as in the public interest? Not on plausible, empirical assumptions. Imagine a system under which the policies in force are generally unobjectionable, by any criteria. The introduction of a policy that treats some people with less than equal respect will not be in the public interest, since it will not be in the interest of each that there be a government that enforces that policy. There is likely to be a rival, non-discriminatory policy that the government could enforce instead, where that has a much more plausible claim to be in the public interest. The empirical assumption behind this judgment is that a government can remain in power, whether or not it enforces this or that particular policy on a given issue; government policies are not a tight package that have to be accepted or rejected as a whole. That plausible assumption is challenged most famously by Hobbes, who argues that there is no alternative to accepting an absolute sovereign, and living with whatever the sovereign dictates as law. According to Hobbes, it is in the public interest that there be such a sovereign, and in the public interest, therefore, that the sovereign impose whatever laws are actually imposed. But this rather outlandish judgment is driven by the assumption that government is available only on a take-it-or-leave-it basis; there is no room for picking and choosing amongst policies in judgments as to what is in the public interest.

So much for the characterization of the public interest. We turn now to the question of how far an authorial–editorial mode of incorporation is likely to force government to track the public interest.

A constitution that is designed to force government in this direction will have to press those in power to advance all policies that are in the perceived, higher-order interests of individuals and prevent government from pursuing initiatives that do not satisfy that condition. It will have to work against two sorts of failure, then: the false negatives involved in missing acceptable policies and the false positives associated with mistaking or misrepresenting unacceptable policies as acceptable.

The authorial constraints on government are the constraints whereby the selection of those in government is determined. They may require the popular, periodic election of at least legislative representatives, for example, and the approval of legislators for appointments to other offices, executive and judicial. They may put constraints on the conduct of elections, ensuring equality at the polls and guarding against abuses in the financing of candidates, in the representation of party positions, in voting and counting votes, and in other such areas. And equally, they may put constraints on the office that should be created and on how they should be filled. They might require the establishment of unelected officials and bodies for determining policies in areas where elected representatives have special interests: this, as with a central bank or an electoral, districting commission. And they might impose strict conditions of public scrutiny, or super-majoritarian support, for appointment to various offices, executive and judicial.

These authorial constraints can serve the purpose of guarding against both false positives and false negatives.[52] This is most obvious on the electoral side, though the point may also hold with unelected appointments. By forcing elected representatives to seek out popular support in competition with one another, they can raise the prospect that where a policy looks likely to be in the higher-order interest of voters, one or another party will espouse that initiative, hoping thereby to increase its electoral support. And by giving voters the power of combining to eject a party from government, the authorial constraints can help in some measure to deter those in government from pursuing policies that do not further the public interest.

Notoriously, however, electoral, authorial constraints do not do very much to guard against false negatives. They may allow the tyranny of the majority under which the members of a stable minority are treated as less than equal. And they may allow the tyranny of an elite whereby those in government, or their immediate cronies and supporters, are treated as more than equal. But it is possible, at least in principle, for such abuses to be reduced or removed by appropriate editorial constraints.

Editorial constraints of the kind I have in mind are prominent in the republican tradition of celebrating the mixed constitution or dispensation. Under this constitution, even in its earliest, Roman form, room is left for electoral, authorial constraints, since the people are given a role in selecting those who will govern in its name (Millar 1998). But the more striking aspect of the mixed dispensation is its emphasis on editorial control, in particular on a sort of control that would force government to treat citizens as equals. Not only can the people collectively check government insofar as they fail to re-elect it. They can check it in other ways insofar as they force government to act under specific constraints. As we saw, government is always to be conducted via the rule of law, not by ad hoc decree; legislation, adjudication, and administration are to be carried out in conditions of public access, on the basis of considerations about the common good; such business is to be pursued in different ways at different centers so that, at the least, there is more than one legislative house, and there is an independent judiciary; and it is to be subject to the contestation of an active citizenry or appointed invigilators: in republican Rome, famously, this role was played by the tribunes of the plebs.

---

[52] I prefer this way of putting things to a formulation I have sometimes used, according to which electoral constraints have both an authorizing and an editorial role. There is no difference of substance involved, only one of presentation.

Further Remarks on Editorial Control and Contestation

This is not the place to explore in detail the sorts of editorial constraint that might be imposed on government, giving us a basis for arguing that the people controls government in the public interest. But it may be useful if I say something on the ways in which the people can enforce editorial, contestatory control, and the currency in which contestation can be made, when contestation is actively pursued.

The people as a whole may contest government in editorial mode when large numbers take part in widespread protests, in manifestations of a hostile public opinion, or in movements of civil disobedience. This represents an exercise of active, direct control over government or, as it may be, an attempted exercise of such power. But there are also other, less melodramatic examples of such control, associated with the imposition of various impersonal constraints on government. Such constraints may require government to rule by general, open, predictable law, for example, rather than by ad hoc decree; to provide suitable reasons in justification of what is done, whether in the legislature, by executive agencies, or in the courts; and to have to persuade a number of bodies, often bodies with different interests, to endorse certain sorts of initiative: this, in the way in which two houses of legislation may have to approve a bill, or a court may have to approve of the measures in some area that an executive proposes to take.

But just as the corporate people can control government actively and directly, so they can do so actively and indirectly or actively and obliquely. Indirect control will involve the use of deputies, oblique control the use of proxies.

Those elected to a legislature serve an active editorial purpose, giving the people indirect control, when they interrogate what government intends to do in congress or parliament. And those appointed as statutory officers will also serve in that way when they call a government to book for a breach of accepted codes in financial accounts, in statistical reports, or in any other aspect of its performance. These sorts of agents are deputies of the people, employed to serve according to a more or less closely defined brief.

Just as active editorship may be indirect, or mediated by deputies, so it can be oblique, or mediated by proxies. A proxy will be an individual or body that acts in a manner that is more or less bound to serve the perceived interests of the people and that is recruited for that purpose by the people: the recruitment may take the form of allowing or protecting or encouraging relevant agents and actions or, in the case of corporate entities, actually creating or contributing to suitable agents. Consider the individual or movement of individuals that takes government to court for breach of the constitution, or challenges government in a public hearing or tribunal, raises a complaint with an ombudsman, or mounts a media campaign. Such agents may often serve as proxy controllers for the people as a whole. They are forced to articulate their complaints in suitable contestatory terms—more on this in a moment—and they are required to make their case before a suitable tribunal, if only the tribunal of public opinion. And so they may be expected to serve fairly reliably as organs whereby government can be kept under appropriate, popular check.

These observations show how the template provided by the mixed dispensation allows for many varieties of popular, editorial control over government. There is active, direct control, as in the mass mobilization of public opinion, in waves of civil disobedience, and in the impositions of various constraints on government. And there are many other forms of active control, indirect and oblique. But it is important to recognize that even if such active forms of control are not undertaken, the people may still enjoy corresponding virtual forms of control over government. Insofar as the collective people can take action against a government and organize disruptive opposition, it will have a degree of virtual control over what government does. And the same is true insofar as private individuals or appointed officials are poised to contest what government claims to have a right to do in the people's name. No government can afford to neglect the impact its policies may have in arousing such protest; and so it will to that extent be virtually controlled by the people.

This brief overview is designed only to give a sense of the battery of ways in which the corporate people, in an extension of the traditional, mixed dispensation, may impose control on government and realize the republican image of democracy. The people authorizes the properly appointed government to speak and act in its name, within the terms of the accepted dispensation. And the range of editorial checks imposed on government helps to ensure—actively or virtually, directly or indirectly or obliquely—that the government does not breach its brief.

So much, then, for the ways in which the people can enforce editorial control over government. An essential part of this editorial regime is that people are able to challenge and contest what government does, in presumptively accepted terms. But what are the terms in which they can do this? Where is the contestatory currency to come from?

The terms of contestation will be set in some part by the recognition of certain rights and constraints in a constitutional document or in a tradition of making and interpreting law; a constraint like *habeas corpus* can have documentary or just customary standing. These terms will be fleshed out by further traditions of judicial interpretation, by the appearance of stable conventions in the legislative branch, and by the terms of reference that come to define expectations for performance in different executive agencies. But still, such terms will facilitate only limited forms of contestation, in particular forms fitted for parliament itself, for the courts, for various tribunals, and the like. If a contestatory regime is to be effectively established, then citizens will need to be able to challenge government on a broader front, in a less regimented currency of protest. And where is such a currency to be found?

My suggestion is that as people in any democracy debate policy, they will inevitably valorize certain common considerations as relevant to the determination of law and policy, and of the procedures for forming law and policy, even if they weight those ideas differently. Unless their discussions go straight to a shouting match, they will take the form of a mutual exchange where each side offers the evaluative considerations supporting its point of view, each side admits at least the relevance of the considerations offered on both sides, and difference is generated and explained by a different weighting of those considerations, or by a different view of certain empirical facts. Such discussions will be pursued across the society, now in this public forum, now in that, now in the context of one private exchange, now in the context of another. And as they are pursued in such diverse but connected settings—even, indeed, as lines of dissensus harden—there will be a common valorization of shared evaluative premises.

The ideas that are widely accepted in advanced democracies today include familiar assumptions: that citizens must be treated as equals; that public opinion should not be ignored; that expert testimony on a range of questions should be taken into account; that there are important limits on the invasion of private space by government; that government has responsibility for helping out the victims of local, natural disasters; that no member of the society should die for want of access to nutrition or shelter or basic medical aid; that those in government should not use public funds for private gain; and so on, through an indefinite range of considerations.

None of these considerations is interpretively closed or determinate; they may look so open, indeed, as to have the character of motherhood statements. But on any interpretation, they will still rule out certain extreme laws and policies, making them close to unthinkable, as they will rule out various procedures for breaking the competition between acceptable candidates. And the very fact that they are interpretively open means that they can supply guidelines for certain groups to push for more specific interpretations and for novel—even radical—departures in policy. The civil rights movement, the women's movement, various multicultural movements, as well as movements of a more conservative character, typically grow out of a particular interpretation of considerations that everyone recognizes as relevant to public policy; they are successful or not, depending on whether they manage to give those interpretations a grip on the imaginations of citizens.

In order for contestation in courts or tribunals to be successful, there has to be provision in law for striking down legislation or policy or even for altering decisions already made. And in order for electoral and parliamentary contestation to be effective, it has to be clear when a government will be put out of office or a bill overturned or a government forced to open its books. But how can more diffuse, popular contestation, framed in terms of putative common values—the sorts of considerations raised—be given force and impact? It will have an impact so far as there is a sufficient sense of fragility and shame among those in government for a high level of public opposition to elicit adjustment and response. It should ideally be possible to expose government to serious pressure, not just by resort to formal channels, but also by less formal kinds of contestation, whether with ombudsmen, or in the media, or on the streets.

The image of a contestatory dispensation in which members of the public have powerful editorial control over government, as well as the authorial control ensured by election, should be reminiscent of the image of the well-ordered society in the later work of John Rawls (1993, 1999, 2001). This is the society that is governed by public reasons that are accepted on all sides as relevant for assessing government; they define the terms in which government can be challenged and forced to justify itself. Just as I have been suggesting that common valuations will emerge as part of the building of consensus and dissensus that occurs in any democratic society, and will be available as a currency of contestation, so Rawls thinks that ideas capable of providing public reasons and of defining the outlines of a public conception of justice will make an appearance in any long-lived democracy. As he says, 'the political culture of a democratic society that has worked reasonably well over a considerable period of time normally contains, at least implicitly, certain fundamental ideas from which it is possible to work up a political conception of justice suitable for a constitutional regime' (Rawls 2001: 34–5).

Not only is the position outlined here reminiscent of Rawls in this respect. It also connects in another way. Rawls (1999) argues that when a society is well-ordered—even, indeed, when it is decent enough to approximate such an order—the state can be seen as representative of the people; it is the people, under a political form of organization. The well-ordered people can speak with one mind and voice, and is capable therefore of taking its place in a dispensation of mutual respect among similar peoples (Pettit 2006*f*). Unlike the disordered people that is subject to a usurper state, and unlike the unordered populace who live without any effective state, the well-ordered people enjoys a corporate control of its own affairs. Although Rawls does not put it this way, such a people, or *demos*, has the power, or *kratos*, sufficient for democratic rule.

Once we recognize the importance of editorial controls in a democratic regime, we can see the possibility of states or peoples forming international networks, or acquiescing in the formation of such networks, without any serious compromise to democracy. We can look without despair at the growth and strengthening of what Rawls describes as a law of peoples. As John Braithwaite emphasizes in his chapter, a conception of democracy in which editorial control is at the center can extend naturally to encompass international as well as domestic centers of power (Pettit 2006*b*). Those centers of power will be on a democratic leash insofar as they are bound by sufficient editorial constraints. And that being so, they can in principle serve as suitably controlled sources of protection and empowerment for ordinary people; they can be part of Braithwaite's widening circle of accountability.

The People can be a Proxy Controller for its Members

And so, finally, to the denouement. On the republican approach, democracy should help to make government non-arbitrary, enabling those who live under its coercive edicts to see such acts of interference as materializing under their control, forced to track their personal interests. We can now see, at least in principle, how government might be established so that this is true.

Let government be controlled by the corporate people in the authorial–editorial mold described, and its policies will be more or less constrained to track the public interest: to avoid the false negatives that lie to one side, the false positives that lie to the other. Thus, on our conception of the public interest, it will be more or less forced to track the perceived, higher-order interests of individuals. And so the authorial–editorial control of the corporate people will represent a form of proxy control exercised on behalf of those individuals. They will be able to look on the government interference under which they live as non-arbitrary and undominating. They will be able to see the government as operating under the control of the people, and they will be able to see the people as a proxy that they help to sustain, that they may even help to direct, and that they will in any case rely on for protection against government abuse. That, at any rate, is the ideal.

It is the ideal, but unhappily, it goes well beyond the reality, of course, even in the most advanced democracies. This gives us reason to deplore how things actually stand in contemporary democracies, though not a reason to resile from the theory. For while the theory presented picks up many strands in democratic institutions and in democratic thinking, it is a virtue of the theory that it provides a normative, potentially critical stance on the ways in which things are actually organized. Take any contemporary democracy, and the investigation of how it can be brought more into line with the requirements of the authorial–editorial model is likely to generate a host of plausible revisions.

But suppose for purposes of our argument that the conditions required for authorial–editorial control by the people are fulfilled, and that the dispensation is in place. The lesson that is important from our point of view is that even if someone were in the minority on a policy implemented under majority support, it would still be in that person's perceived interest that there be a government that imposes the policy. The arrangement would ensure against the arbitrariness of government, even in such hard cases; it would provide reason for saying that still the person commands the respect of those in government. It would do this, indeed, even in the especially hard case where not only is someone in the minority on a policy, but by sheer bad luck, the policy is particularly damaging to the person's individual interests.

You may have voted against setting up a local prison, for example; you may be in a minority on the issue; and the location selected for the prison, as luck would have it, may be in your back yard. On the scenario envisaged, you will not be dominated by the government that taxes you for the prison and then builds it uncomfortably close to your house. The interference of that government in your life will restrict the range or ease of your choices, as natural obstacles might do, but it will not be arbitrary and dominating, or at least not in a serious measure. It will materialize under the control of a corporate body that acts as your proxy, as it acts as proxy for others in the population.

But there is still one dangling issue. Let us suppose that the dispensation and the government of a country is under the proxy control of the *demos* so that the forms of interference imposed on ordinary people are not arbitrary. Even on this supposition, it has to be admitted that people will not generally have chosen to live under such an arrangement and, worse, that they will not generally be able to opt out. They may be allowed to emigrate, and they may succeed in getting another country to accept them, but they will not be able to find any place on earth where they can live as independents, free of the centralized coercion of a polity. Doesn't the necessity of having to live under the centralized authority of a polity—or under the authority of one or another alternative—already impose arbitrarily on people? Doesn't it mean that, no matter how benign the form of centralized government, people are already dominated by the fact of its inescapability?

One reaction to this problem might be to require, with Rousseau, that people unanimously assent to being governed, as signatories to a social contract. But such a demand would make it impossible in the real world ever to have a non-arbitrary polity. For even if one generation unanimously selects a constitution that allows for government, that constitution will come to future generations as something imposed by the dead hand of the past. This fact, notoriously, led Jefferson to suggest that a new constitution should be selected every twenty years or so.

I think that Rousseau's and indeed Jefferson's responses to the problem of the unchosen constitution are misconceived. It is a fact of nature that everyone is born into society with others and, in our world, into a society in which important affairs are managed collectively and in which there is no escape from such a condition: there is too little unoccupied territory to allow dissidents or independents to make a unilateral decision against social and political life. No one imposes that situation arbitrarily on anyone; it is simply a natural necessity. Railing against being born under an unchosen constitution is like railing against gravity, or against the climate: it amounts to treating an impersonally sourced limitation as if it were a voluntarily imposed restriction. It makes sense to rail against a constitution on the grounds that it is sub-optimal, but not on the grounds that it is unchosen.

If individuals were to take their personal baseline options to include the option of living out of society, of course, or of dictating the dispensation under which to live with others, then the fact of not being given a choice over the dispensation under which they are born would represent an arbitrary form of interference. But it would be fanciful of individuals to view society from that solipsistic perspective. Their baseline options, in the nature of human life and history, are confined to options in which they work out their fate together with others. The point is given particularly robust grounding in the argument against social atomism that I sketched in the section before last (see Pettit 1993*a*: ch. 6).

The necessity of being born into society, under a going political dispensation, means that no one can expect to be given a choice as to whether to live in society, or to live under this or that dispensation, or to live under this or that government. No one can make a claim, in the name of freedom as non-domination, to protection against such eventualities. The only claim that people can make is to protection against being subjected to a dispensation that is not under their joint, equal control—say, because it gives all power to a dynasty or to a subset of its members. And that claim is fully respected on what I see as the republican model of democracy.

Regulation in Public Life

It remains to address one final topic. This is the issue of how we can ensure, or help to ensure, that officials in republican democracy will behave to the required standard, and will not abuse the positions of power to which they are elected or appointed. How can we boost the checks and balances built into the mixed constitution, regulating public officials so that they behave as the ideal requires them to behave? How can we guard against the possibility of corruption, with the authorities ruling, not in the common interests endorsed under the accepted dispensation, but in the interests of a faction that they represent, or a pressure group to which they are susceptible, or their own personal welfare?

There are two perspectives from which we might assess the prospect of regulating against corruption. One would suggest that people are all already corrupt, being ready in any position of power to serve their own needs or the needs of those who bribe them most effectively. The other would argue that while people are not inevitably corrupt, while they are generally sensitive to the claims of others, or to the duties of office, they are certainly corruptible (Pettit 1997*b*: ch. 7). Let them be exposed to the temptation to serve themselves with impunity, and few will remain uncorrupt.

The assumption behind this second approach is underlined by the story of the ring of Gyges. Few of us can feel confident that given a ring that enabled us to satisfy our interests and passions without any possibility of redress—the ring would make us invisible to others—we would remain as faithful to law and morals as we may currently be. And similarly, so this lesson would go, few of us can feel confident that given a position of unconstrained power, we would retain whatever humdrum honesty and virtue we now possess. Lord Acton drew on a long republican tradition in saying that all power corrupts, and that absolute power corrupts absolutely.

Were we to assume that all people are naturally corrupt, then we would be tempted to resort to a pessimistic policy for the regulation of public officials. We would look, in the words of Mandeville (1731: 332), for a dispensation that "remains unshaken though most men should prove knaves". But it would be empirically rash to make this assumption rather than the less committal assumption that people are naturally corruptible. And it would be politically reckless. There is now considerable evidence that working with the pessimistic assumption, as with a worst-case scenario, would be bad regulatory policy (Frey 1997; Frey and Jegen 2001). It would support incentives, say of fear or avarice, that can undermine whatever virtue is spontaneously available. And it could lead thereby to a worsening of performance, rather than an improvement.

I prefer to think of the regulatory challenge from the point of view of the less pessimistic assumption of corruptibility. Given this perspective, it is going to be important to have procedures of election and appointment to office that select the sort of people who may be expected to have a high degree of spontaneous virtue and public spirit; the procedures should screen in those we would naturally want in office, and screen out those we would not want there. With suitable personnel in authority, then, the next step would be that of arranging the options they face, and the sanctions to which they are subject, in such a way that whatever motives of public spirit they have will be reinforced, not undermined, by those extra pressures.

The regulatory regime I envisage is not unlike that which is invoked in *The Federalist Papers* (Madison, Hamilton, and Jay 1987), particularly in the papers that were penned by James Madison (White 1987). Both principles are supported in the summary claim, from *Federalist 57*:

The aim of every political constitution is, or ought to be, first to obtain for rulers men who possess most wisdom to discern, and most virtue to pursue, the common good of the society; and in the next place, to take the most effectual precautions for keeping them virtuous whilst they continue to hold their public trust.

There are two aspects, then, to the regulation that a well-ordered republic requires. First, a selectional aspect, involving the election and appointment of officials. And second, a sanctioning aspect, involving the construction of the options over which officials can decide, and the creation of rewards and penalties fit to increase the likelihood of their making decisions in the public interest. The mixed dispensation described already makes a lot of room for appropriate pressures on both fronts. The selectional constraints are relevant in the authorial dimension of popular control, the sanctioning constraints in the editorial.

On the selectional side, as mentioned, the mixed dispensation operates with a system of election and appointment. The system of election can be warped by all sorts of pressures, usually associated with campaign finance needs, as we know from ordinary democratic experience. But it should ideally serve to identify and select those who can pass muster in the public eye and survive the scrutiny that an independent media ought to be capable of bringing to bear. And the system of appointment ought to be capable of finding the best and most reliable people available for various posts. Certainly it will do this if the elected individuals and bodies who make the appointments do so under suitable scrutiny and in accordance with accepted guidelines.

Among the appointments that elected representatives should be required to make are ones that have the effect of limiting their own power. There are many areas in which elected representatives will have a special interest or be subject to special pressures. In these areas, then, there is a serious ground for requiring representatives to set up offices and bodies that operate at arm's length from their control, and that hand down policies or recommendations that it will be hard for them to contest. I gave the example in this context of a districting commission, but I might equally have mentioned a central bank or the sort of body that might give advice on sentencing policy. A central bank body can relieve elected representatives of undue constituent pressure to lower interest rates; a sentencing commission can guard them against the outrage of constituents in the immediate aftermath of any gruesome crime, and the unthinking demand for heavier criminal penalties (Pettit 2002*a*, 2004*b*).

What is there to say about the desirable regulatory regime on the sanctioning side? The important thing is to have sanctions that can target the appropriate personnel, but without inducing a loss of spontaneous virtue. Bruno Frey (1997: 16–17) argues, on the basis of empirical research, that there are three conditions under which sanctions may support virtue rather than supplant it. First, the motivation provided does not suggest that the agent needs to be controlled from the outside. Second, it does not reduce the agent's self-esteem. And third, it does not obscure the presence of virtuous motivation when the agent complies (see too Pettit 1995*a*). Monetary rewards or stiff penalties are likely to violate all three conditions. They certainly suggest that agents need to be controlled externally; they send a negative image to agents as to what motivates them; and their presence means that if agents comply, this will be put down not to virtue but merely to the effect of the sanctioning incentive. The question, then, is whether there is any other sort of sanction that avoids these problems.

My answer to that question, over a long period, has been that there is one particularly striking sort of sanction that measures up very well (Pettit 1989, 1990, 1993*a*, 1997*b*; Brennan and Pettit 1993, 2000, 2004). This is a sanction that does not strictly require the sanctioners to do anything in response to the action rewarded or penalized. It consists in the formation of a good or a bad opinion about the agent, in circumstances where it is more or less salient that such an opinion is formed. The perceived formation of such an opinion will serve as a sanction, negative or positive, insofar as agents care about what others think of them. And that people care about the opinion of others is a platitude of common sense, a routine observation of social psychology, and a centerpiece of Western and other traditions of thought.

Suppose that there are certain criteria that are more or less generally accepted for the evaluation of conduct in a certain domain; within a divided society this condition will not always be fulfilled, as Nicola Lacey points out in her chapter, but it should apply with public officials. Suppose that things are arranged so that how agents behave is subject to the scrutiny of others, as a matter of common awareness. If an agent does well or badly in such circumstances, then we may expect the esteem sanction to come into play; the agent will suffer or avoid shame, even perhaps win a little honor. Those who do the sanctioning in such a case will not be voluntary enforcers of the code; they may not even want to be there, imposing the penalty or the reward. They may be involuntary police in the regulation of the person's behavior.[53]

The economy of esteem, as we may describe this sanctioning regime, satisfies the conditions required for not undermining virtue. Let the economy work to get people to behave well. Since esteem is given out of a belief that agents are acting from relevant forms of virtue, it cannot suggest that they are in need of external control. Since it is precisely a form of esteem, it can only reinforce the self-esteem that agents already enjoy. And since the reward is given on the basis of attributing virtue, it certainly does not hide any virtue present. The economy may activate a dubious motive in people, but the presence of that motive promises to reinforce whatever virtue they have, or indeed to elicit it for the first time, not to drive virtue or the concern for virtue away.

We all manifestly live in a world in which we are exposed to the gaze of others and are expected to behave according to certain standards. Certainly public officials live in a world of such exposure and expectation. Thus, we may confidently expect that those in government will be moved by the sanctions of esteem to live up to what we expect of them. The pressure of the sanctions may not elicit compliance in every case, but it ought to make it more likely that compliance will be forthcoming. Under suitable conditions of exposure and expectation, the desire to be honored, as John Locke (1975: 353–4) predicted, ought to help people to be honorable.

There are a number of conditions other than those of suitable exposure and expectation that are likely to be necessary for the operation of this economy in people's lives (Brennan and Pettit 2004). One, as I have argued elsewhere, is freedom of speech (Pettit 2002*b*: essay 3.4). Take a domain in which people are unfree to speak their minds about certain others, being subject to their power, and now imagine a case in which they say nothing in commentary on something those others do. Imagine, in particular, a case where we expect that did they disapprove, and were they free to express that disapproval, they would do so.

---

[53] Rae Langton is absolutely right to point out, however, that we can easily envisage a scenario in which people, preferring not to be taken to disapprove of certain others—say, others in a position of power or authority—induce attitudes of approval in themselves; only by doing this can they be assured that they will not be taken to disapprove. Such attitudinal adaptation is, alas, all too easy to imagine. But I assume, I hope not too optimistically, that it is not going to be absolutely ubiquitous.

Their not saying anything in such a case will tell us little or nothing about whether they approve or disapprove. Their silence will have been disenfranchised by their lack of freedom, and the operation of the economy of esteem will have been suspended.

Rae Langton discusses my argument about this issue in her chapter. She points out that while the lack of freedom in my sense may indeed be inimical to the economy of esteem, I go too far in suggesting that the presence of freedom of speech will generally be sufficient to unleash the effects of this economy, enfranchising silence. I am persuaded by the points she makes. Even if people are free to speak out in a certain domain, there may still be various costs associated with speaking out, and these can inhibit speech and leave their silence, when they are silent, disenfranchised. The costs may simply be those of making themselves or others unhappy. Why speak out when there is no hope of improving things? If silence is to be enfranchised, and the economy of esteem is to work effectively, then the freedom to speak must not only be uncompromised by the domination of others, to use language introduced earlier; it must also be unconditioned by the impersonal obstacles that can impede and inhibit people.

But if the external requirements for the economy of esteem are more demanding than might be expected, the internal ones are less so. The operation of the economy does not require an active desire for esteem, only its virtual presence in people's motivation. Suppose that people, public officials included, normally act out of habit or routine or whatever; this is surely a plausible hypothesis. The concern for esteem may still have an effect on their performance insofar as it remains the case that should such springs of action fail, or should they lead people to behave against the standards that we expect, then the red lights will go on; people will become aware, with a consequent effect on their behavior, that they may lose esteem or fall into disesteem unless they mend their ways. And if that is the case, then even when they give no thought to considerations of esteem, they may still be behaving within the constraints that a concern for esteem supports. The lash that the economy of esteem lays to their backs may be effective, but intangible.

The economy of esteem holds out the prospect of a regulatory regime that ought to be very attractive, and, understandably, its appeal was long recognized in the republican tradition (Pettit 1997b: ch. 7). It suggests that there is an alternative to the iron hand of the state, which coerces people to behave on a collectively beneficial pattern, and the invisible hand of the market, which wrests a collectively beneficial pattern out of people's self-serving, commercial behavior. Like the first sort of regime, it transforms people's motivation; like the second, its effects are often silent and unfelt. We might describe it as an "intangible hand".

In conclusion, it is worth mentioning one feature of the intangible hand that ought to make it particularly attractive. It avoids the enforcement dilemma that has routinely been raised as a problem facing any proposal to the effect that norms can help people behave in a more public-spirited or virtuous way than they would otherwise do (Buchanan 1975: 132–3; Heath 1976: 156–8; Axelrod 1984: 1098; Taylor 1987: 30). The question raised is why we should expect people to be sufficiently virtuous to enforce norms if they lack virtue to the point of needing to have norms enforced. Let enforcement be required and, since virtue must then be in short supply, it is not going to be available; let enforcement be available, and, since virtue must then be available, it is not going to be required.

The answer to this problem, under the intangible hand, is obvious. Since people do not do anything in applying the intangible hand, thereby enforcing the standards associated with it, they do not have to be particularly virtuous to enforce it. The enforcement of norms under the economy of esteem is costless. So enforcement is likely to be available even when the cost of virtuous behavior is high. The intangible hand may enable people to bootstrap themselves out of failures of virtue, lifting themselves to a level of performance that would otherwise be inaccessible.

9. CONCLUSION: SOME UNIFYING IDEAS

It may be useful in conclusion to highlight some of the main threads that help to join the dots. As I look over this summary presentation of the material discussed in the chapters in this book, I am struck by the prominence of six themes to which I return again and again.

The first is the idea that, while no novel, higher-level forces come on stream at any point in the organization of worldly bodies, there is a program architecture present in the way in which many entities and areas are organized, and this provides reason for not being riveted on lower levels and finer grain. Things are put together in such a way that patterns at higher levels can program for what ensues, even if the events that ensue are ultimately produced by processes at the lowest, subatomic scale, operating by the simplest, most general laws. The boiling temperature of the water can program for the collapse of the closed flask, even when that collapse is triggered by a single molecule. The representations and motivations of agents can program for their actions, even when those actions are the product of neuronal discharge. The policies embraced in common by members of an incorporated collectivity can program for what is done in the group's name, even when those initiatives are always taken by individual agents.

A second theme that bulks large in the preceding presentation is that while agency is a simple and basic phenomenon, it is capable of the most wonderful elaboration, as a result of meta-propositional and meta-perceptual representation. Agency involves the capacity to represent an environment and to act for the realization of certain goals, according to those representations, and is illustrated even in the little robot that moves about a table, setting cylinders upright. But agency becomes ratiocinative as agents come to be able to represent propositions and to seek out meta-propositional beliefs—say, about the coherence of various propositions, or their evidential support—and to use those beliefs as checks on the formation of their attitudes. And agency becomes conscious as agents come to be able to represent perceptions—the perceptual ways things are—and to interrogate them for their representational properties: for how they make things seem to be. The key to each development, on the analysis offered, is the agent's capacity, not just for representation, but for recursive representation: for the representation not just of the properties instantiated in things, but of the properties represented in lower-level representations.

The third theme that stands out is that creatures like us do not come to be able to reason on our own. We depend on our interactions with one another for the capacity to identify stable guidelines—firm meanings—by which to orientate, when we ask what we ought to think in this or that instance. We start from the assumption that, answering to this or that spontaneously mastered word, there is an objective referent, available in common to all; and we use one another in order to triangulate on the identity and implications of that shared concept. Our interactions at this basic level create a tide on which we all rise; resourced by a common fund of interactively tested concepts, we become individually capable of thought and reason. And not only do we depend on one another for the capacity to ratiocinate; we are equally in one another's debt for the ability to operate as persons, speaking for ourselves and assuming responsibility for our avowals and promises. Without other voices we would lack the reality test needed to establish common intellectual markers; without other ears we would lack the conceptual space needed for becoming commissive creatures, capable of giving our word as from one person to another. Trying to reason or personate out of community with others—out of any community, at any point in one's life—would be like trying to clap with one hand.

The fourth theme is that the capacity to reason, scaffolded as it is in human interaction, is the great emancipator. It enables us human beings to identify the personal ideal of exercising orthonomy or conversability—sensitivity to commonly recognized reasons—and to embrace the associated freedom of will and thought. Modulating into co-reasoning, it enables us to rally around the communal ideal of deliberative exchange: a regime of mutual respect in which we deny ourselves access to any mode of influence over others beyond that which is mediated by reasoning together. And, making it possible for us to come to a common mind on the value of enjoying such respect, it provides us with a benchmark by which to determine when it is right, and when it is not right, to live by the strict terms of the regime itself; it gives us a consequentialist criterion by which to regulate our fidelity to that regime.

This fourth theme has a negative as well as a positive side. The control that deliberative exchange may give you over me, as I make a certain choice, will leave me still wholly orthonomous and free. With every option in that choice I will still be able to think, and think rightly: I can do that; it is up to me. You will not have diminished my capacity for choice, and you will not have put any block or burden, real or purported, in the way of the choice; your control will be wholly unalienating. This means, then, that the ideal of deliberative exchange casts into relief the range of actions and relationships in which choice is affected in those negative ways; they will represent alienating or alien forms of control. The ideal provides a standpoint from which to indict exercises of manipulation, force, coercion, and deception; and to indict relationships in which one party has the power to resort to such acts against others, so that whatever the others do is done only so long as the stronger party gives them leave.

The fifth theme that I see in the material evolves from the simple idea that when one factor controls another—when it serves to make the other more probable than it would be in its absence—it need not be the case that there is active or causal influence involved. The control may be virtual rather than active, as when a stand-by factor intervenes only on a need-to-act basis. Such virtual control occurs at different sites: within individual agents, within corporate agents, and between different agents, individual and corporate. Beliefs and desires may often control only virtually for what individual agents do, as when people act on blind habit; and the same may be true indeed of interests, such as people's interest in esteem, or the values that they cherish. Again, the bulk of the membership of a corporate agent may control only in a virtual way for how their organization behaves; they may be stand-by controllers who intervene, on a need-for-action basis, only if the organization departs from its brief. And finally, of course, one agent may virtually control another, as in the case of domination. The agent who has the power of interfering forcefully or coercively in another's choices exercises control over those choices, even when no interference is practiced: nothing that happens in such a case happens without their implied approval or permission.

The sixth theme in the material is the use made of the ideas just rehearsed in thinking about issues of politics. There are two sides to this, both related to what I think of as republican theory. The first is that we should think of the liberty of an individual in society as requiring that others do not have any alien control over that individual. The absence of alien control means the absence of manipulation, force, coercion, and even deception at the hands of others. But it also means the absence of that virtual form of alien control that others will enjoy insofar as they are able to resort to such forms of interference in the life of the person. It constitutes liberty in the republican sense of non-domination.

The other political use of the foregoing ideas is in the articulation of the republican conception of democracy, as I called it. This conception makes important use of the notions of active and virtual control and of the further distinction within each category between direct, indirect, and oblique control. Indirect control involves the use of deputies who track the wishes of the controller, oblique control the use of proxies who may act on their own wishes but are so constituted that what they do tends to satisfy the controller. The corporate people, organized on an authorial-editorial model, may serve as a proxy for individuals, because of a commitment to acting in the public interest: that is, for the perceived common interests of members. And the corporate people may operate on all channels of control, active and virtual, direct, indirect, and oblique, in order to keep the government true to the needs of the public interest. The people may assume such rich lines of control that we have no hesitation in thinking that this is a democracy; this is a regime in which the *demos* has *kratos*, the people has power.

REFERENCES

Axelrod, R. (1984). *The Evolution of Cooperation*. New York: Basic Books.

Bar-On, D. (2004). *Speaking My Mind: Expression and Self-knowledge*. Oxford: Oxford University Press.

Baron, M., P. Pettit, and M. Slote (1997). *Three Methods of Ethics: A Debate*. Oxford: Blackwell.

Barry, B. (1965). *Political Argument*. London: Routledge.

Braithwaite, J. (2002). *Restorative Justice and Responsive Regulation*. New York: Oxford University Press.

——— and P. Pettit (1990). *Not Just Deserts: A Republican Theory of Criminal Justice*. Oxford: Oxford University Press.

Brennan, G. and P. Pettit (1993). "Hands Invisible and Intangible". *Synthese* 94: 191–225.

——— ——— (2000). "The Hidden Economy of Esteem". *Economics and Philosophy* 16: 77–98.

——— ——— (2004). *The Economy of Esteem: An Essay on Civil and Political Society*. Oxford: Oxford University Press.

Broome, J. (2004). "Reasons". In *Essays in Honour of Joseph Raz*, ed. J. Wallace, M. Smith, S. Scheffler, and P. Pettit. Oxford: Oxford University Press.

Bruner, J. (1983). *Child's Talk: Learning to Use Language*. New York: Norton.

Buchanan, J. (1975). *The Limits of Liberty*. Chicago: University of Chicago Press.

Burge, T. (1998). "Reason and the First Person". In *Knowing Our Own Minds*, ed. C. Wright, B. C. Smith, and C. Macdonald. Oxford: Oxford University Press.

Byrne, A. (2001). "Intentionalism Defended". *Philosophical Review* 110: 199–240.

Canning, J. P. (1980). "The Corporation in the Political Thought of the Italians Jurists of the Thirteenth and Fourteenth Century". *History of Political Thought* 1: 9–32.

Carroll, L. (1895). "What the Tortoise said to Achilles". *Mind* 4: 278–80.

Carter, I. (1999). *A Measure of Freedom*. Oxford: Oxford University Press.

Chalmers, D. (1996). *The Conscious Mind: In Search of a Fundamental Theory*. New York: Oxford University Press.

Clark, A. (2006). "That Lonesome Whistle: A Puzzle for the Sensorimotor Model of Perceptual Experience". *Analysis* 66: 22–5.

Cummins, R. (1983). *The Nature of Psychological Explanation*. Cambridge, Mass.: MIT Press.

Dennett, D. (1979). *Brainstorms*. Brighton: Harvester Press.

——— (1987). *The Intentional Stance*. Cambridge, Mass.: MIT Press.

Devitt, M. (2004). "Pourquoi il est si difficile de faire un monde: contre in response-dependence. globale", trans. Olivier Massin. In *La Structure du Monde: Objets, propriétes, étals de chose: renonveau de la metaphysique dans l'École Australienne,* ed. Jean-Maurice Monnoyed. Paris: Vrin.

Dietrich, F. and C. List (forthcoming). "Arrow's Theorem in Judgment Aggregation". *Social Choice and Welfare.*

Dretske, F. (1999). *Knowledge and the Flow of Information.* Stanford, Calif.: CSLI Publications.

Durkheim, É. (1938). *The Rules of Sociological Method.* New York: Free Press.

Dworkin, R. (1978). *Taking Rights Seriously.* London: Duckworth.

Evans, G. (1982). *The Varieties of Reference.* Oxford: Oxford University Press.

Fischer, J. M. and M. Ravizza (1998). *Responsibility and Control: A Theory of Moral Responsibility.* Cambridge: Cambridge University Press.

Fodor, J. (1983). *The Modularity of Mind.* Cambridge, Mass.: MIT Press.

Frankfurt, H. (1969). "Alternate Possibilities and Moral Responsibility". *Journal of Philosophy* 66: 829–39.

Frey, B. (1997). *Not Just for the Money: An Economic Theory of Personal Motivation.* Cheltenham: Edward Elgar.

—— and R. Jegen (2001). "Motivation Crowding Theory: A Survey". *Journal of Economic Surveys* 15: 589–611.

Gilbert, M. (1989). *On Social Facts.* Princeton: Princeton University Press.

Goodin, R. E. (1996). "Institutionalizing the Public Interest: The Defense of Deadlock and Beyond". *American Political Science Review* 90: 331–43.

Goodman, N. (1969). *Languages of Art.* London: Oxford University Press.

Harman, G. (1990). "The Intrinsic Quality of Experience". *Philosophical Perspectives* 4: 31–52.

Heath, A. (1976). *Rational Choice and Social Exchange.* Cambridge: Cambridge University Press.

Honohan, I. (2002). *Civic Republicanism.* London: Routledge.

Hurley, S. (2002). *Justice, Luck, and Knowledge.* Cambridge, Mass.: Harvard University Press.

Jackson, F. (1982). "Epiphenomenal Qualia". *Philosophical Quarterly* 32: 127–36.

—— (1986). "What Mary Didn't Know". *Journal of Philosophy* 83: 291–5.

—— (1992). "Critical Notice, S. Hurley Natural Reasons". *Australasian Journal of Philosophy* 70: 475–87.

—— (1998). *From Metaphysics to Ethics: A Defence of Conceptual Analysis.* Oxford: Oxford University Press.

—— (2003). "Mind and Illusion". *Philosophy,* supp. vol. 53: 253–73.

—— and P. Pettit (1995). "Moral Functionalism and Moral Motivation". *Philosophical Quarterly* 45: 20–40. Repr. in F. Jackson, P. Pettit, and M. Smith, *Mind, Morality, and Explanation.* Oxford: Oxford University Press, 2004.

—— —— (1998). "A Problem for Expressivism". *Analysis* 58: 239–51.

—— —— (2002). "Response-Dependence without Tears". *Philosophical Issues* (supp. to *Nous*) 12: 97–117.

—— —— (2003). "Locke, Expressivism, Conditionals". *Analysis* 63: 86–92.

—— —— and M. Smith (2004). *Mind, Morality, and Explanation: Selected Collaborations.* Oxford: Oxford University Press.

James, S. (1984). *The Content of Social Explanation.* Cambridge: Cambridge University Press.

Johnston, M. (1989). "Dispositional Theories of Value". *Proceedings of the Aristotelian Society*, supp. vol. 63: 139–74.

_____ (1993). "Objectivity Refigured: Pragmatism with Verificationism". In *Reality, Representation, and Projection*, ed. J. Haldane and C. Wright. Oxford: Oxford University Press.

Kornhauser, L. A. (1992*a*). "Modelling Collegial Courts. I. Path-Dependence". *International Review of Law and Economics* 12: 169–85.

_____ (1992*b*). "Modelling Collegial Courts. II. Legal Doctrine". *Journal of Law, Economics and Organization* 8: 441–70.

_____ and L. G. Sager (1993). "The One and the Many: Adjudication in Collegial Courts". *California Law Review* 81: 1–59.

Kripke, S. A. (1982). *Wittgenstein on Rules and Private Language*. Oxford: Blackwell.

Kukathas, C. and P. Pettit (1990). *Rawls: A Theory of Justice and its Critics*. Cambridge: Polity Press.

Lewis, D. (1983). "New Work for a Theory of Universals". *Australasian Journal of Philosophy* 61: 343–77.

_____ (1986). *Philosophical Papers*, ii. Oxford: Oxford University Press.

Lind, J. (1776). *Three Letters to Dr Price*. London: T. Payne.

List, C. (2006). "The Discursive Dilemma and Public Reason". *Ethics* 116: 362–402.

_____ and P. Pettit (2002). "The Aggregation of Sets of Judgments: An Impossibility Result". *Economics and Philosophy* 18: 89–110.

_____ _____ (2005). "On the Many as One". *Philosophy and Public Affairs* 33: 377–90.

_____ _____ (2006). "Group Agency and Supervenience". *Southern Journal of Philosophy* 45 (Spindel supplement).

Locke, J. (1975/1690). *An Essay Concerning Human Understanding*. Oxford: Oxford University Press.

Lovett, F. N. (2001). "Domination: A Preliminary Analysis". *Monist* 84: 98–112.

Lukes, S. (1973). *Émile Durkheim: His Life and Work: A Historical and Critical Study*. Harmondsworth: Penguin.

Madison, J., A. Hamilton, and J. Jay (1987). *The Federalist Papers*. Harmondsworth: Penguin.

Mandeville, B. (1731). *Free Thoughts on Religion, the Church and National Happiness*, 3rd edition. London.

Manin, B. (1997). *The Principles of Representative Government*. Cambridge: Cambridge University Press.

Maynor, J. (2003). *Republicanism in the Modern World*. Cambridge: Polity Press.

McDowell, J. (1996). *Mind and World*. Cambridge, Mass.: Harvard University Press.

McGeer, V. (1996). "Is 'Self-knowledge' an Empirical Problem? Renegotiating the Space of Philosophical Explanation". *Journal of Philosophy* 93: 483–515.

_____ (2003). "The Trouble with Mary". *Pacific Philosophical Quarterly* 84: 384–93.

_____ (2005). "Out of the Mouths of Autistics: Subjective Report and its Role in Cognitive Theorizing". In *The Philosophy and Neuroscience Movement*, ed. A. Brook and K. Akins. Cambridge: Cambridge University Press.

_____ and P. Pettit (2002). "The Self-regulating Mind". *Language and Communication* 22: 281–99.

Millar, F. (1998). *The Crowd in Rome in the Late Republic*. Ann Arbor: University of Michigan Press.

Miller, A. and C. Wright (2002) (eds.). *Rule-Following and Meaning*. Chesham: Acumen.

Miller, D. (1984). "Constraints on Freedom". *Ethics* 94: 66–86.

Miller, R. (1978). "Methodological Individualism and Social Explanation". *Philosophy of Science* 45: 387–414.

Milner, A. D. and M. Goodale (1995). *The Visual Brain in Action*. Oxford: Oxford University Press.

Montesquieu, C. d. S. (1989). *The Spirit of the Laws*. Cambridge: Cambridge University Press.

Moran, R. (2001). *Authority and Estrangement: An Essay on Self-knowledge*. Princeton: Princeton University Press.

Nagel, T. (1986). *The View from Nowhere*. Oxford: Oxford University Press.

Nozick, R. (1974). *Anarchy, State, and Utopia*. Oxford: Blackwell.

Paley, W. (1825). *Collected Works*, iv: *The Principles of Moral and Political Philosophy*. London: C. and J. Rivington.

Pauly, M. and M. Van Hees (forthcoming). "Logical Constraints on Judgment Aggregation". *Journal of Philosophical Logic*.

Perry, J. (1979). "The Essential Indexical". *Nous* 13: 3–21.

Pettit, P. (1989). "Decision Theory, Political Theory and the Hats Hypothesis". In *Freedom & Rationality: Festschrift for John Watkins*, ed. F. D'Agostino. Dordrecht: Kluwer.

—— (1990). "*Virtus Normativa*: Rational Choice Perspectives". *Ethics* 100: 725–55. Repr. in P. Pettit, *Rules, Reasons, and Norms*. Oxford: Oxford University Press, 2002.

—— (1993*a*). *The Common Mind: An Essay on Psychology, Society, and Politics*. New York: Oxford University Press; paperback edn. 1996.

—— (1993*b*). "A Definition of Physicalism". *Analysis* 53: 213–23.

—— (1994). "Microphysicalism without Contingent Micro-macro Laws". *Analysis* 54: 253–7.

—— (1995*a*). "The Cunning of Trust". *Philosophy and Public Affairs* 24: 202–25. Repr. in P. Pettit, *Rules, Reasons, and Norms*. Oxford: Oxford University Press, 2002.

—— (1995*b*). "Microphysicalism, Dottism, and Reduction". *Analysis* 55: 141–6.

—— (1997*a*). "Republican Theory and Criminal Punishment". *Utilitas* 9: 59–79.

—— (1997*b*). *Republicanism: A Theory of Freedom and Government*. Oxford: Oxford University Press.

—— (1998). "Practical Belief and Philosophical Theory". *Australasian Journal of Philosophy* 76: 15–33.

—— (1999). "Republican Liberty, Contestatory Democracy". In *Democracy's Value*, ed. C. Hacker-Cordon and I. Shapiro. Cambridge: Cambridge University Press.

—— (2000*a*). "Democracy, Electoral and Contestatory". *Nomos* 42: 105–44.

—— (2000*b*). "Minority Claims under Two Conceptions of Democracy". In *Political Theory and the Rights of Indigenous Peoples*, ed. D. Ivison, P. Patton, and W. Sanders. Cambridge: Cambridge University Press.

—— (2000*c*). "A Sensible Perspectivism". In *Dealing with Diversity*, ed. M. Baghramian and A. Dunlop. London: Routledge.

—— (2001*a*). "Embracing Objectivity in Ethics". In *Objectivity in Law and Morals*, ed. B. Leiter. Cambridge: Cambridge University Press.

—— (2001*b*). *A Theory of Freedom: From the Psychology to the Politics of Agency*. New York: Oxford University Press.

Pettit, P. (2002*a*). "Is, Criminal Justice Politically Feasible?". *Buffalo Criminal Law Review*, special issue, ed. Pablo de Greiff, 5(2): 427–50.

_____ (2002*b*). *Rules, Reasons, and Norms: Selected Essays*. Oxford: Oxford University Press.

_____ (2003*a*). "Deliberative Democracy, the Discursive Dilemma, and Republican Theory". In *Philosophy, Politics and Society*, vii: *Debating Deliberative Democracy*, ed. J. Fishkin and P. Laslett. Cambridge: Cambridge University Press.

_____ (2003*b*). "Groups with Minds of their Own". In *Socializing Metaphysics*, ed. F. Schmitt. New York: Roman and Littlefield.

_____ (2003*c*). "Looks as Powers". *Philosophical Issues* (supp. to *Nous*) 13: 221–52.

_____ (2004*a*). "The Common Good". In *Justice and Democracy: Essays for Brian Barry*, ed. K. Dowding, R. E. Goodin, and C. Pateman. Cambridge: Cambridge University Press.

_____ (2004*b*). "Depoliticizing Democracy". *Ratio Juris* 17: 52–65.

_____ (2004*c*). "Descriptivism, Rigidified and Anchored". *Philosophical Studies* 118: 323–38.

_____ (2004*d*). "Existentialism, Quietism and Philosophy". In *The Future for Philosophy*, ed. B. Leiter. Oxford: Oxford University Press.

_____ (2004*e*). "Motion Blindness and the Knowledge Argument". In *The Knowledge Argument*, ed. P. Ludlow, Y. Nagasawa, and D. Stoljar. Cambridge, Mass.: MIT Press.

_____ (2004*f*). *Penser en Societe*. Paris: PUF.

_____ (2005*a*). "Consciousness and the Frustrations of Physicalism". In *Minds, Worlds, and Conditionals: Themes from the Philosophy of Frank Jackson*, ed. I. Ravenscroft. Oxford: Oxford University Press.

_____ (2005*b*). "The Elements of Responsibility". *Philosophical Books* 46: 210–19.

_____ (2005*c*). "Liberty in Leviathan". *Politics, Philosophy and Economics* 4: 131–51.

_____ (2005*d*). "On Rule-following, Folk Psychology, and the Economy of Esteem: Reply to Boghossian, Dreier and Smith: Contribution to Symposium on P. Pettit, *Rules, Reasons, and Norms*". *Philosophical Studies* 124: 233–59.

_____ (2006*a*). "Can Contract Theory Ground Morality?". In *Moral Theories*, ed. J. Dreier. Oxford: Blackwell.

_____ (2006*b*). "Democracy, National and International". *Monist* 89: 302–25.

_____ (2006*c*). "Free Persons and Free Choices". *History of Political Thought*, 27, special issue on 'Liberty and Sovereignty'.

_____ (2006*d*). "Freedom in the Market". *Politics, Philosophy and Economics* 5: 131–49.

_____ (2006*e*). "Participation, Deliberation and We-thinking". In *The Illusion of Consent: Essays in Honor of Carole Pateman*, ed. D. O'Neill, M. Shanley, and I. Young. Philadelphia: Pennsylvania State University Press.

_____ (2006*f*). "Rawls's Peoples". In *Rawls's Law of Peoples: A Realistic Utopia*, ed. R. Martin and D. Reidy. Oxford: Blackwell.

_____ (2006*g*). "Response-dependent Theories". In *Encyclopedia of Philosophy*, 2nd edn., ed. D. M. Borchert. New York: Macmillan Reference.

_____ (2006*h*). "When to Defer to a Majority—and When Not". *Analysis* 66: 179–87.

_____ (2007*a*). "Republican Liberty: Three Axioms, Four Theorems". In *Republicanism and Political Theory*, ed. C. Laborde and J. Maynor. Oxford: Blackwell.

_____ (2007*b*). "Responsibility Incorporated". *Ethics* 117.

—— (forthcoming, *a*). "Physicalism without Popout". In *Naturalistic Analysis*, ed. D. Braddon-Mitchell and R. Nola. Cambridge, Mass.: MIT Press.

—— and G. Brennan (1986). "Restrictive Consequentialism". *Australasian Journal of Philosophy* 64: 438–55.

—— and D. Schweikard (2006). "Joint Action and Group Agency". *Philosophy of the Social Sciences* 18: 89–110.

—— and M. Smith (1996). "Freedom in Belief and Desire". *Journal of Philosophy* 93: 429–49.

—— —— (2000). "Global Consequentialism". In *Morality, Rules and Consequences*, ed. B. Hooker, E. Mason, and D. E. Miller. Edinburgh: Edinburgh University Press.

—— —— (2004). "The Truth in Deontology". In *Reason and Value: Themes from the Moral Philosophy of Joseph Raz*, ed. R. J. Wallace, Philip Pettit, S. Scheffler, and M. Smith. Oxford: Oxford University Press.

—— —— (2006). "External Reasons". In *McDowell and his Critics*, ed. C. Macdonald and G. Macdonald. Oxford: Blackwell.

Price, H. (1988). *Facts and the Function of Truth*. Oxford: Blackwell.

Rawls, J. (1971). *A Theory of Justice*. Oxford: Oxford University Press.

—— (1993). *Political Liberalism*. New York: Columbia University Press.

—— (1999). *The Law of Peoples*. Cambridge, Mass.: Harvard University Press.

—— (2001). *Justice as Fairness: A Restatement*. Cambridge, Mass.: Harvard University Press.

Rousseau, J.-J. (1973/1762). *The Social Contract and Discourses*. London: J. M. Dent and Sons.

Scanlon, T. M. (1998). *What We Owe to Each Other*. Cambridge, Mass.: Harvard University Press.

Sen, A. (1983). "Liberty and Social Choice". *Journal of Philosophy* 80: 18–20.

Skinner, Q. (1996). *Reason and Rhetoric in the Philosophy of Hobbes*. Cambridge: Cambridge University Press.

—— (1998). *Liberty before Liberalism*. Cambridge: Cambridge University Press.

—— (2007). *Freedom as Independence*. Cambridge: Cambridge University Press.

Slaughter, A.-M. (2004). *A New World Order*. Princeton: Princeton University Press.

Smith, M. (1994). *The Moral Problem*. Oxford: Blackwell.

—— (2003). "Rational Capacities". In *Weakness of Will and Varieties of Practical Irrationality*, ed. S. Stroud and C. Tappolet. Oxford: Oxford University Press.

Sperber, D. (2000) (ed.). *Metarepresentations: A Multidisciplinary Perspective*. Oxford: Oxford University Press.

Stalnaker, R. C. (1984). *Inquiry*. Cambridge, Mass.: MIT Press.

Steiner, H. (1994). *An Essay on Rights*. Oxford: Blackwell.

Strawson, P. (2003). "Freedom and Resentment". In *Free Will*, 2nd edn., ed. G. Watson. Oxford: Oxford University Press.

Taylor, M. (1987). *The Possibility of Cooperation*. Cambridge: Cambridge University Press.

Tyler, T. R. (1990). *Why People Obey the Law*. New Haven, Conn. Yale University Press.

Urbinati, N. (2006). *Representative Democracy: Principles and Genealogy*. Chicago: University of Chicago Press.

Van Parijs, P. (1995). *Real Freedom for All*. Oxford: Oxford University Press.

Viroli, M. (2002). *Republicanism.* New York: Hill and Wang.

Waldron, J. (1999). *Law and Disagreement.* Oxford: Oxford University Press.

Wallace, R. J. (1996). *Responsibility and the Moral Sentiments.* Cambridge, Mass.: Harvard University Press.

Watson, G. (2003). "Free Agency". In *Free Will,* 2nd edn., ed. G. Watson. Oxford: Oxford University Press.

_____ (2005). *Agency and Answerability: Selected Essays.* Oxford: Oxford University Press.

White, M. (1987). *Philosophy, The Federalist, and the Constitution.* New York: Oxford University Press.

Wittgenstein, L. (1958). *Philosophical Investigations,* 2nd edn. Oxford: Blackwell.

Wolf, S. (1990). *Freedom within Reason.* Oxford: Oxford University Press.

Wright, C. (1992). *Truth and Objectivity.* Cambridge, Mass: Harvard University Press.

Index